Praise for *The 52 Greatest Stories of the Bible*

"Wonderful! This makes other Bible overviews look dull and flat. Up until now, books that start at the beginning were for dummies and books for intelligent adults were for experts. This one is different. John and Ken assume you know nothing without also assuming you're an idiot."

Dr. Conrad Gempf,
lecturer at London School of Theology, England;
author of *Mealtime Habits of the Messiah* and *Jesus Asked*

"Some books about the Bible give us theology, others values and yet others concrete suggestions for life. What we need is a book that brings all three together, and *The 52 Greatest Stories of the Bible* does just that. Here is a book that will jump-start us into reading the Bible so that it gives us what to believe and how to live."

Scot McKnight,
Karl A. Olsson Professor in Religious Studies
at North Park University, Chicago;
author of *The Jesus Creed*

"Not only is this book the ideal follow-up to our Old or New Testament seminars, it is also a powerful stand-alone weapon in the battle against biblical illiteracy. This wonderful resource delivers God's Word in bite-size pieces that are sure to stimulate the appetite and leave you hungry to learn more."

Phil Tuttle,
president and CEO
of Walk Thru the Bible Ministries, Atlanta

THE 52
GREATEST
STORIES
of the BIBLE

THE 52 GREATEST STORIES *of the* BIBLE

A WEEKLY DEVOTIONAL

KENNETH BOA AND JOHN ALAN TURNER

BakerBooks
a division of Baker Publishing Group
Grand Rapids, Michigan

© 2008 by Kenneth Boa and John Alan Turner

Published by Baker Books
a division of Baker Publishing Group
P.O. Box 6287, Grand Rapids, MI 49516-6287
www.bakerbooks.com

Baker Books edition published 2016

ISBN 978-0-8010-1903-6

Previously published by Regal Books

Printed in the United States of America

Library of Congress Control Number: 2016931367

Unless otherwise indicated, Scripture quotations are from the Holy Bible, Today's New International Version®. TNIV®. Copyright © 2001, 2005 by Biblica, Inc.™ Used by permission of Zondervan. All rights reserved worldwide. www.zondervan.com

Scripture quotations labeled NIV are from the Holy Bible, New International Version®. NIV®. Copyright © 1973, 1978, 1984 by Biblica, Inc.™ Used by permission of Zondervan. All rights reserved worldwide. www.zondervan.com

17   18   19   20   21   22   7   6   5   4   3

To our children—
Heather, Anabel, Eliza and Amelia—
who constantly remind us of the power
of a really good story.

Contents

Acknowledgments   11

Introduction   13

1. The First Story   17
2. Warning   24
3. Promise of a Nation   32
4. Birth of a Nation   39
5. Real Freedom   46
6. Promised Land   53
7. Conquest   60
8. The Time of God's Patience   67
9. A Pagan Widow Gets It
   Right   74
10. First King   81
11. A Man After God's Own
    Heart   89
12. The Scarlet Thread   96
13. City on a Hill   103
14. Divided Kingdom   110
15. Just a Regular Guy   117
16. Passing the Torch   125

17. A Farmer and a Plumb Line   132
18. The Fish Story   139
19. Unfaithful   146
20. Holy, Holy, Holy   153
21. A Tale of Two Kings   160
22. Reformation   168
23. Disappointed with Life   175
24. Tears   183
25. Homecoming   190
26. Between the Times   198
27. Savior Born   206
28. A Baby   213
29. A Real Live Human God   221
30. Wilderness   229
31. The Best Sermon Ever   236
32. Miracles   244
33. Transfiguration   252
34. Unconventional   259
35. Telling Stories   266
36. Jesus and Two Women   273

10 Contents

37. One Week to Live   280
38. Love and Feet   287
39. The Last Night   294
40. Crucifixion   301
41. Resurrection   308
42. The Sequel   315
43. The Room Upstairs   322
44. The Ends of the Earth   329
45. A Man Named Saul   336

46. For Gentiles   343
47. Conflict Resolution   350
48. Freedom   357
49. Love and War   364
50. Matter   371
51. Revelation   378
52. The Last Story   385

Notes   393

Acknowledgments

God's plan for humanity has always involved community, so it's no surprise that writing, like life, is best done in that context. That being the case, there are a number of people I must thank.

I had a small army of people who agreed to read the stories as I was writing them (to make sure I stayed on track): David Blackwell, Rick Hazelip, Tony Myles, Kevin West, Andy Sikora, Jeff Sandstrom, Bruce Hopler, Erich Robinson, Melanie Williams, Jennifer Nahrstadt, Daniel Cline, Christopher Green, Craig Jenkins, Marquis Laughlin, Lori Royals, Cindy Bailey, Bobby Valentine, Dee Andrews, Angi Aymond, John Dobbs, Damon DeLillo, Wade Hodges, Keith Brenton, Steven Allen and Sandra Morales. Thanks for your feedback and wise counsel.

Ken and I would both like to express how valuable Andrew Wolgemuth and the rest of the staff at Wolgemuth & Associates have been. You took care of the business side of this project so that we could focus on the writing.

Thanks to Kim Bangs, Alex Field and the rest of the publishing team for believing in this project and being flexible with the deadline.

There are a couple of guys who simply operate as sanity maintenance for me: Dane Booth and Hal Runkel. Thanks for the Monday Night Football and the Tuesday Night Tennis.

My mom and dad, J. J. and Isabel Turner—It was from you that I first heard many of these stories. I am proud to be your son.

Dr. B.—I always leave your presence feeling better than I did before. I am honored to have my name associated with yours on a project such as this, and I treasure our friendship.

And then there's my wife, Jill—You are simply the most amazing woman I've ever met. You're not only my editor; you're my best friend and partner in all things.

Introduction

A generation ago, public discourse was littered with biblical references. Someone who endured painful circumstances without giving in to resignation and despair was said to have "the patience of Job." Someone who demonstrated an uncanny ability to see the true nature of things was said to have "the wisdom of Solomon." Great stories like David and Goliath, Daniel in the lion's den and Balaam's talking donkey were mentioned in stories and songs—both religious and popular. Everyone was at least somewhat familiar with them. But that isn't the case anymore.

Nowadays, people don't know many of the great stories of the Bible. They don't know about the call of Abram from Ur or Ruth from Moab. They've never heard of Elijah, Josiah, Hezekiah or Nehemiah. They don't know much about John the Baptist or Jesus' parents or Paul's conversion on the road to Damascus. These used to be stories everyone knew. But the sad truth is that now, as our society (and our churches) become increasingly biblically illiterate, many people (Christian and non-Christian) simply aren't familiar with them.

The greatest call of the Christian life is to know God and to help others to know Him, too. But where do you begin the task of communicating the gospel to a group of people who do not know the basics? How do you approach people who aren't even sure who God is, what sin is, who Christ is or what a Bible is for? Even more, how do you do these things when you're not sure of their meaning yourself?

Here's how. You learn and tell the Big Story. You go all the way back to the beginning, when God existed in perfect community with Himself. You learn how it was out of that perfect community that God spoke creation into existence, taking time to craft an idyllic place before carefully creating humans to live there in unbroken community with each other and with their Creator. You study how the first act of disobedience toward God brought a curse as a result. You read the stories of Cain and Abel, the Tower of Babel and Noah before you can appreciate the calling of Abram for what it is. Step by step through the Old Testament, you build your worldview, in order to prepare yourself for the greatest story, the story of Jesus.

Unfortunately, few Christians today know how to do such a thing. That's why this book is so important.

In the past, a great deal of effective evangelism was done by teaching key Scriptures about sin, grace and salvation. This was possible because Christians could assume the basic building blocks of a Christian worldview in their listeners. Even when people chose not to believe in God, it was the Christian God they chose not to believe in! Evangelism was rather like hanging wet laundry on a clothesline that was already in place; you could take texts like John 3:16 or Romans 5:8 or Isaiah 53:4–6 and hang them on the line of a Judeo-Christian worldview. The problem Christians have now in trying to reach postmodern people is that there is no clothesline. When we try to hang our texts, they fall to the ground in a heap. The great challenge before us now is to put up a new clothesline.

It is our hope that this book will help you do just that: connect the dots as you read the Bible and see how each individual story is really one chapter in the Big Story. We want to help you establish a Christian worldview through which you will see Jesus as the point of everything. And—this is important—we want to show you that a biblical worldview really can help you understand the answers to the ultimate questions of life.

In a postmodern and post-Christian era, many people are confused about what the Bible is and why it was written. People are looking for spirituality and ways to answer the pressing questions of life—questions of origin, destiny and morality. These people aren't very likely to pick up a commentary set or read many of the scholarly approaches to the biblical stories; they want something practical and easy to understand. We hope our book will become a guide both for people who want to know more about the Bible but don't know where to start, and for those who wish to communicate the truths of the Bible to those who have little or no experience with it but aren't sure they know it well enough themselves to do so.

We intend to take you from beginning to end of the Bible in one year, moving along without getting bogged down in the difficult passages. We'll try to stick with story and narrative, and weave the doctrine in as we go.

But first, a few brief preliminaries must be addressed. First, there's the issue of reducing the Bible down to 52 stories. It seemed like a really good idea when we first thought of it. Then our publisher wanted to know how quickly we could complete the list of stories to be included. We did what most sensible people would do: We started at the beginning.

Creation. Fall. Cain and Abel. Noah. The Tower of Babel. The Calling of Abram. The whole Ishmael debacle. The Birth of Isaac. The Sacrifice of Isaac. Jacob and Esau.

That's when we realized our first problem. We were just over halfway through the first of 66 books in the Bible, and we already had 10 stories!

On our first attempt at the list, we had 45 stories in the Old Testament alone. Clearly, this was going to take some thought.

After consulting several scholars, pastors and teachers, we finally settled on our list. And some pretty good stories got left out. Esther's not in here. Neither is Job. Obadiah and Nahum are important—you should take the time to read their books before you get to heaven and have to have an awkward conversation with them ("You wrote one of the books of the Bible?")—but they're not in here. We chose stories that further the central plotline in significant ways. It was a difficult process, and we know that there will be some who disagree with our list. Those people are welcome to write a book of their own. (And if they do, we'll probably buy it.)

The second issue related to the list we've chosen: details. How do you tell the whole story of Israel's Judges in approximately 500 words? Because we were concerned with moving the story along and limited ourselves to only 26 stories in each of the Old and New Testaments, there are smaller stories—subplots—that got left out. You'll read about King David, but you won't read much about his encounter with Goliath. You'll read about Daniel, but you won't hear about his night in the lion's den.

This has been a difficult but intentional process, and because we've had to leave so many things out, we feel obligated to stress this next point: *This book is in no way intended to replace good, rigorous Bible study.* It is meant to supplement your Bible study. If you're like so many people who have so little time for reading and must choose between either reading our book or reading the Good Book, please put this back on the shelf.

Obviously, we haven't set out to write a textbook here. We've tried to take the scholarly stuff and distill it for mass consumption. This book is intended for use as a personal daily devotional, to help you understand the full scriptural timeline—from creation to eternity—by showing how these great individual stories all come together into a much larger, cohesive narrative. Hopefully, by taking this approach, you'll be challenged to see your life as another part of this continually unfolding Story.

Each week will focus on one story and follow a deliberate pattern:

- Monday's reading will be the story itself. We've tried to tell the story as conversationally as possible, including details about the story's historical context.
- Tuesday will focus on the *orthodoxy* of the story, a description of how the story shapes our *beliefs*.
- Wednesday will key into the *orthopathy* of the story, a discussion of how the story shapes our *values*.
- Thursday will delve into the *orthopraxy* of the story, an explanation of how the story should shape our *actions*.
- Friday will conclude the week's study and will guide the reader through a prayerful response to the story.

As you can see, we've taken a specific approach to unpacking each Bible story. Along with Christians throughout the centuries, we maintain that our faith must not be reduced to merely a set of right beliefs (orthodoxy) or right values (orthopathy) or right behaviors (orthopraxy), but must take all three and intertwine them to form a well-rounded faith that redeems our thoughts, our feelings and our actions.

One final note as to the style you're about to encounter. When two authors agree to write one book, there is always some debate over whose voice to use. We are two very different men with very different backgrounds. Ken is one of the most respected thinkers in all of Christendom. John is . . . well . . . few people have heard of John before. Ken has a doctorate in philosophy from Oxford. John . . . well . . . John is a teaching pastor, and while he likes to talk about Jesus and God and the Bible a lot, he works really hard to make sure he uses language regular folks can understand.

For reasons that aren't even completely clear to us, John ended up writing the material for the first four days of each week, while Ken supplied the guided prayers for each Friday. So you will likely note a difference in vocabulary and style between the Monday through Thursday portions and the Friday prayers.

Now, without further ado, we invite you to buckle up (you may encounter some turbulence) and get ready for the adventure of a lifetime! It is our hope and prayer that you will be changed forever by what you're about to read. We have certainly been changed forever by having written it!

1

The First Story

GENESIS 1–2

MONDAY: Story

Before there was some*thing*, there was Some*one*. Go back as far as your mind will allow you to, millions or billions of years . . . go back beyond the creation of the world, before the existence of matter and energy, space and time . . . drive a stake in the nothingness you imagine and an odd thing happens: From behind the mysterious nothingness steps a benevolent Creator to greet you.

This God revealed (but definitely not contained) in the Bible has always existed and will always exist. He exists as a communion of three Persons—infinite, personal, triune, transcendent and immanent all at the same time. It is from this eternal community of oneness that all others derive life, meaning and purpose. It is from this eternal community of oneness that everything that exists is spoken into existence.

From out of the depths of His love, He spoke light into being, separating it from darkness. He created spiral galaxies filled with innumerable stars, related to each other by distances that can only be measured in light years. And out of all the billions of places He could have chosen, He focused His attention on one tiny planet, lavishing upon that blue marble His love and creativity, giving it sun, moon and stars . . . atmosphere, dry land and water . . . oxygen, cherry trees and grape-vines, hammerhead sharks and falcons . . . wild boars and hairy apes and llamas. "So much beauty around us for just two eyes to see,"[1] Rich Mullins used to sing.

And, at last, the pinnacle of God's creation: humans. Perhaps He created us last as a testament to our inherent dignity—saving the best for last, so to speak. Or perhaps it was so we wouldn't try to tell Him where to put things.

One thing is pretty clear: He didn't need our help. It may sound trite and overused, but it's true nonetheless: God is God and we are not. God created absolutely everything, and into this perfect garden of delight, He placed the man and eventually the woman, giving them dominion over everything else. God was to rule over them, and they were to rule over everything else.

There they lived in unbroken intimacy with God, with each other and with the world around them. It was an idyllic existence.

There was just one rule. Not 10 commandments. Not 613 laws. One rule. They were free to do anything they wanted except this one thing. Obeying the rule would serve as a reminder for them of Who was really in charge. Their Creator, the one who ruled over them, told them to avoid just one thing: *Don't eat the fruit of this one tree.*

How hard could that be?

TUESDAY: Beliefs

The book of Genesis serves as a window, a lens through which we see our world, our place in the world and the rest of the Bible. We look *through* it; we rarely look *at* it. By the time Genesis was written, lots of history had taken place. Adam. Eve. Creation. The Fall. Murder. Exile. Construction. Destruction. Famines. Floods. Dysfunctional families. Genesis was not written as it happened; it was written at least two millennia after the first domino was knocked over.

Before Genesis was written down, Father Abraham—we'll read his story soon—and his frustrating walk of faith had come and gone. Isaac had been rescued. Jacob had been lamed. Joseph had been sold. Patterns had been established. The family had become a nation within a nation. For 400 years, the Israelites languished in slavery under the oppressive hand of their Egyptian taskmasters.

Then, suddenly, into the deafening silence, God spoke to a man, and through that man God spoke (first) to His people, (next) to His people's keepers and (ultimately) to all of human history.

And still Genesis had not been written.

As far as we know, the plagues were visited upon the Egyptians, the Red Sea was parted, the Law was given, the Golden Calf was crafted and the spies were convinced that invading the land of their destiny would be a mistake . . . all of that happened *before* Genesis was writte n.

Perhaps there is a sense in which it is *because* of these stories—and others like them—that Genesis (and the other historical-narrative parts of the Bible) was written. Genesis is written to remind us of what has happened, what God has done and how He has interacted with His people through the first eras of human history. This reminder demonstrates two vitally important principles:

Scripture is always a means to a greater end.

Scripture corrects, reveals and instructs.

It is intended to make us more like the God who authors it. God does not merely desire a transfer of information; He desires our complete transformation.

It is for these reasons that Moses finally put down in writing the stories that had been handed down from generation to generation. He was less concerned with telling us *how* the world was created than He was in telling us that the world was created and by Whom.

And what a world it is! Intricate design (look at a blade of grass under a microscope), balance (four seasons every year), order (the world keeps turning) and controlled mayhem (kick over an anthill sometime). It is a marvelous place of wonder and beauty. If the creation is this amazing, how amazing must the Creator be?

WEDNESDAY: Values

The beginning of the Bible does more than reveal something about God's character and nature (though that should always be among the first things we look for in Scripture); it also reveals something of God's desire and rights. A creator always has rights to determine what becomes of the creation.

The creation story reveals some things that God values. For example, He values creativity balanced with order and design; He does not create things willy-nilly. There also seems to be a structure to His creation process—but the process is not really a model of efficiency. This God values structure and order, but He seems content to take His time, to linger over things without feeling a need to rush or hurry. It's not that He wastes time, but He's not a slave to the clock.

There is order and structure, but diversity seems to be favored over efficiency in God's economy of creation. The things He creates are far from uniform. There is no cookie-cutter assembly line producing leaves in heaven, though that would probably speed the process up considerably. Each leaf is unique, individual, different. Each flower, each snowflake, each person appears to be handcrafted by God.

Furthering our theory that God is not primarily interested in efficiency, it appears that God prefers a rhythm of work and rest to a demanding work schedule. A being powerful enough to create something from nothing could certainly have created everything at once. The God of the Bible did not. He measures Himself, creating just enough for one day, not feeling the need to do too much. And then He rests. He doesn't *need* to rest; He isn't tired. He chooses to rest. He values rest as much as He values work.

The way God's creation of humans is described reminds us that humans are special, unique among God's other creations. Only humans bear the image of God, and as such are to be valued above all other forms of creation. We have an inherent dignity that can only be defended from a correct understanding of the first two chapters of the Bible.

We should notice, too, that it is not merely the male gender of the human species that enjoys this privileged place above all creation. Eve was created to be Adam's companion—his partner—not his maid or his servant. Humans, male and female, enjoy equal status from God's perspective.

Perhaps the most interesting thing to notice is that above everything else God values, He seems to prize community. As God creates, He steps back and declares things to be good. But then He notices something that isn't good: Adam is alone. Amid the beauty and diversity of creation, there is no suitable companion for Adam until another human is made. In addition to being a new creation, Eve brings a new creation into the Garden: the creation of community. God doesn't merely want us to be rightly related to Him; He wants us to be rightly related to one another as well. Community is a prominent theme throughout the Bible.

Creativity. Order and design. Diversity. Rest. People. Community. These are the priorities of God's heart as it is revealed in the first two chapters of the Bible. Are they ours as well?

THURSDAY: Actions

The Creator God revealed in the first few pages of Scripture does not merely create a wonderful garden and place two people in it to lounge around forever. He gives them work to do. First, He calls them to be fruitful and multiply (hooray for sex!). Then He gives them the task of managing the garden. All of creation was under their dominion, just as they were under God's dominion.

Even after many millennia, this idea that humans are stewards of God's creation has never been repealed. We should be custodians of the beauty and diversity of this earth. Those who are in a relationship with their Creator should lead the way in matters of environmental concern. Clearly, we must do this with wisdom and discernment, but do it we must.

In our work, however, we would be wise to follow God's example of resting regularly. In the Ten Commandments given to Moses (more about that presently), God called His people to a weekly period of rest that reflected the pattern He began at creation. We are not obligated to keep the law of the Sabbath any longer, but it is still our goal to manifest an ever-increasing level of godliness in our behavior. One godly thing we can all do is rest, whether we think we need to or not.

Because humans matter so much to our Creator, our fellow humans must also matter to those of us who seek to reflect His glory in our own lives. This may mean fighting for the rights of the unborn and the elderly. But it means much more than that. It means bringing aid to those in need—water for the thirsty, food for the hungry, companionship for the lonely. It means loving our neighbors—those on the other side of the planet, those on the other side of the street and those on the other side of the political spectrum. God not only values human life, He values human community. In our activities, we should not only champion the sanctity of life but the sanctity of fellowship as well.

There are simple things most of us can do to reflect godliness in our behavior. For a starter (and this one is far too often neglected among Christians), married people can have sex. There . . . we stated the obvious! God created sex, and sex is really, really good in the proper context. Enjoy physical intimacy with your spouse as a gift from God. That's godly behavior.

Plant a garden or work in the yard. Physical labor is beneficial for your body, mind and spirit. It gets you in touch with the elemental qualities of life. It reminds you that one of the reasons God put you on this planet was to care for it.

Create a work of art. Paint a picture. Mold some clay. Play a song on the piano. Write a poem. God is the greatest artist in the universe, and you've been created in His image. Do something to reflect God's creative spirit.

Take a nap. God put you on planet Earth and gave you work to do. That work is meaningful, but it is not the end-all-be-all of your existence. God rested. You should rest, too.

Have friends over for dinner. Enjoy their company. Build community with them. Let them know how much you value their friendship. God does not simply want a string of relationships with individuals; He wants a relationship with *a people*—a group that is rightly related to Him and to one another.

Do something for a stranger. Sponsor a child through Compassion International or World Vision. Plan a short-term mission trip. Volunteer in a soup kitchen. Counsel an unwed mother. Adopt a child. Do something out of your comfort zone that shows how much you agree with God that human life and human dignity are worth working to preserve.

While you're having sex, working in the garden, creating a masterpiece, taking a nap, enjoying a great dinnertime conversation or being an activist, remember this: *It's all worship*. The reason you're able to think, speak, walk, draw, plan, rest, breathe and work is because there is a God who created you for a purpose and has called you into partnership with Him to see His kingdom come and His will be done on earth as it is in heaven.

If you can't find cause to worship that Creator, you might need to start over with Monday.

FRIDAY: Prayer

Narrative

O Lord my God, You are exalted above all things we can conceive and imagine. Time and space are a part of Your created order—You brought them into being, and You dwell in all times and places. You are the eternal now, the great i am, the Beginning and the End, the Alpha and the Omega, the First and the Last. You are present everywhere and You rule all things, from the microcosm to the macrocosm. You spoke, and energy and matter came into being. Your boundless power and wisdom are evident in Your works, and all things derive their being from You. The beauty, radiance and wisdom that abound in Your creation all point beyond themselves to You, their Creator and Sustainer. I ask for the eyes to see Your goodness, beauty and truth as I behold plants, trees, animals, insects, sunrises and sunsets, landscapes and the starry sky.

Orthodoxy

What we could not have learned from the glories and marvels of Your world, You have revealed through Your Word. We know from the heavens and the earth that You are all-powerful, utterly wise and everywhere present; Your eternal power and divine nature have clearly been revealed. But it was only through Your special revelation in Scripture that we could know that the One who has dominion over all things is also the Lover of our souls. Your Word is a love letter to the people You created to enjoy forever in loving communion with You. May I be a diligent student of Your Word so that it will renew my mind and give me an eternal perspective as I meditate on your timeless truths.

Orthopathy

Your creation is a magnificent unity in diversity, profound in wisdom, awesome in understanding, marvelous in purpose and rich in elegance. You revel in variety, subtlety, intricacy, information and beauty. All things work together in both the physical and spiritual realms. I thank You for creating and calling me to become conformed to the image of Your Son, and I pray for the grace of holy desire to pursue by Your power what You have called me to become in Christ. I thank You for friendships and alliances with likeminded people, and I am grateful for the manifold gifts and ministries in the Body of Christ. Give me a growing heart for Your people so that I will be embedded in others-centered community as a lover and servant of the people You love.

Orthopraxy

You have called me to participate in Your purposes through the work I have been given to do during my earthly sojourn. May I do my work with care and excellence in the desire to be pleasing to You. I realize that all things become spiritual when they are done in Your name. May I honor You in my choices and activities and view the works of my hands as a mode of worship. I want whatever I do in thought, word and deed to be honoring to You and edifying to others. I ask for a clearer sense of purpose and calling and for the power to accomplish that for which You have placed me on this earth.

2

Warning

GENESIS 3–11

MONDAY: Story

WARNING: *Do not eat the fruit of this tree! If you do, you will die!*

Such an odd warning. What was the big deal about the fruit of that tree? It didn't look poisonous. It looked pretty good, actually. But God made this huge deal out of Adam and Eve not eating this particular fruit off of this particular tree.

Apparently Adam couldn't figure out *why* God said what He said, but he knew God *meant* what He said. So Adam told Eve it would be best to not even touch the tree. And she probably would have been okay . . . if that serpent hadn't shown up asking all those questions.

"Did God really say that?"

"Do you really think you'll die?"

"Why do you suppose God said that?"

All those questions, and no sufficient answers. That's when the doubts began.

Maybe He didn't really mean it. The more I look at it, the better it looks. Maybe God is insecure and manipulative. Maybe He doesn't really have our best interests at heart. He's not even here right now. C'mon, let's just try it.

In that moment, the whole world started to come unraveled.

The hook was set and they swallowed the bait, and nothing would ever be the same again. Sin, which before only existed in theory, was now a reality. Work was hard now, and frustrating. Childbirth was painful. Their relationship was strained. Adam seemed distant, preoccupied with other things. Eve seemed clingy and needy, almost desperate for his attention.

God was still there, but it was different. He pursued them, but they found themselves hiding from Him—terrified at what they must look like to Him, frightened that one day He might decide He'd had enough and wipe them off the face of the earth.

Possibly the worst part was what they saw in their children. Right off the bat, the kids seemed to be leaning away from God, away from intimacy with others, away from their own best interests. They seemed bent on their own destruction. Sometimes they did the right thing, but it usually seemed forced. It didn't seem to come naturally. And then the grandkids came along, and sin started to spread out wider and wider: more and more kids growing up to be worse and worse, plotting new ways of doing wrong, even working together to rebel. The hook Adam and Eve swallowed appeared to have burrowed its way even deeper into their offspring.

It started as a seemingly harmless act: They just ate a piece of fruit they weren't supposed to eat. And now kids were killing kids, swearing vengeance, taking multiple wives. It was as if they lacked the ability to restrain themselves, until every thought was only evil all the time.

Finally, God had enough. He decided to wipe the slate clean and start over. He found one guy, Noah, who seemed better than all the others, and then He flooded the earth, saving Noah and his family. Yet as soon as the water subsided, Noah planted a vineyard, grew some grapes, made some wine, got drunk, passed out naked, embarrassed himself and his sons, woke up, and through his hangover haze managed to curse his unborn grandchildren.

Wow, what a mess!

With just one act of disobedience, God's beautiful creation became the *Jerry Springer Show*. Families torn apart by violence and deception. Brokenness. Frustration. Alienation. Fear. From that first bite, these have ruled the roost, and no matter how hard we try, we cannot rid ourselves of this awful hook that's set deeply in our hearts and minds, corrupting absolutely everything.

WARNING: Do not eat the fruit of this tree! If you do, you will die!

Such an odd warning. Apparently God had His reasons for posting it.

TUESDAY: Beliefs

There is a God.

You are not Him.

You may be good, but you are not God.

The Bible is unique among religious literature in many ways. Most noticeably, from the very beginning, we are given a realistic assessment of human nature in its dignity, its dependence and its potential for total depravity. Only the Judeo-Christian Bible describes each facet adequately.

Here in the earliest portion of the Bible, we read that the Creator decided, "Let us make man in our image" (Gen. 1:26). It is worth mentioning the plural pronoun in this verse. There's a clue as to the nature and character of God, and we'll certainly double-click on that later. For now, we should explore this idea of what it means to be made in the image of God.

An image is a reflection. In this case, it is a person or thing that closely resembles another. We talk about a son being the image of his father. In a similar way, humans have been made to demonstrate something of the character and nature of God. Other parts of creation were good, but nothing else was created in God's very image. Humans are distinct in this. We're not just highly developed animals. We're not just a bundle of body parts and nerve endings. We're not just overgrown germs. We're created in the image of God, and this should bring us a profound sense of dignity.

And yet, it's also very obvious from the first pages of the Bible that we are not God. Created in His image? Yes. But there is a sharp dividing line between the Creator and the creation.

God fashioned the first human "out of the dust of the ground" (Gen. 2:7), and then He called that first human "Adam" . . . which sounds an awful lot like the Hebrew word for "earth," as in *dirt*. It's almost as if God named the first man "Dusty" as a reminder of where the man came from.

Furthermore, that human did not come to life until God had "breathed into his nostrils the breath of life" (Gen. 2:7). In a sense, God continues to do this with each and every one of us, giving "all men life and breath and everything else" (Acts 17:25). If God should decide one day to extinguish the sun or to drain all the oxygen out of our atmosphere, we would be helpless to escape our impending doom. It is only because of the benevolent patience of God that we are able to continue living. Only God is self-sustaining.

We are made in His image, but we are completely dependent on Him.

When we cannot content ourselves with this status of being over something (creation) and under something else (God), we fall prey to all sorts of delusions, the most common of which is the notion that our Creator does not have our best interests at heart. It is this thought that may have led Eve astray, and it lies at the root of most of the sin in our lives.

Can you be content with God's way of being God, or do you secretly think you could do better?

The biblical understanding of human beings provides us with the tension of immense dignity and utter dependence. Any other attempt to understand ourselves and our proper place in the universe will always lead to depravity and confusion. Sin corrupts everything it touches and, unchecked, leaves us in a state of total depravity. In other words, the Bible is very realistic about humans: We're good, but we're not absolutely good; we're bad, but we're not absolutely bad.

Dignity with dependence or total depravity—the choice is yours.

WEDNESDAY: Values

If human beings are just the accidental product of time plus chance, then there is no rational basis for human dignity. If this is the case, then human life should be viewed as a commodity, and we should only value people for what they bring to the party.

Can they tell funny stories or play an instrument well? Okay, let them in.

Do they have money or connections that might be put to good use? They get to join us.

Are they beautiful to look at? Put them at the table in the front.

The smart, strong, talented, wealthy, beautiful people are valuable; all others must stay behind the velvet rope.

In fact, it might be better—since we're all just accidents anyway—to systematically weed certain types out of the garden altogether. If we don't, they'll continue to be a burden on society.

Few people throughout human history have been willing to take this argument all the way to its logical conclusions. Those who have thought things through, almost without fail, ended up either committing some of the worst atrocities in human history or succumbing to utter hopelessness and despair. Without a proper understanding of human nature, though, it's difficult to give a reason why we should not walk down either of those paths as far as we can. But there *is* a reason: *Human beings have such tremendous dignity that we must value human life.*

Meditate today on the implications of humans created in God's image. For most people reading this book, the application will have less to do with issues of abortion or euthanasia and more to do with how you treat the people in your own home or workplace. Do you really value them as ones created in the image of God? Or do you treat them like objects?

The dignity of human life is not the only value we can glean from this story. We've learned that each and every one of us is utterly dependent on God for the very breath that we expect to fill our lungs in the next moment or two. We must also realize that our minds, clouded as they are with mixed motives, must have guidance from an external Source. There is no created person or thing that can help us live above our circumstances. Only something transcendent can provide the perspective we need to navigate our passage through this world.

Because human beings are dependent upon God, we must value His Word.

The Bible is not simply a rulebook or a textbook or a storybook; it is written to shape our thoughts, our feelings and our actions. Without it, we are left to make our own way in the world—to our own demise. The wisdom found in the Bible is like the air we breathe; it did not come from us, but it must come to us—come *into* us, in fact—for us to be sustained.

Unfortunately, our first parents failed to value God's Word and chose to go their own way. Not satisfied to be dependent on God for guidance, they chose to rebel. This decision set in motion a chain of events that has led to despair, anxiety, misery and agony ever since.

We find ourselves in the uncomfortable position of declaring humans totally depraved. There is not one aspect of a human being that is untainted by the devastating effects of sin. Furthermore, there is not one aspect of human society that is pristine or unspoiled. Our own bodies have turned against us, betraying our noblest aspirations, and we often find ourselves feeling trapped in a world without hope. As one biblical writer despaired, "What a wretched man I am! Who will rescue me from this body of death" (Rom. 7:24)?

Thankfully, that same writer answered his own question in the next verse: "Thanks be to God—through Jesus Christ our Lord!" (v. 25).

Because human beings are totally depraved, we must value Jesus Christ.

After all, this Jesus fellow (who is part of the plural pronoun we pointed out yesterday), valued human beings enough to come and die in our place to rescue us from a catastrophe of our own making.

And where do we learn about all that He said and did?

In God's Word.

THURSDAY: Actions

Take a deep breath.

Do you believe there will be enough oxygen for you to take another one in a few seconds?

Why?

Where will that oxygen come from?

What or who ultimately provides it?

Sure, there are trees and all sorts of plants that take in our poisonous gasses and provide oxygen in return. But who or what made the trees?

And how did things get set up so perfectly?

Remember your answer to these questions. You will need them at the end of today's reading.

God's desire is that people live in harmony with Him, with one another and with all of creation. That is precisely how Adam and Eve lived until they gave in to the notion that they could do a better job deciding where the boundaries were than God could.

Their lives had been characterized by meaningful work and a shame-free relationship. They experienced beauty and creativity.

When the consequences of sin began to spread relentlessly further and deeper, they experienced pain and frustration, chaos and alienation. Sin promised greater freedom, but it led to bondage.

And all of that came about because two people failed to do two simple things: *trust* and *obey*.

Of the two, we tend to focus most on obedience. That's what parents stress with their children. We discipline our kids when they disobey. Society has an entire legal system with paid law enforcement officers to punish and restrain disobedient lawbreakers. What we often fail to notice, however, is that disobedience is usually the result of a lack of trust.

If we trusted God to be both great and good—if we believed Him to be as competent as He is portrayed in the Bible—we would be more likely to obey what He says.

As we think about how our behavior is to be shaped by our story this week, it might be easy for us to present Adam and Eve's fruit eating as a cautionary tale about what happens when we fail to obey God's clear commands. But we'd rather encourage you to focus less on obedience to God and more on cultivating trust in Him.

Every command given in the Bible comes from a God who has our best interests at heart. He does not tell us to abstain from sex outside of marriage because He wants to spoil our fun; He tells us because He knows that such behavior will ultimately lead us away from the intimacy we truly crave. He tells us to give money away not because He wants us to be impoverished, but because He knows that true freedom is found in a generous spirit.

Obedience that is not based in trust is short-lived at best and tends to produce resentment. That's not what God wants; it's not what any father wants with his children. Instead, with trust as the foundation of a healthy relationship, obedience comes naturally.

So how do you begin to cultivate that kind of trust in a God you can't see? How do you learn just how trustworthy God is?

Easy: Take a deep breath again.

FRIDAY: Prayer

Narrative

Lord of all creation, You made us for Yourself, and You always take pleasure in granting us every good and perfect gift. Your Word is trustworthy and Your promises are sure. In spite of this, I struggle with trusting You enough to surrender to Your better way. I often succumb to my own devices and desires, foolishly hoping that I can successfully order my life without conscious dependence on You. When I rebel against Your goodness by choosing my will above Yours, I only grasp dust and ashes. Give me the grace to believe that you really do know what is best for me and that I do not. May I cling to Your character and rejoice in Your pursuit of me. I thank You that in spite of my waywardness, You never let me go. May I honor You so that my influence on others will be for their moral and spiritual good rather than their detriment.

Orthodoxy

O God, You are Lord of heaven and earth, and all things come from You and through You and to You. When You spoke the cosmos into being, You remained the infinite and personal One who is forever distinct from Your created order. You alone are God, and we are Your people who have been granted the immense dignity of being created in Your glorious image. You have called me to be like You in my thinking, my choosing, and my desires and emotions. By Your grace

I want to emulate Your character and nature so that I will draw nearer to You. I know that sin and rebellion against Your benevolence only lead to pain, alienation and estrangement in my relationship with You and with others. I want to be content with all You have called me to have and to be, knowing that Your pleasure is my highest good.

Orthopathy

Father, You have loved me and called me to be Your loyal follower, and to find my true pleasure in Your revealed will. You have given all humanity great personal worth and have called us to a high and holy life of other-centered love. As I pursue You, may I also pursue the best interests of the people You have sovereignly placed in my life, so that I will be an agent of reconciliation and of Your grace. You are the eternal wellspring of wisdom, and I want to drink from the water of Your Word and be satisfied. Keep me from being a stumbling block to others and empower me to treat people according to their true dignity in Your image rather than according to the world's distorted view of status and worth. Let my love and service of others be an expression of my love and service to You.

Orthopraxy

God, I ask for a clearer vision of the blessings of obedience and the pain of disobedience so that I will fear You, hope in You and depend on You. Most of all, I want to grow in trust so that I will take the risks of obedience that run contrary to the world system with its temporal values. May I develop a clearer upward perspective so that I realize in my thinking and practice that only the transcendent can give ultimate meaning to life on earth. Without You I am wretched and hopeless, but when I abide in Your loving presence I enjoy the fruit of love, joy and peace. Grant me wisdom from the Word and the desire to renew my mind in Your timeless truth. Then I will walk in the way of life-giving trust and dependence, and then I will learn the blessings of obedience to what You proclaim for my good.

3

Promise of a Nation

GENESIS 12

MONDAY: Story

The world was in a mess, and nothing seemed to help. So God decided to have a chat with a man named Abram, who lived in a town called Ur.

God said, "Hey, Abram, I'm going to make you into a great nation."

"What's a nation?" Abram may have asked.

There weren't any of those around yet. God may have explained that a nation is like a really, really big family.

"Oh . . . okay . . . uh . . . there's just this one thing. I don't have any kids, and my wife is passed the . . . uh . . . well, let's just say that window's closed. Is that going to be a problem?"

God made a crazy promise to a random nobody who lived in the middle of nowhere that his barren wife would give him at least one child and that through his child, a great nation would come and would bless the entire world. God had no reason to choose Abram (whose name was later changed to "Abraham"). There was nothing about him that would commend him to God or indicate that he was a good choice to be patriarch of the most famous people group in human history. But God chose him anyway.

And if you think about it, Abraham had no good reason to obey God. There was no history, no documented evidence that this disembodied voice, speaking from heaven or behind a bush or wherever it came from, was anything other than last night's mutton talking back. The promise was so outrageous, so unreasonable, we would understand if Abram had said, "Yeah, right," and gone on his merry way. But Abram chose to believe anyway.

We have to wonder how exactly Abram explained all this to his wife Sarai (later called "Sarah"). Did Abram go home and try to conceive a child that night? After all . . . it wasn't an immaculate conception! How would he explain his suddenly amorous behavior? *See . . . . there was this voice that said we were going to have a child, so I figured we could maybe . . . well . . . . you know . . .*

But there would be no child conceived that night. Days turned to weeks turned to months turned to years turned to decades. Twenty-five long years went by as the already old couple grew ancient. The temptation was always there to give up. Maybe the old fool had imagined it after all. Equally strong was the temptation to take matters into their own hands (so to speak). Maybe the promise didn't include Sarah but was only for Abraham. Maybe if he found another woman . . .

But Abraham kept believing. He kept trusting. When God said go, he went. And one day, miracle of miracles, the seed did not land on a barren wasteland as it had all the other times before. It found fertility. There were tears of joy and tears of relief and tears of "I can't believe it finally happened." And all three members of the family had to wear diapers!

One random man in the middle of nowhere had enough faith to just keep going and going and going until God came through on His promise. A baby boy was born, and they named him "Laughter."

TUESDAY: Beliefs

Nothing is impossible with God. God can do absolutely, positively anything. The things you think will never happen in a million years can be accomplished in the blink of an eye with God.

Of course, God is also one of the most frustrating people you'll ever meet. He rarely does things when you think He will. He operates on some other-worldly timetable that frequently has you checking your watch, wondering if He's ever going to show up.

Some people say, "God is an 11:59 God."

Abraham probably would have said, "God is a 12:15 God."

Here's the truth: God does what He wants when He wants. He will not be rushed by our impatience, but He will not be slowed by our resistance either.

Sometimes slow, sometimes fast—this God is frustrating, alright. But He's good.

And did we mention that He can do anything? You name it, He can do it. Water in the desert? Just you wait. Food to feed the masses? No problem. He made everything there is, and He started with nothing. If He can do that, then taking a skeptical, old, barren couple and turning them into a great nation is a snap! He can even bring people back to life. Anything you can ask or imagine, He can do and go one better, beyond your wildest dreams.

He can do absolutely anything.

Except one thing: He can't lie. Once He gives his word, He can't go back on it. If He says something's going to happen, take it to the bank, because He simply cannot tell a lie.

It may not happen when you want it or the way that you want it. It may not look like you thought it would. But if God makes a promise, He delivers.

Of course, Abram didn't know this. God didn't have much of a track record yet, and Abram hadn't heard countless stories that attest to the power and faithfulness of God.

But you have.

So, what's your excuse?

God can accomplish far more than you can think of asking Him. He's made all sorts of promises to you about being with you and enabling you to do hard things and protecting you and providing for you. His sense of timing is different from yours. His idea of protection and provision may be different from yours, but His faithfulness and power will more than make up for any delays or discomfort you experience.

WEDNESDAY: Values

People can live without a lot of things. For thousands of years, people lived without cars, computers, televisions and microwave ovens. People can even live without a sense of hearing or sight or taste or smell. People have been known to live without an arm or a leg or even an eye.

But people cannot live without hope.

Life is hard. We don't need a psychiatrist to tell us that; we know it experientially. We all experience the aches and pains of getting older. At some point in time, people let us down and life doesn't turn out the way we thought it would.

Without hope, people give up, sit down and begin the process of dying. Hopelessness breeds despair; hope gives life.

Abraham and his wife, Sarah, did not have an easy path to walk. They'd been barren for so long, bereft of anything tangible. All they had to cling to was a promise from an unseen God. But cling to it theyndid, with all their might, for they knew that without the hope from that promise, they might as well throw in the towel.

Hope is vital to existence. And the truth about people is that, because we *cannot* live without hope, we *do not* live without hope. We all have hope. The issue with which we must all come to terms is where we place it.

Put your hope in another human and you'll be let down. Put your hope in your children and you'll be let down. Wealth, job, status, house, car, golf game, even church—none of these are designed to bear the weight of your hopes.

Only God can fill that role. The God of hope gives us hope in the form of a promise and a track record of faithfulness that remains unbroken for thousands of years. He may have let Abraham and Sarah sweat it out for a while, but He never let them down. In fact, generations later, this God would be referred to as "The God of Abraham, Isaac and Jacob."

That would be Abraham and his son and his grandson, the founders of the Nation of Israel.

And we've never heard of anyone who put their trust in the God of Abraham, Isaac and Jacob getting to the end of life and saying, "I wish I had trusted Him less. I see now how hopeless this whole God-following endeavor really is."

God doesn't just offer hope and sustain hope; He actually *becomes* our hope—the only kind of hope that can see us through the really tough stuff in this life.

THURSDAY: Actions

"We're running out of time! You're going to have to trust me!"

It seems like Jack Bauer says that in every episode of the hit television show *24*. The world is in peril. Jack's the only government agent with the courage and determination to do what needs to be done (even if it means playing fast and loose with the rules), and now there's someone standing between him and saving the day.

"Please. We don't have much time. Will you trust me?" Jack asks, and we know that they will.

At some point, the writers might be clever enough to have a character say, "No, Jack, I don't trust you. Frankly, you haven't been very trustworthy over the past few years. Your success rate is stellar, but your ethics are appalling." (Of course, as soon as they say such a thing, they'll surely become the next casualty of this season's nerve gas or chemical bomb or nuclear warhead.)

What exactly is Jack expecting when he asks for someone's trust? Is he asking them to have an emotional level of confidence in him and his vigilante ways? Of course not. He's not asking anyone to *feel* anything; he's asking for cooperation. In some way, he's asking for obedience. And he knows that obedience comes from trust, not from emotional feelings of security. In fact, emotional security may only come as a byproduct of the kind of trust that feels the fear but does the hard thing anyway.

So it is with God. God comes to us and asks us to trust Him. Does that mean we have to be fearless? Must we stop feeling what we are feeling in order to demonstrate real trust?

No.

Abraham and Sarah were not asked to stop feeling anything they were feeling.

Feel the fear. Feel the disappointment. Feel the weariness and confusion and uncertainty. But do what God says anyway. And know that there is at least one very significant difference between God and Jack Bauer (there are lots, but we'll just stick to one here so you can get on with your day): God not only has a stellar success rate; His ethics are flawless, too.

For God, what gets done is only a fourth of the equation. God does the right thing at the right time for the right reason in the right way. And when you muster up the courage to trust Him like Abraham did, you'll find yourself becoming more and more like that, too.

The question you have to wrestle with today is simple: Will you trust Him? Will you trust Him enough to go where He says go and do what He says do? Will you trust Him enough to give, to serve, to rest, to talk, to listen?

You're running out of time. At some point, you're just going to have to trust Him. How about today?

FRIDAY: Prayer

Narrative

God of Abraham, Isaac and Jacob, You rule the universe but chose to become intimately immersed in human history on planet Earth. You have gradually unfolded the mysteries of Your sovereign plan in the developing stories of Scripture, and You see ends that are impossible for any of Your creatures to fathom. While we are on this earth, we walk by faith and not by sight, knowing that the only worthy object of our faith is Your unchanging character and Your sure promises. As I read Your Word, I see with greater clarity that faith in Your promises runs contrary to appearances, because You call me to hope in the unseen and the not yet. Yet You have given me the holy invitation to risk everything I have and am on the invisible promises that will not be fulfilled in this life but in the new realm You are preparing for Your people.

Orthodoxy

Dear Lord, Your ways are past finding out. Just when I think I understand Your direction, I discover that a new level of trust in Your purposes is necessary. As I look back, I realize that You have never let me down, though it often appeared that way when I was going through the trials. As I look ahead, I rest in Your good will for my life. Mine is only an illusion of control—all things are really in Your hands. Like Abram of old, You change my name and my destiny, and You call me to a country and to a promise that seems impossible to fulfill. But by Your grace, I will believe that what You say is true, even when it makes no sense to me. You have called me to trust in You, not to understand all Your ways. Nothing is impossible with You, and I will confidently hope in what You have promised.

Orthopathy

Lord God, just as You prepared and called Abram out of obscure beginnings, so too You laid Your hand upon me and called me to a glorious destiny. But along the journey I realize that there are times when You will take me to the end of my own resources to teach me that only Your resources are sufficient. You call into being that which did not exist and bring life out of barrenness. You have implanted a living hope within me, and You teach me again and again, sometimes through hardship and uncertainty, that any other hope will let me down. By Your loving power, may I put my hope in those things You have promised and not in the people, possessions and positions of this fleeting world. I thank You for the living hope I have received through the resurrection of Jesus Christ from the dead.

Orthopraxy

Father, I confess that I don't know where You are taking me during this earthly sojourn and that I often try to go my own way instead because I think I understand it. But I also confess that Your purposes and character are perfect, even when they appear to be otherwise. I know that You cannot do anything that is contrary to Your goodness and that You cannot lie. All that You have promised, You will surely fulfill in Your time, in Your way and in Your power. Teach me to take the risks of radical obedience and ruthless trust so that I will honor and please You.

I realize that I can only be truly satisfied when You are glorified. Teach me in my thoughts, words and deeds that trust is a choice. I choose to rest in You and hope in Your perfect character. When I am fearful, I will hold on to You.

4

Birth of a Nation

Exodus 1–14

MONDAY: Story

Abraham had a son named Isaac. Isaac had two sons named Jacob and Esau. Jacob (whose name got changed to Israel) had 12 sons, one of whom was named Joseph (who had an amazing Technicolor dreamcoat!). And Joseph, as you may or may not know, found his way down to Egypt (okay, he had a little "help" from his brothers).

(We seem to be making a lot of parenthetical statements).

It's a good thing Joseph's brothers sold him into slavery. If they hadn't, the entire story would have ended early and badly. A famine struck the land where Jacob lived with his family, and because Joseph was in Egypt, he was able to stave off starvation and save his entire family.

But they were still just a family. They weren't really a nation yet.

The whole family relocated south and lived in relative ease and comfort. They were related to Joseph, after all, and Joseph was the second-most-powerful man in Egypt.

And they started having babies. Turns out the sons of Abraham were a lot more ... er ... fertile than their patriarch. They were so fertile, in fact, that the new pharaoh—who didn't know Joseph or his family like the old pharaoh—started to notice how many of them there were. He started to fear that they might want to take over the place, so he had them enslaved (while he still could). But the people kept growing. Pharaoh, feeling even more threatened, started killing all the baby boys.

The descendants of Abraham were supposed to be a great nation, but they didn't even have their own land yet. They were slaves, powerless to stop a ruthless madman from performing post-birth abortions on their children. They must have wondered about those great promises YHWH[1] had made to Father Abraham. Maybe they were just old wives' tales, stories you tell to children to get them to behave.

But God wasn't finished yet. He was still working, first through a tiny baby boy who shouldn't even have survived, then through the pharaoh's daughter. (You'll see as we go: God loves working through outsiders.) That baby boy grew up to be Moses, the greatest leader in the Old Testament.

Now, it was hardly a straight line from being hidden from Pharaoh in a floating basket made of reeds to leading 2.5 million people (or so) out of bondage and into the land of milk and honey, the land that God had promised to Abraham. Moses tried taking matters into his own hands—which, we already know, never works out well in the Bible—and had to flee from the long arm of the law.

He spent 40 years tending sheep in the middle of nowhere, until he had a conversation with a bush that appeared to be on fire but refused to burn up (how long did it take him to figure that one out?). Out of the flames, God broke the news that He had chosen fugitive Moses to run point on His mission to liberate His people. Moses reluctantly agreed to talk to Pharaoh, and then watched as God miraculously rained plague after plague after plague down on the Egyptians until the oppressors begged the Hebrews to leave. (The Egyptians even threw money at them on their way out.)

And so it happened: God's people become a nation, leaving behind their chains of oppression on their way out the door to the Promised Land.

Here's something we're already learning in this Big Story: God has one central plotline that relentlessly moves the story forward, but He is also content to chase a lot of rabbit trails along the way (He even speaks in parenthetical statements sometimes). He does things at His own pace. Sometimes it's painfully slow and other times it's faster than you can blink.

But it's His story, so He gets to decide when and how things happen.

TUESDAY: Beliefs

By now you've hopefully caught on to a few things about the Bible. First of all, anyone who says that the Bible is boring and irrelevant hasn't read it! Already there's been murder and deception, sibling rivalry, sex and heartache and danger. Themes ripped out of today's headlines come alive in the stories we read about these ancient people.

And we're just coming to the end of the first book!

Something else you've probably picked up on is that the people talked about in the Bible are real people. They're not two-dimensional, cardboard cutouts who always get it right. They're flesh and blood people who struggle with insecurity and anxiety and have mixed motives sometimes—just like the rest of us.

This is important, because it helps us see that their story is, in many ways, our story as well. Adam and Eve aren't just people who lived a long, long time ago in a land far, far away. They're *us*, trying to accept and live within the freedom-inducing boundaries set by our Creator.

Abraham and Sarah aren't just the mother and father of the three major world religions. They're *us*, called to live a life of adventurous, risk-taking faith in pursuit of the land our God has promised.

Joseph isn't just a spoiled brat who hits rock bottom and makes a resounding comeback, saving his family and the destiny of the descendants of Abraham. He's *us*, believing that God is with us in the darkest times, giving us discernment in the midst of confusion, empowering us to forgive those who have wronged us.

The Bible story is *our* story. We don't just read it as an academic exercise; we read it to understand better the true nature of ourselves and the world in which we live.

Third and most important, though, you should know by now that the main character in the Bible is God. As tempting as it may be to read these stories and ask, "What does this tell me about me?" we must first stop to think about what these stories reveal to us about the character and nature of God. Otherwise, the stories become about the people of God instead of being about the God of the people.

When you look at it that way, the Bible reveals to us a God who is in charge, is incredibly creative, solves problems in roundabout ways, takes His own sweet time and manages to deliver His people in spite of overwhelming odds. In fact, it sometimes appears as if God prefers the hard way to the easy way. He doesn't seem to be as interested in efficiency as we are, preferring to lead His people through a character-forming hardship more than along a comfortable, cushy path.

He even seems to prefer working with messed up people rather than someone who's got it all together.

It's rarely a straight line. It's an adventure. But you've already figured that out by now, haven't you?

WEDNESDAY: Values

We live in a parenthesis between what has happened and what we've been promised will happen. But we wouldn't know that if not for the Bible. Were it not for these great stories that have been preserved for us for thousands of years, we might be tempted to think that we're all on our own—at the mercy of the tides, left to scramble and adjust to each random bend in the road.

But the Bible tells us very clearly: *The twists and bends are not random*. Nothing happens to us pointlessly. God uses each and every circumstance to shape us and form within us the kind of character we were originally designed to bear.

Abraham and Sarah were promised a son, but they waited and waited for years before the promise was finally fulfilled. They may have been tempted to give up, but God was interested in more than just getting things done. God is careful about how He does things.

Joseph was sold into slavery, and his brothers meant to do him harm. God, on the other hand, had a much larger plan in mind, and used Joseph in Egypt to save his family.

Moses spent 40 years as a fugitive from the law, tending sheep in the middle of nowhere. He must have thought that maybe God was through with him. But God was using that time to prepare him for one of the greatest missions in human history.

The theme that begins to emerge from these stories is that God values the process as much as the outcome. In some ways, the journey is as important as the destination. God is not merely interested in taking you some*where*; He intends to make you some*one* in the process. The twists and turns, the tempests and trials . . . these are the ingredients He uses to transform you into the kind of person you were intended to be all along.

In our bottom-line oriented society, it's vitally important to remember: *How* we get to the end is every bit as important as *that* we get there, because how we get there—the choices we make and the way we live between now and then—will determine who we are when we arrive.

THURSDAY: Actions

Most married couples either videotape their wedding ceremony or hire a photographer to chronicle the happy day's events. Some do both!

Why?

Well, most couples find themselves caught up in the whirl of emotions and thoughts and find that they have a difficult time remembering the details of the day. Things move so fast; the whole day seems like a blur! Having a video or a photo album allows them to go back and reconstruct the events. It helps them remember. They may not go back and review things every day, but on special occasions it's nice to be able to recall what it was like to be so young and idealistic and in love.

Love fades sometimes—well, the emotional part of it. Marriage is not for the fainthearted. We wear rings as symbols and have pictures to remind us of the commitment we made in front of God and everyone else. We celebrate our anniversaries annually because we must remember our vows to love and honor and cherish "until death do us part."

It's been said that no woman ever forgets that she's married. But a husband or a wife can sometimes fail to act like he or she is married, so having built-in reminders is a good thing. And it's a similar story for people and their relationships with God. It was certainly the case for the Israelites in the Old Testament. It was impossible for them to forget that God had delivered them out of Egyptian bondage and into a land flowing with milk and honey. But they often failed to act like it.

God desperately wanted His people to remember where they'd come from and how He'd delivered them, so He built in some reminders. Every year, they observed the Passover. Periodically, they offered sacrifices. There were special meals, days of fasting and days of feasting. Much of their lives was oriented around activities designed to prompt their memories. God knew that if they failed to live with the memory of deliverance fresh in their minds, they would repeat the destructive patterns of an enslaved people again and again, leading them back into more extreme forms of bondage.

Today, take some time to remember what God has done for you. Specifically, remember the deliverance He has offered you, at no expense to you whatsoever. Remember how He brought you out of your own personal form of slavery—slavery to sin and selfishness and destructive patterns of behavior. Remember how He delivered you from loneliness and alienation, how He brought you into a land of purpose and meaning and relationships, taking you off the path of certain destruction and transplanting you onto a path headed for an eternal home. Remember how He took your sorrow and gave you joy in return, took your anxiety and gave you peace, took your fear and gave you confidence.

Christianity expects certain things of its adherents: Christians are expected to give and serve, love and forgive others and offer thanks to God on a regular basis. It could be that those things would flow more easily from our hearts if we would regularly take time to simply remember.

FRIDAY: Prayer

Narrative

God of our fathers, I give thanks that You have revealed Your great and surprising story of redemption to us in Your extraordinary Word. Through the Scriptures, I see that there is always a purpose in what You do, and that nothing catches You by surprise. You are fully sovereign over human history, and I am grateful that You have embedded Your people in a larger Story. It is this Story that gives me perspective and hope amidst the uncertainties and obstacles of this earthly sojourn. Your creative plans behind the scenes turn the apparently hopeless situations we face into manifestly hopeful outcomes. Your deliverance and Your timing are surprising, but I want to learn to trust in Your wisdom and not in my own. May I hope in Your providential care and not in my own limited plans and efforts.

Orthodoxy

Lord, give me the illumination to see You more as You are rather than what I fancy You to be. I realize that all the stories in the pages of Your revealed Word point to You, Your character, Your ways, Your faithfulness, Your goodness, Your graciousness, Your patience, Your loyal love, Your creative purposes, and to the excellence of Your glorious attributes. Everything is about You and not us, yet You have chosen to make us the recipients of Your boundless grace. May I know You, and may I know myself in light of the knowledge of You. Your progressive revelation of Your person, powers and perfections illuminates my path and inspires me to walk in fidelity and obedience to You, and I ask for the empowerment by Your Holy Spirit to be fully obedient to all that You call me to be and do.

Orthopathy

God, I recognize that I did not determine the circumstances of my birth, my abilities, my opportunities, my pathway. It is You who have called and chosen me for Your inscrutable purposes. My times are in Your hands, and during this season of my temporal sojourn as a pilgrim, a wayfarer and a stranger, I know that You are working all things together for my greatest good. You see what I cannot see—the outcome—and You have called me to be faithful to the process and look to You for where it leads. I acknowledge my own powerlessness and my foolish attempts to do things in my own way, timing and reasons. I thank You that I can learn from the intensely realistic characters of the Bible, because human nature does not change. As I read their stories, I realize that they illustrate the stories of Your people today.

Orthopraxy

Father, You have never left me alone. Even when I feel that You are distant and removed, I know that I am still in Christ, seated with Him at Your right hand. You have allowed seasons of fullness and of dryness, times of abundance and of profound need. I know that You are more interested in my character than in my comfort, and that You use everything to forge godly character in my life. You have called me to fidelity to the process rather than to live only for a product. Give me the grace of holy remembrance, so that I will frequently review all that You have done for me during my journey with You. May I call to mind Your faithful acts, Your provision, Your patience and Your great acts of deliverance. Apart from You, I have nothing and am nothing.

5

Real Freedom

Exodus 20

MONDAY: Story

The people were free! After all those years—centuries—of slavery and oppression, they were finally free and headed to claim their Promised Land.

But there were still a few kinks that needed working out.

For one thing, they had no idea how to live as a nation. They had been an extended family, living under someone else's rules and laws. They'd never really had rules and laws of their own before.

So God decided to teach them how to live.

There is something we should consider about God's communication with people: *How* He says what He says is often an important factor in being able to accurately discern His message. In fact, it could be said that how He delivers the message is part of the message itself.

Imagine: All those people standing around this gigantic smoking mountain. There's thunder and lightning flashing around the top. They have been warned not to touch the mountain, lest they die—and you remember what happened the last time a warning like that was issued!

Most of us probably know how this is going to turn out; after all, the movie re-airs on television every year! But the Hebrews haven't seen the movie yet; they are living it. They have absolutely no idea what's going to happen next. All they know is that this guy shows up saying that a shrub caught on fire and told him to go to Pharaoh to get them free. Then, when Pharaoh didn't want to cooperate (and who could blame him, really?) there was an onslaught of plagues unleashed on those Egyptians. And now here they are on their own in the middle of nowhere, with more money than they know what to do with.

So now this crazy Moses fella climbs up this smoking and shaking mountain. Who knows how long he's going to be up there?

At the top of the mountain, God tells Moses something amazing: If the people will commit to following His instructions, they will be His treasure, a people set apart for His purposes, set above all the other nations. That's pretty impressive, to go from slaves to the envy of all, just by keeping God's instructions. You'd think it would be a no-brainer, right? The deal of a lifetime.

Meanwhile, back down the mountain . . . the people grow impatient and talk Aaron (Moses' brother) into melting all the gold they had received into an idol for them to worship. When he finally climbs down, Moses finds them throwing a giant block party with drinking, dancing and all kinds of sordid stuff that would get you thrown out of your local Bible club.

Fortunately, God had told Moses something no one could have expected. Before He gave even one of the Ten Commandments, God told Moses, "I am the LORD your God, who brought you out of Egypt, out of the land of slavery" (Exod. 20:2). In other words, the law was given *after* their freedom—not in order to gain their freedom. (Don't forget that one.) Obedience was not a means of becoming God's Chosen People; obedience was a response to God's deliverance.

There were consequences for not obeying, of course. Sin is serious and brings about terrible results. Lots of the Israelites died as a result of their terrible choice. Still, God could have chosen to wipe them all off the face of the earth. He could have abandoned them then and there or sent them straight back into slavery in Egypt. But He didn't.

See, God had a plan, and not even the disobedience of His people could stop it.

TUESDAY: Beliefs

Imagine a young couple standing at the front of a beautifully decorated church building. The groom is wearing a magnificent tuxedo; the bride is a vision in white lace. Their friends and families are gathered there, squinting in the candlelight, straining to hear them exchange their whispered promises.

Now imagine the young man turning to his bride. He's written his own vows. He looks at her tenderly and says, "I want you to be my wife, but first I have to make sure you're serious about this. So, after much thought and prayer and consulting people who I believe to be wise, I have come up with the following vow, which I make to you today in the presence of God and everyone: If you will faithfully wash my clothes, cook my meals, clean my house, share my bed and bear my children, then I will marry you."

Any young woman who would go for such a deal ought to have her head examined! The minister ought to call the whole thing off right there. The father of the bride ought to demand his money back. The best man ought to have a word with his friend. It's preposterous.

A marriage is built first on a commitment to relationship and trust. Acts of service are done with that as a backdrop. It's not safe to marry someone without the context of a secure relationship built on mutual submission.

It's the same in our relationship with God (the part about secure relationship—not the part about mutual submission). God does not give us the Law as a condition for relationship; the Law is a confirmation of a relationship. We don't obey in order to become His children; we obey because we are His children. You cannot obey your way into salvation because only perfect obedience would be enough.

You obey God because you are saved. Obedience is your response to His grace.

The ironic thing is, once you begin living a life of obedience, you find your life actually works better. God has set things up to run a certain way; disobedience amounts to sawing against the grain of the universe—it's unnecessarily difficult.

Then a really fascinating thing begins to happen: The more you obey God, the more you trust Him. The more you trust Him, the more you want to do what He says. Ultimately, you find yourself thinking the way He thinks, seeing things from His perspective. You find within yourself a desire to live out the will of God, and you no more think of breaking His law than you think it a good idea to break the law of gravity.

A life of obedience begins to be the only sane way to live; it is, in fact, a life of true freedom. As counter-intuitive as it may seem, real freedom comes only as we submit to God's laws.

WEDNESDAY: Values

Before God gave His people His Law, the world was a rough place. In many ways it still is, but we would be wise to consider the moral baseline of civilization at the time. We live on this side of 3,000 years of the civilizing, restraining influence of the Judeo-Christian ethic. We enjoy the legacy of the Ten Commandments.

The world before God's giving of the Law was an awful, scary, barbaric place to live. People routinely practiced human sacrifice, especially of children. Slaves were killed without any accountability. Women were considered property. Children were disposable resources. Revenge was commonplace.

It was survival of the fittest writ large.

No one—not even the most hardened Darwinian atheist—wants to live in a world like that.

All of us want there to be justice. We want there to be balanced scales. We want there to be a standard of right and wrong, punishment for the wicked and a recourse for the righteous to plead their case. None of that would be possible without the Law of God.

No wonder the psalmist said, "The law from your mouth is more precious to me than thousands of pieces of silver and gold. . . . Oh, how I love your law! I meditate on it all day long" (Ps. 119:72, 97).

People have given their lives to preserve the Word of God. People have gone to jail for possessing a copy. People have traveled land and sea to faithfully translate it into as many different languages as humanly possible. Many of us have multiple copies within easy reach, but do we really value the Bible?

Within its leather-bound, gold-leafed, onion-skin pages, we find more than history and philosophy; we find wisdom for living. The Bible doesn't merely speak to us of "heavenly" things or "spiritual matters." God's Law is holistic, giving us a basis for coherent thought and practice.

As we meditate on God's Word, He shapes the way we think about our world and ourselves, teaching us to think His thoughts and lead an integrated life in which everything we do matters. There is no dichotomy between spiritual and sacred. God intends to govern all of life, rendering it all holy.

How dare we reduce it to trivia or an academic textbook to be studied alongside the *Riverside Shakespeare* or the *Encyclopedia Britannica*! These are the words of life that point us to Wisdom and Truth personified, revealing to us the true character and nature of the true God who desires for us to be His treasured people, a people set apart for a purpose, rightly relating to Him so that we can be rightly related to each other.

THURSDAY: Actions

There really is no such thing as "cold"; there is merely the absence of heat. Likewise, there's no such thing as dark, just the absence of light.

And there's no such thing as evil. There is only the absence of righteousness, a life that honors God by rightly relating to Him and others.

God gave His Law as a means of turning on the lights in a dark room, turning on the heater in a chilly basement. And yet, for some strange reason, many of us continue living in a cold, dark place rather than coming into the warmth and light that God offers.

How do we do this? *We fail to open up and read God's Word.*

Biblical illiteracy is not just an embarrassment for incoming college freshmen. It has infiltrated the Christian community as well. We have the best Story on the planet, and we're largely ignorant of it. Because we don't know our own Story, we can't tell it very well. We settle for bits and pieces told in mostly a *Reader's Digest* format. (No offense to the good folks at that fine periodical, but some books aren't meant to be condensed into bite-sized portions.)

We want to be adamant about this point: We're so very glad you purchased our book and are reading it. It is our hope and prayer that you gain much and grow greatly as a result of our thoughts here. We spent a lot of time and energy producing this, and we would hate to think of that all as a waste. We're honored and humbled that you have read this far.

However, this book is not intended to ever become a substitute for the real thing. You'll never grow into the kind of person who thinks and feels and does the right thing at the right time in the right way for the right reason without picking up God's Word.

Read it. Study it. Learn it. Memorize it. Meditate on it. Live it—not as an end in and of itself, but as a means to a greater end: to become progressively more and more like its Author.

Can you imagine what the world would be like if everyone did? Can you imagine a single day with no murder, no gossip, no child abuse, no deceit, no fraud, no divorce? God intends to create just such a world, and He intends to start with you. Pick up His Word, read it and do what it says, and we can all get on with it!

FRIDAY: Prayer

Narrative

Lord God, where can I find life but in You? Teach me the error of seeking to reduce You to manageable proportions and to make the invisible visible. Protect me from the subtle forms of idolatry in which I worship and serve something in Your created order above You. I know that only one thing can occupy the center of my being and that if it is not You, it is an idol that is not worthy of my allegiance. I thank You that when I do succumb to the sins of disobedience, Your grace always reaches further than my rebellion. Still, I desire to delight in You above all else, and I am grateful for the gift of Your Word that guides me in the way I should go. Your revelation teaches me how to live and gives me the perspective I so greatly need in a world of uncertainty.

Orthodoxy

Lord God, You have revealed Your perfect character and will in Scripture. Your Word teaches the way that leads to fullness of life and provides the wisdom I need to make the right decisions and to value the right things. You have revealed Your Law not to imprison me but to liberate me from the prison of self. You have set my feet on a high place and now You call me to submit to Your will and obey Your commands. And I know that the more I do this, the more I am liberated from the bondage of the world, the flesh and the devil. Thank You for the grace to make me become the person You always intended me to be. Everything You ask me to do is in my best interest, and everything You ask me to avoid is destructive. May I learn more clearly the freedom of submission as I trust in Your character and obey Your precepts.

Orthopathy

Lord, let me increasingly delight in Your Law and meditate on its life-giving truths. I want to be a person of the Word who not only hears it but reflects on it and practices it. As I read the pages of Holy Scripture, I see that all things matter and that there is no dichotomy between the things we call spiritual and the things we call secular. Grant that I may receive a growing wealth of biblical perspective on the circumstances of life so that I will walk in wisdom, in trust, in submission, in obedience and in love. May I express my real freedom in Christ in acts of life-giving obedience and trust in Your ways. And when I slip into disobedience, may I return quickly and be thankful for Your patience and forbearance.

Orthopraxy

O Lord, You have revealed Your will and Your ways in Your Word. In its pages I discover truths about You, about myself, about others and about Your world. Grant me the grace to overcome the spiritual and moral inertia that keeps me from being a regular student of the Bible. May I read its pages, meditate on the words and truths, and hide Your Word in my heart so that I will not succumb to temptation and sin, but be increasingly honoring to You. Grant that I would choose to set my mind and heart on the things above, where Christ is, seated in the heavenly places. I want to be defined by the truths of Your Word rather than the lies of this passing world system. As I learn and reflect on Your truths, I want to respond with unconditional commitment, knowing that I love You because You first loved me.

6

Promised Land

Numbers 13–14

MONDAY: Story

God made a promise to Abraham, and He was working out the fulfillment of that promise. The problem is, He always moves at His own pace!

God's promise to Abraham included two things: a people and a place. It had taken awhile, but the first part had come true. Now the people were gathered together, standing literally at the threshold of their place: the Promised Land.

We might understand if the people had doubted His promise before. They'd spent the last 400 years enslaved to Egypt. But recently, God had gotten a move on and things were progressing at a nice, steady pace.

He had gotten them out of slavery really quickly. The people would never forget those plagues and that dark night when the Angel of Death passed over their houses. They would never forget the blood of lambs smeared over their doorposts. And, of course, how could they forget what God had done at the Red Sea? It's not every day that water stands up like walls and mud turns to a hiking trail in the blink of an eye. It's not every day that you get to see the mightiest army in the world swallowed up by a body of water, helpless before an unseen God.

Oh, and just in case there was any doubt left, let's not forget that whole smoking mountaintop with all the lightning and thunder. This YHWH character made outrageous promises, but He had the goods to back them up! You might say that God had demonstrated both His willingness and His ability to see this whole project through to the end.

Still, slavery tends to breed a sense of inferiority in people.

When they actually saw the land God had promised them, they were overjoyed! The land itself was incredible, better than they ever imagined. If only there weren't already people living there.

God told them it was their land. God told them to go and take it. He had enough firepower to ensure their success. But they backed away. And the reason they give is telling: "We look like grasshoppers in our own eyes" (Num. 13:33).

There are few things in the world more painful than missed opportunities. Here were the Israelites, standing on the verge of finally having their own land, of really becoming the nation God promised them they would be. And they shied away.

It wasn't really because of how big the people there were; it was because of how the Israelites saw themselves.

Over the course of the next 40 years, they would have plenty of time to rethink their position. As they wandered from station to station, walking in the hot sun of the Arabian Desert, eating manna and quail all day every day, they would master two things. First, they mastered the art of complaining (Oy, vey!). Second, they figured out—slowly—how to take their eyes off of themselves and look to the God who had chosen them—inferior as they might feel—to be His people.

Once they did that, they realized He really was big enough to take care of business on His own.

TUESDAY: Beliefs

These days, few people seem to believe that there is such a thing as absolute truth. Fewer still believe we can know it.

Obviously, we've all been influenced by the presence of sin in the world, and that influence has rendered us incapable of absolutely understanding absolute truth. Because we cannot grasp it exhaustively, however, does not mean it doesn't exist.

The truth about us is that whether we express it or not, we all live with a set of beliefs that we take to be "the truth." But how we define truth makes all the difference in how we live.

Moses sent a group of 12 leaders into the Promised Land to gather information. He was going to use the information to formulate his plan of attack. After spending 40 days behind enemy lines, however, 10 of these leaders returned with a bad report, suggesting that there was no way they could accomplish the task of invading and displacing the people who currently occupied Canaan.

Several huge mistakes were made. First, Moses was the one who commissioned the team, but they returned and reported back to all the people instead. They were merely asked to bring back information, but they went beyond that and made a recommendation: "Let's stay out of there!" Most importantly, the report brought back by these leaders failed to consider what God had to say about the situation. And that is precisely what made their report "bad."

Truth is not merely facts. These men reported facts. The land was good. The inhabitants were large. The cities were fortified. Those are all facts. But factual information is only one part of the truth.

Neither is truth popular opinion. In fact, it is often in the absence of an understanding of real truth that opinion polls take on a weight and authority they do not deserve.

Neither is real truth what is doable. Real truth is not our perception. Real truth is higher and deeper and broader than any of that. Real truth is what God says about a particular situation. Real truth corresponds to reality from God's perspective. Only He sees the whole thing, and only He is in a position to make a judgment about it.

Truth is hard sometimes. Truth can be costly. Truth, for these people, would have meant war. It would have meant giving up some of their evenings at home in their tents, some of their peaceful (if nomadic) existence. Because they were afraid, because they had forgotten who they were and how great their God was, they chose to consider only the facts and go with popular opinion rather than doing what God had called them to do.

God's truth would demand too much of them. It was unmanageable. It was impractical, they thought. But whenever a group of God's people chooses to follow the path of practicality instead of listening to and obeying the call of God, they run the risk of spending years wandering about in aimless and fruitless work.

The people had a choice to make. They said, "Let us die in this desert rather than deal with these fierce enemies" (Num. 14:1–2). And that is exactly what God allowed them to do.

Because the people failed to live by God's truth, they ended up dying by their own.

WEDNESDAY: Values

The story of the 12 spies being sent into Canaan is one of the most well-known and instructive stories of the Old Testament. But our understanding of it will be incomplete without a little background information.

Two chapters earlier, we read something that sets us up for greater understanding. According to Numbers 11:1, "The people complained about their hardships in the hearing of the Lord."

Of course, this was not the first time they'd complained. That started early, before they even got to Mount Sinai. They complained about the water. Then they complained about the food. God got their attention by sending fresh water and manna. Then He really got their attention by shaking a mountain with His voice and giving Moses the Law.

But now they're back at it again. Manna isn't good enough; they want meat. Their incessant whining begins to wear on Moses, so he takes to complaining, too.

God is still merciful and gracious in His provision—though He may seem, at first glance, a little passive-aggressive about it. He sends them meat, but listen to what He says: "You will not eat it for just one day, or two days, or five, ten or twenty days, but for a whole month—until it comes out of your nostrils and you loathe it" (Num. 11:19–20).

Here's why we're bringing this up: It's hard to scare people who are filled with gratitude for the blessings they have. If they had spent as much time thanking God for what they had as they did complaining to Him about what they lacked, they would have been less likely to believe the bad report brought back by the majority of the spies.

Gratitude is linked to hope. Gratitude remembers how God delivers on His promises. Gratitude thinks about how God brought them out of slavery, provided water in the desert, and provided manna faithfully every morning.

Their discontent made them almost incapable of believing that God would help them gain possession of the Promised Land. No matter what God gave them—freedom from slavery, supernatural guidance, the civilizing effects of the Ten Commandments, food, water, hope and a future—it was never enough. Discontentment, complaint, ingratitude . . . these are the real killers of God's people. Long before the spies brought back a faithless report, the Israelites had imbibed the toxic spirit of grumbling against God and against His appointed leader.

You are created in God's image. You have a body that probably works most of the time. You have a heart that beats and lungs that breathe, and likely eyes that see and ears that hear. You have a God who loves you and has adopted you into His family. You have a future home with Him forever, guaranteed. You have access to God's Word, God's Family, God's Future. You have been given gifts that can be used in eternally significant ways. Even when you mess up, God loves you and accepts you anyway.

Value what you have. Even more than that, value the God who gave you all that you have. Give thanks to Him for life and breath and food and water and warmth and the means by which you are able to read this book.

You do that, and it'll be harder for you to believe a bad report when one comes along.

THURSDAY: Actions

God could have taken His people right to Canaan and sent all the inhabitants of the land out on His own. It was a 200-mile walk from Egypt to the Jordan River. They could have covered that in just a couple of weeks.

Instead of going northeast toward the Jordan, however, the pillar of fire and smoke, the symbol of God's presence, leads the people south.

Q: Did God just take a wrong turn?
A: Depends on where you're heading.

From our perspective, we think God must have taken a wrong turn, because we think the ultimate destination is Canaan. But, remember, God is far less interested in where His people end up as He is in who they are when they get there.

So God uses the wilderness to train His people, to test them and grow them up. And this is what He's ultimately after, this is His purpose, this is success for His people: *Will they trust Him, even when it doesn't quite make sense?*

That's the definition of a mature follower of God: someone who trusts God—who walks in obedience—even when it doesn't quite make sense from a practical, earth-bound perspective.

Will you follow Me south, even when you know Canaan is northwest?
Will you walk around the city walls instead of attacking it?
Will you be generous even when resources are scarce?
Will you be sexually pure even if no one else will?
Will you do what I ask you to do if for no other reason than it is I who am asking?
Will you trust Me?

That's the essence of faith: choosing to believe and act accordingly in spite of our feelings or experiences to the contrary. Faith is not the absence of fear as much as it is the unwillingness to allow fear to keep us from obeying God's clear command.

Of course, God isn't asking us for a blind leap of faith. He's given us an overwhelming number of reasons why trusting Him makes good sense. He's got an amazing track record of faithfulness and promise keeping. But He's not going to force you into something. He didn't force the people to take the land. They said they'd rather die in the wilderness, so He let them have what they said they wanted. He won't force you to live a holy, generous, pure life.

If you want to miss your real purpose, your true calling, if you would rather die in safety than live the adventurous life your heart really longs for, He'll let you do that. But can you think of anything sadder than a person wandering aimlessly for years and years, just passing the time, waiting to die?

Maybe the only thing sadder would be for a whole group of people—say, a group of God's people like, maybe, a church—to do that.

It happens all the time, but it doesn't have to. And you can break the cycle today by simply choosing to, in the words of an old hymn, trust and obey.

FRIDAY: Prayer

Narrative

Dear Lord, may I frequently review the many acts of deliverance You have accomplished in my life. When I remember Your saving acts, I gain a renewed perspective on Your graciousness and involvement in my life. When I forget to do this, I sink back into a temporal perspective and lose the cutting edge of gratitude and trust. I want to recall Your glorious promises and remember Your creative deliverances so that I will grow in trust and not slip into doubt. With this perspective on my problems, I will not back off in disbelief and miss the opportunities You have provided for me. May I look at things through the lens of Scripture so that I will know how to respond to the circumstances and people in my life.

Orthodoxy

God, I know that truth is what You say about a thing. You alone are the well-spring of the true, the beautiful and the good, and Your unchanging character is the absolute basis for truth. But I live in a culture of growing relativism in which people have increasingly abandoned the idea of objective truth. By Your grace, I choose to stand against popular opinion and affirm that Your Word is truth. May I resist the temptation to define truth in terms of my own subjective feelings, a majority vote or pragmatic results. Instead, I want to make choices that are based on sound judgment, knowing that wisdom is derived from Your inspired revelation. Illuminate my path with Your truth and empower me to walk in it. Then I will interpret the obstacles and opportunities I encounter with a biblical orientation.

Orthopathy

Father, I acknowledge that I often approach life with a deficiency rather than a sufficiency point of view. I realize that when I fail to acknowledge Your many tender mercies, I lose my joy and contentment and slip into ingratitude. Help me to see that when I grumble and murmur, it is not ultimately about my circumstances, but about You and Your provision. Teach me that gratitude must not be left only to spontaneous moments, but must be chosen every day. May I review Your many gifts and blessings in my life, including those I have too long taken for granted. Teach me that gratitude relates to trust and obedience, for I cannot trust You when I am murmuring and grumbling about my life and circumstances. I choose this day to thank You for Your innumerable kindnesses to me, because I have done nothing to deserve them.

Orthopraxy

Lord God, as I read the stories of the Bible, I see again and again that You call Your people to do things that, at the time, don't seem to make sense. I also realize that the reason Your will didn't make sense to Your people is that their vision was limited—they couldn't see the ends You had in mind. Show me in my mind and heart that I cannot know what my best interest really looks like, because I would need to know the future, and only You know that. Because my own perspective is limited, may I learn to trust You and do what You tell me, because it will always work out to my greater good. Then trust will overcome fear, and I will risk everything on Your character and live into the purposes You have ordained for me. As I embrace a biblical perspective, may it change my priorities and my practice.

7

Conquest

Joshua 1–6

MONDAY: Story

How long had it been since the last time they stood there, gazing across the border into the land that would be their new home? Thirty-eight years of wandering, burying their friends in the wilderness, dozens of them every day. Those had been the most depressing years of Joshua's life.

At least Joshua had his mentor, Moses.

When everything seemed crazy and out of control, when doubts began to creep in and displace hope, Moses' rock-solid presence was there to comfort and stabilize.

But Moses wouldn't allow Joshua to go with him on his last trip up Mount Nebo. And Joshua knew why. Moses wouldn't be coming back: He had died up there, and God had buried him in an unknown grave. It was all up to Joshua now. He was the leader. It would be up to him to take these desert wanderers and turn them into city-dwellers.

How exactly would they do it? How would they finally take hold of what was promised to their forefather Abraham all those hundreds of years ago? Would it be through brute force? Would it be through clever tactics and superior strategy? Not exactly.

The first obstacle that stood between the people and their land was this river, this Jordan River. It was at flood stage and had overrun its banks. There was no good place for three million people to cross. How could they invade the fortified cities of Canaan if they couldn't even get across the river that marked its boundaries?

In a scene that must have been meant to remind them of their crossing the Red Sea, God commanded the people to cross the river, promising to stop the water as soon as their feet touched the surface. And it happened. They'd heard stories from their now-deceased parents about stuff like this. They'd witnessed God's protection and provision in the desert, but perhaps they wondered if He was—like so many of the pagan gods—bound by geography.

No, the God of the desert would be the God of their new home as well. He could bring water from rocks and form dry land in the middle of a rushing river.

And that's not all.

They soon found that He could bring down walls without them ever having to lift a finger. Let's face it: Marching around a city like Jericho, shouting and blowing trumpets, isn't a very good military strategy unless you have an all-powerful God on your side. Then (and only then) it makes perfect sense!

And that was the whole point. The children of Israel didn't need to worry about the normal things: numbers, size, strength. They just had to follow this God who has stubbornly refused to abandon them, even in their whining and fear and disobedience.

It's a good thing we've learned that lesson and never worry about silly, trivial things anymore.

Oh, wait . . .

TUESDAY: Beliefs

Here they stood, poised on the edge of their destiny. Before them they could see the land God had promised so long ago, the land they'd left Egypt for, the land that had taken so long and cost so many lives to reach.

But there was a barrier standing between them and the land: a river at flood stage.

The Jordan River starts at the foot of Mt. Hermon, nearly 9,000 feet above sea level. It ends about 90 miles later at the Dead Sea, which is about 1,400 feet below sea level. This makes it one of the fastest-flowing rivers of its size. It runs fast normally, but at flood stage it poses a serious threat to anyone needing to get to the other side.

How would they get across?

For the people who lived in Canaan, the Jordan River wasn't an obstacle; it was a shield. They believed that one of their gods was in control of that body of water and had brought the river to such a high level in order to protect them from any invaders.

Just like God had done in Egypt, when He used the plagues to topple the pantheon of Egyptian gods, He would now take on the Canaanite god of the river. When He divided the rushing waters of the Jordan River, He was serving notice, both to the inhabitants of the land and to His own Chosen People: *I am not just the God of the wilderness, not just the God who brings water from a rock or manna in the desert; I am God of everything and everywhere. There is nothing that is beyond My ability to control.*

Many of the peoples the Israelites would encounter in Canaan believed in regional or limited gods. They believed there was one god in charge of the harvest and another god in charge of the weather. One god helped you have children, another helped you get well if you'd been sick.

YHWH doesn't work like that. He's God of *everything*. He's the same God of the mountains and the sea, the harvest and your health.

Living in that knowledge would be a continual problem for His people. Throughout the Bible, we read that the greatest temptation is not to reject YHWH altogether but to simply add Him to a list of other gods, to worship Him alongside Baal or Asherah or Molech. Let YHWH handle some things; let the other gods handle other things.

In our society, we may not have little statues or funny names for other gods. But we're probably just as guilty as they were of thinking that God is only in charge of some things, not everything. Maybe we'll trust God with our eternity, but we'll handle things between now and then. Maybe we'll trust Him with our Sundays, but we'll take care of Monday through Saturday.

Let God handle "spiritual" areas. Spiritual areas are, after all, priceless. For everything else, there's Mastercard, right?

God wants to be the Lord of your job and your family, how you spend your money, what you watch on television and what you listen to on your iPod. This is how it's going to be with YHWH: He's either God of everything, or He's God of nothing.

WEDNESDAY: Values

If the stakes are high enough, just about anyone will do just about anything at just about any given time. How else can you explain why people do such foolish things? Or such difficult things? Or such risky things?

If a person is hungry enough, he will go to great lengths, take tremendous risks, even be willing to break the law in order to find food.

Why would a person get up before dawn, pull on her shoes, a T-shirt and a pair of shorts to go jogging?

Why would a person stay up late studying when it would be so much easier to eat ice cream while watching Letterman?

People have to want something pretty badly to endure physical or mental distress to get it. They have to value something more highly than comfort.

This is why people get up early, stay up late, put in the extra effort, go without. There is something for which they are willing to pay a price. If it is something desirable enough, they are willing to pay a very steep price—and they do so gladly.

Why? Because the stakes are high enough.

It seems silly—laughable even—that people are willing to make such great sacrifices and pay such high prices to do things like climb mountains or run races when we are simultaneously unwilling to do much of anything to claim the abundant life God has made available for us. God offers us a life of freedom, a life of adventure, a life of security, a life with no regret or anxiety. Will there be pain involved? Of course! But anything worthwhile is costly. If you devote yourself to the relentless pursuit of whatever God has in store for you, it will require huge risk and an alarming level of sacrifice.

What in the world could motivate the Israelites to step into a rushing river? Why would they be willing to march around the fortified walls of a hostile enemy city with nothing but trumpets in their hands?

What in the world could motivate people to give money away when it would be easier to spend it on themselves? What would cause a person to get up early and volunteer to help someone they've never met? What inspires people to forgive, to serve, to turn the other cheek, to sell everything and move halfway around the world to dig wells or teach children to read?

Maybe we've come to a place where we value our comfort and security more than we really value the calling of God in our lives. But we don't have to stay here. In fact, we cannot stay here and go with God over the difficult barrier into the land of His promise.

THURSDAY: Actions

We tend to think of the priests stepping into the Jordan River like going to the beach and tiptoeing your way down to the water's edge, inching closer and closer, maintaining balance the whole time.

In reality, while the Jordan River isn't very wide or very deep, there isn't really a good place to get down close to the water without just jumping in.

And that was sort of the point. When God told the priests to step into the river, He made it clear that the water wasn't going to stop flowing until they went all in.

There are times in life when we know clearly what God's will is. It may not happen all the time; it may not even be a frequent occurrence. But there are times when there's little mystery about what God would have us do. Yet even in those times, there are frequently obstacles in our path, difficulties that must be overcome, in order for us to accomplish what we know to be the clearly communicated will of God.

How do you respond in those times? Too many of us respond by saying, "Okay, God. I know what You want me to do, but there's this obstacle here. You remove the obstacle, and I'll do what You're calling me to do."

Sounds reasonable, doesn't it?

More often than not, however, just like in the Bible, God says, "You take a step first."

In other words, God will take care of a lot of the obstacles in our paths, but He usually waits for us to take a step of faith before He does. This is part of the astonishing humility of God: Sometimes He actually lets us lead.

One step and the obstacles vanish, more completely and more brilliantly than you ever imagined. But there is that matter of the first step. There is that matter of whether or not you are willing to go all-in, not easing your way into things, but jumping headlong into the thick of difficulties in order to get what God has promised.

The people of God, gathered at the edge of the Jordan River, needed a leader. They desperately needed someone who would step forward and say, "Let's go." There were plenty of people in the crowd willing to move, but did anyone want to be first? They needed a push, a prod, a person willing to show them how it was done.

God's people still need leaders, people willing to step up and step out and show us how it's done. What are you doing standing around on the bank? Jump in and see what God does!

FRIDAY: Prayer

Narrative

Dear Father, there have been many times when I have wandered in the wilderness of disbelief, murmuring and rebellion, wondering indeed if You really have my best interests at heart. I know that I make life far more difficult when I question Your purposes and resist what would, in the end, be the smoother and simpler course. Sin against You complicates and confuses my life, and only leads to pain and regret in the end. Please give me the gift of Your wisdom and grace to think biblically in these moments of doubting Your goodness and provision, so that by Your power, I will turn fear into faith. Then I will be increasingly liberated from the oppressive weight of circumstances and view my situation in light of Your perfect character. I desire to grow in faith, hope and love and to cling firmly to Your loving purposes.

Orthodoxy

O Lord, why do I trust You in some areas of my life, but look for other resources when I need help in other areas? How is it possible for me to trust You for my eternal destiny and then look to the world for everything else? Please deliver me from the disease of compartmentalization, in which I merely make You one component of my life and put other things like my work, my family and my friends in other compartments. Give me the faith to truly believe that You alone must occupy the center of my being, my aspirations, my hope, my purpose, my everything. Then I will see other things from an eternal perspective and realize that everything comes from You and is for You. I want to recommit myself to the lordship of Christ in each sphere of my existence and enjoy the holy release of desiring the one thing that is needed above everything else.

Orthopathy

God, I ask that I would experience a growing desire for You and for the things You declare to be important. I also ask that this living desire would express itself in an ever-increasing willingness to take the risks of faith so that I would honor You by treasuring Your will for my life. I want to discipline myself for the sake of Christlikeness so that I will run the holy race with endurance and fight the good fight in Your strength. I acknowledge that this life is no game, that the stakes are eternal. I recognize that there is a cost of discipleship and that spiritual formation does not come naturally. May I be dependent on Your promises and provision so that I will honor You through the risks and price of obedience.

Orthopraxy

Lord, I thank You that You have created me in Your image and have given me the dignity of being capable of moral choices that genuinely affect my journey and destiny. By Your grace, may I exercise this moral and spiritual capacity by taking the steps of faith, especially in times when my flesh resists this process and when fears prevent me from trusting You. I realize that there are times in my life when You ask me to make the first step, because You don't want to force me into obedience but desire my willing cooperation with Your glorious intentions. I recognize that without You I cannot, but without me You will not. May I strengthen my resolve to be Your loving servant and child so that I will pursue the course You have set before me in spite of my fears and natural resistance.

8

The Time of God's Patience

THE BOOK OF JUDGES

MONDAY: Story

God had gone to great lengths to get His people into this land. He certainly took them on the scenic route, but they had finally arrived. They took possession of the land and now it was time to get on with the rest of God's promise—the part about being a blessing to all the nations around them.

But they still had a lot of growing up to do.

When their fearless leader, Joshua, was about to die, he made the people promise that they'd be good.

"We promise!"

"Cross your hearts and hope to die?"

"Cross our hearts and hope to die, stick a needle in our eye!"

But the people couldn't keep their promise. They never could. After Joshua and his generation died, the people started staying out too late, partying with the neighbors' kids, praying to the neighbors' gods.

Thus began one of the most interesting and boring parts of the Bible story: the period of the Judges. Yes—interesting *and* boring, simultaneously. Kind of like college was for most of us, and probably for a lot of the same reasons.

See, there were lots of colorful characters during the period of the Judges, and they specialized in doing strange things. There were obese kings and seductive women. There were feats of strength and barbaric acts. Some people had low self-esteem; others' self-esteem was off the charts and too high for their own good.

It was a crazy time, and you never knew what was going to happen.

Except you knew *exactly* what was going to happen.

It's the same thing over and over and over. It always starts well enough. The land is at peace, and the nation is growing in wealth and influence. But then they get all fat and sassy and start flirting with other gods. YHWH is a highly differentiated person, so He's not easily threatened, but He does consider Himself a jealous God. He'll let Israel go only so far with the philandering. When they cross the line, He's not afraid to let 'em have it.

Peace. Rebellion. Painful (and sometimes embarrassing) correction in the form of an outside oppressor. Remorse. Crying out to God. The emergence of a new leader to overthrow the oppressor. Back to peace.

Lather, rinse, repeat for 400 years, and you get the period of the Judges.

TUESDAY: Beliefs

If you were to just sit down and read the book of Judges, you might find yourself getting so caught up in these fascinating individual vignettes that you would lose sight of the bigger picture. There are so many wonderful characters here: Deborah, Othniel, Shamgar. We relish the quirky details of Ehud stabbing the fat king Eglon; Samson's disgrace at the hands of Delilah; Gideon's torch-bearing, trumpet-blowing army of misfits; Jephthah's rash vow.

But we cannot allow ourselves to get so involved in their stories that we end up thinking that the book is simply a cautionary tale about what happens to people when they divorce themselves from an absolute Source of absolute truth and simply do whatever is right in their own eyes. As valid as that point may be, the book is about much more than that.

From a distance, we can see a different pattern emerge. We are reminded that the Bible is not written to tell us the stories of the people of God. Rather, the Bible is written primarily to tell us the story of the God of the people. With that lens firmly in place, we get a better view of this book and can see two things about God that we would do well to remember.

First, God is remarkably patient. He lets the Israelites grow complacent and lax in their devotion. He allows them to be openly rebellious. He allows them to suffer the consequences and painful sting of His discipline. He hears them cry out to Him in great remorse. He sends them a deliverer and restores peace to the land.

Then He allows them to do the whole thing over again. And again. Each time, He listens as they say, "We'll never do it again, God. This time we've learned our lesson, and this time we mean it."

He could have wiped them off the map. He could have started over with some other nation. He could have done any number of things, but He chose to be patient, to restrain Himself and give them chance after chance. He never says, "I told you so." He never tells them, "This is the fourth time we've done this." His patience is astonishing—and it's a good thing.

But the other side of that coin is that if we are to celebrate the amazing patience of God appropriately, then we must also acknowledge the fact that, clearly, patience has its limits. God is not a doormat here. He doesn't operate like an abused woman who keeps taking back her husband just because he promises not to do it again this time.

God's patience has a limit. He gives his people chance after chance after chance, but eventually He draws a line in the sand and says, "This far and no farther." He is not opposed to discipline, even painful discipline. Just like any good parent, God establishes boundaries and consequences.

Mennonites have a saying: "We are living in the time of God's patience." We are wise to remember that, to thank Him for His patience and celebrate it. But we are also wise to remember that His patience has a limit, and one day judgment will come.

WEDNESDAY: Values

It is probably a safe bet to say that everyone has prayed at some point in time. Even people who say they don't believe in God report praying on occasion. Maybe it's like a rabbit's foot or some other good luck charm; we pray "just in case."

It is probably an equally safe bet to say that anyone who has prayed has spent some time wondering if anyone's really listening. Is prayer just good, positive self-talk? Is it just a psychological exercise? Or does it really fall into the realm of communication between two distinct persons?

The 30,000-foot perspective of Judges reminds that there is a God, and He does actually hear us when we call out to Him. He sometimes even initiates conversations.

God listens to individuals, sharing a back-and-forth dialogue with a woman like Deborah, a nobody like Gideon and a failure like Samson.

God listens to groups and nations, too. And—this is huge—He doesn't require a lot of pageantry and hoopla first. We don't have to stand on chairs and wave our arms to get His attention. No smoke signals or dragon slaying required, just a simple, earnest voice crying out to the God of the universe is all it takes to gain His attention.

God listens and sends a deliverer to help His people when they get into trouble, even when it's trouble they've brought on themselves by not listening to Him in the first place.

It makes one wonder. We have the privilege of speaking with the greatest, most powerful and most generous Being in the universe. And how exactly do we use that privilege? To ask Him to *just* do this for us or *just* do that for us: "God, we're just wondering if You could just help our team just win this one game tonight. If You would *just* help my friend *just* get this job . . . gee, that'd be *just* swell."

Why in the world aren't we asking Him to help us figure out a long-term solution to end poverty or disease, to provide drinkable water for people in Africa or end hunger in our own urban areas? Do we really value the privilege we've been given to speak with a God who hears us when we cry out to Him and has proven Himself willing to respond?

When the people of Israel called out to Him, His response was to send a deliverer. The people He used then weren't exactly pillars of strength. Some of them might qualify for honorable mention, but most of them are of the up-and-down, hit-and-miss variety. Their example should point us to the thing we should value most from our reading of Judges: the once-for-all Deliverer (with a capital "D") who would come hundreds of years later.

We, by virtue of the time in which we were born, are privileged to live under the leadership of that Deliverer, that Judge who also serves as our greatest Advocate and Defender. The Deliverer to whom we pray is now the One through whom we pray, by whom we pray.

THURSDAY: Actions

God takes His people out of Egyptian bondage, leading them through the Red Sea, through the wilderness, right up to the edge of their Promised Land. But they retreat in fear, apparently having forgotten just what God is capable of.

God takes them through a refining disciplinary process and gives them another chance. Moses has the people renew their covenantal vows with God, and they march into the land full of confidence—not in themselves, but in the God they serve.

Moses dies, Joshua takes over, and his first item of business is to lead the people in renewing their covenant again. He wants to make sure they don't forget this time. The people stand and, with one voice, make a promise to love God with everything they have and to pass their faith down to their children.

A promise that lasts one generation.

Joshua dies, and we read one of the saddest verses in the whole Bible: "After that whole generation had been gathered to their fathers, another generation grew up, who knew neither the Lord nor what he had done for Israel" (Judg. 2:10).

The people failed to pass the baton of faith to their children, and it set in motion this depressing chain of events we read about in the book of Judges.

In some ways, this book should never have been written. If the people had simply done what they promised to do, there would have been no rebellion, no punishment, no crying out to God, no need for deliverance. There would have been no Judges. But they didn't keep their promise, so there were and there it is.

And here's the really frustrating part: Every time the people survived their punishment and were delivered by God's appointed judge, they had the opportunity to break the cycle. There was a time of peace that usually followed deliverance. In that time of peace, they had the chance to teach their children, to help their kids avoid making the same mistakes they made.

Do they learn their lesson? No, they do not. If only they'd gone back to the vows of the covenant they had made under Moses and Joshua . . . but they did not love God properly, and they did not teach their children.

Now we find ourselves living in a post-Christian era. We lament the decay of culture, wondering how things could have gotten so far off-track. But with each generational turning, we are given the same opportunity. We can bemoan the loss of Judeo-Christian ethics and values, or we can make a commitment to once again love God with everything—our heart, soul, mind and strength—and pass this commitment down to the next generation.

FRIDAY: Prayer

Narrative

Father, when I read the book of Judges I see that it is a series of warnings that were written for our instruction. Through it, You teach the awful monotony and destructiveness of rebellion and disobedience, and You warn me that to veer off the way of trust and obedience is to take a path that leads to destruction and death. I see in the stories of Judges that it is difficult to hold fast to You when times are relatively easy and peaceful. In such times, I lose the cutting edge of gratitude and dependence and I hope in the things of this world rather than what You tell me to value. The cycles of sin are so predictable and relentless, and when I get caught in this vortex, I lose my peace. By the power of Your Spirit, I pray that I would hold fast to You, not only in times of adversity, but also in times of ease.

Orthodoxy

Lord God, You have progressively revealed Your person, powers and perfections through the course of Your dealings with people in the pages of Scripture. It is through Your revelation that I can see Your glorious attributes of holiness, love, mercy and justice. I find with the passing of time that Your patience with Your people is astonishing. I give thanks for Your forbearance and kindness and for Your willingness to endure my waywardness. But at the same time, I ask that I would not foolishly test the limits of Your patience and presume on Your grace. You discipline me when I stray too far, and I desire to take the better course of staying near rather than straying far. I know that the way of obedience is life-giving and that the way of disobedience is death-dealing.

Orthopathy

Lord Jesus, You are my Hope and Deliverer. In spite of my folly and wayward-ness, You listen to my prayers and work in ways that are too marvelous for me to understand. I give thanks that You really care, and though I live in a broken world of sin, disease and death, I know that nothing can finally separate me from Your love. I give thanks for the privilege of prayer and for the truth that You are my Mediator and Advocate. In spite of the uncertainties of this life, You will never leave or abandon me. You have set me free from the bondage of sin and death, and You have graciously chosen me to accomplish something worthwhile in this life that will endure forever. May I freely lay hold of the benefits of prayer and seek Your wisdom and power amid the adversities and uncertainties of this life.

Orthopraxy

Lord God, as I look back on the stories of Your patience, guidance and many deliverances of Your people, and as I consider the similar story of Your works and ways in my life, I realize that You have put me in a position of great privilege and perspective. You have given me the opportunity to consider and learn from Your many interactions in human history, and You have also given me a personal history of Your many gracious dealings in my own journey. I pray that I would not squander these great gifts, but that I would impart what You have taught me to others so that I would invest in their lives and pass this on to the next generation. I do not want to waste the many blessings You have given me by keeping them to myself. May I pass them on so that Your gracious work in me would be a blessing to others.

9

A Pagan Widow Gets It Right

The Book of Ruth

MONDAY: Story

God promised that Abraham's descendants would bless the rest of the world, but they didn't always cooperate. God, however, is not easily dissuaded from His plans and frequently comes up with the most inventive ways of continuing to push the story forward—even when things seem to have stopped completely.

The Judges of Israel were used in powerful ways, but they were often terrible people with a total lack of impulse control. They were arrogant and violent and stubborn and rebellious. And the people followed their leaders well.

In the end, the Israelites looked an awful lot like their Canaanite neighbors.

What was God to do? This people He meant to make into a special nation insisted on being like the motley crowd around them.

So God went and found someone else.

Her name was Ruth, and she was a Moabite. She married a Jewish man who had moved to Moab with his parents and brother because of a famine in their homeland. But then tragedy struck; all the men in the family died, leaving three widows behind: Ruth, her Moabite sister-in-law, Orpah, and her Jewish mother-in-law, Naomi.

These two Moabite women had never encountered the, uh . . . special blessing that is a Jewish widow. "I'm going to change my name to 'Bitter,' because that's exactly how I feel. God has been bitter to me; I'm going to be bitter to everyone else."

For some reason, Ruth decided to stick it out with this woman. Orpah chose to stay behind while Ruth took Naomi (a. k. a., "Bitter Woman") back to Israel. What a fun trip that must have been!

Now, in those days, wealthy landowners often left portions of their fields unharvested so that widows and other needy people could pick the grain and have some food without having to beg. It was while Ruth was availing herself of this local custom that she caught the eye of a man named Boaz (who also happened to be a relative of Naomi's).

Boaz liked what he saw and asked his workers to be a little extra sloppy when picking the fields so that Ruth wouldn't have to work too hard to find food. Naomi told Ruth, "I think he's warm for your form" (that's a paraphrase you won't even read in *THE MESSAGE*). Ruth made a forward pass that Boaz caught, and they all lived happily ever after.

Oh, and it turns out that bitter turns sweet awfully fast when there's a grandchild involved!

TUESDAY: Beliefs

God's plan for His people wasn't going very well, because they wouldn't cooperate. Time and time again, they turned their backs on God and His benevolent care, choosing instead to do whatever seemed right in their own eyes. The book of Judges is so full of violence and immorality, it's amazing that any of it made it into the Bible.

God's original plan was for His people to live according to His laws and be a guiding light to the rest of the world—to show other nations what it looks like when a people live in harmony with God and with one another for the sake of everyone's highest good. But God's people wouldn't stick with the plan; they wanted to do their own thing—and that always leads to disaster.

Just when you might be tempted to think that God may have to wipe everyone out and start over, we encounter this story about a foreign woman named Ruth. The story of Ruth shows us that God is not above going outside of His original plan to get His purposes accomplished.

Ruth was a Moabite. Moab was not a good place. Its origins can be traced back to a terrible story about a man named Lot and his daughters doing something we shudder to consider, even today. Technically, the Moabites should never have been a nation to begin with. Furthermore, they should have been chased out of the land or killed well before Ruth was born. If Lot had been a righteous man and avoided incest (as even most unrighteous men manage to do), there would have been no Moabites. And if the people of Israel had done as God instructed, the Moabites would have been long gone.

Plus, there's no way God would have advocated that any of His people marry one of those pagan people. They were, well . . . pagans, for crying out loud!

But God had promised Abraham way back when that He would bless everyone, not just the Jewish people. And God never welshes on a promise.

We've learned by now that this YHWH is unpredictable. He doesn't do things the way we would. Just when you think you've got Him figured out, He dips and swerves and goes underground, only to appear where you least expect Him.

And He loves strays, and keeps bringing them in at night even though He knows that if you feed them once they'll keep coming back. He did this with Rahab (who ran the best little whorehouse in Jericho), and now He's doing it again with this Moabite woman, Ruth. Orphans, widows, street urchins, mongrels—they all matter more to God than maybe we think they should.

Ruth's an unlikely character who has nothing much going for her. We expect God to take an interest in a guy like Samson (who lived during this same period of time). Samson was big and strong and powerful. He was born into a good family, had the pedigree. Ruth, by contrast, was a mutt.

Maybe that's the point of the story, though. When the purebred—the physically, mentally, spiritually gifted people, the privileged insiders who have been called by God—fall down on the job, God's not above going down to the pound and picking up a stray. Strays, as it turns out, have really good memories and rarely forget what it was like to be *this close* to death and then be rescued by the kindness of a benevolent person.

WEDNESDAY: Values

The book of Ruth is not flashy. There are no miracles in its pages. There doesn't appear to be anyone remarkably gifted, no feats of strength, no beauty pageants (read the book of Esther for that). The woman herself isn't known for being particularly talented or smart, and the book named for her is sort of the meat-loaf of the Old Testament. The things we see in Ruth, the things that make her stand out, are things like, "She's honest," "She works really hard," "She's loyal," "She has integrity." Not the kind of stuff that Hollywood movies are made of.

Ruth and Naomi were both shrewd, but it was a common-sense, homespun, front-porch kind of wisdom, the kind usually dispensed by grandparents and isn't particularly sexy . . . and isn't valued nearly enough in our time. They got up early, stayed up late, and did the kinds of things you have to do when you live on the edge, barely eking out a living.

This is a pretty apt description of our leading man, Boaz, as well. He was a landowner, but it doesn't seem that he was extraordinarily wealthy. It seems, instead, that he was a decent, middle-class guy. For example, the Law told landowners that when they were harvesting the crops, they should make provision for widows and orphans. Boaz did. There was a little extra generosity on his part, but he wasn't flashy about it. He didn't stand on the street corner and yell out about what he was doing to help the plight of the poor. He just told his foreman to be a little extra sloppy around the edges of the fields.

When he found out that he was related to Ruth, he put together a simple, practical plan to set things right. He had more than a cursory understanding of what the Law says about familial obligation to widows. He went to the right people in the right way at the right time and did the right thing.

This is an ordinary story of ordinary people doing what it takes and doing what is right. All of the main characters are clever, simple, practical, hardworking folks—salt of the earth types who help others and keep their word.

Here in America, we used to call such behavior the Judeo-Christian work ethic. But we don't talk about that much anymore. Our pride is that we live in an age of innovation—and innovation is often a good thing. But nothing will ever take the place of ordinary people doing what it takes and doing what's right.

THURSDAY: Actions

Everybody wants to do the right thing. Okay, maybe not everyone . . . but it's an exceptionally evil person who wakes up in the morning wondering how he can do the wrong thing in new and destructive ways that day.

It's a safe bet that the vast majority of people reading this book—as well as the people you know—want to do the right thing. And when they pray, the bulk of their prayer lives can be summed up this way: "God, could You please make it easier for me to do the right thing?"

There's nothing wrong with that prayer, per se. But what about when it's hard? What about when God sees fit to leave obstacles in your path that make doing the right thing difficult? It's one thing to do right when life's a bed of roses, when the sun is shining and your boss is your best friend. But can you do the right thing even when it's difficult, even when you're stuck with a nagging, complaining, bitter, old mother-in-law who can't seem to remember that *your* husband died, too? Can you continue doing the right thing even when you have to get out early and stay out late and pick up the table scraps from somebody else, just so you can provide food for your own table? Can you do what's right then?

God thinks you can.

After reading the book of Judges, it's understandable for us to have a decidedly pessimistic view of humanity. We may even be tempted to question God's judgment in entrusting His promises to fickle-hearted people who never seem to get it right for very long.

Perhaps that's why God saw fit to preserve the story of Ruth.

Ruth gets it right, even when we might expect her to get it wrong. We would understand if a desperate pagan widow failed. After all, she's got the deck stacked against her. But Ruth refuses to fold, choosing instead to play the hand dealt to her with courage and integrity—and a dash of cunning, as well.

But—and this is important—there's no secret to it. There's no magical incantation to recite, no seminar to attend, no program of seven easy steps to total transformation in just 15-minutes a day. Operators are not standing by ready to take your order.

You already know how to do this. You learned it all in kindergarten. Don't hit. Don't take things that aren't yours. Put things back where you found them. Share. If you see someone who needs help, lend a hand. Take time off to think and reflect and catch your breath. Tell someone that you appreciate what they do. Give someone a hug. This is simple, meat-and-potatoes stuff.

You want to do the right thing? Maybe you could stop looking for a shortcut and just do what you know to do today.

FRIDAY: Prayer

Narrative

Dear Lord, nothing can defeat Your gracious and redemptive purposes. In spite of the frequently profound rebellion of Your people, You continue to unfold Your Story in creative and unexpected ways. You often display the riches of Your grace in ways that we do not understand, and You can use adversity and turn it to good. You can turn our bitterness into joy and our despair into praise when we hold fast to You in times when we are too nearsighted to see the good that You see. I can't control a single day, and I don't know what lies around the next corner of my life. But You do, and You always intend my ultimate good. I ask that by Your grace I would release all bitterness and resentment and embrace a clear and robust hope in You, even though I do not know where my journey is leading me.

Orthodoxy

Father God, I rejoice in the truth that You have chosen the foolish things of the world to shame the wise, and have chosen the weak things of the world to shame the things that are strong. I acknowledge that You have the power to use me in remarkable ways in spite of my inadequacies and weaknesses. You are not impressed with the things that impress people, but You deign to use those who, through humility, are willing to depend entirely on You and not on their position or power. I see that the things that are highly esteemed among people are detestable in Your sight, and that it is foolish to be impressed by the things that impress people. I ask for the grace to live and serve others out of my weakness and thus out of Your strength. Let me be impressed by the things that are truly pleasing to You.

Orthopathy

Dear Lord, I ask that I would apply all diligence to be Your person in this world. As I seek Your will, I don't need to impress or manipulate people. Instead, I can choose the simplicity of quiet service, even when others don't notice. I realize that You often accomplish Your extraordinary work in ordinary ways. I pray that I would learn to welcome You into the routines of my life so that I will see that nothing is too trivial or mundane to be infused by Your grace. May I see my love and service to You in my love and service to the people You have placed in my life. I ask that my faith would be expressed through moral excellence, knowledge, self-control, perseverance, godliness, kindness and love. May I pursue fidelity to You in the small things and little tasks of life.

Orthopraxy

Father, the tasks of this life are so manifold and complex that I can lose the big picture in the details of daily living. Teach me to see with increasing clarity that it is in these details that I am called to trust and obey You. I may be confused about Your ways and timing in my journey, but Your Word tells me that You are working all things together for good to those who love You and are called according to Your purpose. I ask for the grace to see You in all things and to live in the simplicity of willing one thing above all else. May I will to do Your will, love the things You love, and hope in the things You promise. May I have the wisdom to do the right things in the right times and in the right ways. I want to honor You in the many small opportunities of this day and live well before You.

10

First King

1 SAMUEL 8–31

The children of Abraham had developed quite a list of enemies. After all, they had shown up unannounced and proclaimed themselves the rightful heirs to a land that was already occupied. Then they had proceeded to kill everyone who didn't leave peacefully and immediately.

That'll put you on a lot of people's naughty list.

Now, some of these enemies were piddly little people who wouldn't scare anybody. But some of them were fearsome and had names like "Philistines" and "Ammonites" and "Amalekites." And all of them had something the Israelites did not have: a king. Usually that king was an impressive-looking person, the kind of presence that could reassure the people and intimidate the enemies.

When someone asked the Israelites to show them their leader, all they could do was point to a box called the Ark of the Covenant, which sat inside a portable tent called the Tabernacle. That's where YHWH sat but, well . . . YHWH was invisible. And some of their enemies started to wonder if "invisible" might actually mean "imaginary."

So the Israelites wanted a king, a real, flesh-and-blood king. Preferably someone who would strike terror in the hearts of their enemies.

And that's when they found a 30-year-old golden boy named Saul.

He was tall—stood head and shoulders above everyone else—and had that commanding presence that you want in a king. He came from a wealthy family, and he was everything you think of when you think of a leader. Tall. (Did we already mention tall?) Handsome. Quick-witted. He was quickly approved by God, anointed by the prophet Samuel and affirmed by the people.

But none of that was enough to ensure his success as the first king of Israel. Like so many other young men of privilege, Saul had trouble with self-control and responsibility.

Still, whatever doubts anyone may have had were quickly erased after his first military campaign. A foreign king laid siege to one of the Israelite towns, vowing to gouge out the eyes of the townsfolk. Saul raised an army of more than 300,000 men and led them in a pre-dawn attack, utterly destroying the enemy.

Maybe he was going to be alright after all.

But Saul had an internal anxiety that showed up at the oddest of times in the oddest of ways and drove him to do the oddest of things. He hid among the suitcases when it was time to come out and greet the people for the first time. He flew off in a rage at the slightest provocation. He was impatient and impulsive, and when he was confronted, there was always an excuse.

Before long, his mind became completely poisoned by jealousy and fear. Two of his children were estranged from him. His inability to calm the anxiety that boiled within him drove him to attempt the impossible: murder a man God Himself had promised to protect.

Saul's life and reign as king gradually went from bad to worse. The man who had looked so full of promise, so kingly, became a sullen shell of a person who drove those closest to him further and further away. In the end, he lost his kingdom, his integrity, his family and his very life.

The first king of Israel had many enemies, but none was greater than himself.

TUESDAY: Beliefs

Following God is hard. After all, He's invisible. You never know when He's going to show up and intervene . . . or when He's not. His work is constant, but the vast majority of it is hidden from our sight—underground, behind the scenes.

He would spring up when conditions were bad, when the people were being oppressed by some foreign power, and raise up a leader, call out an army and vanquish the foe. But then He would disappear again, waiting for the next crisis.

That's how it seemed, anyway, and it made the Israelites more than a little nervous.

Never mind the fact that they always brought the crisis upon themselves. Never mind the fact that God always came through and always responded when they cried out to Him. Never mind any of that—they wanted something a little more tangible and visible.

They wanted a succession of leaders they could point to, great kings in the history of a great nation. They wanted a dynasty, a royal household with all the trimmings. Pomp and circumstance and high visibility. And a standing army . . . you know, just in case.

But God hadn't given them any of those.

From God's perspective, *He* was their king. He was their fearless and tireless leader. He could trump any of those earthly kings in all ways except one: He wasn't very visible, very touchable. It took something more than a glance at the palace if you wanted to trust Him. It required *actual trust*. You had to believe in something you couldn't see, based on what you had seen in the past.

That's a critical point: God doesn't just ask people to take a blind leap. The Israelites had 400 years' worth of history with YHWH. They had 10 plagues and a Red Sea crossing, manna every morning and water in the wilderness. They'd seen the walls of Jericho come a-tumblin' down. The very fact that they had managed to survive as a nation for over 350 years without a visible king should have given them a sense of security and enabled them to trust God even more.

But the people wanted something else. They wanted following God to be easy.

God never said following Him would be easy. Following Him requires a willingness to do what He asks even when it doesn't make sense. Following Him requires a person to do things that appear counter-intuitive: Give stuff away. Turn the other cheek. These things don't make sense in an economy where what you see is what there is.

But we live in a different kind of economy—God's economy—where there is more afoot than is apparent to the eye.

Following God is hard. After all, He is invisible. But the people who please God are those who make a decision to follow Him even when He can't be seen.

WEDNESDAY: Values

We live in a bottom-line society. From the highest echelon of government to the lowest rung of the ladder, we live with the idea that private morality is just that—a private matter. So long as a person's public performance isn't affected, we make allowances for personal peccadilloes. And if they look the part, that's even better. In fact, shortcomings and flaws matter less than playing the part. What matters is keeping up appearances.

Giftedness and performance are important. It is vital to find diplomats who can negotiate, skilled craftspeople who can make quality products, and business administrators who can do math, and it's necessary for these leaders to do things like bathe and groom themselves (because hygiene and a sense of decorum are also nice). Those things are all important. But make no mistake: *In the economy of God, character is more important than giftedness and appearance.*

The hidden, quiet, internal qualities of humility, wisdom and a willingness to sacrifice personal agenda for the sake of a bigger picture are the character traits of a godly leader. It's important that we review these ideas occasionally, because appearances can be deceiving, and performance without character is often a recipe for disaster.

We've come to value externals over internals. In an image-obsessed society, it's no longer enough for a candidate to have qualifications and good ideas; that candidate must now look "presidential." Some of the greatest presidents in the history of the United States may never have been elected in such a mass-media culture. Likewise, a pastor may be good at turning a phrase and producing a pithy and memorable sound bite, but substance matters. Character makes the difference when push comes to shove.

The story of King Saul is a cautionary tale, not only for those who select their leaders but also for the leaders themselves. If the onus is on the people to do the due diligence of investigating a potential leader's character, the onus is equally on the shoulders of that leader to continue the development of healthy character traits, rather than relying upon giftedness and appearances. The temptation for a leader to look for shortcuts and take the easy way out is always strong.

Simply looking good while you do what you do won't cut it, not in God's economy. Why you do what you do and the way you do it matter.

If Saul looked the part, King David, his eventual successor, was on the opposite end of the spectrum. We'll get to his story next, but for now, suffice it to say that David didn't strike anyone as being particularly "kingly." His own family thought of him as the runt of the litter. But God reminded his spokesman, Samuel, "Do not consider his appearance or his height. . . . The LORD does not look at the things human beings look at. People look at the outward appearance, but the LORD looks at the heart" (1 Sam. 16:8).

Hundreds of years later, Jesus encountered some leaders who had decent behavior but terrible character. They thought that their smooth appearance and spotless performance would be enough to fool God. Jesus told them, "You are the ones who justify yourselves in the eyes of others, but God knows your hearts. What people value highly is detestable in God's sight" (Luke 16:15).

What might Saul have become if he had cultivated the right character? What rewards might God have bestowed on one so gifted and talented, with so much potential? Would it have been Saul's line that produced the Messiah? His throne that was established forever? Would he have been the one to take Israel to unprecedented levels of prosperity and dominion?

We'll never know.

One thing we do know for certain: Saul would have lived a life free of the anxiety and insecurity that eventually destroyed him. God rewards good character, but the greatest reward may be the good character itself.

THURSDAY: Actions

The people of Israel wanted security and stability. They were afraid of being different from all the surrounding nations, forced, as they were, to rely on Someone they couldn't see. Unfortunately, they allowed their fear to prompt a terrible decision, one that produced even higher levels of instability and insecurity.

This is almost always what happens when we make decisions based on fear and anxiety. We end up setting in motion a chain of events that increases the odds of our worst fears becoming reality. Anxiety makes us do foolish things that get us into trouble.

In this case (as in many others), an insecure people selected an insecure leader. At some level, Saul must have known that he got the job because of his looks. Perhaps he wondered if the people would actually accept him if they knew what he was really like. Insecurity usually breeds further insecurity, and at least on some level, Saul's life became about keeping up appearances.

An appearance-based economy will always drive people to duplicity. Saul's insecurity led him first to compromise, then to disobedience.

Eventually, Saul decided to redefine obedience, and in doing so, he became rebellious. Now, disobedience is bad, but rebellion is even worse. God says it's like witchcraft (see 1 Sam. 15:23).

It all began when the people of God let their anxiety get the best of them. They began making decisions based on fear, telling God, in effect, that they knew better than He what was in their best interest. In the final analysis, then, most of our sinful behavior can be traced back to a lack of trust in God's ability and/ or desire to have our best interests at heart. If we could only calm our anxiety, trust in God and do what He says, we'd save ourselves lots of trouble.

We should probably add a word about what to do when you blow it because, you know . . . most of us will blow it at some point in time.

We serve a God who allows us to make decisions, real decisions. He refuses to manipulate us. He's no puppet master, pulling our strings and forcing us to do His bidding. It's important to remember, however, that real decisions, which bring about real consequences, never dissolve our relationship with YHWH. He is always waiting for His people to come to their senses and return to Him.

God wants obedience, even when what He's asking of us seems counter-intuitive. For reasons that are difficult to understand, let alone explain, God allows us to disobey him.

Perhaps you have made some terrible choices, and perhaps you are suffering from the consequences of those terrible choices. Know this: No decision, no matter how terrible it may be, will ever put you beyond the reach of God's grace. You can come back to Him right now. Or you can just say thanks for the last time He took you back.

We'll leave you two alone now.

FRIDAY: Prayer

Narrative

Father God, I know that I am engaged in a spiritual warfare on the three battlefronts of the flesh, the world and the devil. These forces are opposed to Your rule and authority, and the most chilling of them is the flesh, because it is internal. I affirm that the good I want I do not do, and instead practice the very evil I do not want. But if I am doing the very thing I do not want, I am no longer the one doing it, but the sin that dwells in me. There rages a war between my deepest self in Christ and the sinful remnant of what I was in Adam. But thanks be to God through Jesus Christ our Lord! You have given me the power of Your Holy Spirit so that I can put to death the deeds of the flesh. Let me never trust in my own devices and desires, but only in Your power.

Orthodoxy

O Lord, keep me from the folly of following what the world tells me to clamor for. I realize that biblical faith is the assurance of things hoped for, the conviction of things not seen. And I know that it takes a great deal of trust and risk to pursue the invisible over the visible and the not-yet over the now. But hope that is seen is not hope, and if I hope for what I do not see, with perseverance I will wait eagerly for it. I will welcome Your promises from a distance and confess that I am a stranger and exile on the earth. May I trust You enough to treasure Your invisible promises over the visible promises of the world, knowing that only Your promises will endure in the end, and that the world is passing away. You have been faithful to me in the past and I will hope in You for the future.

Orthopathy

God, may I never be more concerned with surface appearances than with inward substance. I long for a Christlike character that will sustain me through the vicissitudes and trials of this life. May I seek integrity over image and holiness over happiness. Protect me from the sin of lost potential that would result from pursuing the wrong things at the wrong times in the wrong ways. Grant me the power to be that same person when no one is looking as I am when I am among my peers. Let me be increasingly impressed with Jesus Christ and less impressed with appearance, posturing and posing. I ask that godly character will inform and empower my daily choices and relationships. Then I will seek the things that really matter and endure over the things that will fade and disappear.

Orthopraxy

Living God, may I never place my security in people or performance, but only in Your character and promises. Deliver me from the plague of insecurity and anxiety that can cripple me and erode my faith in You. I want to be increasingly defined by Your truth and not by the lies of a fleeting and broken world. May I be Your person, even in times of trouble and stress, knowing that from You and through You and to You are all things. Grant that as I cast all my anxiety on You,

I will experience Your peace and make choices that are honoring to You, instead of foolish decisions that spring from fear and disbelief. Thank You for the grace of forgiveness when I do things that are displeasing to You. I am grateful that there is no sin that is so great that it would prevent You from welcoming me back when I come to my senses and return to You.

11

A Man After God's Own Heart

1 SAMUEL 16;
1 KINGS 2

The first king of Israel was the best-looking man in the land. The second king of Israel wasn't even the best-looking man in his own family!

David was the youngest of eight brothers and frequently got the short end of the stick when it came time to divvy up family chores. Consequently, David spent more than his fair share of time outside watching sheep. It was dangerous work, and more than once David found himself face to face with a hungry mountain lion or a bear.

But he seemed to enjoy the solitude. He learned to play the harp and began writing little poems, and putting some of them to music. Mostly they were about this strange God of the Israelites who was always there but sometimes felt absent.

When David heard his father calling for him that day, how could he have known that the odd old man, Samuel, had been sent by that very same God? How could he have known that the crazy old man would pull out a jar of oil and pour it all over David's head? And what would he have done if he could have seen it coming?

From tending sheep to being told he would be the next king of Israel—that's quite a day for anyone, let alone a kid who didn't even have the respect of his brothers or his father.

Turns out David would always struggle with family relationships.

David grew up to be a poet, a warrior, a musician and a statesman. He was a bold and charismatic leader, handsome, fierce, intense. He wrote the prayer book for the human race. He played the harp so skillfully that he was the only one who could calm Saul's jangled nerves. He defeated a giant and gathered some of the greatest warriors of the day to become his "Mighty Men." He lifted Israel to a level of economic wellbeing and political stability that has forever been regarded as Israel's Golden Age—Israel's Camelot.

But he couldn't figure out how to be a family man. He had 8 wives, 11 concubines, rebellious children and adulterated family relationships all over the place.

King David lived large. He felt things passionately. He danced hard, played hard, fought hard, prayed hard and sang hard. Everything he did was done to the fullest extent—even when he sinned. (In one episode, he lusted, coveted his neighbor's wife, committed adultery, deceived the woman's husband and ultimately ordered the man's murder.)

But the one thing that set him apart from Saul was that when he was confronted with his sin, he did not offer a single excuse. He took responsibility for his failures.

King David was not a perfect man—far from it. But it takes more than a perfect man to be called a man after God's own heart; it took this passionate, contemplative, stubborn man to get the title.

TUESDAY: Beliefs

King David is, without a doubt, one of the most prolific characters in the entire Bible. Just about everybody has heard of his story, regardless of their religious background. Who hasn't heard of David and Goliath? Or David and Bathsheba?

This brings up one of the great things about the Bible: It refuses to gloss over the failures of its heroes. The Bible doesn't place them on a pedestal or portray them as two-dimensional cardboard cutouts. These are real people. David most certainly was. He experienced tremendous victories and humiliating defeats (many of which he brought on himself). He was deeply troubled and dysfunctional, a disaster as a husband and father. He had 8 wives and 11 concubines. He was guilty of adultery, deception and murder.

King David was guilty of the kinds of things we want people thrown out of office for today, yet this is the guy the Bible calls "a man after [God's] own heart" (1 Sam. 13:14). How is that possible?

This one reason stands out: While David may have had 8 wives, 11 concubines, uncontrollable children and fractured relationships all over the place, he only had one God. For all the other commandments he ended up breaking (4 of the top 10 in the episode with Bathsheba), he never broke the first one: "You shall have no other gods before me" (Exod. 20:3).

Unlike most of the other kings in Israel's history, David never bent his knee to a false god. He never went over to Baal or Asherah or Dagon. When he failed (which he did often), he took his regret and his brokenness to one Source: YHWH. When he was confused or afraid, he did not seek refuge in the gods of the Philistines or the Moabites. He went to the God of Abraham, Isaac and Jacob.

At the end of his most famous poem, David wrote, "I will dwell in the house of the LORD forever" (Ps. 23:6). Usually we think of this line as if it refers to heaven and eternity. That may not be what David had in mind when he wrote it, however.

Maybe David was an old man when he said those words, with a long, gray beard and a wrinkled face. Maybe he remembered when he was young and handsome and Samuel poured oil all over him and said the mysterious words that started it all. Maybe he remembered how, on that day, so many years ago, the Spirit of the Lord came upon him. Maybe he remembered how he decided when he was a young man—the way young men do—that when he was king things would be different. He'd get things right.

Sometimes he did and sometimes he didn't. But he stayed in the house of the Lord all the days of his life.

He did not write, "I hope I will stay there" or "Maybe I'll stay there." He said, "I'm staying in the house. I'll make a mess of it. I'll spill stuff on the carpet and knock over lamps and break expensive things. It will be a pain having me in the house, but you'll have to drag me out kicking and screaming. I will dwell here, in the house of the Lord, forever."

In the end, that's what God is looking for from all of us. God can handle our failures and our messes. God can handle our most embarrassing episodes. What He cannot abide and will not tolerate is duplicity. David asked God to give him an undivided heart, and it appears God granted that request.

Are we willing to ask the same thing?

WEDNESDAY: Values

David's heart was loyal; some might even say it was stubborn. When he gave his heart to someone, he didn't take it back. When David loved you, you stayed loved—even if he hated you sometimes.

Think about the people in David's life. First, there was King Saul. He was once a promising young king, but then he became increasingly corrupt, tormented by a pathological jealousy of David, paranoid and eaten up by his own anxiety. Several times he tried to kill David, but David just kept loving Saul. Twice David could have killed him, but he wouldn't. He probably would have been justified in doing it; still he refused. And when Saul eventually died, David wrote one of his most heart-rending poems for the king: "How the mighty have fallen," he sang (see 2 Sam. 1:19–27). Knowing everything he knew of Saul, he wept at his death. He loved Saul to the end.

Then, of course, there was Jonathan. He was Saul's son and could have been David's rival for the throne. You might have expected them to be at each other's throats, but instead they had one of the great friendships in all of literature.

Many years later, after both Saul and Jonathan were dead, David started looking for someone from their families, just so he could show that person kindness. Someone eventually found a little-known guy named Mephibosheth, Jonathan's son who had been crippled in a childhood accident. David sent for him and had him brought into the royal court. He treated Mephibosheth like a son because of his intense love for Jonathan.

And his own son, Absalom, who tried to overthrow his father and take the throne. He actually took over the capital city and forced David into exile. As soon as he was in power, he staged an elaborate orgy held in broad daylight on the rooftop with all of David's mistresses involved. That's detestable. But when David was finally restored to power and received word that Absalom had been killed, he did not rejoice in the fact that he was safe and secure. Rather, he cried out that he would gladly have exchanged places with his son. He wished that he had died in Absalom's place.

When David loved you, you stayed loved no matter what you did to him. That's the kind of heart God wants His children to cultivate—a heart that says, "Regardless of what you've done, are doing, will do, might do, you are loved."

That is, after all, God's own heart. When God loves you, you stay loved. No matter what you pull. No matter how much you never realize your potential. No matter how distant and separated you may be. No matter how rebellious you've been. God says, "I wish I could die in your place."

And that is precisely what He did.

THURSDAY: Actions

David's life was characterized by a sense of wild abandon. When he did something, he didn't do it halfway. He jumped in the deep end. He took risks. He felt things deeply and passionately.

When David praised God, he did it with his whole heart (see Ps. 9; 86 and 111). He didn't hold anything back. He wasn't calculating or cautious.

There's a great story of David dancing for joy with all his might. Anyone who has spent time in the company of children has seen their willingness to do this. They dance and get so excited about things that sometimes they just jump up and down squealing. That's what David was like.

Grown-ups are not prone to this kind of activity, unless it's time for March Madness. And that says something about us, doesn't it?

David was like a little kid in his excitement over what God was doing, had done or was going to do. When was the last time you were so overwhelmed with what God was doing that you just had to jump up and down and high-five the person next to you?

You don't want to go to your grave with a heart that is cold and calculating and protected and safe. God wants your heart to be passionate and sold out to Him with a wild abandon.

That is, after all, the kind of heart He has for you. God is not neutral about you. God gives you His heart without holding anything back (see Rom. 8:32). He is *for* you. He cheers you on (see Zeph. 3:17). He longs to lavish good gifts on you. It's almost as if God can't help Himself—He loves you so much that He's willing to go to incredible lengths to restore you and draw you back to Himself.

But there's another feature about David, one that is rare in people whose hearts are so wild and intense. David was also a man of deep reflection. David took time alone with God—out with the sheep, hiding in caves—allowing God to shepherd his heart.

It's uncommon to find both traits in one person. Usually you find in a person one or the other. Either they live with a sense of wild abandon or they are deeply reflective. But David combined both.

In the very first Psalm, David uses this great image of a tree. He says that the godly man or woman is like a tree planted by rivers of water, whose roots go down so deep that producing fruit almost comes effortlessly. The tree can't help but produce fruit because the root system is so deep and the tree is so well nourished that it just flourishes.

Regardless how much you know about gardening, most of us realize that you can't develop a root system in a hurry. It takes time and stillness and waiting. When was the last time you saw someone whose life was always a blur—a rushing, swirling mass of chaos—and they were also deep? You can be hurried or you can be deep, but you can't be both.

Far too many of us live at breakneck speed, squeezing the most out of each day, collapsing in a heap long after midnight, neglecting the command to be still and know that God is God (and by implication, we are not). We've bought into the lie that our worth is determined by our productivity. Our hearts are not often characterized by deep reflection.

Passionate living. Deep reflection. This is one of those cases when we dare not take an either/or approach. We must live in the tension of both/and, allowing ourselves to plunge in the deep end of life with all its messes and mysteries, and carve out time for solitude and contemplation.

That's not just how David lived. It's how Jesus lived (more on Him later). And it's how we were designed to live as well.

FRIDAY: Prayer

Narrative

Father, I desire to be a person after Your own heart. I want to be pleasing and obedient to You, and when I sin against You, I want to acknowledge it quickly with no excuses and waste no time returning back to Your embrace. I know that I will never attain perfection in this life, but I desire to progress in godly character and conduct. You look at the heart and not at the externals that impress people. Therefore I ask that I would guard my heart and walk in integrity before You. By Your grace I would desire what You desire, love what You love and hate what You hate. May I honor my commitments and relationships and not succumb to treachery, dishonesty or immorality. Let me allow You to define my understanding of myself and not the world with its pride and deception.

Orthodoxy

Dear Lord, You alone are the fountainhead of all that is good, true and beautiful. I know that if I want life, I must pursue You above all else. May I say with David, "As the deer pants for the water brooks, so my soul pants for you, O God. My soul thirsts for God, for the living God" (Ps. 42). I have nowhere else to turn, for You alone are the source of all that I want in my heart of hearts. By Your grace I will not succumb to the idolatry of having any other god before You. I will put You first and foremost in my affection and choices, because I know that You alone are worthy of all honor, glory and praise. May I fear to displease You and long to lay hold of that which You want for me. You are my shepherd and I am one of your flock. Surely goodness and lovingkindness will follow me all the days of my life, and I will dwell in the house of the Lord forever.

Orthopathy

Lord God, Your love for me is causeless and ceaseless and measureless. You have loved me because You have chosen to do so, not because of anything I am or have done. This is the wellspring of my true security, and I revel in Your unconditional love and acceptance, knowing that I could never have earned it or merited it. This frees me to be the person You intended me to be—secure enough in Your love so that I can love and serve others. May I show kindness and compassion for people, even when they may turn against me. Give me the grace to be a peacemaker and a reconciler with the people You sovereignly place in my path. Let me learn to see my love, fidelity and service to them as an expression of who I am to You and who You are to me.

Orthopraxy

Dear Father, grant me a childlike enthusiasm and wonder at all that You are and all that You have done in heaven above and earth below. Let me revel in Your many deliverances and kindnesses that You have imparted to me. You have given me vitality, hope and purpose, and I acknowledge that all of life is gift and grace. I ask that I would not merely live on the surface of life, but that I would sink my roots deep into the soil of Your love and draw my vitality from the water of Your Word. May I be rooted and grounded in Your love, and may I take the time I need for reflection, renewal and rest, so that I will know You better and become increasingly like You. Then I will be a contemplative in action, a person of depth and breadth, and one who has learned the secret of living from the inside out.

12

The Scarlet Thread

2 SAMUEL 7

MONDAY: Story

God's intention from the very beginning was to create a people who would live in unbroken relationship with Him and with one another. And they would be stewards of the rest of creation, partnering with God to create a place of meaning and real substance.

But, come to find out, these humans are rebellious. They turn against God and against one another. In the process, the whole world suffers the negative fallout of their sinful choices.

Fortunately, as stubborn as these humans are, God is more stubborn still.

Refusing to give up on the people He loves so much, God makes a promise that one day there will be an ultimate solution to this problem of sin and evil in the world. This promise becomes like a scarlet thread that weaves its way through the rest of the Bible's Story.

The thread often appears as weak as a newborn baby, but it refuses to be broken. And though the Story often comes dangerously close to unraveling altogether, it never comes all the way undone. God simply won't allow it to happen.

Just in case the people forget that there is a larger Story going on, God sometimes reminds them. He does it with the people standing in the desert after wandering around for 40 years, reminding them of the promises He has made to them and asking them to renew their commitment to Him. He does it again at the end of Joshua's life.

Now, years later, there's a good king on the throne. David has brought the nation to a level of unprecedented prosperity and international influence. Their enemies have mostly been dealt with. There is relative peace in the land. It might look like the Story has reached its conclusion.

But there is this one problem: The people are still broken, individually and corporately. There's brokenness everywhere, and as a result of that brokenness, there are these sacrifices that have to be made on a daily basis. That's bloody, exhausting, disgusting work, done because the Final Solution hasn't arrived yet.

God tells David that the once-and-for-all fix is still on its way. In fact, He tells David this bit of great news: *The fix will come directly through David's lineage!* The Deliverer promised to Adam and Eve back in Genesis 3, the One whom the Judges wanted to be, the quintessential King, the Promised One, the ultimate Way the children of Abraham would bless the entire world—the Messiah would be a descendant of David.

There were certainly times in David's life when he must have thought he was part of the problem (and he would have been correct). But in God's strange plan, weaving like a scarlet thread throughout history, David was also part of the solution.

TUESDAY: Beliefs

David had a great idea.

God had blessed him in so many ways. The kingdom was at peace (relatively speaking), the economy was up, inflation and unemployment were down, his approval rating was through the roof and he had this great palace in Jerusalem.

David thought, *Maybe it's time to give a little something back. After all, I'm sitting in this great big house, and God's still living in that rickety old tent. Let's build Him a house, a Temple, a magnificent structure, something that will make people from miles around sit up and take note.*

It sounded like such a great idea. David even checked with his good friend Nathan, who had a direct line to God. The prophet thought it was a great idea, too. There was just one small problem: Nobody bothered to check with God.

Turns out, it was a good idea, but it wasn't God's idea. God had a very different plan, a plan that did not include David building the Temple. In fact, God told David he could not build it because of some sinful things he had done.

We can understand how disappointed David may have felt. This was his chance to demonstrate to God just how thankful he was for how He had used him up to that point. But God had something else in mind.

It's at times like this that we discover something important about God: His plans are not always our plans. They may seem confusing or even disappointing; they may frustrate us and cause us to question God's rationality. But God's plans are always better, always bigger, always longer-lasting. However, it usually requires hindsight to see how true this is. Looking back, what God had in store for David was infinitely better than what David had in store for God.

God promised that one of David's sons would, in fact, build a temple. He promised to establish that son's throne forever.

David was thinking about his own legacy and perhaps the nation's sense of pride. He was thinking about those things in the context of honoring God, and that's a good thing. But he was thinking too small. God was thinking about the whole world.

God made the promise about one of David's sons, but the question remained: *Which son?*

From that point forward in Jewish history, many people assumed that the promise had been fulfilled through David's son Solomon. But as we'll see in the coming weeks, while Solomon did build a Temple, he eventually died. After his death, the kingdom of Israel was split in half, and many of the promises for God's people seem to unravel. What happened to all that stuff God told David?

Well, follow the scarlet thread forward for about a thousand years. There, we find someone in David's line who seems to fit the description in the promise pretty well: Jesus (who so many people insisted on calling "Son of David" [see Matt. 1:1; 12:23; 21:9]).

With so many people suggesting that He might be the fulfillment of that long-ago promise to King David, folks would surely have paid attention to anything He had to say about the Temple. After all, if He were the Promised One, He would have to build God a permanent house in order to establish a permanent throne for Himself.

Jesus never built a single building, but He has built a structure—the Church universal, which is made up of all those who place their faith in His sinless life, atoning death and victorious resurrection. All who do so are the new dwelling place for God (see 1 Cor. 14:25; Eph. 2:21; Heb. 3:6; 1 Pet. 2:5). And because He has built this permanent house for God, He has been given a permanent throne (see Rev. 11:15). But that's not all, because then—and this is so like Him—Jesus shares His kingdom with us, allowing us to participate with Him in His reign (see Rev. 3:21).

God's plans are not our plans. They're always better, always bigger, always longer-lasting.

WEDNESDAY: Values

David wanted to do something nice for God, but God told him not to. David could have gone off and pouted, but he didn't. Instead, he accepted God's plans, even though he couldn't really have understood them. God told David that someone else would do what David proposed doing. Rather than being jealous, though, David was joyful.

That's humility.

David wasn't concerned with who got to build it, as long as it got built. That kind of humility only comes from an understanding that the Story isn't about David. It's not about David's family or David's kingdom. The Story is about God—and David, David's family and David's kingdom get to play a role in a much bigger Story with a much bigger plot and an even bigger central Character.

Embedding your story into God's Story manages to humble you without degrading you.

There's a tricky balance in there. Some folks seem to think that the whole world revolves around them. They're easy to spot, and they tend to cause the rest of us a lot of trouble when they don't get their way.

A lot of Christians respond by saying, "It's not about you." Unwittingly, though, these Christians may, in a knee-jerk sort of way, push the pendulum too far toward the other extreme.

We prefer to say, "It's not all about you . . . not entirely. You do have a part; it's just not the leading role."

That's a more accurate and biblical perspective.

There's a Story going on, a Story as big as the cosmos, bigger even. And the wonderful truth is that you're invited to play a part. The Story is far too big to be rooted in one human being's story, whether that human being is you or Oprah Winfrey or King David. It's bigger than Abraham and Moses and Peter and Paul and Mary put together.

All of these people find their true identities only as they discover the role they were meant to play in the ongoing, unfolding epic drama of God. The process of making this discovery is what infuses life with real meaning and real dignity, all the while keeping our egos in check.

King David realized that there was something far bigger than his legacy at stake. The scope of God's plan and God's Story is huge, extending to all generations, every nation and tribe and language. Yet David also realized that God honored him by allowing him to play a very important role.

Your task is to find *your* role, understanding that only the discovery process can provide you with the proper balance of humility and dignity.

THURSDAY: Actions

There's an old Greek proverb that says, "A society grows great when old men plant trees whose shade they know they shall never sit in."

King David wanted to build a house for God, but God told him not to. David could have lost all interest in the idea after that, and we would understand why. If it was to be the responsibility of one of his sons, perhaps David should leave it alone.

Instead, David spent the rest of his life gathering building materials for the Temple. When David's son Solomon got around to the construction of the Temple, he had an entire warehouse full of supplies and a complete set of blueprints (see 1 Chron. 28). It was like Solomon had a whole Home Depot at his disposal!

David knew that he wouldn't be the one to build the Temple. He knew it would be one of his sons. He also knew that his son would need a lot of wood, stones and fabric to complete what would already be a mammoth task. So David decided to use his remaining days making the task easier for his son—even though he knew that he would never see the building completed!

There's a lesson in there for us. Like David, we live in in-between times—toiling between the first coming of Jesus and the second—enjoying the "already/not-yet-ness" of God's kingdom. We may never live to see the day of His returning. It might happen this afternoon, or He might wait another century. We don't know.

But one day it will happen. One day, people will do God's will as it is now being done in heaven. One day, the lion will lay down with the lamb, swords will be beaten into plowshares, the blind will see, the lame will walk, the poor will be rich and the weak will become strong. One day, everything currently upside-down will be turned right side up again.

It may be for the next generation to see the fulfillment of God's promises. We may never see them, but the way we live our remaining days can either make it easier or more difficult for the generations that follow after us.

So, we long for Christ's return. We join our voices with millions of Christians from the past and pray, "*Maranatha!* Lord, come quickly!" But in the meantime, we wait—and we do more than wait. We gather into the storehouses the materials future generations will need to participate with God in expanding the borders of His kingdom in their time. We put forth our best efforts to leave a legacy, planting those trees whose shade we may never enjoy.

FRIDAY: Prayer

Narrative

God of Glory, the narrative of Your extraordinary and creative program of redemption that is revealed in the pages of Your Holy Word boggles the mind and transcends our imagination. In Your sovereign power and wisdom, you transmute evil into good. What people mean for evil, You turn to ultimate good, and all this without violating the dignity of freedom You have given us as moral beings who, though fallen, are nevertheless created in Your image. You have progressively revealed Your nature and purposes in the history of Your people and in the pages of Scripture. You accomplish Your loving intentions through the obedience of Your people and in spite of their frequent disobedience. I ask that I would be used by You as a willing part of Your purposes so that I can participate in what You are about.

Orthodoxy

Lord God, I so often try to persuade You that my plans and hopes are in my best interests and then ask You to bless them. But when I really think about it, how can I know what is really best for me? I can only judge by appearances, but You look ahead to the outcomes. Only You see and hold the future, and I want to confess that only You know what is truly best for me. Grant that I would become increasingly willing to let loose of my fond aspirations and embrace what You know is really in my best interests. I know I will have to wrestle with this all my life, because I often struggle with what You bring into my life and tell me to do. It is only when I embrace Your goodness and wisdom that I can stop wrestling with Your good plans and purposes.

Orthopathy

Father, I thank You that Your grace humbles me without degrading me and elevates me without inflating me. You have accorded me great dignity and worth, but without You I am nothing and have nothing. I am grateful that You have given me the holy invitation to participate in something that extends so far beyond me that I can only revel in Your kindness, grace and compassion. I fully acknowledge that You can very well accomplish Your intentions without me, and yet You invite me to participate in what will last forever. I ask for a growing clarity about Your unique purposes for my life, so that I can live into those purposes by Your grace and become the person you created me to be, accomplishing the works you have prepared beforehand for me.

Orthopraxy

Lord, I ask for the humility and willingness to live out my life for the sake of others rather than for personal gain or reputation. You have called me to leave a legacy by building Your unbroken truth into the next generation. I want to invest all You have graciously given me in the lives of others so that I will live well and wisely, and not foolishly and selfishly. Let me view every day as if it were my last, knowing that I will either go to be with You or be alive on earth when You return. Let me live each day in light of that day and relish the opportunities You have given me today, investing my time and resources well. I want to abide in You in such a way that when You appear, I may have confidence and not shrink away from You in shame at Your coming.

13

City on a Hill

1 KINGS 5–8

It was hard to believe—impossible for some—but it had happened. God had taken an old, barren couple and from them produced a nation of people—millions of people. He had given them the best land imaginable and placed them right in the middle of civilization so that other nations could come and see what it looked like when a people lived together in harmony under the authority of God.

One promise fulfilled: Israel had arrived.

They had encountered many missteps along the way, but those days were behind them! They had an established monarchy now. Saul had failed, but David had been a success (often in spite of himself). Now the crown had been passed to David's son Solomon, and things really looked bright.

Solomon was the wealthiest man in the world, wealthier than most of us can imagine—sort of like Donald Trump, only with even more wives! Donald Trump, Warren Buffett and Bill Gates combined couldn't begin to touch the amount of Solomon's wealth (or the number of wives, for that matter). And wisdom coming out his ears!

These were bright times indeed, and the brightest spot of all was a gigantic Temple that Solomon constructed for YHWH. He spared no expense, seeking out only the finest building materials and the most skilled craftsmen. The Temple was one of the marvels of the ancient world, and dignitaries from all over came to see the magnificent structure.

It took seven years to build and more than 200,000 workers. And the celebration at the opening put everything before or since to shame. It was New Year's Eve in Times Square, the Opening and Closing Ceremonies of the Olympics, the Academy Awards, the Fourth of July and everyone's birthday all rolled into one! The presence of God was so thick, so heavy, so palpable, so tangible that the priests literally couldn't stand it!

For the Israelites, though, the Temple was more than just a building; it was a visible reminder of God's abiding presence. The Temple was a symbol of just how faithful their God had been—bringing them out of barrenness into fruitfulness, out of famine into abundance, out of slavery into freedom.

Unfortunately, that day was the high point.

From there on out, it was a slow and gradual decline, both for Solomon personally and for the entire nation of Israel. They would never again be this wealthy or this unified. Solomon would allow himself to be led down the slippery slope of idolatry. The people would grow more and more divided, ultimately splitting the kingdom in two. Then they would grow more alienated from each other and their God.

YHWH's ultimate dream of building a city set on a hill would have to wait. But for one brief moment, they actually got it right.

And what a moment it was.

TUESDAY: Beliefs

It is obvious from the first pages of the Bible that God wants to be with these humans He created. In the earliest times, when humans lived in the Garden of Eden, God would join them regularly for walks. They would speak face to face. There was no sin or guilt or shame to mar the connection. Things were ideal.

But then came temptation and sin, and the whole thing started to unravel.

Still, God's intentions never changed. He wanted a relationship with these rebellious and stiff-necked people. He wanted to actually spend time being with them.

So God began arranging ways of meeting with people. He would show up in what are known as "theophanies"—special, divine appearances. They were rare, but Abraham, Isaac and Joseph all experienced a handful of these God-sightings.

Then God appeared in a burning bush to call Moses to get the people out of Egyptian slavery. As they marched out, God was visibly with His people in the form of a cloud by day and a fire by night. Then He led them to a mountain where the people got to see just how terrifyingly powerful and awesome YHWH could be.

But the people rebelled again, so God suggested they just go into the Promised Land without Him (see Exod. 33). The people, realizing that they didn't stand a chance against their enemies without God's presence, refused to go forward unless He went with them.

The next part of God's plan to spend time with people involved Moses building a box—the Ark of the Covenant—and placing it in the middle of a portable tent known as the Tabernacle. The high priest entered the presence of this box once a year, and God promised to meet the people's representative there.

For the next few centuries, the Ark of the Covenant symbolized this abiding presence of God, the special relationship the Israelites enjoyed with their Maker and Redeemer.

Just prior to the reign of King Saul, however, the unthinkable happened: Enemies captured the Ark, causing the entire nation to panic. It was eventually returned, but then Saul did a foolish and unthinkable thing: For an entire generation, he kept the Ark sitting in storage.

King David understood that God's desire was to be in the midst of the people. His first act, after setting up the new capital city of Jerusalem, was to bring the Ark of the Covenant there, with the intent of building a permanent structure for it—a place where the people could always go and meet with God.

David's son Solomon built that place, and it was grand. It was glorious. It was beyond compare.

But it didn't last very long at all. In a short while, the people would rebel again, and in a few generations, Jerusalem was reduced to rubble and ashes, the Temple just a pile of stones. The Ark of the Covenant was lost forever. The place where people could meet with God was gone.

And so, from this point forward, we'll begin to hear more and more about the need for a permanent solution. Prophets will begin to take on a more prominent role in the Bible's Story, calling the people back to their covenant promises and speaking of a time in the future when God would provide a new way of meeting with them.

The meeting point will no longer be a place; it will be a Person. And it is through that Person that God still meets His people. Anyone and everyone who comes to Jesus will find a personal encounter with the God who creates, redeems and restores.

WEDNESDAY: Values

For centuries, God's people led culture. The leading poets and philosophers, artists and architects, musicians and mathematicians were Christians. God's people didn't just influence culture; they created it.
But it's not that way anymore.

Nowadays, it's not uncommon to hear people say things like, "That was pretty good . . . for a church." What they mean is that much of what passes for Christian art, music and thought would never make it in the "real world." The level of excellence (or lack thereof) demonstrated by many churches simply wouldn't cut it in the marketplace.

What's even more shocking is that some Christians reserve their best efforts for their own pursuits while offering God the leftovers of their time, energy and creativity.

Understanding the story of Solomon's building of the Temple can help us counter both of these problems. Look at the care that went into the construction of the Temple. They didn't skimp or scrape or cut corners. They were elaborate and ornate. They didn't settle for unremarkable utilitarian buildings, square bland boxes. They valued beauty and art and creativity, good fabric, real wood and craftsmanship.

Quite a contrast to the nondescript church buildings that dot our landscape, with tile floors, cinder block walls, fluorescent lights and metal folding chairs.

Do we value beauty? Aesthetics? Art and creativity?

Would we decorate our own homes the way we decorate our church buildings? Would we be satisfied if the same level of craftsmanship used on our church buildings was used in the houses we live in?

Solomon wasn't. As magnificent as the Temple he built for God was, Solomon's house was even better. It took nearly twice as long to build and was even more impressive.

It's not that we shouldn't have nice houses. But placing a high premium on beauty and art in our homes or places of business without applying it to our places of worship may reveal more about our misplaced priorities than we realize.

God values beauty; He personifies it. All beauty on earth points beyond itself to the ultimate source of beauty, God Himself. Value it. Prize it. Seek it and allow it to guide you to a finer appreciation of the Beautiful One who wants our best for Himself.

THURSDAY: Actions

The scope of the celebration services in the Old Testament is staggering. Solomon's dedication of the Temple involved hundreds of thousands—perhaps even millions—of people. They gathered and praised God. They prayed and shouted. And—here's the part we like—they had the biggest barbecue cookout you can imagine. They cooked up 22,000 cows and 120,000 sheep and goats. There was food as far as the eye could see. Everyone ate and drank and celebrated for two full weeks.

It was every church potluck and "dinner on the grounds" you've ever been to, and then some!

And what were they celebrating? A building. A fixed place where they could go and find God. They were celebrating the fact that God had kept His promise to them by redeeming them from slavery, giving them a land of their own and blessing them with favor among the other nations.

Those are good things. But think about what *you* have to celebrate. God didn't just redeem you from physical bondage; He redeemed you from a lifetime of spiritual slavery. You don't just have a geographic location to call your own; you have an eternal home in the presence of the One who gives all things meaning and value. You don't just have favor among other nations; you enjoy fellowship and community among God's people. You have more than a fixed place where you can go and find God; if you've placed your trust in Jesus, God actually lives in you. You've been promised an eternity of ever-increasing intimacy with your Creator and other people.

If the people during Solomon's reign had cause to celebrate, what about you?

Life may be complicated. There may be hardships that come your way. Christians are not exempt from sickness and fatigue. Relationships are tricky. Life doesn't always turn out the way you want it to. But think about what God has done for you.

Remembrance is the key to celebration. Sometimes it comes easily; other times it's a discipline. Sometimes, it requires effort on our part. Mostly that effort will be to remember. Remember where you've been and give some thought to what it is, exactly, you've been redeemed out of. Remember how faithful God has been in the past and what His promises are for the future.

Today tie these two activities together: Remember what God has done and has promised to do, and allow that remembrance to lead you to celebration. You might even want to deepen your celebration by involving others in it. Go ahead ... throw a cookout!

FRIDAY: Prayer

Narrative

God of Abraham and David, You have planted a profound longing deep within me that no earthly attainment or solace can satisfy. This aspiration is for Your manifest presence, and it draws me to see the world as You meant it to be. The brief Camelot of Solomon's early reign, with its splendor and its far-reaching influence on the nations around Israel, gives me a hint of what You are planning for the future that will not be ephemeral, but will go on into eternity. When I come in contact with the innermost desires of my heart, I must openly admit that this present world is not enough. You have planted one of my feet in this age and the other in the glorious age to come. Keep me in touch with this hunger and thirst for what You plan to bring, so that I will see more clearly that nothing in this world is enough to satisfy this divinely given restlessness.

Orthodoxy

Dear Father, I rejoice in the revelation that You want to be with me and me with You. The depths of Your grace are unfathomable—I cannot see how You could wish to have such intimacy with me. Yet daily I seem to forget this glorious truth and turn my heart instead to lesser gods that compete with the one thing most needful. Why do I clamor after other affections above Yours? How did I get betrothed to your enemy? I ask that you would untie me and break that knot, and take me to Yourself. Only when I am enthralled by You will I ever be free. Knowing this, I ask for the grace of holy aspiration, so that I will treasure what You declare to be important and stop giving myself to lesser things that cannot satisfy, but only entrap. By Your grace, I would break free from the bondage of the flesh, the world and the devil.

Orthopathy

God of glory and grace, when I reflect on the beauty and diversity of Your created order, I marvel at Your genius, Your creativity, Your personal care, Your exquisite aesthetics, Your glory and order and excellence. May I aspire to excellence in all that I do, in each arena of my influence, so that others would encounter the fragrance of Your manifest presence and lordship. Nothing less than my utmost for Your highness will do. Give me the wisdom to expose myself to those things that build up and nourish the soul rather than those things that denigrate and diminish. Let me be careful and prayerful about what I see, read and do, so that I will not be corrupted by that which is beneath Your vision for my life. Teach me, my God and King, in all things Thee to see, and what I do in anything to do it as for Thee.

Orthopraxy

O Lord, give me the wisdom of spiritual remembrance so that I will never take the riches of Your grace and goodness for granted. Remind me to recall all of Your many benefits and blessings over the years and to realize frequently how much You have done for me. You have carried me through difficult passages. You have comforted me in times of despair. You have encouraged me when I was despondent. You have given me hope when all seemed lost. You have blessed me with freedoms, friends and opportunities that I never deserved. As I review Your benefits in the past, let me also reflect on Your process in my present and on Your prospects for my future. In light of all this, I can fully affirm that Your will for me is good and acceptable and perfect. May this gratitude of remembrance give me perspective and peace in the present moment.

14

Divided Kingdom

1 KINGS 12

MONDAY: Story

God began with a garden and two people. His desire was to create a people and a place where they could all live in unbroken fellowship: God to person, person to person, people to the rest of creation. There would be no alienation, no frustration, no malice, no anxiety.

But it all went awry when these people rejected God's plan and went about trying to accomplish their own agendas.

Still, this God would not give up on His dream. From the day they rejected Him, God began to reveal His larger plan to not only create a perfect world but to redeem that perfect world from its own corruption. Slowly, painstakingly, God began to work with the raw material of fallen and depraved humans—men and women like Abraham and Sarah, Moses, Joshua, Rahab, Ruth, Saul and David. Eventually, under the reign of King Solomon, it appeared as if God's plan might actually reach its fulfillment.

But these humans couldn't stop shooting themselves in the feet.

Solomon, as wise as he was, couldn't keep himself from being seduced by his many wives into worshiping other gods. At first he merely tolerated them doing it. Then he began to endorse them doing it by building them places of worship devoted to the foreign gods. Ultimately, he joined them in doing it and offended the God who had given him everything he had.

As a result of his foolish actions, God told Solomon that his son Rehoboam would lose a portion of the kingdom when he assumed the throne after Solomon's death. In fact, Rehoboam lost most of the kingdom (10 of the 12 tribes). Another man, Jeroboam, would be the king of the northern tribes.

Solomon, hearing this message from God, decided to try to do something to prevent it. He attempted to murder Jeroboam, but Jeroboam escaped to Egypt and stayed there until the king died. Unfortunately, Jeroboam picked up many of the religious practices of the Egyptians while he was down there, and he imported them back into Israel when he returned.

It's hard to believe that some people think the Bible is boring!

The kingdom was officially divided shortly after Rehoboam took control in 931 B. C. His father, Solomon, had imposed a heavy burden of taxation to pay for the construction of the Temple and his personal palace. The people asked Rehoboam to cut back on spending to lighten their load some, but Rehoboam—refusing to listen to his wisest advisors—promised to make things even harder on the people.

Jeroboam saw this as his opportunity, and led a revolt of the masses. The kingdom would be divided from that point on: 10 tribes in the north called Israel, and 2 tribes in the south called Judah.

As you can imagine, it would not end well.

And yet . . . God still had a few tricks up His sleeve.

TUESDAY: Beliefs

It has been said, and rightly so, that the one thing humans cannot live without is hope. Because we cannot live without it, we will always find something in which to place our hope—even when it is the wrong thing.

The people of Israel placed their hopes and dreams on something that could not bear that freight. They trusted in their kings as if Saul, David and Solomon could usher in the fulfillment of God's promises. But they were just men. They couldn't keep their promises to God individually any more than the people could collectively. They were human, and they failed.

All the buildings they constructed eventually fell. All the borders they secured were eventually overrun. All the economic strength and all the glory eventually faded, leaving crushed hopes and dreams behind. Saul unified the people. David subdued their enemies. Solomon built the Temple. But none of them fulfilled God's greatest dream: to build a community of people rightly related to Himself and rightly relating to one another to such a degree that their presence would be a blessing to the entire world.

God wanted His people to be magnetic, to draw others into fellowship with themselves and with Him. Instead, they couldn't even get along with each other. Rather than learning from YHWH how to use the influence they had been given by Him, they used their power to protect themselves, to manipulate others and to further their own selfish ambitions. They did this even at the cost of healthy relationships with others. They did this even when it meant compromising their core beliefs, values and practices, violating their covenant promises to the God who had used His power for their benefit.

They wanted to claim the promise of God—that they would be the most influential nation on earth. Sounds noble and great. But they attempted to claim God's promise by violating their own promises to Him. They trusted in human power and ingenuity rather than relying on the One who had gotten them this far in the first place.

They found out the hard way what happens when you trust a person to accomplish what only God can.

Our trust is terribly misplaced when it is put in the hands of a human being or a program conceived of human initiative or a building constructed by human hands. None of these things are bad or evil in themselves, but none of these things will ever fulfill our deepest longings. We will always find ourselves let down, disappointed and discouraged by the things of this earth.

Only God is strong enough to bear the full weight of our deepest desires, hopes and dreams.

When our trust is appropriately placed, we find an amazing quality of life that is unavailable otherwise. As we allow Jesus to be the fulfillment of our deepest longings and desires, by placing Him at the center of all of our activities, everything we do is not only infused with meaning and purpose, but has the potential to allow us (finally!) participation with God in bringing about the fulfillment of His greatest dream.

The kingdom was divided, but it will one day be reunited. That's what God is doing even now. By embedding our story within His, we are allowed to participate with Him in the greatest adventure of all. That's what it really means to keep hope alive.

WEDNESDAY: Values

When public opinion begins to masquerade as intelligence, we desperately need to prize wisdom.

Do we need authenticity? You bet. Honesty? Absolutely. Should we embrace mystery and paradox? Of course.

But at the end of the day, wisdom must be held in the highest esteem, because an authentic, honest, mysterious, paradoxical fool is still a fool. So where do we turn to find the kind of wisdom that will enable us to see with clarity and conviction? This week's story serves as a sort of cautionary tale for us in this endeavor.

First of all, we are often told that old age brings wisdom. There are even biblical references people cite to back up this theory. For example, Job asks (somewhat rhetorically), "Is not wisdom found among the aged? Does not long life bring understanding?" (Job 12:12).

Well . . . yes . . . sometimes.

However, Solomon himself—the wisest man who had ever lived—disproves the theory that wisdom always comes with age. He actually grows less wise as he gets older! Our elders are often a source of wisdom, but they're not completely reliable.

A second potential source of wisdom is the counsel of our peers. Proverbs 15:22 tells us, "Plans fail for lack of counsel, but with many advisers they succeed."

But Rehoboam got counsel, lots of it. He sought the opinion of his peers and they gave him bad advice.

What about outsiders? Sometimes it's helpful to seek the wisdom of those who are outside our immediate community. Sometimes Christians think that they have cornered the market on wisdom, but that's not true in many areas. It would have been foolish to think that the Egyptians had nothing of value to say about how to govern people; they'd been doing it longer than the Israelites had been . . . well . . . the Israelites. Two whole chapters in the book of Proverbs are taken up with wise sayings from pagan kings (see Prov. 30–31).

But Jeroboam brought back what he thought was wisdom from Egypt, and it ended up ruining the kingdom, driving a semi-permanent wedge between the 10 tribes to the north and the remaining 2 tribes of the south.

Old age, peer groups, outsiders—all of these are potential sources of the precious wisdom we so desperately need. But we must never forget that they are also potential sources of even more foolishness and pooled ignorance. Once again, we are left to consider that only God is completely reliable. Whatever wisdom we think we may have accumulated must be run through the filter of God's Word. Only then do we learn to discern wisdom from folly.

THURSDAY: Actions

Life isn't a sprint; it's a marathon. It's not how you start that determines your success; it's how you finish. This lesson is brought home firmly in both the stories of Solomon and the nation of Israel.

Solomon started so well, so full of promise. He had so much going for him. It seemed like everything he touched turned to gold. He listened to God and responded with obedience. God blessed him with wisdom unlike any other human being who had ever lived before. Solomon amassed a fortune and set a new standard of dignity among the leaders of God's people.

But, as so often happens, his success slowly turned to complacency, opening the door for compromise and disaster. He lost touch with the legitimate needs of his people. He became self-indulgent and began to listen more and more to his pagan wives, catering to their religious desires rather than maintaining his own integrity.

When Solomon began his reign, there was no doubt that there was just one God. But by the end of his reign, there was a hill to the east of Jerusalem with shrines built to just about every other god of the surrounding nations. The magnificent temple that Solomon had worked so hard to build stood as just one of many possible options. A visitor could quickly come to the conclusion that YHWH was but one of many possible gods.

Solomon did so many great things for God during the first half of his life. Unfortunately, he spent the second half of his life undoing a lot of the good he had accomplished. His father, David, had handed him a kingdom that was united and at peace. Solomon handed his son Rehoboam a kingdom that was divided and on the brink of civil war.

It's not how you start; it's how you finish. It is true of individuals, and of nations, churches and corporations as well.

Israel started so well. God brought them into the land miraculously, parting swollen rivers and knocking down fortified cities. The inhabitants of Canaan were terrified of them, and they managed to take possession of the Promised Land with relative ease. They had some bumpy times, brought about because of their own failure to honor God, but they still held together and built an empire that was the envy of all the surrounding nations.

But it didn't last very long.

In less than 50 years, the Israelites went from being united under one God, worshiping in the magnificent Temple and astonishing foreign dignitaries with their society to being a fragmented, confused people who believed that one religious practice was as good as another. They became inconsequential on the international scene and were eventually swallowed up by larger, more powerful nations.

It's not how you start; it's how you finish.

There are examples of people in the Bible who both started and finished well. Those examples, however, are fairly rare. Fortunately, the promise we can cling to is that Jesus, the One who began a good work in and among us, will be faithful to see it all the way through to completion (see Phil. 1:6).

Regardless of whether you started well or have faded somewhere along the path, if there's breath in your body, it's not too late. You can make a decision today to follow Jesus in finishing well.

FRIDAY: Prayer

Narrative

Gracious Lord, Your kindness, patience and lovingkindness have so often been tried by Your people over the centuries. I know that too often I have done the same by taking Your grace for granted and doing what I wanted to do, hoping that You would go along or ignore my actions. Deliver me from the sin of presumption, in which I regard grace as my due. May I maintain fidelity to You and to Your purposes for my life so that I will walk in the way of wisdom rather than in autonomy. Deliver me from the folly of making decisions without seeking Your will and without desiring to be pleasing to You. I want to be vigilant against all forms of idolatry, so that I will not deceive myself into thinking that flirtation with the lusts of the flesh, the lusts of the eye and the boastful pride of life could ever be gratified without dishonoring You.

Orthodoxy

Loving God, You have called us to be born again to a living hope through the resurrection of Jesus Christ from the dead. You are preparing an inheritance for us that will never be corrupted or fade away. Why then do I keep slipping into the blunder of putting my hope in other things? Deliver me from the futility of misplaced hopes that ultimately die. Teach me in experience the wisdom of hoping only in Your unchanging character and the promises You have made that flow out of Your perfections. I do not want to hope in the uncertainties of people, possessions or position, because all of these can change and disappoint. Instead, I choose to hope in You and pray that I will grow in the knowledge, love and trust of You. Then I will experience the security and satisfaction that come from growing conformity to Christ.

Orthopathy

Father of lights, You are the fountainhead of true wisdom, counsel, discernment and understanding. You often mediate Your wisdom through others, but please prevent me from making that my final source. I acknowledge that biblical wisdom is the skill in living life with each aspect under Your governance, and that I cannot attain this skill without the fear of the Lord. May I learn to fear Your displeasure and desire to be pleasing to You, so that I will live my life before You rather than seeking to impress people. I know that when I am more concerned with what You say and desire than with the opinions and expectations of others, I will actually be empowered to serve them better. I want to order my steps before You, to hold fast to You, to aspire to be like You, to hope in You and to pursue You above all else.

Orthopraxy

Lord of all, I truly desire to finish my earthly sojourn well. I know this will not happen automatically, and that many who begin well finish poorly. You have taught me that the most important key to finishing well is intimacy with Christ Jesus, and I ask for the grace to treasure that above all else. Grant that I would grow in fidelity to the spiritual disciplines of renewing my mind with Your Word, with prayer and with times of solitude and silence so that I will grow in the knowledge of the Lord. Give me a biblical perspective on the circumstances of my life, and teach me to pursue a biblical hope and purpose. Please empower me to express the vertical on the horizontal, so that my love and service to You are increasingly evident in my love and service to others. I want to run with endurance the race that is set before me and fix my eyes on Jesus.

15

Just a Regular Guy

1 Kings 17–19

MONDAY: Story

Jeroboam was a bad king. Saul had been a near-disaster. David had his rough patches. Solomon started so well but ended in shame. But Jeroboam didn't even come close. He was bad from beginning to end.

So it is not surprising to find out that his son was bad. And his son's son. And his son's son's son. And just when you think they couldn't get any worse, along comes Ahab, the worst king of them all—a selfish, immature man controlled by his ambitious and overbearing wife, Jezebel. Together they led the Northern Kingdom of Israel into an unprecedented level of idolatry.

Into this awful mix, God sent a prophet named Elijah to deliver a critical message and attempt to persuade Israel to return to YHWH.

And you thought your job was hard!

You'd think God would have picked someone with superhuman intelligence and strength, but He didn't. He picked Elijah, a regular person just like us. Elijah was just a normal guy who struggled with self-doubt, loneliness and acceptance—but when God told him to do something, he did it. Maybe that's the difference between Elijah and many of us.

The first thing Elijah did to get everyone's attention was to ask God to make it stop raining. For two whole years there was no rain, no mist, not even dew in the morning.

As you can imagine, this didn't make Elijah the most popular guy around.

Still, God provided for Elijah through various methods: Ravens brought him food, angels brought him food, pagan widows brought him food. Elijah was a well-fed prophet in a land of famine.

The most famous event in Elijah's life was an event he arranged on the top of Mount Carmel. Jezebel had imported prophets and priests of the false god Baal and supported them with money from the national treasury. Elijah challenged these prophets to a showdown involving two bulls, two altars and two deities: YHWH and Baal. Which one would send fire from heaven to consume the bull on the altar?

The prophets of Baal danced and shouted and howled and cut themselves trying to get Baal's attention. But nothing happened.

When it was his turn, Elijah doused his bull with water and prayed—no dancing, no shouting, no howling like a crazy man, no cutting. And fire came down from heaven, consuming the sacrifice and the altar, the stones supporting the altar and all the water that had collected on the ground.

Sometimes God doesn't leave much room for doubt!

You'd think that after seeing God do such an amazing thing, Elijah would be ecstatic. But you'd be wrong.

Being God's spokesman can be a difficult job, and Elijah often felt scared and alone. Immediately after the big blowup with Baal, Jezebel took out a contract on Elijah's life, and he ran to the mountains to ask God to kill him. Frankly, he got a little whiny about it.

But God is good (even when we're childish) and Elijah received the reassurance that he needed to continue in his calling. God let him know that he was not alone. God promised him that evil would never be allowed to have the last word. And God challenged Elijah to go and find a replacement for himself. In other words, God was saying that the world would go on, long after Ahab and Jezebel were gone—even after Elijah.

God's plan will continue to move forward, and He will continue to use regular people like us.

TUESDAY: Beliefs

Most children reach a stage when they want to know why.

"Why is the sky blue?"

"Why do goldfish die?"

"Why doesn't Daddy have hair on the top of his head?"

It's not just silly, three-year-old questions, though. Sometimes they want to know why their parents want them to do certain things (or not do certain other things).

"Why do I have to eat my vegetables?"

"Why do I have to be home at 10:00?"

"Why can't I go with Lisa and Trish to the beach for the weekend without any parents?"

We tend to operate under the assumption that information will naturally lead to cooperation. Sometimes it does, but most times it does not. It just brings about further attempts to rationalize or justify or cajole.

But here's something we learn from Elijah's story—especially from his whiny conversation with God in the mountains: *If you knew what God knows, you would be more likely to do what God says.*

After Elijah's winner-take-all confrontation with 850 pagan prophets and their false god, Jezebel threatens to kill him and he runs away. Elijah panics and goes on a 12-day journey down to the furthest point in the Southern Kingdom, and then he goes for one more day. In other words, he goes as far as he can and then a little farther. At this point, God shows up and Elijah says, "Okay, God, I've had enough. Kill me now."

Interestingly, God never panics.

God deals with Elijah like you would deal with a cranky toddler: He gives him a drink and a snack and puts him down for a nap. When Elijah wakes up, God shows him all the things He could do at a moment's notice. *Earthquake. Fire. Howling wind.* God's got weapons in His arsenal that we don't know anything about. He's heavily fortified.

Then God lets Elijah in on some things. Ahab won't be king forever. Elijah won't be God's main prophet forever. YHWH was here before Elijah, and He'll be here long after Elijah is gone. He's been at work getting things ready for the next chapter. Elijah can't see things happening, but that doesn't mean that things aren't happening.

"And by the way . . . you're not the only true believer left. There are 7,000 others."

Interestingly, Elijah and God look at the same situation, the exact same circumstances. Elijah panics and quits; God does not.

And why doesn't God panic? Because He has a greater perspective on things than Elijah. See, panic just reveals a limited perspective. God is not nervously pacing back and forth in heaven, wringing His hands wondering what to do. God has got a plan, and nothing in the whole wide world is going to stop Him from bringing it all the way to fruition. God is not going to be surprised by anything.

So we can calm down.

When we think the whole story lives and dies with us, we're liable to panic. We feel afraid, and we stop trusting God. But when we embed our story into the larger context of His Story (history?), our panic subsides. Our fear loses its grip on us, and we can relax, knowing that no matter how messed up things appear to be now, God is still in control.

WEDNESDAY: Values

Elijah was just a guy. He wasn't Superman. He wasn't even Samson. He was just a regular guy like the rest of us (see James 5:17).

When it comes time for us to select a leader—whether a new CEO, a new pastor or a new president—we tend to look for someone special. Backgrounds are checked and records are scrutinized. Anything that hints of impropriety or scandal is enough to disqualify even the most highly qualified person for the job, because we look for that one extraordinarily special person who we believe can and will help to change the world.

God, on the other hand, does not seem particularly drawn to the extraordinary. When God wants to change the world, He usually looks for a regular person . . . someone, say, a lot like you.

Our society values money and education and connections. We want someone with a certain bearing that sets him or her apart from everyone else. We want a leader who will make the rest of us look good and feel good about our standing as a company, church or nation.

But God sometimes goes the other way. It's not that God has anything against wealthy, well-educated people with good networking skills. It's just that God doesn't require any of those things in order to use a person to make an indelible mark on human history.

He certainly didn't require them of Elijah.

Elijah was a regular person who didn't have all the answers. In fact, there were times in his life when it appeared as if he had more questions than answers. He struggled with his confidence. He wrestled with fear and anxiety and depression. And yet more miracles occurred during his lifetime than during the lives of King Saul, King David and King Solomon combined.

God accomplishes extraordinary things through ordinary people.

More often than not, the people God uses are unremarkable until they allow Him to use them. Afterward, we tend to think of them as these incredible pillars of strength, courage and faith. But on the front end, there's often very little to commend them to our attention.

Rosa Parks. Mother Teresa. Dietrich Bonhoeffer. Abraham Lincoln. You would have been hard-pressed to pick these people out of a lineup before God got His hands on them.

So many people feel trapped and helpless, as if the world just happens to them. They're unaware of how much power they actually can have and how much change they actually can effect.

God has a plan, and that plan involves not only the redemption of the world but its restoration as well. He is looking for people who will actively partner with Him in setting everything that is currently upside-down, right side up again—people who will reach out to the widows and the orphans and the poor, people who will tear down corrupt systems and erect righteous systems in their place.

God is at work. He wants people who are willing to work with Him, who will allow Him to work through them. He's not looking for a few good men; He's looking for one willing person.

Maybe today He wants to do something out of the ordinary through a regular man or woman like you.

THURSDAY: Actions

Everybody prays. Some people pray because they know they're supposed to. Some people pray as a way of covering their bases, just in case it might work. Some people pray because they desperately need something and they don't know where else to turn.

Everybody prays. But not the way Elijah prayed.

Still . . . everybody could.

If Elijah really was just a normal, average, everyday kind of person (and not "a strange visitor from another planet who came to earth with powers and abilities far beyond those of mortal men"), then that means normal, average, everyday kind of people like us can pray like he did.

And how exactly did he pray?

Elijah prayed biblically. One time, he prayed for God to make it stop raining. Where in the world did he get that idea? He got that idea from the book of Deuteronomy. Moses warned the people that if they turned away from God and started worshiping foreign gods, it would stop raining (see 11:16–17). Elijah was just asking God to keep His Word and discipline the people like He said He would.

Many times we don't pray like Elijah because we're biblically ignorant and don't know how to pray according to God's revealed will. But we can change that. (Hopefully this book is helping.)

Elijah prayed very specifically. He didn't just offer vague, generic prayers. Because he prayed for specific things to happen, there was no doubt when God answered.

Elijah kept praying even when the answer wasn't immediate. In 1 Kings 18:43, we learn that Elijah prayed seven times for it to start raining again. He didn't just pray once and quit.

Elijah was humble when he prayed. There was no big show, and he didn't seem to need to ramp himself up emotionally. He just asked God for stuff. Perhaps because he had an ongoing, conversational relationship with God, he didn't feel like he had to get worked up to ask Him for big things.

Oh, and speaking of the conversational nature of Elijah's relationship with God, there's another lesson about praying we can learn from him: Elijah complained.

Let's face it: The one thing people do more than pray is complain. Only the Judeo-Christian Scriptures provide us with an example of a people who feel comfortable complaining to their God. That's one of the most unique things about Jewish literature. The relationship they had with YHWH was strong enough to survive unfiltered dialogue—from both directions!

Elijah was just a regular guy—a lot like any of us. But he prayed. And when he prayed, he became extraordinary. What might happen today if you did the same?

FRIDAY: Prayer

Narrative

O Lord, I thank You that You can use ordinary people to accomplish extraordinary things. The source of the power is not from us, but from Your Holy

Spirit. May I not set my sights low, but expect great and wonderful things from You, even things I do not understand. Sometimes I am gripped with fear and insecurity, and these are the times when I have taken my eyes off You. I want to be faithful to the many opportunities You have given me so that I will learn to look to You for all things. May I learn the wisdom of abiding in Christ as a branch abides in the vine, so that I will draw my life and impact from You instead of trying to create life on my own. I ask for Your Spirit to exhort, encourage, comfort and teach me in the times when I embrace the wisdom of obedience, and even in the times when I stray from You.

Orthodoxy

Lord of Hosts, I revel in the truths of Your majesty, power, glory and dominion over all things in heaven and on earth. In spite of so many appearances to the contrary, nothing can happen that comes as a surprise to You or escapes Your control. You order the events of history in ways we do not understand, and in spite of the vastness of human evil, Your plan will be accomplished. I pray for the insight of a growing biblical perspective on the events in my life and in the world. May I move with confidence in Your sovereignty, even when things seem to make no sense to me. I thank You for Your patience and comfort, especially in times when I try to run from You or feel sorry for myself. I want to renew my mind with Your unchanging truth in a changing world, so that my assurance is in Your often-mysterious ways in the affairs of the sons and daughters of men.

Orthopathy

Father God, I frequently find myself slipping into the trap of using the wrong criteria to evaluate success and failure. I want to take my eyes off the things that impress people in this world and fix them on the things that you declare to be important. Trust and obedience and the humility of other-centered service are the marks of true greatness, and I desire to grow in them. May I learn the spirituality of small things, since he who is faithful in a very little thing is faithful also in much, and he who is unrighteous in a very little thing is unrighteous also in much. I know that from a Kingdom perspective, I don't need to make a big splash in this world to be pleasing to You. Grant me the grace of splendor in the ordinary and of fidelity in the little things, because these are the things that accumulate into true greatness.

Orthopraxy

God of power and might, I thank You for the grace-filled gift of prayer. You welcome me into Your presence and bid me to draw near with confidence to the throne of grace so that I may receive mercy and find grace to help in time of need. In prayer, let me lay hold of my true possessions in Christ and exercise the authority You have granted me as a believer in Jesus Christ. I want to internalize and pray Your Word back to You, and I wish to pray at all times by practicing Your presence and acknowledging my dependence upon You in everything. Thank You that I can also be real and honest in prayer without pretence or posing, because there are times when I need to wrestle with Your will in the circumstances of my life. You patiently and lovingly hear my complaints and You succor and comfort me in times of distress.

16

Passing the Torch

1 Kings 19

MONDAY: Story

If only Elisha had stayed where he was, he could have experienced a nice, comfortable life. He was from a wealthy family and had a nice job. Life was pretty good for him.

But God sometimes calls, and, if we have the courage to respond, He leads us in paths we never would have created for ourselves.

Elisha was out working in the field when Elijah came walking by. There was just something about that moment; no words were needed. Elisha knew that God was calling him to leave everything comfortable and familiar to follow this mysterious miracle-worker into an uncertain future.

Elisha had no idea that he would receive twice as much power as his predecessor, Elijah. He could not have known the great things he would do and see, the miracles, the healings, the visions. He could not have imagined the pain he would feel when he pleaded with his fellow Hebrews to repent and return to this God who does such amazing miracles, only to find his message falling on deaf ears.

He only knew that God was offering him the opportunity of a lifetime, and he wanted that more than anything else.

In that moment, Elisha chose to follow. He chose to leave affluence and security behind and become part of a lonely line of prophets that God used to call His people back to Himself. And that one decision marked a turning point for Elisha. His life would never be the same.

Elisha was able to see things other people could not see. But he had no idea that gift would be his when he first signed up to follow God's call. He only knew that he wouldn't be able to live with himself if he ignored the invitation.

He watched as his mentor was taken up into heaven by a fiery chariot and horses. He raised a young man from the dead, caused an axe handle to float on water, took a small amount of bread and multiplied it to feed 100 people, and healed an important Syrian general of leprosy. He even foiled a foreign army's attempt to invade Israel by asking God to strike them all blind.

The strangest miracle involving Elisha happened after he was already dead and buried. A group of people was burying a friend when some bandits from Moab sprang upon them. In their haste, they dumped their friend's corpse into the grave containing Elisha's bones. As soon as the body touched the bones, it sprang back to life.

Strange things happened to Elisha. If only he had stayed where he was, he could have experienced a nice, comfortable life. But he would have missed out on the life he always wanted.

TUESDAY: Beliefs

Elijah invited Elisha to volunteer for a life-changing ministry.

Elisha said, "Let me go home and tell my folks goodbye first." This may have been a polite way of saying, "Give me some time to think about it."

"Hey, take as much time as you want," Elijah replied. "Don't worry about it." And then he let Elisha leave and go home. He didn't feel the need to say, "But if you don't volunteer, think of what you'll miss out on. And if you don't volunteer, think of what you'll be depriving others of."

He didn't say any of that. He didn't pressure Elisha or coerce him or manipulate the deal at all. He didn't use guilt. He didn't use any sales tactics. He didn't insult Elisha by soft-peddling his offer or reducing it to something that involved low levels of risk. ("Hey, why don't you just try it for a while? If it doesn't work out, you can go back to plowing in the field. No hard feelings.")

Elijah didn't do any of that.

Many years later (in another Bible story), a rich young man comes to see Jesus and asks, "What do I have to do to be one of Your followers?"

Jesus tells him, "You know the Law. Don't steal. Don't lie. Don't commit adultery. Honor your parents. All that stuff."

The guy says, "I know all that. I've done all that since I was a kid. Anything else?"

Jesus says, "Well, there is this one thing. You need to trust Me more than you trust your stuff. So go sell everything you own, give the money away to the poor and then come follow Me."

And here's what happens next: The guy walks away. And Jesus lets him go (see Mark 10:17–30).

Jesus doesn't use manipulation. He never uses guilt. He also doesn't lower His standards. ("Hey, did I say everything? What if you just start with half? Or 10 percent?") Jesus doesn't stoop to those kinds of tactics. Neither did Elijah.

And neither should we.

But we should remember this: There is a window of opportunity for each of us. God, in His grace, opens a window for us, giving us each the opportunity of a lifetime: a chance to join our meager resources with His abundance, the prospect of partnering with Him in the greatest adventure of all time.

How long that window will stay open, no one knows. But it does expire. And on the great day of reckoning that is to come, when all accounts are settled and all the questions answered, the only words sadder than "If only . . ." will be "Too late."

WEDNESDAY: Values

Elisha had it pretty good. He was the son of a wealthy landowner. When Elijah found him, he was plowing in a field with 24 oxen. Most families at that time would have been lucky to own a chicken or a goat! Owning an ox was like driving an SUV, and having 24 oxen was almost unthinkable. Elisha came from a family of means.

But there's more to life than comfort and affluence, and Elisha—rich as he was—recognized this.

He had no idea what exactly he was getting into when he agreed to become Elijah's protégé, but he knew it was something bigger, something better, than just living for the moment, living for a paycheck.

He left behind a comfortable life (even burning the plows and cooking his oxen as a sign of his total commitment) to pursue God's calling on his life. The life he was choosing would be difficult. He would challenge powerful people and be hunted by entire armies. He would live hand to mouth, sometimes not knowing where his next meal would come from.

Elisha did not believe that following God would keep him well-fed and wealthy, and he had no guarantee that things would turn out well, that he would be rewarded in this life. He must have known the potential danger he might encounter by choosing the narrow path.

But Elisha chose it willingly because he valued the calling of God more than he valued the comfort of this world.

Embracing an eternal perspective like that is never easy, but it's often especially difficult for people who have an abundance of material possessions—in other words, the vast majority of people reading this book (including the two authors and all the editorial staff). We may not feel wealthy, but statistically speaking, we are. That wealth is one of the primary reasons we have a hard time valuing the unseen calling of God over the tangible benefits and comforts of "the good life." It's quite a risk to let go of everything we've been taught to clamor after!

But at some point in time, a thoughtful person must ask, "What do I *really* want?"

People are sometimes fooled into believing that they want status, prosperity or popularity. Elisha had all of these things in spades, but he knew something was missing—or at least he recognized when an opportunity to find out presented itself. Ultimately, our pursuit of things leads to emptiness and a lack of fulfillment. As counter-intuitive as it seems, the pathway to the life we've always dreamed of—a life of true freedom, meaning and purpose—is found in the conscious choice to pursue the things of God, even when that pursuit brings us to difficult circumstances, trials or hardships . . . even when it calls us to give up everything.

Few people on their deathbeds lament, "I wish I'd accumulated more money, more land, more wealth, more status." People at death's door know they can't take any of that to the ultimate show-and-tell.

When we value calling and character over comfort, we find out what real comfort is. We find a better comfort than we could ever have imagined for ourselves.

If you don't believe us, wait 'til you get to heaven and ask Elisha.

THURSDAY: Actions

From the very beginning, God had one burning desire: to create a community of people rightly related to Himself and rightly relating to one another in such a way that their presence would be a blessing to the surrounding world. And sometimes, God's strategy for fulfilling His plan to create a special community of people who will bless the surrounding world seems very strange indeed.

God chose to pursue His goal by lighting a torch and handing it to a human being, with the understanding that the person holding the torch would, in turn, pass it to someone else before he died. Abraham passed it to Isaac who passed it to Jacob. Moses passed it to Joshua. Eli passed it to Samuel. Jesus would eventually pass it to the Twelve. Late in his life, Paul would pass it to Timothy.

More than likely, you're reading this book because someone passed the torch to you. And the question you must answer is now: *Will you pass it to someone else before you die?*

In their conversation in the cave, YHWH told Elijah it was time for him to pass the torch to someone else. So that's precisely what he did with Elisha . . . even though Elisha was something of an unlikely candidate.

When Elijah found Elisha, the latter was plowing in the field. The prophet went to Elisha and handed him a cloak as a way of inviting him to be an apprentice. This was probably difficult for Elijah for a number of reasons.

First, it meant that Elijah would no longer be the only prophet. Up until then, Elijah had been *the* man of God; now he would be one of the men of God. You have to figure that required some humility on his part.

It might also have been difficult for Elijah because of Elisha's great wealth. Elijah the Tishbite from Tishbe was from the other side of the tracks, and sometimes not having much can breed suspicion about wealthier people.

Elijah had depended on birds to bring him food. He had relied on a widow with just enough flour and oil to make a single loaf of bread. It might have been easy for him to look at Elisha and say, "God, You've made a mistake. There's no way this guy is going to give up all that stuff to pursue the lifestyle of a prophet. I'm not even going to ask."

But he did ask. Because the man of God stopped one day to have a conversation with a wealthy farmer about volunteering for a ministry, widows and servants and kings and whole armies were changed forever—all because he simply asked.

Is there someone in your life who you think is such an unlikely candidate for God's program that you've been saying no for them?

Maybe that person is the best choice of all.

FRIDAY: Prayer

Narrative

Father, Your ways are mysterious and past finding out. I cannot comprehend Your purposes even for my life, but I know that You have implanted deep longings within me that correspond to Your intentions for the life I should live before You. The world is too much with me, and it is difficult for me to hear Your voice amidst the din of activities and obligations. May I learn the wisdom and sanity of solitude in which I retreat long enough from the claims and lures of this world to hear Your voice, Your call. I am willing to follow You into the unknown—I acknowledge that You really have a better plan and purpose for my life than I do. As I renew my mind with Your truth during these times, give me the grace to respond to Your invitation and turn away from the things that keep me from becoming the person You want me to be.

Orthodoxy

Lord, You have given me the great dignity of inviting me to participate in what You are doing in the world. I realize that I cannot contribute anything to You, because You lack nothing and have no needs. Yet you call me to participate, and You affirm that this decision will have everlasting consequences. I do not want to miss out on Your call or wait until it is too late. But I also know that it will take a real risk on my part to treasure and implement Your call, especially because there are so many visible alternatives that compete for my allegiance. You lead me in graciousness without compelling or coercing me to do what You know is in my best interests. I am willing to do Your will, and I ask for the power and spirit of obedience and trust that I need to realize Your loving intentions for my life during my earthly sojourn.

Orthopathy

Lord God, every day I wrestle with the visible versus the invisible, the now versus the not-yet, the goods of this world versus the currency of the next world, the temporal versus the eternal. As I reflect on the things the world system tells me to pursue in its definition of the good life, I understand that none of them can satisfy my soul, because I was made and meant for so much more. I must admit that no amount of wealth, pleasure, success or prestige can ever contend with even the simplest gift that comes from Your hand. You are the architect of true pleasure and satisfaction; these things flow out of the personal knowledge of You. What I really want is You, because I realize that when I seek first Your kingdom and righteousness, everything else will fall into its proper place.

Orthopraxy

Dear Lord, I ask for the grace to be winsome and attractive to others who wish to know You better. May they sense the fragrance of Christ in me and see increasing evidence of the fruit of Your Holy Spirit in my life. I know this is only possible as I pursue You and apprentice myself to Jesus by following Him wherever He leads. Show me the people You want to touch through me, and grant me the willingness to love and serve them with no hidden agendas or manipulative expectations. I wish to impart what You have so freely given me to the people You have called me to bless. May I become a conduit of Your love and grace and never an end in myself. I know that as I give myself to others I will discover the true satisfaction and spiritual wealth that You encourage me to pursue.

17

A Farmer and a Plumb Line

The Book of Amos

He didn't look like much. He was a farmer. He tended some sheep and watched over a grove of fig trees. It wasn't very exciting, but it was a living.

And then—for some reason only God knows—Amos was called to go to his northern cousins and deliver a message.

The Northern Kingdom of Israel was experiencing a time of economic growth and affluence, a golden age. They lived in large houses and had the financial margin to enjoy leisure activities previously unknown. The people were prosperous, so they figured that God must be pleased with them.

Sounds kind of familiar, doesn't it?

Amos showed up in Israel and wasted no time getting down to business. He delivered a scathing message that was intentionally designed to sneak up on his audience. He began by telling them how angry God was with their neighbors, the pagan nations surrounding them—the Syrians, the Philistines, people from

Tyre, Edom, Ammon and Moab. He practically drew a circle right around Israel on the map, naming all of Israel's major rivals. God was really angry and was finally going to let 'em have it!

Whatever skepticism the people of Israel may have felt toward this southern prophet must have melted away as they heard him rail against their enemies. They had a little pep rally going!

Then it got even better: Amos started to speak out against his own land, the Southern Kingdom of Judah. The people of Israel never expected a prophet to come from Judah and pronounce judgment on his own homeland. This was great! It served to confirm what they thought all along: God was pleased with them and angry with Judah. Judah wasn't keeping the Law. God was going to destroy them. This was vindication for the Northern Kingdom.

Except the prophet wouldn't stop talking. If he had stopped right there, things would have been okay. But it turns out that all the stuff so far was mostly a setup for the *real* message.

The real message was that God was angry and disgusted with Israel. The gap between rich and poor was growing. Wealthy people learned how to work the system and keep the underprivileged in line. God had blessed the people in many ways, and they were using those blessings to indulge themselves rather than to be a blessing to others. Furthermore, they gave lip service to the idea of serving YHWH while blending a lot of idolatry into their worship.

It *does* sound a little familiar, right?

Amos startled them by suggesting that God wasn't measuring Israel against the nations around them; He was measuring them with His own plumb line: the Law He had given them. Compared to other nations, they might be able to say, "We're not so bad." But when compared to God's Law, it was easy to see how crooked they had become.

The scariest part of the message from Amos was that while Israel was looking for God to punish the surrounding nations, God meant to punish them first.

Of course, God gave them a chance to avoid the punishment. Amos's message was a warning; there was still hope for them if they would heed it and straighten up. If they would listen and return to God and do the right thing, they could continue to live in peace. If not, destruction was inevitable.

Amos never got any positive response. The priest at Bethel even told him to shut up and go home! So he finished up his message and then he did. He went back home and wrote down his message for a future generation to read. And the crooked nation continued on its crooked walk toward judgment.

TUESDAY: Beliefs

Obviously, the similarities between Amos's time and our own are startling. This book feels like it has been ripped from today's headlines, and its message carries a stinging rebuke for the consumerist mindset that is rampant in our own society. Because of this, there are some vitally important lessons we can learn from this little-known part of God's Story.

The first and foremost is this: *Don't mess with the people God loves.*

God's love for people—all people, but especially those who find themselves marginalized by society—is so fierce that mistreating them is something YHWH simply cannot tolerate. He doesn't seem to be as bothered by people mistreating Him as He is with people mistreating others; He simply cannot let it go on for very long without intervening. Amos's message makes it sound like God values how we treat other people as much as (if not more than) how we treat Him. And if it's *that* important, we'd better listen up!

It also seems that the lower the social status a person has, the more interested God is in how that person gets treated. Children, women, single mothers, foreigners, day-laborers, migrant farm workers—these tend to be the people God stands up for most vigorously, the people who cannot stand up for themselves. God is sacramentally present among the poor.

Amos delivers a message that makes it sound as if God's own people have become His enemies. The people of Israel are described in the same kinds of terms Amos uses to describe the Philistines, the Edomites and the rest of the pagans living around them. It's almost as if Amos is saying that the Israelites are no better than anyone else.

Actually, there's no "almost" about it. From God's perspective, the Israelites are just as bad as their neighbors—in some ways even worse, because they should know better. And God calls them on the carpet. It's not the manner or location of their worship. Although their worship has obviously been corrupted, God seems not to mind that so much as He minds the way they are treating people—particularly the widows, orphans and foreigners that He loves.

Hundreds of years later, an "expert" tried to test Jesus' knowledge of the Law by asking Him, "Which commandment is the greatest?" Jesus couldn't just offer one; He offered two: "Love God with everything you've got, and love other people like you love yourself" (see Matt. 22:34–40).

Jesus didn't give two answers because He was looking for extra credit. He offered them because the two are inseparably linked in the mind of God. You simply cannot love God if you don't also love others. In fact, the level to which you fulfill the second command is the level to which you can claim to have fulfilled the first (see 1 John 4:20).

WEDNESDAY: Values

It takes chutzpah to do what Amos did. He delivered a message that he knew would be unpopular, and he delivered it with prophetic force. He called the people back to the way things were supposed to be from the very beginning.

God's dream has always been for a community of people who can relate to one another correctly, and that means demonstrating compassion. Throughout the centuries, however, some of God's people have demonstrated a remarkable ability to receive acceptance and grace from God while doling out immense portions of rejection and condemnation to their fellow humans.

We're supposed to be kind, but we're often among the most hurtful and apathetic people around. The need for justice in our society is unfortunately far greater than is found in most Christian circles.

Amos railed against the people of Israel who cared more about their own comfort than they did about others. He made no bones about it, using intentionally inflammatory language. In our day, we prefer a more diplomatic approach.

Now, there's a time for diplomacy. There is a time to be tactful. But there is also a time to stand up and call people to stop going in the wrong direction. Amos was a simple man standing firm in the face of fierce opposition. We could use more folks like that, people willing to deliver unpopular messages with such boldness. Unfortunately, Christians who are most willing to deliver hard words are often sorely lacking in compassion. In fact, there are some who willingly volunteer to be the stick God uses to smack people with.

The reason the way we deliver the message is so important is because *how* the message is delivered is part of the message itself. God's message—especially here through Amos—is fierce . . . but it's really a message of compassion. Amos brings a sharp rebuke, but it's a rebuke directed toward a people who have failed to look after one another, to care for one another, to make sure no one goes hungry and no one is lonely, to bring orphans into families and make sure widows aren't being taken advantage of.

It would be terrible for the message of compassion to be negated by the lack of a compassionate messenger.

And yet that is precisely what happens all too often.

Somehow, we must strike that delicate balance between boldly stating our convictions and gently offering compassion to those who are most in need of hearing them. It will be tricky, but maybe you could start right now by asking God for a little chutzpah and a little gentleness at the same time.

THURSDAY: Actions

God told Amos to set out a plumb line and use it to judge the people. Plumb lines are interesting things. Tie a piece of string to a weight of some sort and let it hang down. Gravity works to create a straight line with no deviance.

So simple, a child could use it.

Plumb lines are still used today by carpenters and construction workers, because they're inexpensive, effective and completely reliable. There's no room for some relativist carpenter saying something ridiculous like, "Well, what's plumb for you isn't plumb for me." There are no pluralist carpenters saying, "Let's take a poll to see whose plumb is the real plumb."

Plumb is plumb. Gravity doesn't lie.

Christians are fond of using the analogy of the plumb line. And in an age of relativity, where objective truth is often downplayed for the sake of political correctness or popular opinion, Christians *should* feel the need to advocate some sort of standard of right and wrong. Usually, we equate God's Word—the Bible—with the plumb line.

And that's okay in most situations. But that's not what this story tells us. According to Amos, plumb is something else. Plumb isn't God saying, "Read My book." Plumb is God saying, "Treat others the way you treat Me." God even goes so far as to say, "The way you treat others *is* the way you treat Me" (see Matt. 25:31–46).

So simple, a child could do it.

Are there hungry people? Feed them. Sick people? Heal them. Lonely people? Befriend them. That's how God plans on judging His people (and He refuses to judge on a curve like Israel was hoping).

You may have gained all the knowledge you can squeeze out of the Bible. You may attend lots of church services, volunteer to serve on committees and sell cookbooks for your women's ministry. But do you have God's heart for the poor and marginalized in your own society? That's plumb.

Later in the Story, one of Jesus' closest friends writes, "If anyone has material possessions and sees his brother in need but has no pity on him, how can the love of God be in him? Dear children, let us not love with words or tongue but with actions and in truth" (1 John 3:17–18).

Do we love people? Do we really, really love people? This isn't about feeling warm fuzzies for them or getting choked up when we see late-night infomercials about hungry children. Does our love for them really show in our actions? Having the right beliefs and values (Tuesday and Wednesday) are of little good until they begin to direct and change our behavior.

What if everybody took God seriously on this one? What if God's plumb line of compassionate behavior toward widows and orphans and strangers began to take root in you? In your small group or your whole church? What if everybody in your neighborhood or in your school began to plan and act to feed the hungry, heal the sick, visit the prisoner, clothe the naked?

If everyone jumped in and started acting according to God's plumb line, we might just see God's kingdom come, His will being done on earth as it is in heaven, the upside down turned right side up—the crooked set straight.

FRIDAY: Prayer

Narrative

Lord God, You have called me to be among the followers of Jesus who will prove themselves to be blameless and innocent, children of God above reproach in the midst of a crooked and perverse generation who appear as lights in the world. This is a high and holy task that is difficult to fulfill because of the pressures and obstacles of this present darkness. The world has such powerful lures that seek to seduce me to play by two sets of rules and serve two masters. As I renew my mind with the timeless precepts and principles of Your Word, may I see through this web of deception and not mistake material abundance for Your blessing. In Christ, I want to become increasingly different from my culture so that I will treasure the goodness of Your kingdom above the goods of this world.

Orthodoxy

Father, I want to pursue a lifestyle of love. I wish to display Your *agape* to the people I encounter today so that they will see Christ in and through me. Keep me from playing favorites so that I will not succumb to the blunder of viewing people according to their social and economic status. Just as You show special concern and kindness for those who are downtrodden and overlooked, may I also treat such people with special love and consideration. In spite of appearances to the contrary, You have accorded great dignity and worth to all who have been created in Your image, and by Your grace I want to imitate You. I ask You for the power to love the unlovely and notice those who are overlooked. In this way, I will display my love for You in the way I love the people You love.

Orthopathy

Dear Lord, in the prophets and apostles whose words are recorded in Scripture, and most fully and clearly in Your incarnate Son's earthly ministry, You have perfectly balanced the combination of truth and love. I also want to speak Your truth to my generation and to do so in a gracious and loving manner. Keep me from the poles of cold orthodoxy and warm sentimentality. I ask for the courage to be forthright and honest when it is needed and for the compassion to consider the needs of others before my own. In Your way and through Your guidance, may I become a source of blessing to people who are in need, and may I be increasingly concerned about the plight of the lost, the last and the least.

Orthopraxy

God of glory and grace, You have spoken timeless truth through Your servants the prophets, and through them You have called and inspired Your people to be concerned about the things that are of concern to You. You have revealed Your compassion for the poor, the orphans and widows, the destitute and the oppressed. Please enhance my compassion for these people as well and show me the specific things You would have me to do in order to manifest the Spirit of Christ among the needy. Let me not love with word or with tongue, but in deed and truth. Open my eyes to the opportunities You have already placed before me, so that I will become an agent of grace and reconciliation to those whom You love. Let me make a difference in this world by being faithful and obedient to Your heavenly calling.

18

The Fish Story

THE BOOK OF JONAH

MONDAY: Story

Jonah was lounging around his house, minding his own business, when YHWH showed up and told him to travel 500 miles to the city of Nineveh. "Tell them I'm not happy about the way they're living up there. In fact, tell them that if they don't straighten up and fly right, I might just get rid of them."

Jonah immediately got up, packed a few of his belongings . . . and ran the other way.

He didn't argue. He didn't beg. He didn't complain. He just went to the shore and hopped on the first ship out of town—heading nearly 2,000 miles in the exact opposite direction!

He chose to run from the God of the universe by getting on a boat for several days. A boat. In the middle of the ocean. Where he would be completely helpless.

Jonah was not the smartest of God's messengers.

He paid his fare and went below deck and fell asleep, thinking he had managed to escape from God. But God isn't that easy to escape.

A huge storm came to wake Jonah up (literally and figuratively), and after confessing to his shipmates that he was the cause of the bad weather, he asked to be tossed into the sea. Maybe he thought God would let him die and he would still manage to get out of his assignment.

See, Nineveh was one of the largest cities in the world and the people there were known to be ruthless pagans. They might not like Jonah or his message very much. They sure weren't going to welcome him with open arms. They might, in fact, decide to silence him for good! Better to sink to Davy Jones's locker than face a city full of angry Ninevites.

But God wasn't going to let Jonah off the hook so easily. As incomprehensible as it must have sounded to Jonah, God actually cared about those crazy pagans up there in Nineveh. He didn't want them to continue in their ignorant ways. He wanted someone to go and warn them. Maybe they'd turn to Him and He would finally get to have a relationship with them.

Instead of letting him drown, God sent a big fish to swallow Jonah. It swallowed him whole, in fact, which gave Jonah some time in timeout to think about what he had done. It was there, in the belly of that fish, that Jonah came to his senses and told God he was sorry.

After a few days, the fish started to wonder if maybe he'd eaten some bad human—he started to look a little green around the gills. Soon Jonah became the first person to see up close and personal whether or not a fish's eyes water when he throws up.

Then he went to Nineveh and delivered his message, secretly hoping the people wouldn't pay much attention. He wanted to see some divinely inspired fireworks! Maybe God would do to Nineveh what he had done to Sodom and Gomorrah (see Gen. 18–19) and he went to the edge of the city to watch the destruction firsthand.

As things turned out, though, the pagan people of Nineveh thought that maybe this God of Jonah's would be compassionate if they turned things around. At least it was worth a try. And so they did—they took God's message seriously.

And God turned out to be a lot more like they hoped—and a lot less like Jonah hoped—He would be.

TUESDAY: Beliefs

For a lot of us who grew up going to church, Jonah's story was primarily about two things.

First, it was about proving to people that a fully grown man could actually be swallowed whole by a fish and live to tell the story. After all, if a person didn't believe this story literally happened, they might not believe anything in the Bible literally happened. And it had to be a fish, not a whale. It seemed very important, in a lot of churches, that God got His animal classification right.

Second, the moral of the story was that if you run from God, He'll get you. (Ever hear a message like that in Sunday School class? What a horrible portrayal of a God so full of grace!)

Now, we believe this story did literally happen, and we believe it for a variety of reasons. (Mostly because Jesus seemed to think it literally happened [see Matt. 12:40]. And because He also figured out a way to come back from the dead, we tend to side with Him in situations like this.) But as to the moral of the story, we think there's something much bigger than what many well-intentioned Sunday School teachers told us.

In the story of Jonah, we see him hit rock bottom and cry out to God. God, in turn, does an amazing thing: He hears and He answers. No "I told you so" lectures. God is amazingly compassionate, and His love extends to all people—to runners, to sailors and to Ninevite pagans.

He warns the pagans. He spares the sailors. And He disciplines the running prophet. He warns, He saves, He disciplines—and He does it all (and more) because of His great love.

Jonah ran, and God stopped him in his tracks. But God didn't discipline Jonah out of vengeance. He disciplines people because He loves them. He doesn't do it to *pay* them back but to *bring* them back.

Sometimes God actually causes pain, but that pain is always dealt out of redemptive purposes and loving intentions. This is a unique quality of YHWH. The pain He allows is always potentially redemptive, because it offers to bring us closer to God—to help us understand Him better and understand our need for Him, as well. Suffering gets our attention. Suffering well builds character. Suffering reminds us of our need for Him, makes us turn to Him.

In that sense, God's discipline—like the fish in this story—is part of His provision. Interestingly, the text says, "Now the Lord *provided* a huge fish to swallow Jonah, and Jonah was in the belly of the fish three days and three nights" (Jon. 1:7, emphasis added). We usually associate the provision of God with something really great, some big blessing. God provided food in the midst of famine. God provided money in the midst of poverty. God provided a child for a barren woman. God provided water in the desert.

But being swallowed by a fish? That hardly fits our idea of provision.

Sometimes God loves us enough to provide painful consequences that stop us in our tracks and force us to deal with things.

What God wants to communicate to us in a whisper—lessons we desperately need to learn but stubbornly refuse—often are only learned through painful situations. God allows us to endure pain—deliberately brings pain on us sometimes—but only because He knows pain is what is required to bring us back.

He wants us back that much.

WEDNESDAY: Values

God values people—all people.

Unfortunately, people often value things above people. Take Jonah, for example. At the beginning of the story, God tells Jonah to go and warn a whole city full of people about the judgment that they are about to incur. Jonah doesn't value those people as much as God does. In fact, it becomes increasingly clear that Jonah doesn't want to warn them, because he thinks that they might actually repent and be spared.

Jonah would rather see them die than have them united with the God who created and loves them.

By the end of the story, we see Jonah, resigned to doing the will of God but doing it through gritted teeth. He sits atop a hill, hoping for the chance to see some divine fireworks of judgment. He values the plant providing him shade more than he values the eternal souls of the Ninevite people.

To Jonah's mind, the Ninevites are outsiders, so he shouldn't have to care about them. As a prophet, he knows that God wants him to "love your neighbor as yourself" (Lev. 19:18). Jonah just figures the Ninevites aren't his neighbors.

It's a lot easier to put a whole group of people in the "not my neighbor" category than it is to figure out how to love them. Loving others can get messy. It can cost you something.

Jonah's not the first person to do this in the Bible, and he's not the last. As a matter of fact, it happens all the time . . . even today. We look at a group of people or one person in particular and think, *I know God wants me to love everyone, but God never met* him!

God is not suggesting that we should love Muslims. Or is He? What about feminists? Homosexuals? Liberals? Fundamentalists? Illegal aliens? Lawyers?

God loves each and every human being, even those who fall into categories we don't even want to think about. He sent His Son to live and die and come back from the dead on their behalf, and He does not want any of them to spend eternity separated from Him. He loves them as much as He loves you, and He calls those of us who have entered into a personal relationship with Him to turn and show the same kind of love to them that He has shown to us.

Remember the song from Sunday School? "Red and yellow, black and white, they are precious in His sight." God values all people. Do you?

THURSDAY: Actions

God is Ultimate Reality. He is the source of everything good, true and beautiful. He is wisdom. He is love. He is faithfulness personified.

But when you run from God, you run from all that. You run from goodness and truth and beauty and wisdom and love and faithfulness. And as a natural consequence, when you run from Him, you make really foolish choices.

Think about Jonah, for example. When Jonah ran from God, he decided to get on a boat. How foolish is that? A boat? In the middle of the sea? You have to admit that's pretty foolish.

People who run from God never run to safety. They run toward self-destruction and danger financially, relationally, vocationally. People who are running from God do things that make everyone standing by and watching shake their heads, wince and wonder, "How can such a smart person do such a dumb thing?"

Eventually their lives begin to unravel, and they think it's a result of all the bad choices they've made. And it sort of is. Their relationships come apart, and they trace the demise of the relationship, trying to figure out where they went wrong. The truth is, they went wrong when they left the Ultimate Source of love and acceptance. Ever since then, they've been looking for something from people that people aren't designed to give.

Sometimes when a business goes under, its owner tries to trace the demise of his career. Where did he go wrong? The truth is, he went wrong when he left the Ultimate Source of meaning and purpose. Ever since then, he's been looking for something from his job that a job just isn't designed to give.

A lot of us, if we were in Jonah's shoes, would have thought, *If only I'd gotten on a different boat. If only I'd sailed to a different place. Maybe I should have gone to Egypt instead of Tarshish.* But Jonah's life didn't start to unravel because of that city or that boat or that storm. Jonah's life started coming apart the moment he started running away from God.

The story of Jonah is the story of each and every one of us. We've all run from God in one way or another. As much as we like to think that our situation is unique, it's not. We're all runners, and we all run for the same reason: We wanted something other than what we thought or even knew God wanted for us.

And at some point in time, we've all got to acknowledge our rebellion—whether it's the big, outright, running-away kind or the subtle kind of rebellion no one but we (oh . . . and God) can see. In either big or small ways—we all need to turn around and run the other way, back toward God in humble repentance and obedience, knowing that God is always willing to receive us again with open arms.

FRIDAY: Prayer

Narrative

O God, why do I so often wrestle with Your will? Why do I argue and grumble and complain? Many is the time, it seems, when You have asked me to say or do something and I have quietly or stubbornly refused to obey. So frequently I find myself arguing with You over what my best interests look like, and I foolishly suppose that I have a better understanding than You of what I really need. Yet Your right hand will still lay hold of me even when I am seeking to escape Your presence. You will always be faithful, even when I am faithless, because You have gripped me with Your grace and because Your love is a holy love that will not be satisfied with mediocrity in those who are members of Your family. Give me the boldness and courage of holy desire to want what You want and love what You love.

Orthodoxy

Faithful Lord, You know me intimately, and You know all my real needs even when I am unaware of them. I find that I am too often concerned with things that don't really matter in the long run, and that I am anxious about things that are of no lasting consequence. But Your love is too great to let me languish in compromise and disobedience, and You sometimes use hard measures when I fail to hear Your message in easier ways. I know that Your severe mercy brings me to repentance and renewal, and that I cannot thrive when things always go my way. In Your wisdom and power, You use suffering in a redemptive way and allow the pains and problems of this life to teach me and draw me closer to You. You are preparing me for an eternal destiny, and You graciously use temporal adversity to transform my character into the image of Your Son.

Orthopathy

Father, I confess that too often I am highly selective in the way I approach people and put up barriers against those I find unattractive. Would that I could learn to see people more as You see them, and recognize no one according to the flesh, but according to Your view of them. I might not like everyone, but You call me to love everyone with the love of Christ, a love that transcends emotions and barriers and that sees each person as uniquely valued in Your eyes. May I grow in this love of the will by desiring the highest good of those I encounter every day. May I break through the stereotypes and prejudices that I have absorbed from my background and culture, and may I learn to view my love and service of others as my love and service of You.

Orthopraxy

Lord God Almighty, You created the heavens and the earth, and all that is visible and invisible. You are the fountainhead of all that is good, of all that is true and of all that is beautiful. You are the wellspring of true pleasure and delight, and nothing this world has to offer even comes close to what You intend for those who love You. But because I so frequently forget these truths and get caught up with the worries of the world, the deceitfulness of riches and the desire for other things, I lose sight of Your glorious intentions and settle instead for scraps that can never satisfy. Nothing in this world can bear the freight of what You desire for me, and when I turn to things, accomplishments, wealth and success, these things can never fill my soul. Only You can do that, and I am tired of running away from You. May I repent, turn around and run back to Your loving embrace.

19

Unfaithful

THE BOOK OF HOSEA

God—as it turns out—has a soft spot for hookers.

He used Rahab to save the Israelite spies in Jericho (see Josh. 2; 6). Jesus spent time with "women of ill repute" while He was here on earth, and said quite clearly that prostitutes "are entering the kingdom of God" (Matt. 21:28–32).

God is not above using prostitutes to further His mission. He'll even use one to make a point. Such was the case of a woman named Gomer, who married a prophet named Hosea.

From everything we know, Hosea was a good guy, a man who wanted to be faithful to YHWH—which was something of a rarity in his era. For the most part, the people around Hosea didn't honor their commitment to God; they used Him when it was convenient, and then two-timed Him by serving other gods on the side.

Imagine Hosea, minding his own business, trying to honor the God who made him. Now imagine the cognitive dissonance when Hosea heard this God very clearly tell him to marry Gomer.

Maybe she was beautiful. Maybe they knew each other. Maybe they were in love. But God told Hosea how the whole thing was going to turn out. She would be unfaithful. She would be worse than unfaithful. She would intentionally enter into a lifestyle of infidelity.

Gomer would become a whore.

And God told Hosea to marry her anyway. Hosea married Gomer "for better or worse," knowing full well that it would be mostly "worse." He listened as she promised to love him, honor and obey him, forsaking all others and keeping herself only for him as long as she should live. And Hosea knew she was lying.

They had a few good years after the wedding, had three beautiful children. But the names given to the children indicate there were some serious problems. The kids were called *Jezreel*, which was the place of a massacre; *Lo-Ruhamah*, which means "not loved"; and *Lo-Ammi*, which means "not my people."

After a while, Gomer began to stray. Perhaps it was subtle at first, but it wasn't long before everyone knew what was going on. Hosea must have been humiliated. Eventually, she left altogether and ended up being sold into slavery.

Divorce was a legitimate option for him, but Hosea wouldn't pursue that. It was as if his heart had grown attached to this wayward woman. As angry and hurt as he must have been, his love for his wife overpowered his desire for justice.

Rather than paying Gomer back for the pain she inflicted, Hosea took a different approach. He pursued her until her found her, and then bought her back from the slavery she was in. He purchased her out of bondage and brought her back home.

And so the question remained: Would she stay faithful this time? Could love and acceptance accomplish what judgment and condemnation never would? Would this wandering woman allow herself to find the unfailing love she really desired in the arms of her one true husband?

God has a thing for hookers. As it turns out, it's a good thing for us that He does.

TUESDAY: Beliefs

God's love is irrational. It defies common sense. It causes Him to do things we would never do.

Think about it: When God made His covenant with the Israelites, He said, "If I'm going to be your God, I have to be your only God. This is an exclusive deal" (see Exod. 20:3). But even then, God knew the Israelites wouldn't keep their end of the bargain.

Imagine standing in front of a room full of people, dressed to the nines, staring into the eyes of your beloved, and all the while knowing that the vows you're exchanging mean more to you than to the person you love. If you knew that your spouse would be unfaithful, would you still say "I do"?

Throughout most of Hosea's life—throughout most of the Old Testament—God's people had been two-timing Him. They had this covenant relationship with YHWH, but they also had other gods on the side. Hosea's marriage became a mirror in which the love of God for His people could be seen in heartbreaking detail.

This is what God has done for us: He said "I do" even though He knew that we would be unfaithful and bring Him unspeakable pain. He even knew that deliverance would ultimately be up to Him, and would involve Him taking on human flesh, entering into our world and being rejected by it.

And He did it anyway.

God's love seems crazy to us, but He knows a thing or two about love that we do not. Primarily, He understands that love and acceptance can accomplish what judgment and condemnation never can.

God could have divorced Himself from His people. They had, after all, adulterated their covenant promises. In fact, the Old Testament Law prescribed the death penalty for both parties involved in an act of adultery (see Lev. 20:10). By violating the relationship, the people of God had earned nothing short of death. And in the book of Hosea, God seems to waver for a moment (see Hos. 11:5–7). But He can't seem to live with that course of action, so He relents (see v. 8). He cannot allow judgment to be the last word. God's sense of justice demands that something be done. God's prevailing love refuses to give up on these people.

Back in the Garden of Eden, when Adam and Eve sinned for the very first time, God's justice and love began a long, slow march toward one another. Eventually, the two characteristics of God would meet in a terrible collision on a hill just outside of Jerusalem.

There, His love would cause Him to do the most irrational thing of all.

WEDNESDAY: Values

Our world is not as it was intended to be. We are not who we were intended to be. Things have gone awry.

And the real danger is that we now assume it to be normal.

The brokenness, the upside-down-ness of it all, is expected and common—but it is not normal.

The only thing worse than assuming that it's normal is shrugging our shoulders and going on with our lives without any sense of hope that this problem might have a solution or that we may even be asked to play a part in fixing this mess.

When we muster up our courage enough to accept the valid diagnosis, an amazing thing happens: When we acknowledge that the problem is sin—not particular sins, not someone else's mistakes or shortcomings, but our own personal and corporate evil in our thoughts, values and behavior—then and only then do we recognize that there's hope. Something can be done for sin. Something *has been* done for sin.

But we'll never receive the prescription as long as we continue to debate the diagnosis.

God's solution to our problem is not that we should love Him better but that we should receive the love He offers us. Such a great depth of love cannot help but restore us to our intended state. Once internalized, love begins its relentless work of transforming, a work that stubbornly refuses to be done until we look like we are meant to look, until we are sound, whole, holy.

Ah, that last word is loaded, isn't it?

The concept of holiness brings up all sorts of images, mostly negative. Smoke and incense. Burning sacrifices. Strict, regimented, joyless lifestyles. These are the kinds of things we often associate with being holy.

But holiness simply means being set apart for God's purposes. It involves abstaining from things that pollute and striving after things that purify. But this is the most important thing: Holiness isn't the end; it's a means to a greater end. We are called to be holy so that God can work in, among and through us to accomplish His purposes.

Holiness must be valued not as a means of gaining God's good graces but as a way of fitting into God's plan of action to restore what has been so deeply corrupted in the world, in our own hearts and minds, in our relationships with others, and with our Creator. Holiness matters because God doesn't just take our sin seriously; He takes it personally. Our sin is an offense to Him, not because God is touchy or overly sensitive, but because it adulterates our covenantal relationship with Him.

The world is not as it was intended to be. It's been spoiled, and it often seems to be growing worse with each passing year.

The problem is sin. The solution is God. The goal is personal holiness and cooperation with God in a wholesale restoration of all things.

THURSDAY: Actions

The story of Hosea and Gomer isn't about why it's bad to be an adulterous whore. There is more at stake here than just the sanctity of marriage. This is an allegory about faithfulness and about sin and the pain it causes.

Gomer doesn't represent unfaithful spouses; she represents *us*. That's distasteful and we don't like hearing it. We want to be Hosea in the story and think of all the people who have betrayed us. We prefer a lesson on how we must go on loving the unlovable.

But we are the adulterers and harlots. God is the one who remains faithful while we are so often faithless (see 2 Tim. 2:13). We sin and we hurt the One who loves us. Sometimes we do this in big ways, sometimes in small ways that are hidden and quiet. In one way or another, we've all violated our relationship with God.

The question that faces us is this: When faced with our own infidelity, will we return to our first love? Will we turn from our waywardness and run to the arms of the One who purchased us out of slavery and eagerly awaits our return?

The biblical word for this is "repent." Like the word "holy" we looked at yesterday, this is one of those words that carry a lot of baggage. It's been misused in many places. It's been used to manipulate and coerce. But "repent" simply means to recognize that you're headed in the wrong direction and turn around to go the right way again.

Once we acknowledge our spiritual adultery, we must repent and make a commitment to return to the path God has chosen for us.

Part of walking that godly path is loving others the way God has loved us. From the story of Hosea, we learn that true love isn't just an impulse; it is a decision. It is a firm commitment to act in the best interests of the beloved, regardless of cost. Hosea made a decision to love Gomer, knowing the awful cost he would have to pay.

That's why he went ahead and married her, even though he knew she would be unfaithful. That's why he stayed married to her, even though he would have been justified pursuing a divorce. That's why, when she was at her lowest point, he paid her price and brought her home.

Later in the Bible story, we'll read that "God so loved the world" (John 3:16). That doesn't mean He felt warm fuzzies about us. In fact, God sees our sin, and it bothers Him. It repulses Him. But God has chosen to act in our best interests regardless of personal cost, even to the point of sacrificing His Son to redeem us.

God's love for us has been demonstrated not only in the sacrificial death of His Son, but in this: "God has poured out his love into our hearts by the Holy Spirit, whom he has given us" (Rom. 5:5). The Holy Spirit pours God's love into our hearts so that we can personally experience it in our lives today. Moreover, once we have internalized this love, then we can choose to act (painful as it may be), by the power of the Holy Spirit, in the best interests of others.

Just like Hosea. Just like God.

FRIDAY: Prayer

Narrative

Father, I give thanks to You because You are the lover of my soul; You pursue me and desire an intimate relationship with me; You lift me from the morass and put my feet on high places; You care so much for me that You take great measures to bring me back to You when I stray. Your love is causeless, measureless and ceaseless; Your righteousness overcomes my guilt; Your holiness informs all of Your purposes; Your compassion reaches out to the lowly and downtrodden; Your mercy and grace extend far beyond my sin. May I delight in You, draw nearer to You, hold fast to You and remain faithful to You. I know that my soul cannot flourish in disobedience and opposition to Your loving intentions for my life. When I am tempted to wander from You, may I recall Your character and remember Your many blessings.

Orthodoxy

Loving Lord, over the millennia, You have gone to unimaginable lengths to display Your love, grace and mercy to a largely disobedient and rebellious people. I cannot begin to grasp the richness of the breadth and length and height and depth of the love of Christ that surpasses knowledge. If You gave us justice, we would all be alienated from You and suffer the consequences of Your holy judgment. But You have given us mercy, and mercy triumphs over judgment. You have given us grace, and grace is wholly unmerited. In Christ, the righteous requirement of justice and Your compassionate offer of love were perfectly blended and satisfied in His redemptive work on the cross. I praise you that through His blood, You justify those who have faith in Him.

Orthopathy

God of holiness, You have commanded that Your people be holy because You are holy. But none of us can fulfill this command without being infused with Your power and grace. The problem of sin runs as deep as the inner recesses of the human heart, and only a new heart in Christ can make it possible for us to experience the fullness of restoration with You. But even with a new heart and with Christ now living within me, I still struggle with the temptations of money, sex and power that are so much a part of the human condition on this earth. Yet by Your power, I can always choose the way of walking by Your Spirit rather than the flesh, and because of this, sin no longer need be master over me. I am no longer under law but under grace. Thank You that I have become the righteousness of God in Christ Jesus.

Orthopraxy

Faithful God, You have called us to enjoy a relationship with You even though You knew from the beginning that we would often turn aside to other lures and lovers. Though You have no needs, You have extended Your profound desire to Your people, and it is Your pleasure that we become increasingly conformed to the image of Your Son. Our waywardness hurts You and our obedience pleases You. May I grow in the apprehension of Your deep love, so that I will fear Your displeasure and love the fruits of trust and obedience. When I commit spiritual adultery by giving my heart to the allures of this world, may I quickly repent and return to You. I know that I will never find rest or fulfillment unless I discover these in You. Thus, I want to make it my ambition to be pleasing to You.

20

Holy, Holy, Holy

ISAIAH 6

MONDAY: Story

Uzziah was the king of the Southern Kingdom for more than 50 years, and his reign was a time of tremendous wealth and prosperity. Some considered it a return to the golden age of King David and his son, King Solomon. The people were safe and secure. Their northern cousins had long since given up any pretense of keeping their covenant with YHWH, but the south had certainly risen again!

Then an unthinkable (yet inevitable) thing happened: King Uzziah died. The entire nation was reeling. How could they go on without the fearless leader who had brought them to this place? For half a century, the people had relaxed, knowing their king was in charge. Then, overnight, he was gone. Who knew what kind of king his successor might be?

All of this led a man named Isaiah to the Temple. Perhaps God could provide some answers for such a time as this.

God's answer to Isaiah's uncertainties was simple but direct: No matter how dark things seemed (and things were going to get very dark indeed), a time was coming when YHWH would provide an ultimate solution for Israel's infidelity, through the Person and work of His appointed Deliverer.

This must have been good news for Isaiah to hear after the death of his beloved king. God was still in control. His plan was still intact.

But there was still this matter of how dark things were going to get in the meantime.

God's message to (and through) Isaiah included a warning as well as a promise. God said that if the people would return to Him, He wouldn't have to discipline them the way He was disciplining the Northern Kingdom. If they would go beyond external religious practices and draw near to God with their hearts, they could continue to enjoy their status on the world's stage.

Isaiah took the message seriously and set out to warn enough people (or at least the right people) so that they could avert some kind of national disaster. Because Isaiah grew up as a member of the royal court, he had direct access to the king. Perhaps he could persuade the new king to follow God and keep covenant with Him.

At first it worked. And then it didn't.

During the reign of Hezekiah, Isaiah's message was well received. The Southern Kingdom was spared the same kind of humiliation their northern cousins endured . . . for a while. Hezekiah ruled for 29 years, and he led the people well.

Then his son Manasseh took the throne. And Manasseh was a horse of a different color. He was quite possibly the wickedest king in the history of Judah. Not only did Manasseh dislike Isaiah's message, but, according to Jewish tradition, he had Isaiah killed by sawing him in half.

When we first meet Isaiah, he's a young man who is distraught because of his circumstances. Just before he dies, he's an old man whose circumstances have taken a serious turn for the worse—yet he bravely faces them.

The change for Isaiah comes with his understanding that no matter what, God is ultimately in control.

TUESDAY: Beliefs

Isaiah and the Southern Kingdom were in a time of turmoil. Uzziah had been in power for 50 years. (That's like having one person in power while Eisenhower, Kennedy, Johnson, Nixon, Ford, Carter, Reagan, Bush, Clinton and Bush II all serve out their terms!) Most of the people in Judah had never known another king, and Uzziah's reign had been characterized by security and prosperity. He had brought technological advances in the field of agriculture and irrigation. He had restored the people of YHWH to a place of prominence again.

But now Uzziah was dead, and no one knew what the next leader would be like.

The prophet Isaiah was confused and afraid. Where do you go when what's next is uncertain? Where do you go when the future is frightening?

Isaiah went to the Temple, and got far more than he bargained for!

Imagine being Isaiah. He was young and still relatively new to his role as a prophet. He went into the Temple and suddenly saw God—huge and holy and scary. His fear of whatever the future may have held was suddenly overwhelmed by his fear of the One who held the future.

And then there were the angels calling out, "Holy, holy, holy is the Lord Almighty" (Isaiah 6:3).

Today when we want to emphasize something, we have plenty of options at our disposal. We can, for example, <u>underline</u> something or put it in *italics*. We can make the word **bold**, or we can do some combination of ***<u>all of the above</u>***.

The writers of the Bible could do none of those things. But they could repeat themselves. To let the readers know something was especially important, they often repeated the word or phrase. (Jesus used a similar approach when He would say, "Truly, truly, I say to you . . .").

No other attribute of God is ever stated as emphatically as this thrice-repeated word.

Holy, holy, holy is the Lord Almighty.

Not mercy, mercy, mercy (sounds like a song).

Not patient, patient, patient.

Not angry, angry, angry.

Above all else, God is holy—and not only in a morally pure sense of the word. God is set apart, wholly other, unlike anything or anyone else.

In a sense, holiness is best understood by seeing its effect on whatever it comes into contact with. Like fire. When fire comes into contact with something, it heats, it burns, it consumes. When holiness comes into contact with something, it silences, it stuns, it inspires awe.

When you see Niagara Falls or the Grand Canyon, it silences you. These things are unlike anything else. It's simply amazing that such a thing even exists. Multiply that by infinity, and that's what it would be like to encounter the holiness of God.

The angels continue by saying, "The whole earth is filled with his glory."

The earth can no more contain the glory of God than a thimble can contain the Pacific Ocean, than a child's sand bucket can contain the Sahara Desert. He's too big for this earth. He's bigger than all my cares and anxieties, bigger than the known and the unknown, the knowable and unknowable. Big enough for this year and big enough for next. Big enough for today.

God is huge and holy. No king could ever replace Him. Nations may rise and fall, but God has dominion over all. A God this big cannot fail. He is in charge. His plan will continue unhindered. He will sustain His people.

His arm is strong. His plan is sure. When you don't know where else to turn, God is always the best place to start.

WEDNESDAY: Values

As Isaiah comes face to face with the awesome holiness of God, he can't help but realize something: He, Isaiah, is terribly *unholy*.

When Isaiah sees God, his first reaction is not excitement, as if he's happy to have been chosen for this wonderful honor of seeing something no one else gets to see. He doesn't immediately begin to think about how he can include this story in his monthly newsletter to all his ministry partners (like so many modern-day prophets might).

No—his initial response is, "Woe!"

This isn't the "Whoa!" that means "Hey, that's really cool." This is "Woe!" as in the word used by prophets to pass judgment on the nations. This is "Woe!" as in "I'm in a lot of trouble here." "Woe!" as in "Help!"

Isaiah's not being melodramatic here; this is simply an honest evaluation of the state of humanity in the clear light of God's glory. When you see what true holiness looks like, you cannot help but recognize the extent of your own damage. There's no use pretending things are better than they are, attempting to hide your flaws from a God who sits high and exalted on a throne surrounded by multi-winged angels declaring His holiness night and day. There is no rationalization now. There is only confession.

Confession is not something we value much anymore, even though we should.

The Greek word for confession is *homologeo*. It's a compound word: *homo* (same) and *logeo* (speak). The word literally means *to say the same thing* as God.

What else is there to be done when you come into the presence of a holy God but to agree with Him in His assessment of your life? He says you have missed the mark and fallen short of His glory. Now that you have caught a glimpse of His glory, you find that you're not in much of a position to argue with Him about that.

Isaiah realizes that he is called to carry God's message to God's people, but he is unclean—he lacks the integrity necessary to be God's messenger. He needs cleansing and forgiveness, but he cannot receive it until he is willing to fully own his brokenness and turn back to God (that's a good working definition of "repent").

Isaiah learns that this process of repentance and confession is often painful when an angel flies down and places a hot coal on his lips. (That's gonna leave a mark!) But the sting is redemptive and must be embraced.

Our society has elevated rationalization and justification to an art form. We hardly ever value remorse or tears of confession. Perhaps that's because we rarely reflect on what we've done from the perspective of the one we've hurt. Perhaps it's because we rarely stop to think about how sin keeps us from being holy like our Father in heaven is holy.

THURSDAY: Actions

There is an already-but-not-yet-ness about God's plan. The angels in Isaiah 6 say that the whole earth is filled with the glory of God. However, a later prophet tells us that there is a day coming when the whole earth will be filled with the knowledge of His glory as well (see Hab. 2:14).

We live in the in-between times. The earth is full of God's glory, but not everyone realizes it or acknowledges it yet.

Isaiah found himself living in times like ours. There was anxiety and uncertainty, wars and rumors of wars, economic upheaval, moral decline, and ritualism instead of righteousness. But he caught a glimpse of a God who is bigger than he ever could have imagined. The train of His robe filled the enormous Temple. The whole earth could not contain the gravity of such a God.

In that moment, Isaiah realized that he was woefully corrupted and in need of cleansing and forgiveness. He also realized that he had a part to play in letting the whole earth know what he had seen.

And so it is with each of us. Personal worship begins when we seek God, acknowledge our personal inadequacies, and endure the painful process of repentance and confession in order to receive cleansing and forgiveness. But it does not end there. Authentic worship culminates in our willingness to take the message to others, after submitting our lives fully to God. Worship necessarily leads us to say, "Here am I. Send me" (6:8).

Isaiah spent the rest of his life telling people the message of God, reminding the people of the awesome holiness of God, calling them to repentance and confession, assuring them of God's promised Deliverer. Some listened; most did not. But that wasn't the point.

Isaiah had become consumed with YHWH. He couldn't help but tell others. He wasn't concerned with their response as much as he was concerned with his own faithfulness to do what he knew God had called him to do. He had seen some things that he could no longer keep to himself.

And that's the best way to think of evangelism. It's not some sort of compulsory duty to be carried out grudgingly or to appease a guilt-ridden conscience. When a person comes face to face with the glory of God and hears the words the angels spoke to Isaiah, "Your guilt is taken away and your sin atoned for" (6:7), that person finds it impossible to keep this good news to himself.

FRIDAY: Prayer

Narrative

Heavenly Father, I am grateful that You have blessed me with access to the oracles and wisdom of the Scriptures. In them I can learn of You and of Your creative and redemptive work in human history. You raise up kings and depose kings, and regardless of their intentions and actions, You remain the sovereign Lord over all things. Although this is a sinful and fallen world, Your great plan and purposes will not be thwarted. You are the righteous judge of people, nations and empires, and You work all things together to accomplish what is to come. Your promises are rich and trustworthy, and I look with anticipation to the consummation of all things under the rule and reign of the Lord Jesus. In spite of the foolishness and turmoil of my own time, I can look with expectant confidence to the future You have promised.

Orthodoxy

Thrice-holy Lord, Your person, powers and perfections are beyond all human and angelic comprehension. Holiness informs all that You say and do, and holiness is what most becomes Your people. You have sanctified me in Christ Jesus—set me apart from malice, deceit, wickedness and all other forms of sin. And You have set me apart from these things to You and to Your lordship and likeness. Grant me a growing vision of Your great holiness and a clearer sense of the deceitfulness of the flesh. As I realize that You are so much greater than I thought and that my flesh is so much worse than I thought, let me translate this awful distance into an increased vision of the magnitude of Your grace that overcomes this barrier. The more I am consumed by Your greatness, the less I will be anxious about other things.

Orthopathy

God of heaven and earth, You dwell on a high and holy place, and also with the contrite and lowly of spirit. I ask for the grace of true contrition so that I would humble myself under Your almighty hand and put no confidence in the flesh. Keep me from the self-deception and rationalization that would make me think more highly of myself than I ought. I acknowledge that You know all my thoughts and motives even more fully than I can know them. Even my best deeds can be tainted with the selfish desire for recognition and applause. But as I learn to make You my audience instead of playing to an audience of many, there is no place for pretense or hiding or posturing. All things are open and laid bare before Your eyes, and only Your assessment will matter in the end.

Orthopraxy

God of eternity, You have no beginning or end; You dwell in all places and times and yet You transcend all places and times. You are incomprehensibly transcendent and yet marvelously immanent. As I learn to fear You in holy love and awe, I also learn to fear my circumstances and challenges much less. My confidence is in Your promises, and though they will not be fully manifested until the King of glory comes to rule and reign on earth, I know that it will ultimately be true that every knee will bow, of those who are in heaven and earth and under the earth, and every tongue will confess that Jesus Christ is Lord, to the glory of the Father. I ask for a greater vision of Your glory and a growing desire to share that vision with the people I encounter during this earthly pilgrimage toward the celestial city of God.

21

A Tale of Two Kings

2 KINGS 16; 18–19;
2 CHRONICLES 28–32;
ISAIAH 7; 36–37

MONDAY: Story

For centuries, there hadn't been a major superpower on the international scene. The usual suspects (Assyria, Babylonia, Egypt, Persia) had all been in a season of decline, and this is one factor that allowed Israel to become a nation of prominence.

But bullies are resilient, and it can be hard to keep them down for long.

After Israel split into two kingdoms, during the lifetime of Isaiah, Assyria roused from its slumber and began gobbling up smaller, weaker nations like they were deviled eggs at a church picnic. Needless to say, anxiety was spreading in the hearts of people everywhere—especially down in the Southern Kingdom of Judah.

The Southern Kingdom had enjoyed a time of great wealth and prosperity under their king Uzziah, but his son Ahaz seemed to be taking the wrong path. Assyria was marching their way, and people were getting nervous.

It didn't make things much better when the king of the Northern Kingdom came to Ahaz with a plan: "I'm going to join forces with the king of Aram to fight against Assyria. Why don't you join us as well? Maybe the three of us put together can beat them!" Ahaz refuses the offer. His northern cousin turns on him, hoping to have him overthrown and install a new king who will join the alliance.

Ahaz needs help, and God knows it. So God sends a message through Isaiah: "Don't panic. Trust Me, and I'll get you through this." But Ahaz isn't buying what God is selling. Instead, he comes up with the crazy idea to go to the biggest bully on the block. He asks Assyria for protection.

Isaiah practically pleads with Ahaz to just trust God instead of trusting the military might of the Assyrian army. He even tells Ahaz to ask God for a sign, but Ahaz has already made up his mind. A sign will only confirm his blatant disobedience and disregard for God's command.

Ahaz chooses to ally himself with Assyria, and it ruins him. He becomes a puppet king, a slave to Assyria, a figurehead, king in name only. He ends up sending the gold and silver from the Temple in Jerusalem to the Assyrian king (his new master), to build altars to pagan gods. He even makes a burnt offering of his own son.

Fear and anxiety drive people to do foolish things.

Fortunately, kings don't live forever—well, the kings of this earth don't, anyway. Hezekiah, another of Ahaz's sons, eventually takes over, but the Assyrians are still on the prowl. It isn't long before they come knocking on the door of the Southern Kingdom, looking to intimidate and conquer this upstart kid who thinks he can do better than his father did.

Once again, God sends a message to the king through His prophet Isaiah. It's pretty much the same message: "Don't panic. Trust Me." But Hezekiah's holding in his hands a letter from Assyria detailing exactly what's going to happen to him if he doesn't surrender.

What do you do when you get the worst news imaginable?

Hezekiah takes the letter to the Temple, spreads it out in front of God and prays. God hears. God answers. God strikes the Assyrians with such force that they never really recover.

Fear and anxiety still make people do foolish things. A person's got to trust in something. The question is: Will we give in to panic, or will we take our biggest problems to God and trust in Him?

TUESDAY: Beliefs

It's odd, isn't it? Two different people can go through almost exactly the same circumstances and come away with vastly different conclusions. One thinks the world is out to get them; the other thinks they must have done something to deserve this. One finds reasons to give up; the other finds reasons to continue fighting.

We've all been in situations like that. Two people who have so much in common find themselves sharing a difficult time, but approach their lots in life from opposite perspectives and respond not only with different attitudes but with different behaviors.

What's the difference?

Usually the difference lies in what each individual believes—about their circumstances, about themselves, about other people, about the world, about God.

We often think that our circumstances dictate our actions, but it's not true. In between what happens to us and what we do in response lies what we tell ourselves about what just happened—that is, our beliefs.

Ahaz and Hezekiah were both threatened. Someone from the outside wanted to remove them from power and take away what was rightfully theirs. They found themselves in precisely the same situation, but their responses could not have been more different. Ahaz panicked. Hezekiah prayed.

What was the difference? They believed fundamentally different things about themselves, about other people, about the world and, most importantly, about God. Whether Ahaz believed that God could not help or would not help, the bottom line is that Ahaz assumed God was no help to him in his situation. In spite of the fact that God wanted better for Ahaz than Ahaz wanted for himself, the king thought—for some inexplicable reason—that he was on his own in figuring out what to do next.

Worse, Ahaz made up his mind what to do and not even God could talk him out of it.

Hezekiah found himself in the same situation: The Assyrians came knocking at his door, just like they did with his father. But Hezekiah interpreted his circumstances differently. He believed God trustworthy and available, and his response to his circumstances reflected that belief.

Similar circumstances. Different responses. Different outcomes. What is the point of departure? It lies in their core beliefs.

This is precisely the bridge between their story and ours. We all must decide what we believe on some core issues.

Is God as competent as He is portrayed in the Bible? Is He both willing and able to help? Is His default disposition toward His children that of an angry and petty dictator or of a patient and loving heavenly Father? When we disagree with Him over what's in our best interests, will we trust Him enough to do what He asks—even when it doesn't seem to make much sense?

WEDNESDAY: Values

No one sets out to kill a child, placing an infant into a glowing hot oven and ignoring his cries for help. Such a thing is repugnant for normal human beings. And yet that is exactly what Ahaz did.

Ahaz probably grew up wanting to do the right thing. As a little boy, he would have been taught—like all little children—to share and tell the truth. He would have heard these fantastic stories about YHWH, the God who brought His people out of slavery in Egypt into this magnificent land flowing with milk and honey. This God wanted His people to trust Him and love others.

We might wonder if any of those childhood memories were swirling around in Ahaz's mind when he picked up his own son, walked toward the altar and offered the child's life to appease a god who didn't even exist.

Ahaz didn't just wake up one morning and decide to kill his child. These things happen gradually, slowly, steadily, terribly. One tiny compromise is made, and then another, and then another, and before we realize what's happening, the whole thing has snowballed out of control.

Small things done consistently over time have a cumulative effect. That's true positively or negatively. In the case of Ahaz, the consequences of his compromise weren't limited to himself. Eventually, his whole family, his whole community, his whole nation suffered. A man destroyed a child, and the world was forever changed because of it.

It all started when he turned to the wrong source of strength. He turned his back on God, seeking strength from a pagan king instead. Then he turned his back on God again, giving up control of his kingdom (for all practical purposes). Then he turned his back on God again, stealing from the Temple. Then he turned his back on God again, using what he stole to build altars to idols. And then he found himself marching toward one of those altars with a crying baby in his arms. By then, killing a child was no longer the farthest thing from his mind—it was the next logical step.

Compromise destroys a little at a time, gradually eroding the ground beneath our feet until we find ourselves in a full-on free fall.

There are all sorts of things we could say about how to avoid compromise, but no single thing will ever be as effective as valuing the honest accountability of a few close friends. The word "community" is very popular in churches, but it's hardly ever actually put into practice, because we chafe at the restraints of true community. It is a costly endeavor and one that stands in stark contrast to the Lone Ranger ways of modern society.

Honesty demands confession. We all have our blind spots, and if left to our own devices, compromise becomes all but inevitable. Without the availability of a few close friends who are willing to tell us truth even when it's painful, we are all that much more susceptible to the slippery slope of compromise.

THURSDAY: Actions

The insurance ads are right: "Life comes at you fast." It's in the heat of the moment, when everything's a blur, that it's easy to do things you end up regretting.

Maybe life was like that for Ahaz.

Maybe Ahaz had good intentions but just got caught up in the rush and panic of life. The wolves were gathering around his door; storm clouds of impending doom loomed on the horizon. The clock was ticking, and he was running out of options. (There are so many ways to say it.)

Panic and anxiety cause people to do irrational things. Maybe that was what got Ahaz into trouble. Given the limited options he could see, Ahaz chose an irrational path that eventually led to his destruction. We could understand it better if it was just a poor decision made in haste.

But if all that was true of Ahaz, it was equally true of Hezekiah.

Hezekiah faced the same situation; perhaps the danger was even more acutely felt under his reign. If time was short for Ahaz, it was even shorter for Hezekiah. Assyria was stronger now and Judah was weaker than ever. Yet Hezekiah was able to find the pause button and gain some perspective. When he did so, he found that God lives in that pause, in that moment between feeling panic and acting in panic.

When the Assyrian attack was first imminent, God wasn't far away somewhere, nervously pacing back and forth, wondering what Ahaz would do. He was right there. Waiting. Offering help. If only Ahaz had been willing to pause for a moment and reflect before acting, perhaps he would have enjoyed the same outcome as Hezekiah.

We'll never know.

It's easy to criticize Ahaz for doing something foolish, but how often do we find ourselves following the same pattern? We find ourselves under attack or in the midst of chaos and a flurry of downward-spiraling activity. We wonder what we're to do as we feel the icy grip of panic take hold of our throats.

In those moments, can we summon the resolve to hit the pause button instead of fast-forward or rewind? Only in doing so will we be able to regain the perspective and composure necessary to navigate the uncharted waters of our day. Maybe we've got it wrong. Maybe in times of confusion the maxim should be: *Don't just do something; stand there.*

Stand there for a moment. Wait. Take a breath. Count to 10. Think. Reflect. Pray.

Trouble is never far, even for Christians. (Odds are, anyone who says that God wants to exempt you from suffering and hardships is getting ready to ask you for money.) So what's a person to do when life gets hard?

Thinking people do just that: think. Pause. And strengthen yourself. Do what it takes to bolster your trust in God. Prepare yourself to view circumstances from an eternal perspective and make choices based on the faith in God you claim to possess.

If you haven't worked on building up your trust in God, then you're more likely to give in to panic like Ahaz did. But if you trust, you'll find the time to pause. And if you stop and pray, you'll find that God is there, in that quiet moment, just as He was for Hezekiah.

FRIDAY: Prayer

Narrative

My Rock and my Deliverer, this life in a fallen world is so uncertain and often frightening. I cannot even control today, let alone what will happen tomorrow or next year. I would be a fool to trust in my own abilities and resources, because these are too meager to provide any real security. I know that my basic choice in life is fear or faith, disbelief or trust, autonomy or dependence. I therefore choose the wisdom of radical trust in Your character and promises instead of my own inadequate resources. May I always turn first to You in the midst of life's challenges, knowing that the arm of the flesh is wholly inadequate. Disobedience to

Your desires always leads to greater pain than the prudence of trusting obedience. May I grow in the desire to honor and please You by putting You first in all things and making You my refuge and stronghold in times of need.

Orthodoxy

Living Word, I affirm that all things come from You and through You and to You. You have made the cosmos and all that is in it, and You hold all things together. All truth is derived from You, and You tell me to love You with all my mind as well as all my heart. May I renew my mind with the timeless truths of Your Word and cultivate an ever clearer biblical worldview so that my thinking will be in accordance with truth. Give me the wisdom to test everything according to the truths of Scripture so that I will think clearly and make sound judgments that are not based on emotions or wrong thinking but on the sure foundation of the written and living Word. I know that only as I think biblically will I be in a position to make the right decisions about my circumstances.

Orthopathy

God of light and love, You want what is really best for me, but I find myself resisting Your will because it challenges my autonomy and self-dependence. But I know that if I seek to order my life according to my own devices and desires, I will end up making a growing number of compromises and lapse into folly. It is in the small decisions of life that my character is forged. Small acts of infidelity lead to ever-increasing acts of unfaithfulness, just as small acts of faithfulness lead to greater acts of faithfulness. Nothing is really neutral, as decisions in even the smallest arenas are cumulative. Give me the wisdom and true desire to seek accountability and honesty with a few people I can trust so that they can protect me from myself. In this way, we will encourage one another so that we will not be hardened by the deceitfulness of sin.

Orthopraxy

God of all comfort, I thank You for the rich ministry of Your Holy Spirit in my life—for His encouragement, counsel, teaching, conviction, comfort, empowering and filling. You have given me all the resources in Christ that I need to live a life of fidelity and ministry to the people You have placed in my life. Still, it is easy to neglect Your resources and to panic when times become difficult. In those times, I am more tempted to run than to rest and to react than to reflect. Please keep me from making decisions out of fear and haste, and direct me to Your wonderful resources in problematic times. Like Jesus, I want to live with the poise, peace and patience that are derived from time spent in Your presence. May I treasure times of being so that they will empower me in times of doing.

22

Reformation

2 KINGS 22–23;
2 CHRONICLES 34–35

MONDAY: Story

Who says kids can't change the world? Josiah proved them wrong.

Well . . . maybe he wasn't just a kid. He was also a king. Never mind that he was only eight years old when he started out; he was the king of Judah. He could do whatever he wanted. That was, after all, what his father and his grandfather before him had done.

Josiah's family hadn't exactly prepared him to be a great leader. No one had taught him the value of things like faithfulness, personal integrity, sacrifice or generosity. His grandfather, Manasseh, was known as the worst king of all time. His father wasn't much better. Josiah didn't exactly grow up in a godly household. Actually, he hadn't really even grown up yet.

Take a kid who hasn't been taught the importance of following God and give him nearly absolute power. That's usually a recipe for disaster, right?

But Josiah was different.

He could tell things weren't right, and he knew that God had given him the authority to do something about it. So little Josiah set about implementing a campaign of national reform. Not bad for a kid.

He ordered that all of the places where pagan gods were worshiped be torn down. He passed laws that reflected his kingdom's heritage as a godly nation. He even developed a plan to remodel the Temple, which had been grossly misused and sadly uncared for during the reign of his forefathers.

And it was during the remodeling of the Temple that someone made an amazing discovery: They found the Bible. Apparently, their one existing copy of the Word of God had been misplaced, stuck in a closet or something while Grandpa Manasseh was setting up altars to every god he could think of. Imagine their shock and surprise when they found it!

But it begs the question: What in the world had they been doing in the Temple all those years without the Bible?

We must conclude that it's possible to hold a lot of religious services, committee meetings and community activities without the Bible. (Why anyone would want to do such things is difficult for us to understand, but there it is.)

Josiah was very excited by the new discovery. He asked that the Law be read to him in its entirety, and when he realized how far short the people had fallen on keeping its covenant with God, he ordered the entire nation to repent. Having seen the lengths to which God is willing to go to discipline His children in the Northern Kingdom, Josiah tried desperately to avoid such a tragic end.

But it proved too little too late. The people obeyed Josiah while he was alive. They went through the motions of putting away their idols and offering sacrifices and prayers to YHWH. But as soon as Josiah died, they went right back to their old ways. The national revival was a farce. The people were still as far away from truly following God as they had ever been.

In fact, the people couldn't even remember what it looked like to get it right anymore. If only there was a way to show them, to demonstrate up close and personal what an obedient lifestyle really looked like.

Fortunately, God had such a plan. It was still several hundred years off, but the day would come. First, though, there was a matter of discipline that needed to take place. The people needed to learn that God does not make empty threats.

TUESDAY: Beliefs

Before Josiah became king, the Southern Kingdom of Judah had gone through more than 50 years of rebellion against YHWH. Clearly, the Word of God spoke against their practices.

When Manasseh, the most wicked king in the history of the Southern Kingdom, was in power, everyone had certainly heard about what the king and queen
of the Northern Kingdom had done with the prophets who dared to speak in
opposition to their YHWH-less policies: Ahab and Jezebel had killed them all.

There was little doubt Manasseh would do the same if anyone dared to speak
against him, so we can understand why the priests may have simply ignored
Scripture. If they had actually spoken from the sacred texts, they would have
been considered politically incorrect. And in a corrupt political system where
absolute power corrupts absolutely, incorrectness is intolerable and might result
in the death penalty.

Apparently, the high priest chose to store the Bible somewhere in the Temple.
Perhaps after he tucked it away, he gave short "fireside chats" laced with happy
thoughts about practicing random acts of kindness. But half a century with none
of God's Word being taught bred a whole generation of people with absolutely
zero knowledge of God's Law. They had no idea what righteousness was anymore.

It's a good thing that doesn't happen today. Oh wait . . . it does.

In far too many places, the Bible has been labeled politically incorrect and has
been removed from its place of prominence, shelved for more favorable texts laced
with happy thoughts about being nice to our friends. Perhaps this is one reason
why so many younger people long for a relationship with God and despise the
local church. They're seeking God. They go to church. They don't find Him there.

Without God's Word filling a prominent place in our lives, we lose a sense of
what is really right and really wrong. We have little understanding of God as He
actually exists and begin to worship God only as He exists in our imaginations.

Josiah took Scripture seriously. He heard it read and made a choice to put it
into practice, beginning with his own life. As a result of his efforts to bring the
people of God back into line with the Word of God, judgment was spared during
his lifetime. And when he died, this was his epitaph: "Neither before nor after
Josiah was there a king like him who turned to the Lord as he did—with all his
heart and with all his soul and with all his strength, in accordance with all the
Law of Moses" (2 Kings 23:25).

Unfortunately, Josiah's revival was pretty much limited to his lifetime. We'll
talk about that more tomorrow. For today, understand that there is often a direct
correlation between biblical knowledge and morality. It is primarily from the
Bible that we can even understand what morality is.

The sobering news is that it only takes one generation to lose that.

The good news is that a revival can start with one person . . . like you.

WEDNESDAY: Values

Throughout the book you're reading, we've broken out the lessons we can learn from these stories into three categories: *orthodoxy, orthopathy* and *orthopraxy*. You can think of these three categories as *beliefs, values* and *actions*, or you can think of them as *head, heart* and *hands*.

In reality, human life cannot be separated as neatly as that. Your mind is not distinct from your heart. And your behavior doesn't exist in isolation from your thoughts and feelings. In fact, the Bible frequently speaks of how important it is to guard your heart above all else, "for it is the wellspring of life" (Prov. 4:23).

In other words, as your heart goes, so goes the rest of your life.

Now, when the Bible talks about our hearts, we must not only think about our feelings. We must realize that the heart reveals our primary disposition. Biblically speaking, the heart comprises our will, our intellect, our conscience and our emotions. Your heart is the you inside of you that makes you you. When we talk about the heart, we're talking about the foundation of your whole being.

This is why King David, when he was confronted with his sin, prayed for God not only to "cleanse me with hyssop, and I shall be clean; wash me, and I will be whiter than snow" (Ps. 51:7). He knew that he needed more than forgiveness, so he continued, "Create in me a pure heart, O God" (v. 10). David realized that what he had done was a direct reflection of the state of his heart, so he asked God to deal with the root of his bad behavior: his thoughts and feelings.

God has always wanted more from us than behavior modification. He wants a true change of heart.

Josiah's revival lasted just one generation because, while the people's behavior changed, their hearts did not. God told Jeremiah, who was a prophet during the lifetime of Josiah, "Judah did not return to me with all her heart, but only in pretense" (Jer. 3:10). God's solution? "I will put my law in their minds and write it on their hearts" (Jer. 31:33). In other words, God would transform us from the inside out.

Which do we value more? Good behavior or a real renovation of the heart?

Lest we answer too hastily, we must consider the implications of our response. It's a lot easier to gauge behavior than it is to measure the level of internal righteousness in our spouses and our children. You can't see heart change. You can see when someone stops swearing or drinking. It's easy to conclude that someone's changed behavior means they are a changed person.

Jesus was not so easily fooled, however. He understood that there were weightier matters of the Law, such as mercy and compassion. Those things are difficult, if not impossible, to quantify.

Behavior is important. Morality is very important. But if the behavior is not motivated by a true change of heart, behavioral change is short-lived at best.

Real life-change happens from the inside out. Jesus wants us to hand our hearts over to Him so that He can replace our old, sin-soaked hearts with brand-new ones, setting in motion an internal process of renovation that will lead us to something better than better behavior. Jesus plans on making us into the right kind of person who does the right thing at the right time in the right way for the right reason.

That's true righteousness. And that's Jesus' aim for us. Is it your aim as well?

THURSDAY: Actions

Two kids get into an argument. You can make them apologize. You can even make them shake hands or hug or say they're sorry. But you can't make them feel remorse. That's got to come from something inside of them.

A nation has been practicing idolatry and gross immorality. You can call them to repentance, tear down their altars and legislate national reform. You can make it illegal to worship foreign gods and proselytize through persecution. But you can't make them surrender their hearts to God. That's got to come from something inside of them.

Government, in one sense, is downstream from society at large. And society, in the grand scheme of things, is downstream from individual hearts and minds. That means that if we want to fix what's wrong with this world, we must stop trying to fix it through legislation and focus on the true source of the problem: individual people and the way they think about their own identities, about God and about the world in which they live.

Josiah had such wonderful intentions. He led the nation to repent and live according to God's laws. He even called on the people to renew their covenantal vows to YHWH. But his reforms died soon after he did.

Structures can change for a season, but unless people's hearts are changed, they will inevitably revert back to their old ways. Government cannot bring about lasting change. Fear of punishment won't do it. Prosperity won't do it. Religion won't do it.

Perhaps it's natural for us to want a program. Five steps to a changed heart! Seven easy ways to bring about lasting change! Change the world in just 15 minutes a day! We could probably sell a lot more books if we proposed such a programmed approach to life change.

But the truth is that lasting change is something that only God can bring about. If you really want to experience this kind of change, you must do something counter-intuitive: You must give up. You must cast yourself upon Him and ask Him to do what you cannot do for yourself through sheer force of will.

You may be able to change your circumstances. You may even be able to change your behavior. But you can't change your own heart. Only God can do that. And He has promised He will, if you're willing to submit to Him and trust Him.

Looks like the ball is in your court now.

FRIDAY: Prayer

Narrative

Dear Lord, where would I be without Your Word? What would guide me and teach me the answers to the fundamental questions of origin, purpose and destiny? Human speculation is utterly inadequate for this task, because the answers to these and other questions require a word from without, a revelation that is not under the sun but from above the sun. Teach me to treasure Your Word, and give me the wisdom to read, meditate and memorize Your revealed truths—this is the sure foundation upon which to live and flourish. May I be different from the corrupt culture in which I live and value the things that have eternal rather than passing worth. Then I will order my steps with wisdom, prudence, discernment and good counsel. I want Your Word to make a difference in my life and to be evident to all.

Orthodoxy

Lord, I live in an age in which the media, entertainment and public education have become the shapers and purveyors of culture and popular opinion. Your Word has been marginalized and rendered irrelevant in these arenas, and secularization continues to grow in my time. Nonetheless, Your Word is alive and will endure forever, and it will accomplish what You desire in spite of the rebellion of men. I ask for the grace to apply it more fully in my life so that I will not merely be a hearer, but a doer who applies Your truths in each area of my life—my family, work, friends and finances. This wisdom of application will enrich not only my life but also the lives of everyone I encounter. May people see the living Word in me, and be drawn to the Person and work of the Lord Jesus who lives and reigns in me.

Orthopathy

Father God, Your Word addresses the deepest issues of human existence and penetrates beneath the surface of things to the matters of the inner person. People are impressed by appearances, but You look at the heart. People notice changed behavior, but you look at transformed being. May I be increasingly strengthened with power through Your Spirit in my inner self so that Christ would dwell in my heart through faith. I want to live from the inside out so that genuine inner growth in Christ would become increasingly evident in my practice and choices. I don't want to put on a good show, but to live out the genuine integrity of a growing congruence between what I believe and how I live. Instead of imitating people, I want to imitate Christ, and You have given me the power to do this through my new identification with Him.

Orthopraxy

God, Your revealed Word is so radical and countercultural that no one could have made it up. It goes beyond the ceiling of our own comprehension and reveals truths that are utterly unique. While every religion and cult teaches variations of work systems in which we are told to merit salvation or deliverance, the Bible uniquely teaches that it is impossible for us to attain any real merit before You, and that salvation is given to us by grace through faith in the redemptive work of Your Son. I cannot change my heart, turn over a new leaf or earn Your favor. Instead, I have come to see that spiritual life is impossible through human attainment. I ask for the grace to surrender myself entirely to Your work and power in my life and to realize that the spiritual life is the life of Christ reproduced in Your people by the power of Your Holy Spirit.

23

Disappointed with Life

2 Kings 24–25;
2 Chronicles 36;
Jeremiah 39; 52;
The Book of Ezekiel;
The Book of Daniel

MONDAY: Story

Daniel never thought he would end up in Babylon. And Ezekiel never imagined he would live out his days near the Kebar River, 700 miles from his hometown, either. They were supposed to live in Jerusalem—the city of their people, where God had put His name, the city where the Temple was, the city of God.

But sometimes God's plans are not our plans. In fact, that's often the case, as we've seen so far in this Story.

Daniel was intelligent and wealthy. He had a bright future, to be sure. He would get a good education, marry a good woman, raise some good kids, hold down a good job. He would do good things for God.

Ezekiel was going to be a priest and serve in the Temple. There was no higher aspiration for a young man growing up in Judah.

But both Daniel and Ezekiel lived in an unfortunate time—the time God chose to discipline His people.

See, the people of God had continued in a steady slide away from their covenant with Him since the death of Solomon. There had been glimpses of hope, brief episodes of promise keeping. But idolatry had become increasingly commonplace, and the whole basis for morality was lost when the Law of God was literally lost for a while and utterly disregarded even after it was found. The people of God mostly lived like their pagan neighbors. They may have engaged in some religious practices, but those were mostly just for show—hollow ritual at best.

The clouds of God's judgment began to gather.

Again and again, God sent prophets to call the people back to faithfulness, with little or no lasting effect. Finally, God drew a line in the sand and judgment began during the reign of King Josiah's son, Jehoiakim.

Nebuchadnezzar, the king of Babylon, laid siege against Jerusalem. He rounded up the best and brightest people in the city. Daniel was one of those who was carried off to the Babylonian capital. All of the young man's dreams were dashed as he left his home behind, never to return.

When the cream of the crop is gone, mediocrity ascends to leadership. After this initial loss, Jehoiakim's son Jehoiachin (a. k. a., Jechoniah) became the new ruler. He reigned only three short months before the Babylonians returned to take the next batch of best and brightest away.

Ezekiel was in this second group, as was King Jehoiachin, who was so young that he did not have an heir to replace him. His uncle Zedekiah had to take Jehoiachin's place, and Uncle Zed quickly proved why he wasn't considered dangerous enough to be taken away with either the first or second batch of smart kids.

These were dark days, indeed! Daniel and his friends lost everything—their customs, their language, even their given names. Ezekiel never got to serve in the Temple. These young men found all of their hopes and dreams shattered. But they hung on to God and to the idea that He isn't random. God is intentional—even about something like this.

They knew that God was up to something in Jerusalem and in Babylon. Even by the Kebar River. Even in times of discipline and distress. Even when life didn't turn out the way they thought it would.

God is always up to something.

TUESDAY: Beliefs

It's called the doctrine of divine retribution, and it goes like this:

If you're good, then you will receive blessing and prosperity.

If you're bad, then you will receive misery and poverty.

In other words, God treats people the way they deserve. If you're suffering, you have no one to blame but yourself. If you will just repent, then you will suffer no more. After all, God doesn't allow good people to suffer, does He?

Well, Daniel and Ezekiel throw two Major Prophet-sized monkey wrenches into the divine-retribution machine. After all, they didn't do anything wrong. They were good guys doing the right thing. Ezekiel wanted to be a priest, for crying out loud! (Come to think of it, Job, Joseph and Jesus might have something to say on this topic as well.)

Sometimes good guys end up living out their lives in a foreign land, serving a foreign captor, their hopes and dreams unfulfilled. God doesn't always balance the books in this life.

The really scandalous thing is when this terrible theology gets taught in Christian churches (and it happens far too often). It makes a mockery of human suffering—the same human suffering that God Himself entered into on the cross. Talk to someone who has suffered, and they'll tell you that people who inflict more harm than good are usually Christians. Christians who say things like, "If you just had more faith . . ." or "God is refining you" or "This is a wake-up call from heaven."

It was said after 9/11. It was said after the tsunami in Sri Lanka. It was said in the wake of Hurricane Katrina: *They must have done something to deserve such a tragedy.*

This belief breeds a kind of death—the death of hope, the death of gratitude, the death of joy, the death of grace. Life becomes just one endless cycle of reaping and sowing.

You can call that many things, but you sure can't call it "good news."

It is neat and tidy, though. No muss, no fuss. If you suffer, it's because you deserve to. If you succeed, it's because you earned it. That's probably part of the appeal: It just makes so much sense to us. It's how we would run the universe if we were in charge.

Another part of its appeal is how close to the truth it is. God loves to bless obedience, and God does discipline His children. And we often bring terrible things on ourselves. If you smoke two packs a day, overeat and refuse to exercise, don't go blaming anyone but yourself for the health troubles you have later in life.

But God rejects a simplistic one-to-one correlation like divine retribution because it inevitably turns Him into some kind of vending machine, and righteousness becomes a means to an end rather than an end in and of itself. Righteousness is never something we use to gain something; righteousness is *the thing* gained. And if we think God is dealing in tit-for-tat tactics, we will eventually stop pursuing God and start using Him to get what it is we really want.

If that's our theology, then good circumstances don't breed gratitude; they breed pride. And bad circumstances don't build character; they build despair.

It's called the doctrine of divine retribution, and it's one of the deadliest forms of heresy there is.

WEDNESDAY: Values

We like God . . . most of the time. Granted, He's the most frustrating Person we've ever encountered, and just when you think you've got Him figured out, He takes a hard right and "goes dark," leaving you groping around for Him.

Still, we like God.

But do we really? Do we actually like God as He exists? Or do we prefer God as He exists in our imaginations? That's a tough question, because it's difficult to get at the true nature of this One who exists outside of space and time. Our minds are, after all, finite. Grasping infinity is, well . . . impossible.

Still, we like God. Or at least we like what we think about God. When it suits us.

Here's the pinch: What do you do when the God who actually exists isn't like the God you want? It's one thing to embrace a God who is relevant and contemporary, yet when we find that God can also be irrelevant and old and difficult to follow, will we still love and obey Him? What will we choose when we find that the God of the "easy yoke" is also the God who demands that we take up the instrument of our own death and follow Him wherever He chooses?

What do we do when the God who is there is not the God anyone is looking for? Do we still proclaim Him? Will we be tempted to hold on to a God who wants His people in Jerusalem even after He has allowed us to be carted off to Babylon?

Basically, it comes down to whether or not we value God as He is. He is, after all, the Absolute One in the equation, regardless of our ability or inability to understand Him completely. This is the God who deserves our praise whether in sickness or in health, for richer or poorer.

Do we value God for who He is, or do we value him like a farmer values his cow? Just for the milk and the cheese? Do we love God like kids love the ice cream man? Is it just about the stuff He provides? Just about what He can do for us?

If so, what happens when the milk runs dry and the ice cream man's truck breaks down? What do you do when you find yourself hundreds of miles away from home, your hopes and dreams shattered? What if those dreams were even good dreams about serving God?

At times like that, you need a faith in the God who is actually there, the kind of God who says, "If you're looking for God, I AM the God you get, because I AM who I AM."

And that will have to be enough.

THURSDAY: Actions

We are fascinated by aliens. Television shows like *My Favorite Martian*, *The X-Files* or *Third Rock from the Sun*, movies like *E. T.* or *K-Pax*—we love stories about strange beings from another world.

Perhaps one reason we love these stories is that there are times when we all feel a little out of place. Who hasn't found herself watching the evening news and wondering, "What planet am I on?" As odd as it sounds, it's probably normal to feel a little strange when we hear about some of the crazy things happening in our world.

The Bible affirms this, too, calling us "aliens and strangers in this world" (1 Pet. 2:11). There's something in us that feels like a fish out of water, something that knows we don't belong here, that we were made for something other than this, bigger than this. We resonate with stories of aliens because we all know that, to some extent, we are aliens ourselves.

That's one reason why the stories of Daniel and Ezekiel are so important for us. These two godly men spent most of their lives in a land they never intended to inhabit. They lived and died as strangers in a strange land, and—in doing so—they showed the rest of us how to live as resident aliens.

Throughout the centuries, Christians have debated the best way to live out our calling in a land that is not our permanent home. Some have cautioned against becoming too comfortable here and have advocated a strategy of isolation. Others have pushed the pendulum to the other extreme, suggesting that we must immerse ourselves completely in the culture in order to redeem it. All in or all out; which is it?

Jesus' desire for His followers was that they learn how to be *in* the world but not *of* the world (see John 17:13–18). That is to say, Jesus wanted His followers to figure out how to be fully engaged in this world without allowing this world to shape their beliefs, values and behaviors. Imagine such a thing: a group of people who maintain their integrity in terms of their distinctive beliefs, values and behaviors while having conversations with "outsiders"—helping them, living in community with them—all the while never demanding that they agree on all things, never coercing or manipulating them into uniformity.

Sounds an awful lot like Jesus when He was here on earth.

The only way to do this is by remembering that God is the God of everywhere.

Yes, He's the God of Israel and the One who blesses Jerusalem. He's the God whose presence overwhelmed those serving in the Temple when Solomon dedicated it. But He's also the God of the Kebar River and the God of the Babylonians (whether they realize it or not).

If you have to leave your home, He goes with you. When you find yourself in a strange place or strange circumstances, He's still with you. The Bible tells us that there's nowhere we can go to get away from Him, nowhere we can go that He cannot save us. The One who knit us together in our mother's womb will still be with us, even while we dwell here in the land of our sojourn.

How are we to live as strangers in this strange land? We are to live with the confidence that God is with us—even in Babylon. And we are to live with the hopeful expectation that, unlike Daniel and Ezekiel, we will one day be brought home again.

FRIDAY: Prayer

Narrative

O Lord, when I consider how fragile and uncertain my world is, I realize that there is no real refuge but You. I make my plans, dream my dreams and hope for things whose outcome is uncertain. I cannot control this day or any other day. I am often frustrated by disappointments and setbacks and uncertainties. It is only when I turn back to You and release my fears and concerns to You that I will discover real peace. Therefore, I will be anxious for nothing, but in everything by prayer and supplication with thanksgiving I will let my requests be made known to You. And I know that as I do this, Your peace will guard my heart and mind in Christ Jesus. For You are my confidence and stronghold, and You never change. You always want what is best for me, and in spite of the difficulty of the journey, You will bring me safely home.

Orthodoxy

Lord God, Your ways are past finding out. Just when I think I have a handle on Your will and work and plans, unexpected outcomes and events crowd into my life and dispel my illusions. Who but You can know what an hour will bring? There is no simplistic one-for-one correspondence in this fallen world between obedient behavior and positive consequences. In fact, it is painfully evident that unrighteousness sometimes leads to apparent gain in this world. Give me the wisdom of an eternal perspective that will enable me to see that the Story isn't over in this life, and that Your divine justice will fully prevail in the next. Let me live today for You and not for apparent gain; let me pursue You and not the things I think I can get from You. For You are my hope and my life. Whom have I in heaven but You? Nothing on earth can compare with You, the strength of my heart and my portion forever.

Orthopathy

Lord in heaven, I confess that You are high and lifted up and that Your purposes are past finding out. I also confess that I often want You to be more understandable and comprehensible so that I might behold more than just the fringe of Your ways. There are many things in Scripture that do not appeal to my mind, and I often struggle with hoping in the God I want more than in the God You really are. But You have called me to trust and hope in You, not to understand You. You have made it clear that Your thoughts are not my thoughts and Your ways are not my ways. They are utterly beyond human attainment, and in Your transcendent glory, You will always abound in mystery. Therefore I choose the way of trust, not that of understanding. May I hold on to You and Your character even in the vicissitudes and unexpected turns of this earthly life.

Orthopraxy

God of grace and hope, I am embedded in this world as a participant and agent, and yet I realize that my true citizenship is in heaven and not on earth.

In this life in Christ, I know that I am really a stranger, an alien, a sojourner and a pilgrim. Like the men and women of faith in Hebrews 11, I know that I will not receive the promises in this life, but that I can see them and welcome them from a distance, confessing that I am a stranger and exile on the earth. I acknowledge my identity as a steward and an ambassador. As a steward, I own nothing, but only manage Your possessions; as an ambassador, I am not here on my own business, but on the King's business. Wherever I am, I can be Your agent and Your steward as salt and light in an insipid and dark world. May I use this time and opportunity in Your service.

24

Tears

The Book of Lamentations; Jeremiah 52:31–34

MONDAY: Story

The building of the Temple during the reign of King Solomon had been the high point for the people of God in the Old Testament. People had traveled from the far corners of the known world to see the beauty of God's city. The people of God had become a city set on a hill, a light to all the other nations, an example of what it looks like when a group of people are rightly related to their Creator and rightly relating to one another.

The promise God made to Abraham all those years ago was fulfilled in those days.

The destruction of that same Temple, during the reign of King Zedekiah nearly four centuries later, was the low point. The city of Jerusalem, the city where God had put His name, was reduced to smoke and ashes. The people of the Northern Kingdom had been scattered to the far corners of the Assyrian empire, and now the people of the Southern Kingdom had been taken into captivity too, exiled to the far corners of the Babylonian empire.

The prophet Jeremiah must have wondered if there was any hope left for the purposes of God. He must have wondered if God was through with keeping His end of the bargain. Certainly the people had failed; perhaps YHWH was finished with them for good. Jeremiah sat down and began to weep for the broken-down state of affairs surrounding him.

But God had a plan (sounds familiar, right?). Oddly enough, the plan involved a young man who had been king for three short months before he surrendered and was carted off to be imprisoned in exile in Babylon. Jehoiachin was eventually released from prison and became a member of the royal court in his new home. Because his life was spared, the royal lineage of David continued. In fact, Jehoiachin (sometimes known as Jeconiah) found his way into the genealogy of Jesus.

Obviously, Jeremiah didn't know anything about this plan when he surveyed the landscape of Jerusalem and saw how it had been decimated by the Babylonian army. He hadn't the foggiest notion how God's plan would be fulfilled. But he believed that God was faithful.

And so it was that 70 years later, a small band of people would return to this devastated city of Jerusalem and rebuild it. As the years passed, walls would protect it again. People would once more travel the busy streets of the market. The Temple would once more be a meeting place for God and His people.

The Babylonian captivity would not be the end of the Story of God. God was still at work, even if Jeremiah was unable to see how any good could ever come from the circumstances in which he found himself.

God has always shown Himself faithful and will continue to do so until the day when all His people are gathered in His presence. Then His purpose for all eternity will begin.

TUESDAY: Beliefs

The once busy streets of Jerusalem were quiet at midday. The Temple, the place where God's presence had once been so tangible, so heavy that people couldn't even stand up, was destroyed. The dwelling place of God was reduced to a pile of rubble. The walls that had provided such secure defense against the enemies of God's people were completely destroyed. There was hardly one stone left on top of another. All the king's sons were dead, murdered before his very eyes. The people of the Northern Kingdom were scattered, and now the people in the Southern Kingdom were taken into exile in Babylon.

Jerusalem was a ghost-town.

This was the lowest point so far in Jewish history and, not surprisingly, when the book of Lamentations was written. The prophet Jeremiah walked through hushed alleys, the smoke still rising from the ashes of the formerly beautiful Temple where God's presence had been known. The prophet began to weep, his heart broken over the torn-down state of the work of God in the world. What hope was there now of God's dream becoming a reality? God had set out to build a community of people rightly related to Himself and rightly relating to one another, a people placed in a strategic setting, a community that would be a blessing to all nations.

And now look at this mess. This is what people did with God's great plan: They threw it all away to be like everyone else.

And yet . . .

God's discipline—painful though it may be—lasts for a moment. God is never content to allow destruction and misery to have the last word. He promises to bring beauty in place of the ashes. Life had crashed down around the weeping prophet's ears, but that didn't mean God was through. God had a dream, and He meant to turn it into reality.

Obviously, we read this story from a privileged perspective. We know that God's plan continued long after Jeremiah sat down and cried.

God remains sovereign. His plan transcends all apparent defeat and destruction. Despite the devastation Jeremiah felt about what had happened to his people and his hometown, God's plan continued moving forward toward its inevitable fulfillment.

Even now, the state of God's work in this world may seem broken down, thwarted by the rebellion of God's own people or brought to ruin by His enemies. But don't you believe it. In times like these, it may be impossible for us to see how His plan will come to fruition. Perhaps the only way to see it will be in retrospect.

But rest assured, the plan continues to this day, and our God will not rest until things have come full course.

WEDNESDAY: Values

"In this world you will have trouble" (John 16:33). No less an authority than Jesus Christ Himself tells us that following Him is not an exemption from pain and sorrow and troublesome times.

Sometimes pain comes when people, in their brokenness, turn and hurt others. Relationships are difficult to maintain and bring with them the certainty of heartache. The only way to avoid it is to avoid people altogether—an impossibility for those of us who want to lead healthy and productive lives.

Sometimes pain comes as a result of living in a fallen world. Storms happen. Cancer strikes innocent people. Wildfires wreak havoc. Bad things happen to good people, and so much seems beyond our control.

There is no escape from this kind of pain, no alarm system that will warn that the doctor is about to give you bad news, no gated community that will prevent life from crashing down around your ears.

Sometimes pain comes as a result of our own poor choices. We eat too much and exercise too little and reap what we've sown. We spend years pushing people away and wonder why no one wants to visit us when we're old. Wisdom (especially the wisdom found in the book of Proverbs) may help you minimize those poor choices, but there's no escaping the pain we bring upon ourselves.

Sometimes, though this is not a popular thought, God actually inflicts pain on us. The writer of Hebrews assures us, "The Lord disciplines those he loves" (Heb. 12:6).

His discipline is perhaps the most painful to endure, but it is also the most redemptive. The writer of Hebrews goes on to say, "No discipline seems pleasant at the time, but painful. Later on, however, it produces a harvest of righteousness and peace for those who have been trained by it" (Heb. 12:11).

The problem with pain is that sometimes it becomes all we can see. In our hardship, we lose sight of the goal and fail to understand that suffering may actually be an integral part of the path we're called to walk. The pain God inflicts on His people is never merely punishment; it is always ultimately redemptive, if for no other reason than that our pain should drive us closer to Him. When we draw close to God in our pain, we find the words of Jeremiah to be true: "Because of the Lord's great love we are not consumed, for his compassions never fail. They are new every morning; great is your faithfulness" (Lam. 3:22–23).

Hundreds of years earlier, King David knew something about this. He wrote, "For his anger lasts only a moment, but his favor lasts a lifetime; weeping may remain for a night, but rejoicing comes in the morning" (Ps. 30:5).

Hundreds of years later, James, the half-brother of Jesus, also had something to say on the subject. He advised the early followers of Christ to consider it pure joy when they faced all kinds of troubles, because those troubles happen for a reason: so that our faith may be mature and complete (see James 1:2–4).

What would happen if we stopped crying for help every time we experienced difficulties and instead sought to value the difficulties, rejoice in our sufferings and esteem the discipline as a means of developing character?

We don't mean to minimize the pain and suffering we all encounter. We merely want to point out that, while we continue in our own personal lamentation, we must embed our story into the larger narrative of God's unfolding Story. This (and only this) is how suffering can make sense.

Remember that God values the tears of a person who cares about the state of His work in this world. A broken heart is often a sign of spiritual health. In fact, our deepest and most effective ministry may come out of brokenness.

THURSDAY: Actions

Jeremiah was a good guy. He didn't waver in his commitment to God. He faithfully carried out the duties of his calling as a prophet of YHWH. He did crazy things, was willing to make a fool of himself, preached the Word in season and out of season, never failing to do what God asked. Days became weeks became months became years. Thirty-five of them went by.

And no one ever responded favorably to his message—not one single person.

In fact, things just seemed to go from bad to worse until God allowed a pagan nation to invade the land He had promised to His people, driving them from the land of milk and honey, scattering them to the four corners of the known world.

To be sure, Jeremiah wasn't the last person to experience the sting of despair.

Anyone who has ever attempted to do something for God—whether to plant a church or raise a child or be a witness at school or on the job—has been tempted at some time to give in to hopelessness. How is a person to live when her work for God nets her nothing but heartache and rejection?

In those dark hours, we've got to cling to God's character in the midst of our pain. We may not understand what He is doing, but He is the only anchor of hope we have.

And that brings up something important: You have hope. Hope is the one thing human beings cannot live without. You have hope somewhere. The question is not, *Do you have hope?* The question is, *Where is your hope?*

Is your hope in success? It will fail. Is it in the way people respond? They will let you down. The only secure hope you will find is in God's unfailing commitment to see His plan all the way through to completion, to finish the work He has begun in you and in this world. God's unchanging character and unwavering commitment to His people and His plan are like "an anchor for the soul, firm and secure" (Heb. 6:19).

Things may appear dark, but we must not give up. We must keep working toward the time when God's people, who are called according to His purposes, will eventually live in the place of His provision.

We can do this because we remember that Lamentations isn't the last book of the Bible—Revelation is. And in it, we see that the time is coming when all those promises will be fulfilled (see 21:3–5). God will create a new heaven and a new earth, and when He does, the old order of things will pass away. Cancer will pass away. War will pass away. Terrorist activity will pass away. Pain and sickness and death will all pass away when God makes everything new.

In the meantime, the people of God will bravely serve in this fallen world as it is. We will shed tears, but we know it will not be like this forever. One day, perhaps one day soon, God will wipe away our every tear.

FRIDAY: Prayer

Narrative

Faithful Father, as I reflect on the redemptive history recorded in the narratives and oracles of Scripture, I see so many surprising setbacks and breakthroughs. The wisdom of Your Word invites me to view events and circumstances with a long-term perspective. When I only look at the short term, I get muddled, confused and doubtful, because I allow my immediate circumstances to shape my understanding. But when I contextualize the events of my life in the long term, I can see that You are indeed causing all things to work together for good to those who love You and are called according to Your purpose. Teach me to affirm that the sufferings of this present time are not worthy to be compared with the glory that is to be revealed to Your children in Christ.

Orthodoxy

Lord of history, Your name is to be blessed and exalted forever. Your dominion is everlasting and Your kingdom endures from generation to generation. Wisdom and power belong to You and You rule over all the times and the epochs of human history. It is You who removes kings and establishes kings, and no one can withstand Your will and purposes. Therefore, in spite of all appearances to the contrary in this rebellious time in history, I know that You will bring about Your kingdom of righteousness even upon this earth. I ascribe all glory, majesty, dominion and authority to You and exult in hope of the fullness of Your reign. I will embed my time and my culture in this larger whole as I wait on You to fulfill Your glorious promises. *Maranatha*—come quickly, Lord Jesus.

Orthopathy

God of redemption, You have given me the inexpressible grace of being justified before You through faith in the Person and work of Jesus Christ. You have overcome my enmity and given me the gift of peace with You and the hope of Your glory. But You have also taught me in Your Word that I will encounter tribulation in this world, especially as I seek to live godly in Christ Jesus. In spite of my natural disposition to the contrary, please make it more evident to me that affliction can be redemptive, because it can forge proven character and draw me away from misplaced and ill-defined hopes. I want to hope only in You and not in the goods and benefits of this passing world. My experience of suffering will be brief in light of eternity, and I know that You will perfect, confirm, strengthen and establish me in Christ.

Orthopraxy

Father, may I grow in my desire to love and honor Your name in all things. I want to be faithful to You in this fallen world and not be lured away by cheap substitutes and futile hopes. I will fix my hope completely on the grace that will be brought to Your people at the revelation of Jesus Christ. I want to live in holy anticipation and long for the fullness of Your purposes. The only sure anchor for my hope is in the promises You have made to those who have made You their refuge and confidence. Your lovingkindness and compassion will never diminish, but will go on into eternity. In spite of the adversities and uncertainties of this life, You have offered me a living hope that will never disappoint or fade away. My hope is in Your perfect character and Your steadfast faithfulness, and these will never let me down.

25

Homecoming

THE BOOK OF NEHEMIAH;
THE BOOK OF EZRA

MONDAY: Story

Nehemiah was a Jew, but he didn't live anywhere near Jerusalem. In fact, he'd never even visited the land of his forefathers. He lived in Persia, hundreds of miles away from the Temple. He was a servant, and—even though he was a high-ranking servant—he didn't have much clout.

But he had this idea of one day being able to walk where King David had walked, to touch the stones that Solomon had set in place, to see the same hillsides that Elijah and Elisha had seen. He sometimes tried to imagine what these places looked like—the rough stones of the walls around the holy city, the smell of the Mount of Olives.

It became something of an obsession for Nehemiah. And he could not stand the idea that the once-great city of God had been reduced to rubble and ashes and abandoned. He felt a gnawing sense of responsibility, even though he was a nobody, just a servant in a distant land. He would sometimes form plans to restore the city of Jerusalem, daydreaming about what he would do if he ever found himself in a position to do something.

Of course, he had heard reports about how Ezra, Zerubbabel and 50,000 others had gone to restore the Temple. But he had no idea how his story would intersect with theirs. God often works on multiple fronts, weaving different threads together to create something that is greater than the sum of its parts.

One day, out of the blue, the Persian king Artaxerxes asked him, "What's wrong? Are you feeling well? You look like something's bothering you."

Taking a deep breath, and believing that God must have somehow put him in this place at this time, for this purpose, Nehemiah spilled everything. Then, unbelievably, the king asked, "What can I do to help?"

"Send me to Jerusalem," Nehemiah blurted out, "and let me rebuild the wall around the city."

Nehemiah must have held his breath while he waited for a response. Imagine his shock when the king's next words were, "How long will it take and when will you return?"

Nehemiah had played out so many scenarios in his mind, dreaming of a moment like this. He had mapped the whole thing out a thousand times and was fully prepared to answer all of the king's questions. For the next several hours, the king helped Nehemiah get together everything he would need to make his journey.

Amazingly, the biggest obstacle to Nehemiah's dream coming true was not logistical factors (such as his foreign captors, the length of travel or the cost of materials); it was something far more difficult to conquer: discouragement.

The task of rebuilding the walls was enough to sober up Nehemiah and his party, but soon there was the added hardship of dealing with two bullies, Sanballat and Tobiah. Initially these two engaged in verbal taunting, but that eventually gave way to threats of outright sabotage. In response, Nehemiah divided his workers into those who would stand guard with swords and spears, bows and arrows, ready to defend against an attack, and those who would work directly on the wall. Even the workers dealing with bricks and mortar kept their weapons close by.

Because of Nehemiah's dogged trust in the God of his forefathers, the city soon stood strong once again. The walls were set in place and, 500 years after the glory of God filled Solomon's temple, the people stood together to renew their covenant with YHWH.

But this is more than just a story about one man whose hard work allowed his dream of rebuilding God's city to become a reality. This is a story about a faithful God who works through ordinary people (a builder like Zerubbabel, a Bible teacher like Ezra and a strategic planner like Nehemiah) in absolutely extraordinary ways when they are willing to be used by Him.

TUESDAY: Beliefs

God gave Adam and Eve everything they could have wanted, and they threw it all away by rejecting Him. Still, God was not content to leave it at that. We have seen the lengths to which He is willing to go to restore a relationship with His people.

God promised that He would use the family of a childless nobody named Abraham to bless the entire world. His commitment to see that promise through to completion transcended their disobedience and stubborn rebellion. How else could we explain the fact that this one family eventually became a great nation?

God gave them His Law and showed them how to live in harmony with one another. They became the envy of kings and queens from all over the world, but they succumbed to the seduction of other gods. They never stopped believing in YHWH; they simply added other gods to the mix.

God warned them that He would discipline them, as any loving parent would discipline a disobedient child. Through prophets, He sent His message, but the people refused to listen. The 10 northern tribes were scattered across the known world. Later, the 2 remaining tribes in the south were carried away into exile as well, where they remained for 70 years.

God is relentless and more stubborn than His children. He never gave up on them or His dream. A small community eventually resettled in Jerusalem, and God's people began to gather again in God's place. They rebuilt the Temple. They rebuilt the walls. They made sacrifices. They read the Law. They wept and prayed and celebrated.

But something was missing: the visible, tangible presence of God.

God had promised to be among His people. The visible reminder of His presence would be the Ark of the Covenant. This golden box was to be placed in the center of the Temple . . . but it had been lost. The Most Holy Place, the Holy of Holies, was an empty room. Great building; no God.

As the first act of God's Story comes to a conclusion and we reach the intermission, we're left with a combination of feelings: We can see clearly how God keeps His promises, but we're still looking to see how God will ultimately deliver His people from evil.

The people are broken and the Law is inadequate to fix them. No amount of sacrifice or obedience can repair the damage that has been done. Forty years in the wilderness couldn't undo the damage; neither will 70 years in captivity. The Story is incomplete. Something cosmic is going to have to happen for all this to have a happy ending.

And that fact points us forward. The people would wait 450 more years until the time when the Author and Finisher of this Story showed up, embodying the visible, tangible presence of God: appearing in the Temple (actually replacing and becoming the Temple), endowing those who trust Him with Temple-like status, enabling those who follow Him to be the dwelling place of YHWH.

It is only when we realize that Jesus Christ—His sinless life, His sacrificial death, His victorious resurrection, His ongoing work—is the dénouement of the Story that we understand the first act. Then we see Him as the One promised in Genesis 3. We recognize Him as the boat that carried Noah's family to safety, the ram sacrificed in Isaac's place, the Passover Lamb that secured life for the people in Egypt, the manna that sustained them in the wilderness. He is the sacrifice, the Temple, the Ark of the Covenant, the Holy of Holies, the fulfillment of everything hoped for and promised.

WEDNESDAY: Values

Nehemiah was not a weak man. But his heart broke when he thought about the plight of his homeland, and he wept like a baby. He was burdened, and his burden drove him to a prolonged time of prayer and fasting.

This eventually led to the formation of a plan, and that plan eventually led to his place in God's Story. He took his plan and turned it into a reality. Without Nehemiah, the city of Jerusalem wouldn't have been rebuilt. Nehemiah's name isn't mentioned in the genealogies of Jesus, but he had a part in preparing the world for the coming of its Messiah.

And it started with a burden.

It's been that way throughout human history. God gets a person's attention. That person sees something he doesn't like about the way things are or the direction things are headed. It gets stuck in the craw, refusing to pass. He finds himself thinking about it throughout the day, turning it over and over in his mind, wondering what he might be able to do about it. He can't let it go, because it refuses to let go of him.

Sometimes that burden is something that you don't have the resources to fix. You may know what needs to be done, but you may not have the faintest idea how to get things from where they are to where they should be. What do you do then?

Nehemiah's concern began to consume him. He became obsessed with what could be, what *should be* versus what actually *was*. He saw the gap clearly, and he began to formulate a plan to close it. It changed his life. It changed his appearance. People around him could tell that his mind was elsewhere.

But he didn't do anything hasty. He didn't assume that the burden was a green light from God. Neither did he ignore the issue that was tugging on his heart. Instead, he chose to wait, to allow things to percolate for a while, to have this burden give birth to a clear vision and a solid strategy. He knew he wouldn't be able to do anything other than pray about the situation until God opened a door for him. But he wanted to make sure he was ready to walk through that door when the time came.

He had passion, but passion is never enough. He began to understand the goal. But neither is having a goal enough. He needed a plan, and that is what he set about discovering.

It started with that burden.

What's yours? What makes you weep? What makes you pound the table in disgust? What does your mind keep turning over and over? Do you have a burden?

Value that burden. Allow that burden to mature into a moral imperative. Spend time cultivating that passion, stoking it into a full-blown fire. Then ask yourself: Do I have a plan?

THURSDAY: Actions

"This day is sacred to the Lord your God. Do not mourn or weep. . . . Go and enjoy choice food and sweet drinks, and send some to those who have nothing prepared. This day is sacred to our Lord. Do not grieve, for the joy of the Lord is your strength" (Neh. 8:9–10). When the walls and the Temple were finished, Nehemiah, Ezra and the priests told the people, in essence, "Throw a party! Have a cookout! Eat the really fat pieces and drink something good—something with a cork or with one of those little umbrellas in it!"

One of the prophets of an earlier period predicted, "On this mountain the Lord Almighty will prepare a feast of rich food for all peoples, a banquet of aged wine—the best of meats and the finest of wines" (Isa. 25:6).

God is, apparently, in favor of good food (and we don't necessarily mean "good for you") and good wine. He wants us to eat the red meat, the marrow, the good stuff.

Oddly enough, this doesn't get taught in a lot of places. Those verses in Nehemiah and Isaiah are never the memory verses for Sunday School. It may be for precisely this reason (and a few others) that we've lost touch with the discipline of celebration.

Oh, yeah . . . we did say "the discipline of celebration."

We normally associate the word "discipline" with being deprived of something fun or enjoyable. But God is so concerned that humans learn how to celebrate properly that He actually built specific days into the Old Testament calendar on which people had to party. They were called "feast days," and they were mandatory.

They were balanced by days of meditation and days of fasting, but there's no getting around the fact that they were in there. They involved all the things you would normally associate with partying: gathering with people you like, eating, drinking, singing, dancing.

And it was always a corporate thing, never done in isolation. All of these activities were to be done in the company of others while reflecting on the goodness of the God who had given them such wonderful gifts.

This wasn't pleasure seeking for the sake of seeking pleasure. On the contrary, this was intensive training for joy. When we practice celebration—real celebration, from a biblical perspective—we find the exact opposite of hedonism. When we merely seek pleasure, we end up following a path of diminishing returns. The things that made us happy last night won't work tonight. We have to constantly raise the stakes.

But when we really celebrate, we find ourselves noticing things today that we did not notice yesterday and taking delight in them. Those things that formerly went unnoticed become catalysts for joy in our lives. Celebration actually exercises our ability to see and feel the goodness of God in small things.

So celebrate! Throw a party. Gather your friends together and rejoice in the fact that you have friends. Thank God for your taste buds, for the availability of creamy, buttery sauces and medium-rare beef. Play your favorite music loudly. Sing along at the top of your lungs. And when someone asks you what in the world you're doing, tell them it's worship. And if they look at you funny, consider that an invitation to tell them about your amazing God.

FRIDAY: Prayer

Narrative

Lord of all things, Your sovereign will and purposes cannot be thwarted by human or demonic opposition. You revealed to Your prophets the things that were to come, and You have been working in history to bring these things to pass just as You predicted and promised. May I have a growing sense of confidence and assurance in all Your promises and rest in the realization that setbacks and opposition and disappointments will not defeat Your purposes for my life. I ask for a broader perspective that sees things in light of eternity and contextualizes the present in light of the ultimate future. May I have a zeal for the things that You have declared to be important and a desire for that which You want to accomplish through me for Your good pleasure. When I am anxious, I will give my burdens back to You and rest in Your assurances.

Orthodoxy

God of glory, in wisdom You have made the heavens and the earth, and nothing is too difficult for You. You rule over the cosmos with its hundreds of billions of galaxies and hold all things together. You created all things for your good pleasure, and the heavens proclaim Your glory, majesty and greatness. Your glory and wisdom are also manifest throughout the manifold flora and fauna of this rich, though bent, world. In spite of the transgression of the Fall and the consequent spread of sin and of death, Your redemptive work will overcome the ravages of sin. Your Word clearly reveals that no amount of human effort could conquer this alienation and bring about peace with You and with humanity. I thank You that You have paid the only price that could bring this about through the redemption that is in Christ Jesus.

Orthopathy

God of wisdom, Your plans and purposes are lofty and unattainable by human comprehension. Even though the world is in rebellion against You, all that You have planned in Your perfect wisdom will be fully accomplished. It amazes me that You will do this through the choices both of those who know You and those who have rebelled against You. You have given me the dignity of being a moral agent whose decisions will matter. I pray that the choices I make would be in conformity with Your good and acceptable will, and I ask that You would clarify Your desires for me through the burdens and aspirations that You implant within me. May I seek Your guidance and power in transforming these burdens into plans that You inspire so that I will honor Your name by accomplishing what You have prepared for me to do.

Orthopraxy

Father of lights, teach me to enjoy You as never before. I want to delight in Your goodness, glory, grace, beauty, perfection, wisdom, justice, holiness, compassion, omniscience, omnipotence, omnipresence, majesty, truth, love, patience, transcendence and immanence. Teach me the wisdom of acknowledging You in all things, including Your often-overlooked tender mercies in the small things of life. May I celebrate Your many gifts and graces and delight in Your will. I affirm that my service to You is perfect freedom and that delighting in You is so much better than delighting in passing things. May I will to do Your will, love the things You love and desire what You desire. Only as I do this will I find the true fulfillment You want for me, because all good things come from You, and in Your right hand there are pleasures forever.

26

Between the Times

Imagine what it would have been like to be born a Hebrew slave in Egypt. For more than 400 years, your people were held captive, forced to follow someone else's orders. You might go home, weary from a long day's work, and hear some old fool telling stories around a campfire about a God who made outlandish promises to your forefather Abraham.

He had promised to make Abraham's descendants into a great nation with a land of their own. He had promised that through Abraham's descendants all nations on earth would be blessed.

But you're one of those descendants and you're a slave in Egypt. You don't feel blessed.

It might have been difficult to believe the promises of this God who seemed so far away. This YHWH didn't seem to mind your pain, your heartache. His promises might have sounded to you like some sort of fairytale, the kind of story you tell children at night before bed.

But you would have been wrong.

Now imagine what it would have been like to be born a Hebrew slave in Persia. For more than 70 years, your people were held captive and forced to follow someone else's orders. Again, you might head home, worn out from the kind of backbreaking labor only slaves have to do, and hear some old woman recounting (again) the stories of Israel's God and the promises He had made to King David.

He had promised that there would always be someone from David's lineage to sit on the throne. He had promised that someone from that lineage would eventually fulfill all the promises He had made to Abraham.

It might have been difficult to trust that God keeps His word, even though you had almost the entire Old Testament story to reflect on. It seemed as if YHWH had turned a deaf ear to the cries of His people. His promises might have sounded like old wives' tales, the kinds of things you teach children in school to remind them to be obedient.

Again you would have been wrong.

Now imagine what it would have been like to be born in between the two testaments of the Christian Bible, in the period often referred to as "the 400 years of silence." You may have lived in Jerusalem, but you were hardly a great nation. You were passed around like a hot potato from one superpower to the next, from Persia to Greece to Rome, with little or no say about your own laws, no foreign policy of your own, forced to pay taxes to a government that practiced the most abominable things imaginable.

The last thing you'd heard from YHWH was some cryptic message about sending the prophet Elijah back to earth and how He would turn the hearts of fathers back to their children and vice versa, or else God Himself would strike the land with a curse.

That was it. After that, nothing but a long, deafening silence for 400 more years. Clearly God was angry, but had He finally had enough? Was this the curse?

It must have been difficult for people to hold on to any kind of belief that God had anything good in store for the children of Abraham. It would have been easy to think that YHWH had given up on them and on His promises.

But once more, you would have been wrong.

TUESDAY: Beliefs

By the time we reach the end of the Old Testament, God's list of promises is so long, it's understandable that people might begin to wonder when or if He's ever going to get around to checking things off the list.

It had been nearly 2,000 years since God told Abraham, "I will bless you . . . and all peoples on earth will be blessed through you" (Gen. 12:2–3). Abraham had been confused about how this would happen because he had no children, but God miraculously intervened and caused Abraham and Sarah to have a baby boy named Isaac. But God's blessing didn't come to the world through him, so that promise was still unfulfilled. It hadn't been broken, but it hadn't been kept yet either.

It had been nearly 1,000 years since God promised King David that one of his descendants would build a house for God and reign forever. David's son Solomon built a spectacular Temple, but that wasn't what God was talking about. That Temple had been destroyed, and the Nation of Israel had been split in two after Solomon's death. Another promise unfulfilled—not broken necessarily, but not kept either.

It had been nearly 600 years since God had told Jeremiah and Ezekiel that He would create a community of people who wouldn't live God's Law out of a sense of obligation but because of an internal desire. Again, this promise was so far from reality that people began to wonder if God would ever make good on His word.

Perhaps you wonder about things like this. Jesus promised to return and set everything right once and for all. But one look at CNN provides enough evidence to know that there's another promise that's been left unfulfilled.

Beyond that, God has promised rest and joy and security to His people. And many of us know what it's like to ache for those promises to be fulfilled in our personal lives. We live with stress and anxiety. Our relationships are fractured. Our health is failing.

We may join others in wondering when or if God will ever see fit to keep His promises.

But here's something to keep in mind: Your circumstances do not reveal God's character. In fact, the challenge of living Christianly in our world is to view our circumstances in light of God's unchanging character.

You see, God is patient (and that's a good thing); He does things in His own sweet time. He makes promises and He keeps them. But He doesn't always keep them when or how we want Him to.

If you think about it for more than a moment, He's got a pretty good track record. He has never broken one of His promises. And the promises He has fulfilled have always exceeded the expectations of people.

Most of the people who have ever lived on this earth have lived during one of the periods of silence or hidden activity. They've lived during the 400 years of Egyptian captivity or during the 70 years of exile or during the 400 years of inter-testamental silence or, like us, between the advents of Christ.

Knowing that we might struggle with His timing, God calls us to live with hope and trust in that which He has promised—in spite of the fact that we don't see it yet. He calls us to look back at His track record. He calls us to look forward to the coming fulfillment of His promises.

God has, in fact, decisively acted in our past. He has made startling promises regarding our future. Only by combining the backward glance with the forward gaze do we have sufficient perspective to live in the now.

WEDNESDAY: Values

"We are a New Testament church producing New Testament Christians."

Ever heard that? The sentiment may not always be expressed in these same words, but it's a prevalent mindset in our time. We spend so little time studying the Bible at all that when we do go to God's Word, we tend to reach for the Gospels or one of Paul's letters (usually the second half of one of Paul's letters; you know . . . the really practical parts). The Old Testament is often relegated to children's Sunday School (where it serves as a good source for morality tales) or adult Bible studies related to biblical prophecy (where it serves as a kind of Oijua board, giving us shadowy clues for the future of our nation and our world).

It hasn't always been this way. Christians throughout the centuries understood the profound sense of unity and harmony between the two testaments. But when Nazi Germany officially forbade the study of the great "Jewish book," it was only reinforcing what many people already thought: *We don't need the Jewish parts; we just need the Christian part.*

Here's the problem with that statement: You can't really be "New Testament" anything without being "Old Testament," too. Just try to understand Hebrews or Revelation without the Old Testament background. When the apostle Paul told Timothy, "All Scripture is God-breathed and is useful for teaching, rebuking, correcting and training in righteousness, so that the man of God may be thoroughly equipped for every good work" (2 Tim. 3:16–17), what "Scripture" do you think he was talking about?

He was talking about what we now call the Old Testament.

To be clear: It is our belief that the Old Testament is incomplete without the New. It is also our belief that the New Testament is incomplete without the Old. Apart from the Old Testament, we have an incomplete understanding of what God is really like. Without the Old Testament, we couldn't understand the origins of our truest problem—our alienation from God and others—and we would have an incomplete understanding of what people are really like.

The Old Testament constantly reminds us that God is the center and source of life. The world does not revolve around us. We are not the center of the universe. The earth is not ours to do with as we see fit. We are given the task of being stewards of God's creation, and our lives are sacred—meaning we belong to God and are set apart by Him for His purposes.

We learn from the Old Testament how life with God actually is, not necessarily how it should be. Its stories are alarmingly real, refusing to gloss over life with all of its humanity and brokenness. Abraham, Jacob, Job, Moses, David, Jeremiah, Jonah—God refuses to wait until a golden boy hero comes along with his perfect teeth and broad shoulders and spotless character. He deals with people as they are, enduring arguments and complaints and wrestling matches and moral failures, and He is not unmoved by our problems.

The Old Testament gives us a history to join and a promise that God doesn't kick us out at the first chance, but chooses instead to enter into a relationship, with all that involves. We know from the Old Testament that we can actually interact with God, that He prefers an honest argument to dishonest compliance.

More than anything, Christians should value the Old Testament because Jesus did. These are the stories He learned and the prophets He quoted. These are the psalms He prayed and the Law He lived.

Without a good understanding of the Old Testament, it is impossible to become like Jesus.

Before you launch into the second half of our book, you might want to pick up your Bible and do some reading from the first half. Read the psalms. Read the Proverbs. Allow yourself to steep in the wisdom of the same Bible Jesus read.

THURSDAY: Actions

We hate to wait.

We don't like lines at the grocery store. We don't like traffic. We don't like conventional ovens. "Take a seat and the doctor will be with you shortly" is among our least favorite sentences—not only because it stretches the definition of the word "shortly" beyond credibility, but because it implies something we don't want to think about: *There are things beyond our control.*

Waiting is so . . . passive. It feels weak. It means we're not in charge of the process.

We hate to wait.

We eat fast food, eschewing restaurants that require us to make a left-hand turn across traffic, scanning drive-thru lanes to see who would be in line ahead of us, trying to predict the likelihood of them being one of those high-maintenance customers who special orders everything and presents the high school student at the window with a coupon and a two-party, out-of-state check that will most certainly require a manager's approval.

We hate to wait.

But we *have* to wait. The message of the Bible, the Old Testament in particular, is this: *There is a God; you are not Him.* Living in-between times, which we do as much as the folks who endured the inter-testamental period of 400 years' worth of silence, forces us to wait.

Are there things that are in your control? Of course. You can choose whether or not you'll keep your wedding vows. You choose how you spend your money. You choose how much television you watch and which programs. You have a lot of say over a lot of things.

But you don't get to say when Jesus comes back. For that, you will simply have to wait.

Should you make good use of your time? Of course. You should be diligent, refusing to live like foolish people (who tend to waste time, killing time). You should live like a wise person, redeeming the time. You should make the most of your time by investing in those things that will last into eternity. But you must recognize that there are a few things out of your control. When you discover one, your best move is to do nothing for a while—to wait, to learn the wisdom of Psalm 46:10: "Be still, and know that I am God."

If you do, you will find out what a blessing it is to have some things that are completely out of your control. More than that, you'll probably find out how trustworthy is the One who holds the future in His hands.

FRIDAY: Prayer

Narrative

Lord in whom I trust, I freely acknowledge that I am often tempted to question Your ways and to wonder why You allow difficult and grievous things to happen not only in my life, but also in the lives of the people I love. But I must also admit that I simply do not have the knowledge or perspective that I would need to understand

Your purposes in these events. When I consider the history of Your people in preparation for the coming of the Messiah, it is remarkable how little of that time they flourished and how many mistakes and enduring consequences dogged their lives and shattered their dreams. But when I see it from the broader perspective of the New Testament, it becomes clear that all of that contributed to a far greater good that will continue into eternity. May I never lose hope in You and Your works.

Orthodoxy

Lord God, in this life I can only see in a mirror dimly and I can only know in part. I cannot know fully just as I have been fully known by You, but the time is coming soon when I will see You face to face. In that glorious day when I stand before You by the grace AND merit of Christ, my questions will be answered and I will be satisfied. I will fully proclaim that You have done all things well. It is good for me, Lord, to reflect on that future reality so that I can contextualize my circumstances in this present darkness. It is also good for me to review Your faithfulness to Your people in the past in spite of their disobedience, and to review Your many blessings and mercies in my own life's journey. Then, as I look back on what You have done and look ahead to what You will do, I will grow in confidence in what You are doing today.

Orthopathy

Dear God, I know that the stories, prophecies and wisdom of the Hebrew Bible are critical for our instruction, so that through perseverance and the encouragement of the Scriptures we might have hope. You have made it evident that we cannot understand Your great Story without the witness of inspired Scripture prior to the coming of the Lord Jesus. May I regularly expose myself to the full counsel of Your Word and drink deeply from the well of both Testaments. I give thanks for the profound wisdom and marvels of Your revelation through the people You inspired, and ask that I would make the time to read, meditate, pray and rest in Your Word so that I will walk in the path of righteousness, trust and obedience. May the life-giving seed of Your truth bear much fruit in and through me.

Orthopraxy

Author and Ruler of all things, I confess that I am often impatient with the processes of life that force me to cease striving and know that You are God and

I am not. My resources, wisdom and power are so bounded that I control very few of the things that happen in my life. I get frustrated and impatient with the challenges and unexpected troubles that crop up so often. But when I think more deeply, I realize that these setbacks and circumstances can accomplish more in my character formation than in having things go my way. It is through such things that patience and forbearance and steadfastness and fortitude are forged by Your wise and loving hands in my life. May I learn to wait on You, to hope in You, to trust in You, to delight myself in You and to unreservedly commit my ways to You.

27

Savior Born

MATTHEW 1:18–25;
LUKE 1:26–38

MONDAY: Story

He probably didn't have wings and a halo. But there was something about him—Mary knew he was an angel.

Mary was young and idealistic. Joseph was a good guy, the kind of man any father would be glad to welcome as a son-in-law. They had their whole lives ahead of them. They would get married, settle down and start having children—in that order.

Or so they thought.

But then came the strange visit from the strange visitor who announced such troubling things. He knew her name, and he said she was going to have a baby . . . but that couldn't be true! She and Joseph were going to wait until after they were married before they . . . you know . . . did the thing that leads to having babies.

Still, this odd person—this angel—said she would have a child, even though she was a virgin. The baby was going to be God's Son, and His conception would have nothing to do with the normal processes.

How in the world was she going to explain this to Joseph?

Joseph—the man with the upstanding reputation—did not take the news well. He didn't get angry and yell at her; he was too much of a good guy for that. But he certainly wasn't going to marry her now. She was damaged goods. Once people found out (and Nazareth was too small a place for them *not* to find out), it would cost him that upstanding reputation.

If he wanted to maintain his status, he would have to dissolve their relationship. There was no need to make a big fuss over it. He could handle this quietly. He didn't want to embarrass her.

But, he may have wondered, *what if she is telling the truth? No, that's crazy! There's no way an angel showed up to a teenage girl in the middle of nowhere to tell her that she's carrying a miracle baby. In Jerusalem? Maybe. In Nazareth? Never.* Joseph decided to sleep on it.

Little did he know that YHWH would invade his dreams, sending a messenger to let him know that Mary was telling the truth. Joseph need not be afraid to marry her, the angel said. He didn't need to worry that Mary had been unfaithful.

And so Joseph and Mary, neither of them knowing how it would all work out, embarked on their journey together.

And you thought your engagement and wedding were stressful!

Together, they would endure the onslaught of insult and ridicule. They would hear the whispers and see the smirks. They would answer the questions they could and ignore the rest. Sometimes they doubted themselves and wondered if they had imagined the whole thing.

But then there was this baby, who became a boy, who became a man who was really a Person who had always existed. And it was all so strange and new and unheard of that it had to be true.

And it was.

TUESDAY: Beliefs

The New Testament opens by re-emphasizing a theme that runs through the Old Testament: *This is God's Story*. He's been writing it since before the beginning. He accomplishes it through bizarre events, miraculous activity and unlikely people. It always exceeds our wildest expectations and stretches the limits of believability.

Mary and Joseph had dreams of their own—dreams they'd been dreaming since before God started meddling in their business. They were modest dreams, to be sure, of raising nice kids and having a nice home.

But then God showed up and invited them into a larger Story, a dangerous Story that would demand more of their time and energy than they could have ever imagined. Signing on to play their roles in this Story would be compelling, but it would also be costly. It promised a greater adventure than they could have found anywhere else—the kind worth living and dying for—but they would have to become supporting characters, rather than stars.

Life is not all about you. Obviously, you're in there. You're significant. Your life has meaning and purpose and all that. But let's be honest about this: There's a much bigger Story playing out around you.

You have a couple of options. You can choose to be the star of your own story. It's a relatively small story with a miniscule budget, and you have to write, direct, produce, act and do your own hair and wardrobe.

It's exhausting just thinking about all that.

Or you can choose to play a supporting role in Someone else's masterpiece; to be precise: God's Story. His story has no beginning and no end; it has an unlimited budget, and the wrap party promises to be something we can't even begin to imagine.

The only problem is that you don't get to be the star.

Of course, it's a much better movie, and—because there's Someone else writing, producing and directing this thing—you don't end up running yourself ragged and driving everyone around you insane.

The greater the story, the larger the narrative, the more able it is to withstand hardships and the more likely it is to answer the foundational questions that keep us up at night. *Where did we come from? Where are we going? How are we to live in the meantime?*

As it turns out, nothing less than this Big Story will really satisfy our deepest longings. What we find when we allow our stories to be absorbed into God's larger Narrative is that we can embed our time into eternity.

The choice is yours. Do you want to star in your own little show? Or do you want to play a supporting role in the greatest Story ever told?

WEDNESDAY: Values

Salvation is free. It costs you absolutely nothing at all. In fact, if you try to pay for your salvation, you'll find yourself on the outside looking in.

In the Bible, there is only one category of people eligible for grace: the humble. That's kind of the point. You have to humble yourself in order to receive the grace of God that brings about your salvation.

But there's so much more involved in the gospel than just that. God has saved you for a purpose. He has a plan for you. He wants you to partner with Him in the redemption of the whole world. He wants to change the course of human history through you—through the money you give, the time you invest, the conversations you have, the talents you use.

God's got something for you, something far greater than anything you could ever imagine on your own.

Yet what God has in mind for you will cost you something. It may cost you everything. Of course, it will be worth the price tag. You'll find yourself repaid in spades. You'll look back on life and wish you'd invested even more. And this is how it should be; anything worthwhile is costly. The higher the potential reward, the greater the upfront costs usually are. It's this way in your personal finances. It's this way in your relationships. It's this way just about everywhere in life.

How badly do you want to see God's plans come to fruition? Badly enough to pay the price? Badly enough to make sacrifices and do without in the short-term for the sake of long-term gain?

Think of Mary and Joseph. They were members of God's Chosen People. They didn't have to do anything to achieve that status. God graciously endowed them with that blessing.

But then He invited them into something deeper, something richer, something heavier. He invited them to participate in His Story, to play major roles in furthering His purposes in a powerful way. Accepting His invitation would cost them everything—their reputations, their standing in the community. They would be ridiculed. Their families would be embarrassed. Their children would grow up with a stigma.

And still they said yes.

Salvation is absolutely free; that's one of the things the Incarnation is about.

But furthering the plotline of God's unfolding Story—actually *playing a part* in that Story—can be a very costly endeavor. Are you willing to pay that price?

THURSDAY: Actions

God always takes the initiative. He is the Prime Mover, the Uncaused Cause. He banged the Big Bang, lit the fuse that eventually exploded everything into existence. He set the dominoes up and knocked the first one down.

We are given the honor of responding to Him—without coercion, without manipulation, without any strings attached.

God initiates; then He waits for us to respond.

YHWH comes to a childless old man and calls him to leave his homeland. Then He waits to see if Abram will say yes.

YHWH comes to a fugitive in the desert and calls him to go back to his homeland. Then He waits to see if Moses will say yes.

YHWH comes to a young boy tending sheep for his family and calls him to become the next king of Israel. Then He waits to see if David will say yes.

Think of it: the astonishing humility of a God who waits for a response rather than forcing one, who places His plan into the hands of inconsistent and inadequate people, promising His assistance if they seek it.

YHWH comes to a young woman in a backwater village and calls her to bear a child who will be the Savior of the world. Will Mary say yes?

YHWH comes to a frightened and embarrassed carpenter and calls him to raise a son who will never truly be his. Will Joseph say yes?

They could have said no. Abram could have stayed where he was. Moses could have ignored that burning bush. David could have stayed out there with the sheep. Mary could have run away from the angel. Joseph could have divorced her quietly.

God did not force His plan on any of them.

But if they had said no, think of what they would have missed!

God has a plan, and He will see to it that it comes all the way to fruition. He does not need your help, but He invites you into the Story as a way of honoring you. You don't have to do it. He can find someone else.

But if you say no, think of what you might miss!

If you listen closely, you may just hear the voice of YHWH calling you (not as unlikely as you might think) to something extraordinary, placing a portion of His plan into your inconsistent and inadequate hands, promising His assistance if you seek it.

FRIDAY: Prayer

Narrative

O Lord, You are the God of the unexpected. Often when I think I have a clear idea where my life is heading, You intervene in surprising and creative ways. When this happens, I am reminded again that my field of vision is so bounded that I can only see as far as the first bend in the road ahead. You have said that my faith in You is the assurance of things hoped for, the conviction of things not seen. When I hope in You, I hope in what I do not yet see, and I pray that I will persevere in waiting eagerly for the realization of all that You have promised. To trust in what You call me to do and to obey Your direction often does not make sense in the eyes of the world. Nevertheless, having come to faith in Christ Jesus, I know that I have no other viable option than to echo Mary's words: *Behold, the bondslave of the Lord; may it be done to me according to Your word.*

Orthodoxy

God of might, majesty and dominion, when I consider the billions of people on Planet Earth, it is difficult to conceive how You could want to be intimately involved in the lives of all people who would welcome You now and in ages past. Yet Your Word reveals that this is somehow so, and that You want us to live our little stories in light of Your Story in human history, the greatest Story ever told. Rather than playing the lead role in a self-made drama, I choose to play a supporting role in the great Narrative that begins and ends with You, the Alpha and the Omega, the Beginning and the End, the First and the Last. Only in this way can I be assured that it will end well, not as a tragedy, but as a part of the Divine Comedy. May I embed my life in Yours and do all things with the holy ambition of being pleasing to You.

Orthopathy

Father, may I never live my Christian life carelessly or casually. May I never compartmentalize my faith through the blunder of drawing a thick line between the secular and the spiritual. All of life becomes spiritual when I do even the most mundane things for the sake of Christ. May I grow in the wisdom of welcoming You into all the facets and details of my life, so that whatever I do will be for You. May I find the pleasure of surrendering to Your Story and relating everything to Your desires and purposes. Then I will know the holy relief of being carried by You rather than trying to strive on my own. I want to humble myself under Your mighty hand and cast all of my anxieties on You, knowing that You care for me and always want what is truly best for me. I acknowledge Your goodness and thank You for Your grace, mercy and compassion.

Orthopraxy

Lord God, You are the sovereign, majestic and transcendent Ruler of all things, whether visible or invisible, past or present. The angelic hosts of heaven serve You continually and go to and fro to accomplish Your perfect will. You have established Your throne in the heavens and Your sovereignty is over all. Nevertheless, You are also immanent and intimate in the lives of those who respond to Your loving initiatives, and You give us the incredible dignity of participating in Your purposes. I know that there is nothing I can contribute to You as though You lacked anything; yet You invite me to participate in what You are doing and be a part of the eternal things You are bringing about. May I always will to do Your will and receive what You invite me to do as my greatest good.

28

A Baby

MATTHEW 2:1–12;
LUKE 2:1–20;
JOHN 1:1–14

MONDAY: Story

God does a lot of things—many of them seem strange to our admittedly limited perspective. Without a doubt, the single most unsettling, irrational, illogical thing He has ever done is come to earth *as a baby*!

If God came to earth as a fully-grown man, we might understand that a little better. If He came to earth as an angel, a ghost, an apparition or a disembodied voice, it might make more sense or fit our expectations a little better.

But a *baby*? He was totally helpless! He couldn't feed Himself or talk or walk or control His own bladder. And have you ever been to a birth? There's blood and sweat and mucous and screaming . . . and that's just the dads! The whole process is uncomfortable, to say the least. It's unseemly. It's unsanitary. As much as we may not want to admit it, birth—for all of its wonder and amazement—is a yucky process.

This is how God chose to enter the world.

He could have chosen any way He wanted—something miraculous and exceptional, regal and majestic. But He chose the ordinary way.

Worse than that, He chose the *peasant's* way. He could have chosen a major city with doctors, nurses or midwives and their sterilized equipment. Instead, He chose a barn in a backwater town with nothing but a carpenter's rough and calloused hands to usher Him into the world. There were more animals than people looking on.

We would understand if royal officials were there eagerly awaiting His arrival. But no one important showed up save a few dirty shepherds—oh, and some strange men from the East several months later.

It doesn't make much sense to many people—the God of the universe humbling Himself in such a way, emptying Himself of so much for so little in return. But the Bible leads us to believe that this is exactly the way God wanted it.

A young couple, miles from home, are unable to find a decent place to sleep. They are forced to spend the night in a stable when she goes into labor, where she delivers a baby that has already caused so much pain and will cause even more in His attempt to bring true peace, true healing, true joy. She wraps Him in strips of cloth to keep Him warm as her husband makes room in the feed trough. They are both unaware that, even now, magi are headed their way from afar and shepherds are receiving the shock of their lives in the form of a heavenly chorus.

This is our God, this tiny baby with fists for hands and squinting eyes, depending on and trusting in two scared newlyweds for His survival. He risks everything in order to rescue the people who have never been able to keep their promises to Him.

The storyline doesn't make much sense to us because it is we who are so out of synch with the way things ought to be.

TUESDAY: Beliefs

Question: If you were a shepherd 2,000 years ago and were outside watching the sheep one night when an angel showed up with a message from God, well . . . what would you do?

Answer: *Panic!*

Shepherds were not highly regarded in those times. It wasn't considered a very noble profession. You practically lived outside with animals (*stupid* animals, at that). You were constantly coming into contact with . . . animal stuff.

"Unclean" was not merely a description—it was a condition. Shepherds were unclean hygienically *and* ceremonially. They weren't allowed to testify in court. They weren't allowed in the synagogues or the Temple. Ironically, the lambs they helped come into the world—the very animals that would be sacrificed for Passover—rendered them unfit to make sacrifices in the Temple.

So what must they have thought when they saw the angel? They probably thought, *Oh, no! What did we do now?*

They had been told that God didn't like unclean people, so they might have assumed the angel was there to tell them God was mad at them—or worse. Maybe God had finally reached His limit with all the uncleanness in the world and was ready to do something about it—starting with them!

But instead the angel began with these words: "Fear not." It's a familiar refrain if you've read much about angels, who were always having to preface their conversations with people this way.

"God's not angry," the angel continued. "In fact, I've got Good News for everybody—even dirty shepherds like you. You know all the stuff that's wrong with the world, all that stuff you wish could get fixed but looks hopeless? Well, God's going to do something about it. He's sending Someone to save the day. This Savior is also going to be the King. You can go see Him now if you want. Here's how you'll know Him when you see Him . . ."

Okay, wait. Don't hurry on here.

If you're that shepherd, how do you think that sentence should end? Think about it: This is the one sent from Almighty God to turn everything that is upside-down right-side-up. This Guy is supposed to deliver. He's going to be the greatest King you've ever seen. How will you know Him when you find Him?

"He'll be wrapped in satin and lying in a hand-carved ivory crèche. In His hand will be a golden rattle and in His mouth will be a silver spoon." Right?

Wrong!

"He'll be wrapped in rags, lying in a feed trough, surrounded by stinky animals—kind of like one of your kids would be." In other words, here's how you'll know the Messiah when you see Him: *You'll find Him in the middle of a big mess.*

The whole reason this is Good News—to the shepherds that night and to us right now—is that we're all messy people. Every night, people appear on television (under the label "News") and tell us how the world got a little messier today. We manage to mess up every single area of life: relationships, finances, work, family, the environment, the Church (especially there), our consciences, our habits.

There's not a single place we haven't managed to mess up. And we can't seem to fix any of it. Try as we may, we cannot put Humpty together again.

So the angel says, "Here's the Good News: God is not afraid of your mess."

Our God doesn't care how messy your life is. It couldn't be any messier than His was. He was born in a mess—wrapped in rags, laid in a manger—and He died in a mess—stripped of His rags, hung on a cross. And in between His first day and His last day, He mostly spent time with messy people.

We make Christmas really pretty, with red velvet bows and evergreen branches and all that. But the real story of Christmas proves that you don't have to clean up for Him. Cleanliness, it turns out, is far from godliness. If anything, it's in the middle of our messiness that He shows up.

WEDNESDAY: Values

When we talk about the birth of Jesus, we always turn to Luke's or Matthew's Gospels. That's where we read about angels and shepherds, a star and a stable, wise men and visitations. That's where all the familiar images of Christmas have their origin. Mark's Gospel skips the beginning and starts in the middle of the story. John's Gospel goes too far back, to before the beginning of anything, and is hard to read and understand. John and Mark don't get much play during December. They don't smell enough like a stable.

But by the time he wrote his Gospel, the apostle John had had a lifetime to reflect on the events surrounding the life of Jesus. He had been the one asked to look after Mary, Jesus' mother, so (assuming she had become part of his family) they must have spent time talking about Jesus' birth and all the craziness surrounding it. Her face, her laugh, the way she turned phrases—these things may have been reminders to John of what Jesus was like.

When John finally sat down to write his version of the story, he must have thought about where to begin. His mind must have played and replayed the details of that night in Bethlehem. Instead of starting there, though, he went beyond it and beneath it. His version begins by telling us about the One called the Word and how this Word came into a dark and dying world. In fact, as we read through the prologue to John's Gospel (1:1–14), two words surface more than any others: *light* and *life*.

Jesus is many things to many people, but to John He was Light and Life. The apostle must have remembered where Jesus was standing and what He sounded like when He referred to Himself by those words.

"In him was life," John wrote (v. 4). Jesus wasn't just alive; *He was Life.* Life was in Him. More than just a being with a beating heart and contracting lungs, Jesus produced beating hearts and contracting lungs. He was Life, so Life was His to give. John's Gospel reminds us that giving life was what Jesus had come to do. Jesus was the bringer of life.

"That life was the light of men," John continued. What was going through John's mind as he read back over his own words? He could recall watching men and women who were dark and full of death coming to Jesus, and then seeing how one touch, one word from Him sent them away forever changed—forever filled with the Light and Life of the One who came to conquer our fear of death and beat back the darkness. He could remember how that Light broke into his own darkness with a simple question: "What do you want?" Jesus had asked (see John 1:38).

Life and Light . . . that was Jesus.

There *is* a little inkling of the birth to be found in John's Gospel after all. It is one short sentence, but it says as much as Matthew or Luke do (without the gory details): "The light shines in the darkness, and the darkness has not overcome it" (v. 5).

This verse should be read before Matthew and Luke. It prepares us to receive the full version of the story. The Light that is Jesus shines in, around, through, behind, beneath, beyond the darkness of the manger, the darkness of the stable, the darkness of the world, the darkness of our own hearts.

And yet we still do not understand it any more than the shepherds or the wise men did. Who can grasp this idea of Light and Life being contained in a body?

Like those first witnesses to the Christ-child, we are left to worship, adore and ponder the mystery. We pray for His Life to come to life in us. And we ask for His Light to shine forth from our hearts forever.

THURSDAY: Actions

Think back to the most comfortable place you've ever been. Remember the warm sun or the soothing sounds, the aroma of fresh-baked bread or roasting meat over an open fire, the knowledge that everything is under control or that there's not one thing to worry about. Have you ever been waited on hand and foot, surrounded by people telling you how wonderful you look, how wonderful you smell, how wonderful you are?

Label that place "A."

Now, have you ever been to a working dairy farm? Remember those smells and those sights? You have to watch your step everywhere you go, and you might not want to touch anything unless you're wearing gloves. Have you ever seen a feeding trough? The edges of them tend to be smooth because of all the cow tongues that have lapped up every kernel of corn and grain and table scrap. Did we mention that cows do their business standing up, often while eating? The very fact that you are looking at a cattle trough means you're probably standing in the waste created by the cattle. (We're trying to be delicate.)

Okay, label that place "B."

In one moment, Jesus went from the most comfortable and beautiful place that has ever and will ever exist to one of the grossest, germiest places you can imagine. From A to B in a heartbeat.

Have you ever seen a baby being born? It's not exactly a noble way to enter the world. Even with the best medical attention and technology, it's a gross thing to watch. When Jesus was born, there weren't any nurses or doctors with sterilized instruments and medicine, no clean linen or machines that go "ping!" to assure you that everything's going to be okay.

There were just two peasants in a cave among the flies, barnyard animals and manure. When God was born, they wrapped Him in strips of cloth and laid Him in a feed trough. The Author of Life, the King of kings, the Prince of peace lying there among the spittle and leftover feed.

That's the Incarnation.

That's grace.

Before He spoke a word, He built a bridge. He came from heaven to earth to make a way for us to get from earth to heaven. That's what we mean when we say that Jesus built a bridge. He brought us grace, and without grace there's no salvation. Without grace, there's no hope. Without grace, there's nothing beyond the grave except misery and punishment and the full extent of our human depravity without restraint in one, unending, monotonous, tortuous eternity.

That's where we were headed. And that's where we'd still be headed if it weren't for Jesus and the grace He provides. He built a bridge to make a way back for us to return to our heavenly Father. And after He built that bridge and demonstrated its ability to return us home, He turned on a light. After He came in humility, awkwardly learning to walk and talk and navigate life in our world, He asked us to humble ourselves, awkwardly learning to walk and talk and navigate life in His world.

He could ask us then.

He had earned the right.

That's the length to which He was willing to go for our sakes.

How far are you willing to go for His sake, and for the benefit of others?

FRIDAY: Prayer

Narrative

Father God, I marvel at the mystery of the Incarnation. It is utterly unique in the history of the world—the God-Man, the eternal Logos become flesh, the self-emptying of the Lord and Creator of all in order to become one of us. The radical and profound measures You took in order to save Your people from their sins and bring about a reconciliation with those who were alienated from You amazes me. The story of the first Advent is so marvelous that no one but You could have conceived of it. The weakness and vulnerability of the One who holds the cosmos together is incomprehensible. Having made the world, He came into the world, knowing that He would be betrayed, rejected and crucified by the people He came to save. I praise and magnify Your Name, thanking You for Your indescribable gift.

Orthodoxy

Dear Lord, I praise and bless Your Name for the boundless magnitude of Your love in sending Your Son to be the Lamb of God who takes away the sins of the world. He endured degradation, malice, betrayal, mocking and an agonizing and ignominious death so that we, who would have no hope of being acceptable to You, could receive Your forgiving and welcoming embrace. I thank You that there are no preconditions and qualifications that we are required to achieve before coming to Christ. Instead, we can come to You as we are in all our uncleanness and corruption, and humbly receive the gift of life that we could never merit. I am grateful that whoever will call on the name of the Lord will be saved. May I always be thankful for Your glorious gift and recall the awful price You paid to make it possible to bestow.

Orthopathy

Lord of Life and Light, I rejoice in the fact that the Word became flesh and dwelt among us, displaying the glory of the only begotten from the Father, full of grace and truth. We enter into this fallen world with physical life that begins to decay early, but You sent Your Son so that we could receive a new and enduring kind of life, the spiritual life of the new birth in Jesus. Now the wellspring of life indwells all who have received Him, so that as the Word became flesh when He came into the world, so the Word becomes alive in the people He has redeemed and adopted. May I glorify You by displaying that new life that now indwells me, so that people will see the beauty of Christ in me. As a bearer of His life and light, may I share it with the people You have sovereignly commissioned me to love and serve.

Orthopraxy

Lord Jesus, You have gone to such amazing lengths to make it possible for us to have life in You. You have transferred me from a condition of depravity, alienation, futility, emptiness and hopelessness to an entirely new position of purity, fellowship, meaning, fullness and hope. I give thanks for Your grace, in which You exchanged the boundless glory and majesty of heaven for the poverty and suffering of earth. Your poverty has made me rich; Your love has lifted me up; Your grace has given me hope; Your suffering has given me life. I thank You and bless Your Name, the Name which is above every name, at which all who are in heaven and on earth and under the earth will bow and acknowledge that You are Lord. You have called me to a life of fullness and purpose as I derive these from Your life in and through me.

29

A Real Live Human God

MATTHEW 2:13–23;
LUKE 2:21–52

As Jesus grew up, He increased in wisdom and in favor with God and other people. That's all we know for sure. Everything else is speculation.

Did He play tag with other children? Did He scrape His knee and run to His mother? Did He wrestle with His younger brothers? Did He ever notice the girl next door and her sparkling eyes?

We don't know.

He grew taller and wiser, and He had a way with people. He had a good relationship with YHWH. That's what we know.

Jesus was born while the family was on the road, and there was something of a commotion immediately after the blessed event of His birth. Angels sang and shepherds came out of the woodwork with a crazy story. Strange travelers from the East showed up to worship the newborn King of the Jews, sending the current king of the Jews into a jealous tirade. Babies were killed—at least a few. The family had to relocate to Egypt until the whole thing blew over.

When they returned, they settled in a town called Nazareth, in the hill country of Galilee. Jesus was—in some respects—a hillbilly. Probably had a funny accent and everything!

He would have gone to school, learning to read and write, memorizing portions of the Torah (the Jewish Law). The educational system in His neck of the woods was pretty good. He spent time reading and pondering words from Deuteronomy (more on that next week), and a fair amount of time meditating on the psalms. From an early age, He had a keen understanding of things, a way of asking questions nobody had thought about. He listened well and gave thoughtful answers when He was questioned.

Once, He got lost in the big city of Jerusalem. His parents were frantic, but Jesus didn't panic. He told them, "You should have known where to find Me" (see Luke 2:49). But sometimes parents just don't understand—not even the parents of the Messiah!

He would have learned a trade from His father, carpentry (probably including masonry of a sort). He and His father may have participated in the construction of a huge amphitheater in the city of Sepphoris, a few miles away from their home in Nazareth. (When Jesus was a teenager, maybe younger, a man named Judas broke into an arsenal in Sepphoris and led a revolt. When the Romans found out about it, they captured Judas and crucified him, showing everyone in Galilee what happens when a hillbilly dares to stand up to them.[1])

That's all we know. Mostly what stands out about Jesus' childhood is how normal it was. He was born. He went to school. He learned a trade. Nothing really remarkable about any of that.

Except for this one thing: He was God in a human body.

TUESDAY: Beliefs

Faster than a speeding bullet. More powerful than a locomotive. Able to leap tall buildings in a single bound. Look! Up in the sky! It's a bird. It's a plane. It's ... Jesus! Yes, it's Jesus—strange visitor from another planet who came to earth with powers and abilities far beyond those of mortal men. Jesus, who can change the course of mighty rivers, bend steel with His bare hands and who—disguised as a mild-mannered carpenter from a tiny village in Galilee—fights the never-ending battle for Truth, Justice and the American Way.

Okay, Jesus was one of a kind. There's no debating that here. Jesus was the Son of God, the only begotten Son of God, totally unique, preexisting, eternal member of the Trinity.

And yet . . . Jesus was not Superman.

The first heresy of the Early Church was that some people thought Jesus only *seemed* to be a real flesh-and-blood person. But the Bible goes to great lengths to correct this misperception (see 1 John 4:2). Jesus fully entered into humanity. He really did become a human being. He got physically fatigued. He endured physical pain. He experienced emotion.

One of the few things we know about Jesus' childhood is that He "increased in wisdom and stature, and in favor with God and men" (Luke 2:52). Jesus *increased* in wisdom? What does that imply?

Jesus was God—let's be clear about that. However, when He came to earth, He fully embraced human limitations. He could no longer be everywhere at once (He wasn't omnipresent). He willingly gave up His power to do anything He wanted (He was no longer omnipotent). He surrendered the knowledge of certain things (He was not omniscient).

He wasn't faking His humanity.

The writer of Hebrews says that Jesus became like us in every way (see Heb. 2:17; 4:15). He was not the Six-Million Dollar Man with a computerized brain, supersonic hearing and bionic limbs. He was not impervious to the limitations that accompany humanity. He was not the Man of Steel with a microchip in His head. He was physically and mentally limited. He knew human existence . . . but He knew it without sin.

Here's why that's so important: You can never become like Superman. You can never learn to fly or concentrate hard enough to have X-ray vision. But you *can* become like Jesus.

Jesus is more than our Savior and our Lord. He's not just a teacher. He is a model of what life can be like when it's fully surrendered to the power of the Holy Spirit.

Jesus did what He did because He was filled with the Spirit (see Matt. 12:28; Luke 3:21–22; 4:18–19; Acts 10:38). This means something absolutely astonishing for those of us who follow Him: *It is actually possible for us to live like He did, to live a life totally surrendered to and empowered by the Spirit of God.* This means that we are able to carry out God's plans, to continue the mission Jesus began during His earthly life and ministry. We are able to live in harmony with God, in touch with His power.

WEDNESDAY: Values

Jesus had a body—a flesh-and-blood, physical body with a heart, two lungs, kidneys, a spleen . . . the works. He had teeth and a tongue, a digestive tract and all that goes with it. He ate. He drank. He slept. He worked with His hands and He walked on His feet. He sweated. He bathed. He blew his nose. He sniffed and He scratched and He spat on the ground.

This isn't grossing you out, is it?

Jesus was a man with a body, and it's high time we take His physical presence seriously . . . because if a body was good enough for Jesus, it ought to be good enough for us.

The very first heresy the Early Church encountered wasn't that Jesus was only a human and not God. The first heretical development was called *docetism*, and docetists believed that because Jesus was God, He couldn't really be human. They believed that matter—the stuff your body is made of—is inherently evil.

But the writers of the New Testament want to make it clear that "the Word became flesh" (John 1:14). That's an affirmation of matter. "Jesus grew in wisdom and stature" (Luke 2:52, NIV). He grew up in a body, hit puberty. His voice probably cracked. He grew hair in all the appropriate places.

Let's not shy away from this. Let's celebrate this. The Son of God didn't just create the physical world (see Col. 1:16); He became part of it. There's no stronger affirmation of matter than that. There is no room for some kind of over-spiritualized notion that this physical world doesn't matter, none of that nonsense about "spiritual" things being prioritized over mere "physical" things. God made matter and called it good, no less than seven times in the very first chapter of the Bible. If matter is good enough for Him, then (whether we acknowledge it or not) it is plenty good for us, too.

Has matter been corrupted? You better believe it has! But despite how cosmic the ramifications of the Fall are, they are not enough to eradicate the inherent goodness of God's creation. Besides, God's plan is to eventually redeem it all, to restore creation to its original, pristine state.

> This is my Father's world—
> O let me ne'er forget
> That though the wrong seems oft so strong,
> God is the Ruler yet.
> This is my Father's world!

The battle is not done;
Jesus who died shall be satisfied,
And earth and heav'n be one.[2]

Let's not disparage God's physical creation with all its physical inhabitants of various physiques. Let's cultivate it and enjoy it properly, giving thanks to the Father, from whom all of these good gifts come!

THURSDAY: Actions

Jesus grew in wisdom and stature, and in favor with God and men.

Now, most of us have reached a place where our stature is what it is. We're as tall as we're going to get; in fact, some of us have reached the place where it's starting to go the other way. At some point, we just can't grow any taller. So let's take stature out of the equation for a minute.

Jesus grew in wisdom and in favor with God and men.

Those are three pretty good target growth areas: wisdom, favor with God, favor with men.

Jesus grew in wisdom. He always made the wise choice and frequently cited biblical passages as explanations for His behavior. He didn't quote Scripture in some rote, mechanical sort of way; He actually understood how to apply to His own life verses that had been written hundreds of years before His birth. (And it's a safe assumption that He didn't quote the Bible because He was there when it was written; He quoted it because He had actually spent time studying it, thinking about it, memorizing and meditating on it.)

Jesus grew in His ability to see the true nature of things from God's perspective. His actions were informed by a deep understanding of His heavenly Father's nature and desire. Maybe you could stand to grow in wisdom, too—not just your Bible knowledge, but your ability to see things from God's perspective and act accordingly.

Jesus grew in favor with God. The writer of Hebrews tell us that "without faith it is impossible to please God" (11:6). Just after Jesus was baptized, God said, "This is my Son, whom I love; with him I am well pleased" (Matt. 3:17). We can infer from reading these verses in tandem that Jesus must have had faith. Growing in faith is linked to growing in favor with God.

But how does one grow in faith? Well, there are several different methods. You can read a book like this one and see how faithful God has been over the centuries. You can get together with a group of other people and ask them for stories about how God has been faithful to them. Or—and this is probably the best bet—you can test Him out and see what happens. What happens when you follow His advice for money-management? What happens when you follow His advice for marriage? What happens when you follow His advice for living?

Jesus grew in faith because He learned just how faithful His heavenly Father could be if Jesus totally trusted Him and followed His will. Maybe you could stand to grow in favor with God, too—not just in your level of obedience, but also in your level of trust in the God who knows how things are supposed to operate.

Finally, Jesus grew in favor with others. He followed the Golden Rule: "Do unto others as you would have them do unto you." He honored others, treating them with dignity when others did not. He touched lepers. He taught women. He hung out with hookers and IRS agents. He answered their questions and went to their parties.

Jesus was the most righteous human being who ever lived, but He had not a trace of self-righteousness about Him. He was approachable in a way that His followers have not imitated often enough. The most important person to Jesus seemed to be the person who was right in front of Him. For many of us, the person right in front of us is just in our way.

Jesus treated others with love, kindness and respect. He redefined the Golden Rule so that now we are called to treat others *the way He has treated us.* Maybe you could stand to grow in favor with others, too—not just treating people well to get something in return from them, but treating others the way Jesus has treated you.

FRIDAY: Prayer

Narrative

Lord God, You are the God of the extraordinary in the ordinary, of heaven on earth. When Your Son took on human flesh and pitched His tent in our midst, He became one of us and genuinely experienced the human condition from the inside out. He showed us what it is like to be fully human, and He did this in innumerable small things as He prepared for His public ministry. In the same way, You teach me to glorify You in whatever I do, even in the most mundane areas of life. You call me to honor You in the way I listen and speak to people, in the way I do my work, in the way I relate to my family and friends, and in the way I think and choose. Even the most routine tasks can become great when done in Your Name. May I seek to practice Your presence not only in the big issues of life, but also in the small and often overlooked areas.

Orthodoxy

Heavenly Father, You have chosen us to obey Jesus Christ by the sanctifying work of the Holy Spirit. In Christ, You have granted us everything we need to manifest the fullness of life that is empowered by Your indwelling Spirit. I know that it is impossible to live out the spiritual life in my own resources and power and that only as I abide in Jesus and walk by the Spirit is it possible for me to display a life of godliness and righteousness. As I live by the Spirit, may I bear the fruit of love, joy, peace, patience, kindness, goodness, faithfulness, gentleness and self-control. May I be strengthened with power through Your indwelling Spirit so that I can live a life that will be pleasing to You and edifying to others. May the love of Christ overflow in my thoughts, words and deeds this very day.

Orthopathy

God of all creation, You have embedded me in a physical existence on a planet perfectly fine-tuned for life that orbits just the right kind of star in just the right kind of galaxy. But more extraordinary than all the wonders of the hundreds of billions of galaxies with their hundreds of billions of stars is the human body. We are fearfully and wonderfully made, a marvel of Your handiwork. I thank You for the mysteries of human existence and the ability You have given me in Christ to present to You the members of my body as instruments of righteousness. And though in this life I am subject to the conditions of the curse, I know I can anticipate resurrected life in a body that will be conformed to the Body of the glorious resurrected Christ. May I use the opportunities You have given me in this life to accomplish what will endure in the next.

Orthopraxy

Dear Lord, just as Jesus is Your beloved Son with whom You are well-pleased, so I also want to be pleasing to You as Your beloved child. May I pursue the wisdom of treasuring relationships above all other goods, and may I put You uniquely above all relationships. It is as I love You more than others that I will be empowered to love them more. May I learn to know You better through meditation on Your Word and through the actions of trusting obedience. May

I learn to acknowledge You in all things and to welcome You into my thoughts, decisions and actions throughout the day. And may I learn to be an other-centered person who expresses the fullness of life in Christ in the way I treat people with kindness and concern. Empower me to edify, encourage and exhort others to enjoy a closer relationship with You.

30

Wilderness

MATTHEW 3–4:11; LUKE 3:1–22; 4:1–13

MONDAY: Story

John the Baptist seemed, to the watching world, a crazy man. Unkempt. Unshaven. He ate God only knows what—locusts, bugs, wild honey (maybe even the camel whose skin he wore as a coat). He called people names, telling them that they needed to turn back and get right with God. He must have looked as strange to them as that guy who stands shouting outside U2 concerts and basketball games. You know the guy—the one with the "Turn or Burn" placards.

The Baptizer attracted a following, though. And people came from miles around to see the spectacle of a man set on fire for God, burning from the inside out with a message he absolutely had to deliver.

John's cousin Jesus had lived a quiet life. He burst onto the scene 30 years or so before, but hadn't yet lived up to all that potential. (How do you live up to your potential when a chorus of angels shows up at your birth and announces that you're the One who will bring peace on earth? The bar was set pretty high.) Jesus hadn't done much to confirm John's suspicions that the angels might have been right.

Still, there had always been something about Jesus. There was that time in the Temple when He was 12—when He confounded the brightest religious scholars of the day with His insights. But after that, He seemed content to stay in Nazareth, working with His dad, providing for their family.

Until now.

Now here He is, all of a sudden, demanding that John baptize Him. John's dumbfounded, just like his dad had been all those years ago (see Luke 1:5–25).

"Me? Baptize *You?* You must be kidding! If anything, You should baptize me."

"Just do it, okay, John? It'll make sense later."

Down He goes. Up He comes. Something comes out of the sky like a bird. It lands right on Him, and then a Voice from nowhere says something probably no one besides Jesus could really understand.

And then He's gone, into the wilderness by Himself for 40 full days. Not eating. Fasting. Praying. Thinking.

The wilderness had long been thought of as a place of testing. It certainly is for Jesus. There in the sparse, dry countryside He faces down the devil, proving that God and His Word are more than a match for the most evil forces in our world. Not once but three times, Satan himself comes at Jesus, doing his crafty best to trip Him up. Not once but three times, Jesus uses the book of Deuteronomy to fend off the evil one's attacks.

Satan leaves, a defeated enemy. He's down but he's not out—not yet, at least. He's got a plan, and he's content to bide his time. Jesus has won this round, but will He have what it takes when the pressure gets a little more intense?

TUESDAY: Beliefs

Ancient Greeks loved power. They loved to talk about power and think about power—specifically what they would do if they had absolute power! For them, power was the highest attribute of all, greater than anything else. They idealized this love of and longing for power in their gods. When it came to gods, power was more important than morality.

The Greeks reasoned that if a god were to submit to a code of morality, then that god would be inferior to that code or whoever might enforce that code or whoever codified the code in the first place. And a god couldn't be inferior to anything.

So the gods in Greek mythology periodically broke their promises, just to prove that they could do whatever they wanted and no one could say a word to them about it. They were capricious. They said they'd do one thing but then did another. They flexed their muscles just to prove who was in charge. They were unstable and unpredictable. They threw a lightning bolt down on some poor, unsuspecting mortal just because. They made laws, and then they broke their laws. And if you questioned them on it, they sent a pox on your house for questioning them.

But the God of the Bible isn't like the Greek gods. The very fact that YHWH approached Abraham with a covenant promise meant that God was intentionally willing to limit His power. In making a promise, God eliminated a great deal of possible actions on His part. God could no longer *not* bless Abraham's descendants. He committed Himself to a particular course of action.

For the God of the Bible, the willing restraint of power—in other words, *humility*—is an even greater attribute than the possession of absolute power.

An immature person feels the need to constantly flex and parade his power to impress people. A mature and differentiated person feels comfortable enough to practice self-control. There is no better example of this principle than the life of Jesus. In the story of His temptation in the wilderness, we can clearly see His determination to maintain His self-imposed limitations.

Think of it: Satan tries to get Jesus to do three simple things, things that would not have been difficult for Him. "Turn stones into bread. If You can make stones out of nothing, how hard would it be to change them into something different? If You're really all that powerful, c'mon . . . show me Your muscles."

But Jesus refuses.

"Okay, throw Yourself off the top of the Temple. Prove to everyone that You're not subject to the laws of gravity or cause-and-effect like everyone else. You know God's not going to let His Son die like that. If You're really who You say You are, prove it."

But Jesus refuses.

"Okay . . . if You won't prove it to me, I'll prove it to You. I have the power to transfer power over all the kingdoms of the earth to anyone I choose. Wanna see? Wanna see me flex my muscles?"

Once more, Jesus refuses.

Jesus understands that people don't need a God who can flex His muscles for His own benefit. People need a God who will keep His promises and use His power for *their* benefit.

Ancient Greeks loved power.

YHWH loves people.

WEDNESDAY: Values

There were no eyewitnesses to Jesus' temptation in the wilderness. It was just Jesus and Satan out there, two cosmic warriors duking it out in the barren landscape.

Yet we can read about it all in the Gospels of Matthew and Luke.

So how did the story get out?

Jesus must have told His followers about it; how else could they have known? Jesus thought it was important for them to know this story, so He told them. Then the Holy Spirit thought it was important for us to know about it, so He told Matthew and Luke to write it down.

And that brings up an interesting point: There are things about this Story (the one God has invited us to be a part of) that we could never figure out on our own. There are things about the God who created us and redeemed us that we could never figure out in a million years unless He clued us in.

So He did.

And that's important.

God does not want to keep us in the dark (though it may sometimes feel as if He does). He wants us to understand some things about Him. He wants to see us live well and thrive. He is not content to hide in the shadows, allowing only those who endure hardship and adversity to approach Him. Rather, He takes the initiative to reveal Himself to us so that we can enjoy the relationship with Him that He so badly desires.

The apostle John wrote, "No one has ever seen God, but the one and only Son, who is himself God and is in closest relationship with the Father, has made him known" (John 1:18). In other words, one of the most fundamental reasons Jesus came to earth was to explain—better yet, to demonstrate—what the Father is like.

The apostle Paul argued that there are some things about God that ought to be obvious to the least observant people—mostly His power and creativity (see Rom. 1–2)—but there are qualities that would never have been known if it weren't for Jesus (see Rom. 8). For example, we could never have known just how humble our God is without Jesus. We would never have really understood how approachable He is, how far His love extends or how deep His grace reaches. We could have known how great He is, but we could never have guessed how good He is (see Matt. 11:25–30). Jesus told the story of His temptation in the wilderness to His disciples; they wouldn't have known about it otherwise. He must have wanted them to know about it because He wanted them to know that He wasn't putting on a show. He wanted them to know how high the stakes are. He wanted them to know that He had the ability to overthrow evil itself, through the power of His gentle, humble love.

Jesus matters for lots of reasons. Without His resurrection there would be no hope. Without His crucifixion there would be no forgiveness. Without His life there would be no example. Without His teaching there would be no instruction. Without His existence there would be no understanding the true nature of our Father, the One true God, who is both great and good.

THURSDAY: Actions

Temptation comes. There's no getting around it. If you live on Planet Earth, you will encounter temptations and trials. It comes with the territory.

You can try to avoid temptation. Lots of people have tried. Through the centuries, people have castrated and blinded themselves and lived in isolation and deprivation, all in hopes of freeing themselves from temptation . . . all to no avail.

Temptation is part of life on this fallen planet. More than that, we often find ourselves faced with temptations that seem custom-designed just for our own unique weaknesses. The evil one we face is sinister and shrewd; he knows our vulnerabilities well. That's why the apostle Peter warns us to "be alert and sober of mind. Your enemy the devil prowls around like a roaring lion looking for someone to devour" (1 Pet. 5:8).

So, what's a good Christian boy or girl to do?

The most effective way to counter temptation is by relying on the truth of God's Word (just as Jesus did) and allowing it to stop us from rationalizing. King David knew how effective this approach was. That's why he wrote, "I have hidden your word in my heart that I might not sin against you" (Ps. 119:11).

This method requires some preparation. If you wait until you're undergoing temptation to start seeking out the Bible's wisdom, you'll find it's too late. To resist temptation, you must cultivate a deep and abiding knowledge of God's principles for living wisely.

The first line of defense against temptation is wisdom, and wisdom comes from God. But though we can find strength in God's wisdom accumulated through good, solid study habits of His Word, we are still human. And as much hope as we find in the empowerment of the Spirit-filled life as exemplified by Jesus Himself, we will also find that our hearts are at best a mixed bag, our motives are jumbled and our fallenness goes deep.

234 The 52 Greatest Stories of the Bible

It is for these reasons that God has seen fit to put us with other people. God never planned for people to deal with Him solo. He has no special provision for those who say, "I want a relationship with God but not other Christians." A relationship with God requires us to have a relationship with other Christians; it's a package deal.

And in times of temptation, that's a very good thing.

Many college campuses have signs posted warning students: *Don't jog alone*. A single jogger (especially a single female jogger after dark) faces potential danger that a group of joggers do not face. Likewise, someone who embarks on a relationship with God without the assistance and accountability provided by a Christian community is more likely to give in to the dangerous temptations crafted specifically for them by the enemy.

There are inevitably times when we fail to resist temptation as we ought. In those times, we are wise to throw ourselves fully into confession and repentance, trusting God to not only forgive and restore us, but to increase our sensitivity and resolve.

FRIDAY: Prayer

Narrative

Father, out of Your glorious workmanship You have created each of Your people for good works, and You prepared these beforehand so that we would walk in them and find fulfillment in them. Life without You would have its transitory joys and setbacks, but none of this would have any enduring meaning in a godless world. You are the true Source of meaning and of purpose and of hope in this life, because You have made it clear that we live in a soul-forming world that is preparing us for our eternal citizenship in heaven. Therefore I will rejoice in hope, knowing that both the joys and setbacks of this life are part of a much larger whole, and that nothing in heaven or on earth can thwart Your purposes. You have invited me to participate in a grand and glorious drama that will conclude with the death of death itself.

Orthodoxy

God of grace, I give You thanks and praise that You desire to have an intimate relationship with me as an adopted child in Your heavenly household. Your power and might are boundless and transcend human comprehension. I cannot fathom even the fringe of Your ways. And yet You have chosen to use Your power to love and serve people who are weak and insignificant apart from You. You have restrained Yourself to accommodate the needs of Your people, and the clearest display of the humility of restrained strength is the Lord Jesus Christ. I am amazed that He never did anything to impress people, but that all His actions were intended to serve them. He came in humility, walked in humility and died in humility, and yet He was the most powerful person the world has ever known or could ever know. Thank You for the gift of Your other-centered love and grace.

Orthopathy

Father in heaven, You have graciously revealed rich and wonderful truths about Your nature and plan that we could never have known on our own. The heavens declare the glory of Your invisible attributes—Your eternal power and divine nature. But nothing in Your created order could prepare us for the revelation that the God of majesty and sovereign glory is also the God who humbles Himself to make it possible for us to enjoy a living relationship with Him through the merits of His glorious Son. What we could never learn in nature, You have revealed in Your Word, which centers on the Person and work of Christ Jesus, the Alpha and the Omega. May I grow in my love and obedience to the Lord Jesus, who has given Himself to rescue and draw me to You, and may I become more like Him in my spiritual journey.

Orthopraxy

Gracious God, may I learn the wisdom of quickly calling on Your Name whenever I encounter temptations, rather than attempting to deal with them in my own resources. I will draw near to You and submit to You so that I will be in a position to resist the enemy. I know that I live in the midst of a spiritual war and that I can only succeed on the battlefronts of the world, the flesh and the devil through Your divine power, which works in and through me when I turn to You and walk by Your Spirit. Thank You for Jesus, the great High Priest who has been tempted in all things as I am, yet without sin. He understands what I am experiencing and offers His mercy and grace to help in time of need. As I approach Your throne of grace with confidence, I also thank You for the gift of other believers who can strengthen and encourage me so that I will not be hardened by the deceitfulness of sin.

31

The Best Sermon Ever

MATTHEW 5–7;
LUKE 6:17–49

Jesus walked everywhere He went—from village to village, healing the sick, spending time with people, laughing, talking, eating, listening. He was equally at home with wealthy landowners, sharecroppers, religious teachers, lawyers, tax collectors, prostitutes, widows, grandmothers and children. He dealt with them all the same.

This endeared Him to some and estranged Him from others.

Impossible to pin down or categorize, He moved easily among the people and had the same message for all of them: *This is it! This is what you've been waiting for! The Kingdom is at last so close that you can reach out your hand and grab hold of it!* And, oh, the people wanted to hear it, wanted to believe it! But they had no way of understanding what He meant, so He was constantly misunderstood.

Finally He decided to sit down and explain it all in as much detail as He could. So He went up on the side of a hill; He wanted everyone to be able to see and hear what he had to say. He needed some elevation because the crowds had grown so thick lately.

From His vantage point, perched on a hillside in rural Israel, Jesus surveyed the people. These are the faces He had in mind before the foundations of the world were in place, the people to whom He knew He would inevitably come, the people for whom He knew He would inevitably die. He saw crutches and pallets, hungry and well-fed, men and women, young and old, Jew and Gentile. They were staring up at Him with a look of hope, a desire to know (from someone who seemed to know things) that things were going to be okay. Life wouldn't always be this uphill struggle with more questions than answers, more bills than money, more darkness than light.

He saw them all before He said a word.

Who knows whether what He said next took several hours or just 15 minutes? In one sense, it doesn't matter, because what He said is still ringing in our ears. We are unable to rid ourselves of its awful and strangely inspirational message.

The Creator of the universe spoke definitively and confirmed our suspicions: *Life is not as it should be, not as it was intended to be, not yet as it will be.* But a time is coming—in fact, that time has already come to some pockets of this world—when the poor will have unimaginable wealth! The hungry will eat until they are stuffed! Those who are sad will break out into laughter and applause!

The grandest reversal of fortune ever is under way, and we are invited to participate in it. Life in God's kingdom is available to everyone, regardless of social status. But beware: The rules are all different now. There's a new operating system in place. Everything you thought you knew about life on earth is changing. Up is the new down. Rich is the new poor. Strong is the new weak.

By the time He was done, He had not only delivered the greatest sermon ever preached, He had changed the entire world forever.

TUESDAY: Beliefs

There's a lot of talk these days about "the gospel" and how it ought to be defined. The word itself means "good news," but what exactly is it?

For the apostle Paul, the gospel is that Jesus came and died and rose from the dead so that we could be reconciled to God (see 1 Cor. 15). For Martin Luther, the gospel is that we are justified to God by faith alone in Christ alone. For Mel Gibson, the gospel is that Jesus suffered on our behalf. For Rick Warren, the gospel is that Jesus restores us to God so that we can live a purposeful life.

But the New Testament Gospels have a different take. The Gospel of Mark was the very first of the four Gospels written, and the first person to use the phrase in that book is none other than Jesus Himself. For Jesus, the word "gospel" means, "The kingdom of God is here—so close you can reach out and touch it with your hand. The time you've been waiting for has now arrived. Now act like that's so."

Of course, this brings up an important follow-up question: What exactly is the kingdom of God (or Kingdom of heaven in Matthew's Gospel)? Well, by definition, a kingdom is wherever the king's will is realized—where that king's thoughts determine reality. In that light, God's kingdom is wherever His will is done fully and completely—wherever what God wants to happen happens.

Jesus' Good News was this: *Your life can be lived in such a place. Your life can actually be that place where God's will is done fully and completely.*

Imagine that! This God we've learned so much about, this God who wants to bless people, wants people to live free of regret, fear or anxiety, this God who wants you to live in such harmony with Him and with others that your very presence is a blessing to the whole world—He's made a way for it to happen.

Jesus has come to give us a chance at life—really living life the way we always wanted to live. We have a shot at being that person we always wanted to be, to have the power and freedom we always wanted to have. Because of Him, it's possible for love to conquer fear; for security to defeat anxiety; for ordinary, fallen, broken people like us to be extraordinary people of integrity and strength. It's possible to not only do the right thing now; it's actually possible to do the right thing in the right way at the right time for the right reason.

It's possible to be completely transformed into the people we were created to be.

Because God's kingdom has broken into our world, the momentum has shifted once and for all. And this kind of life is available to absolutely everyone. And—this is the best part—*it's absolutely free.*

That's what we'd call "good news."

The only question that remains is this: *If that kind of life is really available, why are so few of us living it?*

WEDNESDAY: Values

At the turn of the twentieth century, a debate that had been brewing in academic circles spilled out into the mainstream. The debate was about Jesus, and it has shaped much of theology for more than 100 years now.

One side of the debate said that the Jesus of history was simply a good, wise and moral teacher. He was a very important teacher—possibly one of the greatest teachers ever. But that was all. He was not the Son of God. He did not really do miracles. Virgin birth? Please. Nope, Jesus was just a fantastic teacher, and we could all learn from His teaching. That's as far as it goes.

The other side of the debate said, "No! Jesus is the Son of the living God, eternally pre-existent member of the Trinity, spotless Lamb of God sent to offer His life as a ransom for many. He was born of the Virgin Mary, conceived by the Holy Spirit. He lived a sinless life, died a sacrificial death and was vindicated by God the Father through His bodily resurrection. He ascended into heaven, where He sits at the right hand of the Father, interceding on our behalf."

A bad thing happened as a result of this brouhaha. People who believe in the deity of Jesus began to de-emphasize the role of His teaching. In fact, there came to be a kind of suspicion among some of them; when folks started talking about Jesus' teaching, these suspicious types automatically assumed they were on the other side of the debate. Some sects of Christianity went so far as to suggest that large portions of His teaching—such as the Sermon on the Mount—don't apply to us anymore. The importance of Jesus' teaching was gradually pushed aside to make room for Jesus' redemptive work on the cross.

To be clear here, we contend that the Jesus of the New Testament was both fully human and fully divine and is today living and vitally involved in human affairs. We affirm the historical creeds of orthodox Christianity when it comes to the Person and work of Jesus Christ.

Yet we also firmly believe that teaching isn't something Jesus did to pass the time until it was time for Him to die. Jesus' teaching isn't an optional, dispensable part of His ministry. His teaching was an integral part of His ministry. He didn't just come to die for us (though He did do that, and we're eternally grateful for it); He also came to teach us about life in God's kingdom. He was the wisdom-bringer, the one who showed us what God is really like, what people are really like, the way the world really operates and how to live as citizens of the Kingdom of heaven.

Jesus' earliest followers were drawn to Him initially because of His teaching. He was, among other things, the smartest man they had ever known. His instruction made so much sense; it had that ring of truth that you don't get from human wisdom. Crowds flocked to Him, amazed at His teaching. They watched Him live out His message with integrity, and they were astonished.

They'd never seen anyone live like Him—they had no idea such a life was even possible.

And then He told them an unbelievable thing: *If you will trust Me and do what I tell you to do, one day you will live like Me.*

This part is really, really important: Because they felt that they could trust Him as their teacher *during His life*, they learned to trust Him as their Savior after His death and resurrection.

So, if you want to fully experience the love of Christ, you must come to value one of the most important gifts He offers: His teaching. You must trust that He is right about absolutely everything. This means that when you disagree with Him (and it will probably happen every once in a while), you're either wrong or you don't fully understand what He was saying.

To really follow Jesus, you must allow Him to teach you how to live. He was, after all, the greatest Teacher of all time.

THURSDAY: Actions

In Luke's version of the Sermon on the Mount (often called the Sermon on the Plain), Jesus says:

> No good tree bears bad fruit, nor does a bad tree bear good fruit. Each tree is recognized by its own fruit. People do not pick figs from thornbushes, or grapes from briers. Good people bring good things out of the good stored up in their heart, and evil people bring evil things out of the evil stored up in their heart. For out of the overflow of the heart the mouth speaks (Luke 6:43–45).

People have strange ways of reading the Bible sometimes, looking for either a command to obey, an example to follow or what is often called a "necessary inference." When the Bible doesn't give an explicit instruction, we make necessary inferences by using logic and inductive reasoning to determine what we are supposed to do. This method of Bible reading, which focuses solely on what we should do in response to the Scriptures, brings up all kinds of issues. First, it doesn't help us understand what the text *means*; it's only a method of applying the text to our lives. Second, one person's "necessary inference" is hardly universal.

There are other problems with this form of Bible study, but the most important issue of all is that this method of reading the Bible is ungodly. We mean that last word in a precise way; approaching Scripture in this manner is ungodly in that it's completely unconcerned with God. It's what could be called an "anthropocentric" (man-centered) way to read the Bible, because it is completely concerned with humans and what we should do. Or (even worse) it's concerned with others and what you think they should do. God is hardly even a factor.

A theocentric (God-centered) approach first asks what a particular text reveals about the character and nature of God. Then it asks how we might apply this text to our lives in such a way that we become more like Him.

Of course, reading the Bible that way takes a lot more work, and that's probably why some people prefer the other approach. But those folks often have a really hard time trying to figure out what in the world Jesus wants them to do. Take the above paragraph from Luke, for instance. There's no command. There's not even an example. And the whole necessary inference thing is confusing for most people anyway.

So what does Jesus want us to do?

To ratchet up the tension even further, He adds: "Why do you call me, 'Lord, Lord,' and do not do what I say?" (Luke 6:46).

Because You haven't told us what to do, Jesus!

This gets to one of the most frustrating things about Jesus' teaching: He rarely gives an outright command. And sometimes when He does, it's outrageous. Does Jesus really want you to pluck out your eye or cut off your hand?

How do you obey Jesus when He won't give you a decent command?

While we're here, let us ask this: Have you ever heard someone say that before you can follow Jesus you have to "obey the gospel"? Well, if the gospel is the Good News that Jesus came and lived a sinless life, died a sacrificial death and rose victorious over the grave to secure your pardon from sin and purchase for you a new life characterized not by fear and shame but by hope and peace and joy—if the gospel is the availability of life in God's kingdom—if it is an historical event, well . . . how do you "obey" an historical event?

The answer to both questions above is the same: *You live as if it were true.*

How would we live if we believed Jesus' words in Luke 6 to be an accurate depiction of reality? How would we live if we believed the Good News were really true?

Maybe that's what Jesus was getting at in His teaching ministry—not some tutorial offering new and improved rules for living, but a better picture of reality, sharing with us what life would be like in this Kingdom He was bringing. And maybe what He desires of us most is that we begin to live as if it were true.

FRIDAY: Prayer

Narrative

Lord Jesus, all the Scripture that was written prior to Your Incarnation pointed directly to You and anticipated Your Person and work. You are the perfect fulfillment of the Messianic prophecies that spoke of Your redeeming work as the Savior of the world, and of the prophecies that remain to be fulfilled when You come to judge the world and rule in righteousness. May I be a herald of Your kingdom, in which You call us to enjoy the blessed release of submitting to Your lordship in this life. I want to be an agent of change in this world by obeying Your commands and walking in Your power. The values of Your kingdom invert those of the world—You teach that the last will be first, the humble will be exalted, the giver will receive, the poor in spirit will be rich, the downward way is the way up and the servant of all is the true leader.

Orthodoxy

Father, I anticipate the day when Your will shall be fully realized not only in heaven, but also on earth. Even now, I want to be a follower and doer of Your will on this earth as I live between the present age and the age to come. Only in You can I discover the resources to become the person You intended me to be and to live the life You have called me to live. I ask You for the grace to fulfill Your will in my relationships, in my work, in my aspirations and with my possessions. I willingly affirm that Jesus is Lord of all, and that there is no part of my life that should not come under His guidance. Whenever I am tempted to retreat from Your loving rule, may I recall anew where I was without You, where I would be without You and where I would be destined without you. Apart from You I can do nothing.

Orthopathy

Jesus, may I learn to take Your yoke upon me, to follow You wherever you lead me to learn from You. Although You have said many things that I do not fully grasp, I wish to submit to the authority of Your teachings and learn to trust You when I do not understand. Your words bring life—Your message is unique and authoritative, and Your wisdom surpasses anything the world has ever heard. I acknowledge that without the new birth in which I was regenerated by the Holy

Spirit, it would be impossible for me to live as You ask me to live. But You have not only revealed the way to go; You have provided me with the resources that will empower me to travel along that way. I give thanks for the power of Your indwelling Spirit, for your life-giving teaching, and for the new quality of life to which You have called me.

Orthopraxy

Holy Father, Your Word is truth. It brings life, hope, purpose, fulfillment and power to all who submit to its authority and put it into practice. I want to receive it, reflect on it, internalize it and apply it. Your Word gives me the wisdom that leads to salvation through faith in Christ Jesus, and it teaches, corrects, reproves and trains me in righteousness. Your magnificent promises are sure. Your perfect character is unchanging. Your loyal love is unwavering and Your boundless grace is constant. I can lean with full confidence on Your promises and precepts, because they are the anchor for my hope and the foundation for my wellbeing. Teach me the way in which You want me to order my steps so that I will fulfill Your benevolent desires for my life. By Your grace may I follow You, trust in You, hope in You and please You.

32

Miracles

MARK 5–9

This Jesus is quite a character. He moves about with a strange fluidity, at ease among a very diverse group of people who have begun to follow Him around the countryside. He speaks with authority, flouting religious rules, revealing hypocrisy and corruption, alternately alienating and endearing Himself to the powers that be.

And then there are the miracles.

There can be no other way of explaining the things that happen when He's around. They're miracles. Demons leave people alone. People who had once been prone to seizures or dangerous and destructive behavior are calmed by a single sentence from Him. No big emotional ramp-up seems necessary. Just a word or a wave of His hand. Sick people are healed with a touch—sometimes it doesn't even require a touch, just a word spoken from a distance. There are even reports of dead people being raised to life again.

Demons are one thing. Sickness is another. Death . . . well, that's a whole different ballgame.

People are fed—food seemingly materializes out of thin air. Storms are calmed just because Jesus tells them to. Some say He walked across the surface of a lake. It's crazy. No one has ever seen anything like it.

Well, that's not entirely true.

Miracles have happened before. But they only seem to happen during the really pivotal times in God's Story: just prior to and following the Exodus, during the life of Moses, just after the nation split in two, during the lives of Elijah and Elisha. Those were special occasions, times when God was showing the world something new about Himself and the way He wanted to interact with people.

Miraculous events give a special level of authority to the one through whom such signs and wonders occur. If these miracles Jesus performs are legitimate, that means . . . well, that means something is going on.

It means that YHWH, the God of Abraham, Isaac and Jacob, is trying to show His people something new about Himself and how He wants to relate to us. It means that this Jesus guy has some sort of special authority. His ability to perform miracles could be seen as validation from God.

But that can't be the case. Look at Him. He doesn't look right. He doesn't act right. He didn't study with the right rabbis. He doesn't hang around the right kind of people.

But these things that happen everywhere He goes . . . what should we make of them? You don't suppose it means . . . ?

TUESDAY: Beliefs

"Do you believe in miracles?" Al Michaels provided the world with this famous sound bite when he called the 1980 U. S. Olympic Men's hockey team's improbable victory over the Soviet Union. As the final 10 seconds ticked away, he asked this rhetorical question and answered it at the buzzer: "*Yes!*"

Do you believe in miracles?

Yes!

But was it really a miracle in 1980? Was it a miracle when the 2004 Boston Red Sox finally broke the Curse of the Bambino and won their first World Series in 86 years? What about last Christmas when it was so cold outside and you prayed for a parking space near the front of the mall and one opened up just as you turned the corner? Was that a miracle? Or the time that guy at work found out he had cancer, and then everyone was praying, and when he went back the doctors said the cancer was totally gone . . . was that a miracle?

Sometimes people say that a miracle is when God intervenes in the world. But this assumes that God isn't active in the world on a regular basis. Others say we can make our own miracles by looking within ourselves and calling upon the hidden resources of our own mysterious humanity.

For the sake of accuracy, one might say that a miracle occurs when God—who is always at work in our world—deviates from His usual pattern and does something extraordinary. The more extraordinary it is, the more confidently we can say, "That's a miracle!"

The 1980 U. S. Olympic Men's hockey team outplayed their Soviet opponents. The 2004 Red Sox made some good trades, stayed healthy and played well down the stretch. People eventually leave the mall, relinquishing choice parking spots.

Cancer . . . that's closer to what we're talking about when we discuss miracles.

Healing the sick, walking on water, raising the dead, feeding thousands with five loaves of bread and two fish . . . these are miracles for sure.

If you believe in miracles.

That's the question we've got to start with: Do you believe in miracles? Not coincidences. Not random events. Real. Bona-fide. Miracles.

Do you believe in miracles?

If you do, seeing miracles happen is just a matter of refining your definition, knowing what to look for and understanding the purposes of God's miraculous activity. But if you don't, no amount of experience or evidence will be enough to suffice. There were witnesses to the resurrection of Jesus who lied about it and never put their faith in Him (see Matt. 28:11–15).

Those of us who do believe in miracles are wise to remember that God's purpose is not merely to help people. God has a purpose far deeper than that. He means for us to look beyond the miracle—to the Miracle Worker Himself.

WEDNESDAY: Values

In your opinion, what is the greatest miracle in the Bible?

Is it Creation? God speaking everything into existence? One second there was nothing; the next second there was everything. Pretty great, but that doesn't get our vote.

What about the Incarnation? The Creator of the universe coming to earth as a tiny, helpless baby? Again, it's astonishing, but it doesn't get our vote.

The Resurrection? It's certainly the pivotal event of human history. The Resurrection of Jesus is the single event that makes sense of all the other events of His life and ours. If there's no Resurrection, it's every man for himself. Eat, drink and be merry, for tomorrow we die—and after that there's nothing. The Resurrection certainly is an amazing miracle. And yet . . .

None of the miracles above get our vote because we wouldn't know about any of them without the Bible. Maybe the greatest miracle of all time isn't *in* the Bible; maybe the greatest miracle of all time *is* the Bible.

Approximately 40 different authors, writing in three different languages over the span of about 1,400 years worked with God to create, in 66 books, one Story.

There was a group of people who lived during Jesus' lifetime called the Sadducees. They didn't believe in any kind of resurrection. As far as the Sadducees were concerned, when you died, you were dead and that was that. They didn't believe in angels or spirits or anything that sounded supernatural.

If you took off a Sadducee's robe, put him in a tailored suit, gave him a laptop in exchange for his scrolls, took him out of the Temple and put him into an office building, you'd have a pretty typical white-collar American—a good, solid, tax-paying, church-attending guy.

But Jesus had a question for Sadducees, both old and new: "Are you not in error because you do not know the Scriptures or the power of God?" (Mark 12:24). In other words, the reason people don't believe in supernatural activity is because they are ignorant of the Bible. Lots of people claim to believe in God, but the god they believe in is not the God found in the pages of the Bible. They never expect God to do anything in their lives.

Jesus goes on to say that the God of the Bible is the God of Abraham, Isaac and Jacob (see Mark 12:26). If we want to know what He's like, we should look at how He dealt with those three patriarchs.

Abraham worshiped idols until God intervened, calling him to leave everything behind and go to a new land. When God says He's the God of Abraham, He means that He intervenes in our lives to call us to follow Him.

As a young man, Isaac's father bound him to an altar on Mount Moriah. He was about to be sacrificed when God intervened to save him by providing a substitute. Isaac was released and an animal was offered in his place. When God says He's the God of Isaac, He means that He intervenes in our lives to save us from death.

Jacob lived a twisted life filled with lies and deceit. He ran from his family and he ran from God. But God never gave up on him. One night, the angel of the Lord appeared to Jacob and wrestled with him. The struggle changed Jacob forever, moving him from a posture of resistance to a posture of dependence. When God says He's the God of Jacob, He means that He is the God who is willing to fight for His people.

The God of the Bible—the God of Abraham, Isaac and Jacob—is the God who calls and saves and fights for us. He is the God who intervenes to change things. Once you know this God of the Bible, miracles aren't so hard to believe.

That's why we've spent so much time and energy writing this book. We believe that once you come to value God's Story and embed yourself in it, you'll be able to see God's hand at work all around you.

THURSDAY: Actions

Okay, so if God still does miracles (and He does), how do we get in on that? Is that what prayer is for? Do we pray in order to get God to show us some of His fancy stuff? From the sound of it, that's how lots of people approach this thing called prayer.

But that kind of praying puts you in a tough spot. If you get what you want, then prayer works. But if you don't get what you want, then what? Did you get the sequence wrong? You put the change in the slot, pressed the button and nothing came out. Did God just eat your quarter?!

Sometimes people quit praying because God didn't do a miracle for them. Most of us are too religious (or maybe superstitious) to stop praying altogether. We may not be completely convinced that it works every time, but what if it works *this* time? Maybe it's every other request or some other intricate pattern. How it works or why it works—who knows? But it's better to have it close by just in case, like a rabbit's foot or a four-leaf clover.

One other thing that's really confusing: Have you ever noticed that God sometimes answers a small prayer and ignores a larger one? Maybe you had a friend who went without a job for a long time. You prayed and prayed and prayed and nothing happened. But your Aunt Edna often asks God to help her find her keys and it always works! Ask God to heal your sick mother and she might get worse. Ask Him to cure AIDS or end world hunger, and nothing happens. But ask Him to help you get a parking spot near the front of the mall . . . lo and behold!

What are we to make of all this? Is there some hidden secret? Is there a requisite level of faith required? Is it about saying the right words in the right way with the right feeling?

You've seen those guys on TV in their expensive suits and bad hair, shouting and crying and wiping the sweat from their faces and pounding on big black Bibles. They're on nearly every night, standing in front of crowds numbering in the thousands, building them into a fever pitch, yelling about faith and what faith does and how if they have enough faith they'll be wealthy and healthy.

What do you do with the idea that people in wheelchairs are there because they lack the faith to stand up and walk? Jesus said, "You just need faith the size of a mustard seed" (see Matt. 17:20). That's not much faith at all; you'd think they could rally at least a mustard seed's worth!

One time a guy came to Jesus and said, "If you can do anything, will you help my son?"

Jesus said, "What do you mean, *if*? Don't you believe?"

The guy said, "I do believe; help me overcome my unbelief" (see Mark 9:14–29).

That's where most of us live: on both sides of the semicolon. We do believe; but we don't believe all that much.

But is that really the key to getting God to do a miracle for us? Do we have to muster up some kind of confidence or bravado before God will give us what we want? That can't be right, can it?

Here's a more important question: What if none of this is the point of prayer to begin with? What if prayer isn't about getting in on God's miraculous activity? Or what if that's just one tiny part of prayer? How tragic would it be to spend your entire life thinking that one tiny part of prayer was all there was to it?

Miracles are never meant to be ends in and of themselves. Miracles are meant to point beyond themselves to the Miracle Worker. What makes a real difference in our lives is not how much miraculous activity we experience. What makes a real difference is how well we know the One to whom these miracles point.

That makes all the difference in the world.

FRIDAY: Prayer

Narrative

Lord Jesus, the Gospels proclaim the abundance of marvelous things You said and did during Your brief public ministry. You made claims no one else ever made before or since, and You had the authority to back up those claims by Your extraordinary works. You demonstrated Your supremacy over nature, demons, disease and death. Yet You did all this in a context of profound humility, never calling attention to Yourself but instead pointing to Your heavenly Father. You came not to judge the world but to save it; but the time is coming when You will return in manifest glory and power as the Judge and Ruler of heaven and earth. I thank You that You have the power to grant eternal life to all who come to You, and I wait in anticipation for the day when I will receive a resurrected body that will be in conformity with the body of Your glory.

Orthodoxy

Lord God, I live in a time when skepticism, naturalism and secularization have gripped my culture as never before. More than any other ideology, Christianity has become the target of media, entertainment and our educational system. But rather than wring my hands over these things, I gladly acknowledge that this comes as no surprise to You, and that the real issue is one of the heart and the will. You have provided enough evidence to satisfy the minds of those who make You the source of their trust, but You have also allowed enough ambiguity so that unbelievers can rationalize their disbelief. You have given us the dignity of choice, and those who choose to humble themselves under Your mighty hand recognize that You can and have intervened in miraculous ways in human history. I thank You that You have displayed Your greatness and beauty most clearly in the person of Your Son.

Orthopathy

God, where would I be if You did not reveal Yourself in Your Word? My knowledge of You would be limited to inferences I draw from the natural world, and I could never have known that You love me and have gone to unfathomable lengths to draw me to Yourself. Your revelation of Your works and ways in Scripture is the foundational authority for truth in my life, and it bristles with implications for how I should order my steps from day to day. Grant that I will seek more diligently to expose myself to its teachings and counsel, and that I would meditate on and memorize truths from the Bible. As I read and reflect on the Scriptures, I gain a wisdom and perspective I could never attain otherwise, and my soul is nourished with great thoughts about who You are and what You have done.

Orthopraxy

God of grace and glory, in Christ You have welcomed me into the profound intimacy of the "You in me and I in You" relationship. I want to want You more than anything else, and I realize that I can never really know You apart from spending time in Your presence and welcoming You into each of the facets of my life. May I come to see the reading of Your Word and prayer as profound vehicles for real communication with You. May I never resort to using prayer in an attempt to get You to do what I want. Instead, I desire to see prayer as a means to intimacy with You and of learning how to align myself with Your will for my life. May I learn to listen to Your voice and to be responsive to the subtle prompting of Your Holy Spirit so that I will live in the fullness of Your presence.

33

Transfiguration

MATTHEW 16:13–17:13;
MARK 8:27–9:13;
LUKE 9:18–36

MONDAY: Story

Jesus was confusing—even to His closest followers. After spending so much time with Him, they still didn't really understand what was going on. So He decided it was time to get a little more explicit.

He began by asking them a question: "Who do people say I am?" (see Mark 8:27–30).

They responded with three very common views about Jesus: "Some say John the Baptist; others say Elijah; and still others, one of the prophets." John had been a wise and moral teacher. Elijah was a miracle-worker. The prophets spoke to the people on behalf of YHWH.

But Jesus pressed, "What about you? Who do you say I am?" In other words, "Do you think I fit into any one of those three categories? Or is there something more?"

It was Peter who finally stepped up and said what many of them may have suspected: "You are the Messiah."

Bingo! Bull's eye! For once in his life, Peter got it right on the first try!

But then an odd thing happened. Jesus went on to explain the implications of this whole "Messiah" thing—about how He would suffer and be rejected and die (see Mark 8:31–33). Such a thought did not sit well with Peter, so he took Jesus aside and scolded Him for bringing everybody down. Jesus responded with some scolding of His own. He even called Peter a really bad name and accused Peter of trying to sabotage His plan.

Awkward.

We don't know how the whole thing was resolved, but we can assume there was some tension among them. It's possible that not a word was spoken for a full week (see Matt. 17:1; Mark 9:2; Luke 9:28). Jesus knew His mission would ultimately lead Him to the cross, but now He knew that those closest to Him did not understand. It must have been a lonely time for Him. And the disciples must have felt like they were walking on eggshells, wondering what the future held.

After a full week, here's how Jesus broke the silence: Gathering His three best friends—Peter, James and John—to Him, He climbed a mountaintop and gave them the clearest picture imaginable. His face began to change ... glowing ... and His clothes did, too. It was as if Jesus reflected—or better, radiated—some bright light.

In the coming days, the disciples would see Jesus beaten beyond recognition. The light they now saw would be extinguished, but they needed to know that the darkness would not have the last word. Jesus' light radiated from within, and no amount of suffering and humiliation would ever be able to permanently snuff it out.

Interestingly, Moses and Elijah showed up and started talking to Jesus. And the topic that surfaced? "They spoke about his departure, which he was about to bring to fulfillment in Jerusalem" (Luke 9:31). Moses and Elijah understood something that Peter failed to grasp: Jesus' death (His "departure") was how YHWH's promises were going to be fulfilled.

Then a cloud appeared and a voice boomed out of the cloud: "This is my Son, whom I love; listen to him!" (Mark 9:7). If there was any doubt at all about Jesus' identity, or any thought of correcting His theology or His methodology, this erased it!

The cloud evaporated. Moses and Elijah vanished from view. The befuddled disciples were left alone with Jesus again, but now, when they looked at Him, He didn't look quite the same.

TUESDAY: Beliefs

When we use the phrase "son of," we mean something specific. Assuming we aren't prone to profanity, we mean to mention a given person's parents. "He's the son of J. J. and Isabel" or "He's the son of the pastor." We use the phrase to give information about a person's origin: "He owes his existence and wellbeing to J. J. and Isabel."

But ancient people used the phrase differently. Rather than using it to describe a person's origin, they used it to describe his character or his likeness with someone or something. For example, two of Jesus' followers, James and John, were called "sons of thunder." A character we meet later in the New Testament, named Barnabas, was known as the "son of encouragement." They didn't mean that Thunder and Encouragement literally gave birth; they were being descriptive: James and John were like thunder; Barnabas was like encouragement.

So when the Bible says Jesus is the Son of God, it doesn't mean that YHWH literally gave birth to Jesus. (The Bible is clear about who Jesus' birth parents were.) It means that the Son is exactly like the Father; Jesus is exactly like God. God the Father and God the Son are both eternal, self-existing and fully equal in their Persons. Neither owes His origin or wellbeing to the other. Neither brought the other into existence. Neither is superior to or greater than the other. They are alike.

Whatever the Father is, God the Son is also. Any glory or praise or worship the one is entitled to receive, the other deserves as well. That's why praying to Jesus is acceptable and so is singing to Him.

To say that Jesus is the Son of God is to say that His nature is one and the same with the Father and the Holy Spirit, that He is divine in His very essence. Father, Son and Spirit are united by virtue of Their shared deity.

Jesus' three closest friends stood there on the mountain, mouths agape, watching the whole thing unfurl before their eyes. What were they supposed to think? Here stood Moses and Elijah, talking with their friend Jesus as casually as you might chat with your next-door neighbor over the fence on a Saturday afternoon. The author of the Law and the greatest miracle-working prophet in Jewish history—they were rock stars, and they were standing so close that the disciples could hear them talking.

Once again, Peter blurted out the first thing that popped into his head: "Let's build some kind of monument to mark this momentous occasion. No, wait! Three monuments; one for each of you!"

And then came the Voice: "This one is my Son. He's the one I love. Listen to Him." Moses was great, but he wasn't the Son of God. Elijah was great, but he wasn't the Son of God.

There's only one Son of God—the One and Only—sent from the Father to save the world. That's Jesus. He's the one we should listen to.

WEDNESDAY: Values

History is moving, slowly but steadily, toward a day when the glory of the Lord will be revealed and recognized. The whole earth is already filled with His glory (see Ps. 72:19), but the whole earth is not yet filled with the *knowledge* of His glory (see Hab. 2:14).

One day, however, it will be.

In the meantime, we must often persist through suffering and darkness in this world. We persist in hope, though, because we know that God is moving toward the day when His Son will be revealed, and every person who has ever lived will see His glory.

But wait! There's more!

According to the story of Jesus' Transfiguration, *we will share in His glory.*

Moses and Elijah appeared alongside Jesus in glorious splendor, and they shared in the glory that radiated from Jesus. The sight must have been staggering for His young disciples. For almost three years, they had witnessed some of Jesus' glory in His miracles and teaching. But this time, they were seeing something altogether new; they saw what He will look like when His kingdom comes in its fullness.

But they saw more: Moses and Elijah were humans, but when they stood in the light of Jesus' glory, they radiated His light. Evidently, regular human beings can be transfigured into something glorious as well. As the Son gave His closest friends a glimpse into His future, He was giving them a glimpse into their own future as well.

Elijah and Moses were great men, but they were men. They had their share of failures. Moses had quite a temper; he murdered a man and was kept from entering the Promised Land as a result of his inability to control himself. Elijah saw one of the greatest miracles of the Old Testament—calling down fire on Mount Carmel—but he got so depressed when he was persecuted that he actually asked God to kill him!

They were two great men, no doubt. But they were human beings with baggage and failures and despair—just like us. But on the top of that mountain, they shared in the glory of Jesus Christ. And if they can do it, so can you.

Because you were created for eternity. Once you come into existence, you never stop existing and you never become someone else. Moses was still Moses. Elijah was still Elijah. You will still be you. Think about it: Somehow Peter recognized who these guys were. We have no idea how that happened; there weren't any photos of them! But somehow God allowed Peter, James and John to know the identities of Jesus' visitors. Odds are, your identity will not only remain intact in the Kingdom that is coming, but you will be known as well.

After all, God's plan has always been to create a community of people who don't just relate to Him but relate to each other, too. One of the great joys of the next life will be the joy of seeing the glory of God reflected in ourselves and the light of Jesus shining through people we love.

THURSDAY: Actions

The story of Jesus' Transfiguration has a command in it, spoken directly from God the Father to the three disciples. It may be one of the most neglected commands in the Bible: "This is my Son, whom I love. Listen to him!" (Mark 9:7).

Every person who claims to be a follower of Jesus must reckon with these two questions: *What do you think Jesus is saying to you right now*? and *How do you know it's Jesus and not someone else*? Obviously, answering requires a high level of discernment, but as followers of Jesus, we can know that He wants us to know His voice and do what He says (see John 10:27).

But how does that happen? How does Jesus speak to us today? The three disciples standing there on the mountaintop could follow Him literally and speak with a human. It's a little more difficult for us.

Still, it's possible.

Broadly speaking, there are three primary ways Jesus speaks to us now: (1) through His words; (2) through the inner witness of the Holy Spirit; and (3) through the collective wisdom of the Body of Christ—that is, the Church. Let's take a closer look at each of these.

It's probably obvious by now that we like the Bible. We advocate Bible reading. We've written a book about the Bible, because we believe there is great wisdom to be had by reading from all portions of Scripture. But there is something special about reading the words of Jesus Himself, allowing your mind to steep in the wisdom of the smartest man who ever lived. We neglect the "red letters" to our own peril.

The Spirit has come in place of the bodily presence of Jesus, so a person follows Jesus only to the extent that he or she follows the leading of the Spirit. But the Spirit of God rarely shouts; He simply will not clamor for our attention. If we want to hear His voice, we must shut out the noise that so easily and often distracts us. Turn off the television and the iPod, the computer and the Xbox and ask the Spirit to speak.

Finally, as communities of faith, we must develop the capacity to listen together for the voice of Jesus. When we come together, there is so much to do—songs to sing, announcements to be made, sermons to deliver. But is there ever time to pray and listen collectively for what Jesus might want to tell His people? If we are to hear Him and discern together that He is truly speaking, there must be.

God the Father said, "This is My Son. I love Him. Listen to Him!" What could happen if His people took Him seriously and did what He said?

FRIDAY: Prayer

Narrative

Lord Jesus, I aspire to know You better, and I recognize that at present I am only dimly aware of who You really are and what You are like. Scripture reveals wonderful truths about You, but You are unimaginably more than those words can communicate to me. I affirm that You are the Christ, the Son of the living God, but my capacity to understand what that means is bounded. Your majesty and glory are beyond human comprehension, and even in heaven the journey into the knowledge of You will be limitless. And yet You invite me to know You even now. Because intimacy with You is related to trust and obedience, may I respond by obeying what You command me to do as an expression of my love for You. In this way, You will progressively disclose Yourself to me and enlighten the eyes of my heart.

Orthodoxy

Jesus, You are the wonderful Counselor, mighty God, eternal Father, Prince of peace, holy One, Lamb of God, Prince of life, Lion of the tribe of Judah, Root of David, Word of life, Lord of all, Son of God, Shepherd and Guardian of souls, the Messiah. You are the I AM, the bright morning Star, the chief Shepherd, the Head of the Church, the Sun of righteousness, the Resurrection and the Life, the Alpha and the Omega, the Beginning and the End, the First and the Last, and the Way, the Truth and the Life. May I willingly submit to Your lordship over every area of my life; may I abide in You, hope in You, trust in You, love You, obey You and follow You in all You tell me to do for Your sake. Then I will see, with greater clarity, that Your service is true freedom, that Your yoke is light, and that Your cross is glorious.

Orthopathy

Father, I give thanks that You foreknew me, that You chose and called me, and that You have declared me righteous in Christ. My desire is that I become fully conformed to His image in spirit, soul and body so that I will display the beauty of His light as it shines through me and blesses others. I eagerly await the fullness of my adoption as Your child through the redemption of my body. I long for the day that will come when we put off mortality and are clothed with immortality. In the resurrection of our bodies, we will enjoy the fullness of our salvation. You will do away with death, sickness, suffering and grief, and this perishable will become imperishable. We will manifest Your life and reflect Your glory through the prisms of our unique personalities, so that each of us will contribute to the whole at the great feast and in the great dance.

Orthopraxy

Lord, teach me the wisdom of taking the time and care to listen to Your voice and seek Your wisdom and will for me. May I pause to hear what You want to tell me, and may I regularly make room for this to happen in my life. When I am busy and driven, I cannot hear what You want to tell me, and I crowd You out as I rush from one thing to the next. Instead, I ask for the grace to expose myself to Your Word and listen to its life-giving counsel. I also ask for a greater capacity to give attention to the quiet voice of the Holy Spirit as He counsels, comforts, exhorts, convicts, encourages and inspires me. May I additionally listen to the collective wisdom and insight that is available through the communion of saints, so that I will not endeavor to live the spiritual life on my own, without these rich resources that You have given to me.

34

Unconventional

LUKE 10:38–41

MONDAY: Story

Unconventional. That's the word for it. *Unseemly.* That's another good word for what is going on in the other room.

Maybe things were different in Nazareth or Bethlehem or Egypt or wherever this itinerant rabbi was raised, but here in Bethany, women keep to their places and men keep to theirs. Outside where the children play, there might be some interaction (and of course, in the bedroom). Other than that, though, men talk about men things in the men part of the house. Women keep to themselves.

But Mary . . . she's in there with her brother, Lazarus, and the rest of the men, sitting on the floor, listening to Jesus. Learning from the rabbi as if—it's laughable, unthinkable really—as if she intends to become a disciple herself.

And she's left poor Martha in the kitchen all by herself. No one to talk to. No one to help her prepare refreshments.

It's unconventional. Unseemly. Unwomanly.

Martha continues to stew, the heat slowly rising, her thoughts simmering for a while until they burst into a rolling boil. Convention flies out the window as she bursts into the room, demanding that Jesus tell her sister to get back into the kitchen where she belongs.

A woman, telling Jesus that women have no business exchanging ideas with men.

Ironic. That's the word for that.

But Jesus, gentle and firm at the same time, refuses to be cowed by Martha. He affirms Mary's choice, giving a divine stamp of approval to women and learning, liberating countless generations of women who will follow her to assume unconventional roles in His kingdom. And after opening that door to the sisters, He becomes as close to them as He is to their brother.

Unconventional. Unseemly. Ironic. These are all words that describe the things Jesus did during His life on earth. These are also words that accurately describe the ongoing activity of Jesus through His people. Wherever Christianity has gone, conventions have been broken, stereotypical roles have been redefined. Men and women serve side by side, for the harvest is plentiful but the laborers are so few.

Liberty. Approval. Affirmation. These are also words that describe Jesus and His followers. At least they should be.

TUESDAY: Beliefs

Jesus was a teacher, a rabbi. He is referred to as "Rabbi" 14 times in the New Testament—40 times as "Teacher." That was His job, and it's important to note that there were standards associated with His chosen profession. Not just anyone could go around calling himself a rabbi. There was a system in place, a fairly intricate system.

For a young boy growing up in Israel, being a rabbi was the greatest aspiration. Beginning around the age of six, male children began learning the Torah. From the age of 6 to the age of 10, a little boy would sit at the feet of a teacher from dawn until afternoon, memorizing and learning about Torah. Day after day, week after week, chanting and reciting the Law of Moses. Around the time a boy reached the age of 10, it was time to learn the family trade, and that was the end of his studies.

But some showed a special aptitude for learning, and these were invited to learn from rabbis how to apply the Law to everyday life. The rabbinical method of teaching was focused primarily on asking the students questions, such as "How do you honor your father and mother?" and "What kind of work is acceptable on the Sabbath?"

By the time a studious boy reached the age of 14, he had the entire Old Testament memorized, Genesis through Malachi. If, at that point, the student wanted to continue his studies, he went to find a rabbi he admired and asked if he could become one of the teacher's followers—a *talmidim*.

A rabbi never recruited students. That was considered beneath a rabbi's dignity. Students came to the rabbi; the rabbi never went to the students. In fact, students had to apply and submit to a series of screening tests. They had to prove that they were good students, that they had memorized large portions of the Scriptures and were able to rightly interpret portions of the Law. They had to interact with various schools of rabbinical interpretation.

If the student was good enough, the rabbi allowed him to become a follower.

If a rabbi accepted the student, the young man left everything behind for a once-in-a-lifetime chance to learn from a master teacher. The goal wasn't just to gain information from the rabbi, but to study him, observe him, learn how to live like he lived. A good student never let the rabbi out of his sight for fear of missing something he could learn.

Jesus was a rabbi. He taught with great power. Everywhere He went, He caused a great stir, and people were amazed at His teaching.

But—and this is amazing—Jesus went out and recruited followers.

Jesus not only recruited followers, He went out and recruited people no self-respecting rabbi would want: uneducated fishermen, tax collectors, rebels and revolutionaries.

And *women*!

He allowed a woman to sit at His feet! There was a saying back then: "Better to burn the Torah than to teach it to a woman." But Jesus was a rabbi of a different kind. He went to people who had been told that they didn't have what it takes to really know God. They had been told that they didn't have the mental aptitude or that they were born the wrong gender. And this rabbi with amazing authority told them, "I believe in you. I think you've got what it takes. You come follow Me. No prerequisites. No admission tests. I'll be your rabbi; you'll be My apprentices. Learn from Me. Watch Me. And one day, you'll not only know what I know; you'll live the way I live."

He calls the most unlikely people. He's even calling you.

WEDNESDAY: Values

The story of Mary and Martha is often used to beat up on busy, fast-paced, achievement-oriented, multi-tasking people. However, those adjectives pretty well describe the two authors of this book, so we're going in a different direction!

As we've seen, Jesus was staying in the home of Martha and her sister, Mary. Mary was sitting at Jesus' feet, just like a disciple would sit with a rabbi. Martha was busily working in the kitchen, complaining about having to do everything herself; she was in the same house with Jesus, but they might as well have been on other planets. Proximity does not always equal intimacy.

Jesus said to her, "Martha, you're all tied up in knots about so many things. Only one thing is necessary. Your sister has chosen the best thing, and that will never be taken away from her."

What exactly is Jesus saying here? Is He saying that Mary's personality is better suited for discipleship than Martha's?

That's the lesson that some have taught from Jesus' words. Teachers use this story to say, "See, the quiet, introspective types have an advantage over those busy-bee, type-A folks with their constant activity. If only they would learn to sit quietly, then they would know the joy of true discipleship."

It's easy to say that when it's your job to study the Bible. But what about folks who actually work for a living? What about the mother with three kids under the age of five? What about the guy who just got his first big promotion and is trying to overcome a huge learning curve at work while continuing to keep his commitment to coaching his son's little league team?

Does spending time with Jesus mean we have to stop everything and sit really still? Because if so, it may just have to wait for a lot of us. Maybe when the kids are out of the house and we're retired from our jobs, living on a beach in Florida—maybe then we'll be able to sit still long enough to have a relationship with Jesus.

Now is when it's important to remember that one of the names Jesus bore is "Immanuel," which means *God with us.* Not "God with us when we stop doing things and sit quietly." He's God with us while we prepare the meal. God with us while we do the dishes. God with us while we drive. God with us at work. God with us at rest. God with us once and for all.

The obstacle to intimacy may not be our busyness; it may be our unwillingness to believe that He wants to be with us while we do the things we do every day.

THURSDAY: Actions

Anyone who has ever delivered a sermon or a Sunday school lesson has heard this: "That message was so good. I know just the person who needed to hear it."

As professional Bible teachers, we've certainly heard our share of it. So many of our listeners want to get copies of a CD they can give to someone else, someone else more in need of correction than themselves. Or they want to know what next week's lesson will be so that they can bring a certain friend who really needs to hear what we're talking about. No one wants to apply the message to him- or herself. Many sit and wonder if that person across the aisle is listening, or they practice "the ministry of the elbow" to make sure that their spouse is paying attention.

Martha seems to have suffered from this affliction—this preoccupation with what others were doing. She was certain that Mary was doing the wrong thing; she was so certain that she felt comfortable saying, "Excuse me, Jesus? Isn't there something You'd like to tell my sister?" She just assumed that Jesus would agree with her. Who wouldn't agree with her? She was right, of course, and it never occurred to her otherwise.

But Jesus refused to endorse her perspective.

This certainly caught Martha off guard. Perhaps that was His intention. Sometimes you have to jar someone to get her attention. It wasn't the first time Jesus used this tactic, nor would it be the last.

It's easy to spend too much time evaluating the actions of others and too little time looking in the mirror, practicing the all-important task of self-evaluation. Jesus asked, "Why do you look at the speck of sawdust in someone else's eye and pay no attention to the plank in your own eye?" (Matt. 7:3). The apostle Paul echoed Him: "Each of you should test your own actions. Then you can take pride in yourself, without comparing yourself to somebody else, for each of you should carry your own load" (Gal. 6:4–5). How much more effective might Christians be if we spent as much time looking at ourselves as we spend pointing the finger at others? After all, pointing out what's wrong with our world is kind of like shooting fish in a barrel. And who really changes their ways because Christians look upon them with disapproval?

Rather than grading the performance of others (especially with the assumption that God will surely agree with us) an effective church empowers its members to take individual responsibility for their own walks, allowing the faith community to be an encouraging force.

That doesn't mean we have to ignore sin in the camp, but it does mean being slow to pass judgment, especially in areas that don't have anything to do with sin. Martha crossed that line and Jesus refused to hear her complaint. Let's not make the same mistake she did.

FRIDAY: Prayer

Narrative

Holy Father, all glory, honor and praise are Yours not only because of who You are but also for what You have done. You have broken the yoke of sin and of slavery in the lives of those who trust in You, and You have overcome the enmity and alienation that plague relationships among those who embrace your rule and authority. Wherever the true gospel of salvation and sanctification by grace through faith has spread, people have been transformed in the wake. Because of the Good News, the old distinctions that separated and estranged people need no longer rule our hearts. In Christ, there is neither Jew nor Greek, there is neither slave nor free man, there is neither male nor female, for we are all one in Christ Jesus. I praise You for the gift of freedom that overcomes the bondage of sin and unites us together into one Body, of whom He is the head.

Orthodoxy

Holy Son of the living God, You did what no one ever did and taught what no one ever taught. Unlike other teachers and rabbis in Israel, You taught out of your own authority and revealed truths that were previously unknown. You taught that the standard of righteousness the Father requires is nothing short of His own perfection. When the religious leaders were trying to externalize the moral law and reduce it to manageable proportions, You taught the radical truth that the Law concerns not only what we do, but also what we say and even what we think. You revealed that the problem is not external but internal; it concerns the corruption of the human heart. Our only hope is the new birth in which You implant a new heart and nature within us. I praise You that You perfectly fulfilled the Law in thought, word and deed and that You impute your righteousness to all who trust in You.

Orthopathy

Lord, I want to echo the words of Your servant George Herbert when he prayed, "Teach me, my God and King, in all things Thee to see, and what I do in anything, to do it as for Thee."[1] You are intimately involved in our lives, and everything we do matters when it is done in Your Name and for Your good pleasure. Grant me the biblical perspective that reveals the importance of everything, so that I will grow in the realization that all things should be done to the glory of God. May I come to see my work as part of my ministry and that when I do it with excellence in the service of others, it becomes a form of worship. I want to offer all the areas of my life to You and seek to be pleasing to You in all respects. May I grow in the wisdom of practicing Your presence in the most mundane and ordinary activities, knowing that is of value because it is done in Your Name.

Orthopraxy

God of grace, Your Word often convicts me about things that need to be changed; yet I often resist it, supposing that others need this message more than I do. I am often tempted to focus my attention on the errors and shortcomings of others because these are so easy to spot, and it costs me nothing to observe. But You have made it clear that I must first examine my thoughts and actions before criticizing others. Like the psalmist David, I ask You to search me and know my heart; try me and know my anxious thoughts; see if there be any hurtful way in me, and lead me in the everlasting way. I thank You that when I invite the Spirit to search my heart to reveal any areas that are displeasing to You, Your conviction comes not in generalities but in specifics. You graciously reveal the things I need to deal with one at a time, and You give me the power to respond in obedience.

35

Telling Stories

MATTHEW 13;
MARK 4:1–34;
LUKE 15

MONDAY: Story

John the Baptist had exploded on the scene, a whirlwind spitting fire and brimstone at the gawking crowds who came to witness the spectacle of it all. And he never failed to put on a show for them, with his astonishing claim that the Kingdom of heaven, the long-awaited fulfillment of all of God's promises, was finally close at hand.

And then Jesus showed up. John pointed to Him and said, "There He is. He is the Kingdom-bringer!"

Jesus didn't look like the Kingdom-bringer; He looked like a homeless rabbi, roaming the countryside and surviving by the kindness of strangers. But Jesus knew something no one else knew: that the Kingdom of heaven did not look like what they were expecting. Still, He wanted them to understand what the Kingdom is and what life is like for a citizen of that Kingdom. Mostly, Jesus wanted them to understand what the King of that Kingdom is like and what He wants for His people.

So Jesus devised a brilliant strategy: The Kingdom-bringer became the Story-teller. He told them stories about a plucky widow who wore down a judge with her persistence and about a farmer whose seed found several different types of soil in the same field. Two men went out to build two houses in two very different locations. A traveler was jumped by bandits and left for dead until a stranger showed up and offered assistance. A middle manager was caught cooking the books and forced into an audit. A king offered to let three servants manage more money than they'd ever seen in their lives.

He moved. He healed. He told stories. His teaching was amazing. Folks came from miles around to hear His captivating tales of ordinary people who had sons, served as attendants at weddings, threw extravagant parties. The stories were mesmerizing. They stuck in people's heads. They found themselves repeating them to people who hadn't heard them firsthand.

Sometimes the stories were about human nature: We all procrastinate, getting caught up in doing foolish things and frittering away our lives (even though we know we shouldn't). Sometimes the stories were about the community God has been trying to build since the beginning of time.

Mostly the stories were about what kind of God this YHWH is. He's like a shepherd who goes out looking for that one little sheep who keeps getting himself lost. He's like a woman who loses a coin and refuses to give up looking for it. He's like a father whose son has gone far, far away. He may wish he could be content to sever that relationship once and for all, but he just can't bring himself to do it. He catches himself looking to the horizon in the afternoon sun, his breath catching every so often. *Is that him? Is he coming home?*

Jesus' miracles were explained away by many. His teaching and understanding of the Scriptures were called into question and disputed. But these stories of His . . . they stick in your head.

TUESDAY: Beliefs

Up to this point, we've made a pretty big deal about Jesus. That is as it should be. He's the main character of the whole Story. He's the hero; we're the damsel in distress.

We've made bold assertions in previous weeks that Jesus was the greatest teacher of all time, the smartest man who ever lived. We stand by those statements. And yet . . .

His teaching can't really be considered data-rich, and He didn't convince many people. Jesus' teaching has had deep impact over the past 2,000 years, yet He was probably considered a fairly ineffective teacher during His own lifetime. He was more likely to ask you a question than give you an answer. He never revealed the theory of relativity to anyone, never spouted off about the sun being the center of the solar system.

Wise? Absolutely. Knowledgeable? Er . . .

As for all the stories He told . . . well, let's talk about those for a minute.

Most folks think Jesus used stories in order to communicate difficult things to simple people. And there's probably something to that.

But there's something more going on with these parables of His. In fact, Mark's Gospel sets up a distinction between the parables and plain teaching, saying He used parables with big groups of people but spoke plainly when He was with His disciples (see Mark 4:34). It appears, on closer inspection, that Jesus may have used these stories to obscure rather than illuminate what He was really saying (see Mark 4:10–12). At least that's what it sounds like from Mark.

Consider this: Jesus wasn't letting His friends in on a little secret that had to be kept from others as much as He was helping them solve a mystery. The clues were everywhere around them, but they lacked the perspective to piece them all together properly. They were Watson to Jesus' Sherlock Holmes. He wasn't providing them with missing pieces of information; He was helping them connect the dots of information they already had into a meaningful pattern.

Once they got all the dots connected and were able to step back and discern the pattern, that's when they really got frustrated. Jesus hadn't been giving them information or enlightening them at all! Instead, He was telling these thorny stories that got inside their heads and went off like little time bombs to force them into making a choice about Him: *You're either inclined toward God or away from Him. You either have ears to hear and eyes to see, or you do not.*

The stories that He told came together to form a wedge; a wedge that could find a crack in your heart and, little by little, force you off the fence.

WEDNESDAY: Values

Many churches today are filled with people who have placed their trust in Jesus to take care of what happens to them after they die. Few Christians have really placed their trust in Jesus to teach them what to do before that. Many of us have decided to follow Jesus into eternity, but we haven't decided to follow Him here and now. This explains why there is so little evidence of Christlikeness and transformation among us on a consistent basis.

Jesus once told a couple of stories about this very dynamic. He said, "The kingdom of heaven is like a treasure hidden in a field. When a man found it, he hid it again, and then in his joy went and sold all he had and bought that field. Again, the kingdom of heaven is like a merchant looking for fine pearls. When he found one of great value, he went away and sold everything he had and bought it" (Matt. 13:44–46). In other words, God's kingdom is so valuable that any sacrifice necessary is worth it. In fact, any necessary sacrifice—getting rid of anything that stands between you and the life offered by Jesus—is done with joy. It's a no-brainer. Get rid of something in order to gain that which is infinitely more valuable? Gladly!

So many people in our world today have made a radical commitment to excellence. Steve Jobs is so determined to make Apple, Inc. the industry leader when it comes to innovative and practical uses for technology that he draws a salary of $1 per year. Do you think he ever breaks that down into hourly increments and wonders whether or not he made the right decision when he signed that contract?

Of course not!

Everyone from sports franchises to paper manufacturing plants to candy bar companies sacrifice and stay awake at night and put in extra hours to ensure the quality of their product. They do this because they really believe that what they will get in return is of much greater value than what they give up.

Here's a simple question for you: Have you made the same level of commitment to following Jesus as Steve Jobs has to Apple, Inc.?

The earliest followers of Jesus did not leave everything behind to tag along with Him because they were afraid they might end up in hell if they didn't. They followed Him because they were fools not to. If what He was saying was true, they would never forgive themselves for rejecting it and missing the opportunity of a lifetime to learn firsthand how to live in God's kingdom.

Living life in God's kingdom—living out the gospel according to Jesus—isn't easy. It will probably require a complete restructuring of life as we currently know and experience it. It may involve difficulty and pain and sacrifice and long hours. It will most certainly require a clean break from some of the loyalties and affections that keep us divided in our hearts and minds.

But anything worth doing is worth doing well. And if it's really all it's cracked up to be, life in God's kingdom will prove to be well worth it.

The question is, *How badly do you want it?*

THURSDAY: Actions

Jesus' stories have a way of drawing us in, captivating us, forcing us to identify with one of the characters. We find ourselves in His stories about irresponsible young women or hard-working day laborers. We're attracted to their side of the story because we can relate so well to their plight.

One of Jesus' most famous stories begins this way: "There was a man who had two sons" (Luke 15:11). Of course, this is widely called "The Parable of the Prodigal Son."

You know how it goes. The younger son comes to his father and says, "I want what's coming to me after you die, but I don't want to wait that long. Can I have it now so I can leave and get on with my life?"

Astonishingly, the father agrees to this presumptuous plan. The son leaves, goes out into the wide world and wastes all his money. He hits rock bottom and is forced to get a job feeding pigs (which would have been repulsive to a good Jewish boy). It is there in the pigpen that he remembers the generosity of his father, and he begins to formulate a plan: He'll return as a hired hand to the family estate. Perhaps he can make enough money to repay what he owes to his father.

He makes the long journey home, rehearsing his speech. But while he is still a long way off, his father sees him and takes off in a mad dash to meet him. Before the son can get his speech out of his mouth, the father calls the servants to bring some decent clothes for the boy and orders a giant block party to be thrown in his honor.

Meanwhile, the older brother is at work out in the fields. He hears the singing and the dancing and wonders what's happening. He starts toward the big house and asks the first servant he finds, "What's going on?"

"Your brother's back and your dad's throwing a huge party."

The older brother is infuriated and refuses to go in to the party, and his father comes to find out what the problem is.

"This son of yours comes back and this is how you treat him?" (Note that he doesn't say "this brother of mine.") "All this time I've been working like a slave for you, and you never threw me a party!"

The father is distraught. He has just received one son back, but now he's alienated from the other. Why can't the big brother be happy for his younger sibling?

And that's where the story ends.

There are many people who have written about this famous story; there are lots of great books and articles you can read about it. But for today, think about this: Jesus' stories have a way of drawing you in. You find yourself identifying with one character or another, sort of siding with one or the other.

You might identify with the prodigal son. You spent years in the distant land, far away from the God who loves you. When you finally returned, you were overwhelmed at how ready He was to accept you—not to the status of a hired hand but to the full status of a beloved son or daughter. You'll be forever grateful for His generosity and grace.

Or you might identify with the older brother. You spent years doing the right thing even when others didn't. You may find yourself wondering if serving God actually pays dividends. You're reluctant to receive your prodigal brother back into the family.

Or maybe you know from personal experience that it's hard to be the prodigal and return home without turning into the older brother. In a strange twist of irony, you find it difficult to accept others the way you, yourself, have been accepted.

But this is the point of the story: Regardless of whether you identify more readily with the prodigal or the older brother, *you are called to become like the father.*

Jesus did stuff like this a lot. He left this story unfinished.

You get to decide how it ends.

FRIDAY: Prayer

Narrative

Lord Jesus, You are the most wonderful Teacher the world has ever known. Your words, which have been recorded for all time in the Gospels, reveal wisdom and truths that are unprecedented and unparalleled. And because of Your boundless understanding of human nature, You knew that many would scoff at and reject the gospel of the Kingdom because the human heart in its natural state is opposed to Your rule and authority. I marvel at the way You used parables to conceal truth from those who would reject it and at the same time reveal truth to those who would receive it. Your stories penetrate the heart and cause us to see things we could not see directly. I ask that I would be a part of the good soil in which the seed of Your Word penetrates and sends roots into my inner being so that it bears fruit on the outside.

Orthodoxy

All wise God, You have made us for Yourself, and You know our natures and ways far better than we do. In ways that are mysterious to us, we are an integrated unity out of the diversity of spirit, heart, soul, mind, will, emotions and con-science. We are fearfully and wonderfully made in our material and immaterial existence, and Your Word speaks to every component of our being. I am thankful that You have revealed both propositional and personal truth and have called us to integrate our minds and our hearts. May the principles and precepts of Your Word not only illuminate our minds but also enflame our hearts as we realize that the way, the truth and the life is a Person whom we can know and love. I pray that the truth of Your Word will inspire our minds to seek true greatness and our hearts to seek Your goodness.

Orthopathy

Lord, why is it so much easier to pursue excellence in our work or in sports or in knowledge than it is to pursue greatness as You define it? Why do believers typically trust in You for their eternal destiny but trust in the world for every-thing else? Why do we treasure the temporal over the eternal and aspire to success in this life more than rewards in the next? I know that it takes risk and trust to desire the unseen and the not-yet more than the visible and the now. But You have exhorted us to seek first Your kingdom and Your righteousness, and not to be anxious about material things because You know our needs and will sustain us when we value You over them. May I pursue the pearl of great price and the treasure hidden in the field and give everything I have in exchange for that which Your Word proclaims will endure forever.

Orthopraxy

Lord Jesus, I thank You for the wonderful parables and stories You told that force me to wrestle with the issues of life that really matter. Your stories grip my mind and my imagination, and as I begin to understand what You are saying, I am penetrated by the barb of truth that reveals my true condition. Just when I realize that I am the prodigal son, I discover the self-righteous older brother in me as well. But I know that the person You most want me to identify with is the loving father. For You are the One who waited for Your son to return, who felt compassion for him when You saw him at a distance, who ran and embraced him and kissed him and celebrated his return. Because that is who You are, I can trust You, love You and return to You whenever I stray from Your gracious embrace.

36

Jesus and Two Women

John 4:1–42; 8:1–11

MONDAY: Story

Once upon a time, they were two little girls with hopes and dreams. They thought about what it would be like to grow up, get married and have children of their own. They imagined what they would wear on that day, who would be invited, what the party would be like and how long it would last. Like so many little girls, they played that scenario out in their minds as the day drew closer and closer.

They never stopped to think that their lives might end up the way they did.

One woman went through five husbands. We don't know why. Maybe they all died. Maybe they all left her. Maybe she left some of them and some of them left her. We don't know, but there are several possible scenarios, all leading to the same outcome: Her heart had been broken more than once.

The end of a marriage is like a death in the family. Nothing prepares a person for it. And to some extent, it doesn't matter whose fault it is; when a marriage ends, a heart breaks. Maybe it was her fault; maybe it wasn't. Maybe it wasn't anyone's fault; maybe it just happened. Regardless, she must have been devastated.

Now imagine what it was like to go through it again . . . and again . . . and again . . . and again. Five times she gave her heart away. Five times it was broken. We can understand if she was willing to only go halfway now; she might live with a guy, but get married? No thanks.

The other woman had been caught, the door broken down just as dawn was breaking. She was still in bed with the man when they came in and dragged her out. Did she even know his name? Was he a longtime friend? We know nothing of the man; it was the woman these religious ruffians wanted to shame.

They hustled her through the streets to the Temple, throwing her to the ground at the feet of Jesus. To them, she had ceased to be a person; she was an object, wielded for their purposes. They were using her to make a point, to win an argument, to defeat the enemy they found in this traveling rabbi.

Two little girls—full of innocence and wide-eyed wonder—had grown up to be two women who knew the pain of this world. Their eyes had been opened, and they shuddered at what they were forced to see . . . until the moment they saw *Him*.

In this strange man, whose name they did not even know, they found the ultimate fulfillment of all the hopes and dreams they had carried in their hearts since childhood. They found a faithful Man who didn't want them because of what they could do for Him. They found a Rescuer who refused to condemn. They found a Provider who would never abandon them. They found a Messiah who knew everything about their pasts and loved them anyway.

TUESDAY: Beliefs

He could have taken a stand. He could have told the Samaritan woman exactly what was wrong with her, how she'd taken her life and thrown it away and how badly she had been misguided in her approach to God. He could have told that woman caught in the act of adultery just how wicked and sinful she was. He could have been the one to cast the first stone, but He didn't.

After all, Jesus was better than good; He was the best. He was sinless. He was perfect in thought, in word and in deed. He never told a lie. He never stole. He never gossiped. He never said or did things just to impress or make others feel inferior. He never manipulated or used people. He never harbored a grudge or had a lustful thought. He always did the right thing in the right way at the right time for the right reason. He was the most righteous human being of all time.

Yet (and this is huge) He had not one whiff of self-righteousness about Him. Rather, He was the most approachable person imaginable. Those who were despised and regarded as riff-raff seemed to enjoy His company, and when they were in His presence they found a level of acceptance and grace they had never experienced before.

Maybe that's the cause and effect right there.

See, Jesus could have come to earth to take a stand. You know—the kind of stand lots of Christians think they are obliged to take in the world. He could have taken a stand against immoral people. He could have taken a stand against impure people. Being the only perfect person around, He could have thrown lots of stones.

But He didn't.

He accepted them with a completely undeserved acceptance. Rather than taking a stand or casting stones, Jesus chose to build a bridge from this sin-sick planet to our heavenly Father. And He did that because He knew something that we seem to have forgotten: Sometimes grace and acceptance can accomplish what judgment and condemnation never can.

He knew that offering people the kind of dignity they deserve and desire is often the key to real life-change. By refusing to condemn the adulterous woman and the divorced woman, Jesus opened up the opportunity to really speak into their lives, to reach into their hearts and begin the amazing transformational process He came to initiate. His acceptance inspired the kind of change from within that we long to see in ourselves.

WEDNESDAY: Values

It's a familiar fairytale storyline. *Once there was a beautiful girl, born to be a princess. Her heart was pure. Her love was true. But, alas! She fell into the evil clutches of some malevolent villain who placed her under a curse. Now trapped, her only hope was for a handsome prince to set her free.*

This prince, when he arrives, is not only physically strong, but also spiritually pure; he has to be to defeat her oppressor and win the fair maiden's hand.

Just as she begins to despair, he appears. With bravery and cunning, the prince lays siege to the tower where she is held by the curse and breaks the icy grip of the sinister force holding her captive. Blood is shed, and more than once the prince appears overmatched. But he is valiant and relentless. Eventually, all is well in the world. The dragon is slain, the villain destroyed. The object of his heart's desire is rescued.

They ride off to his castle on the hill where they live happily ever after.

This story—or some variation of it—is buried deeply within our collective conscience. Every little girl dreams that one day her prince will come. Little boys intuitively rehearse their parts with cardboard paper-towel tubes, jousting with one another in preparation for the day when they will be called upon to dispatch some real enemy. No one has to tell children these stories. Somehow, this idea is already in us. The brave man risking life and limb to rescue the beautiful woman is as close to universal as it gets.

And that's why there are few times more devastating in the life of a woman than when she is told the opposite—that she is not valued. She is not wanted. No one is willing to fight for her. She is no man's treasure. Rather, she is ugly and unloved.

What happens to a woman who hears these words? The worst things you can imagine. And she's likely to tell herself that she deserves them. A little girl who has been abandoned or abused is often willing to do nearly anything as an adult to get the attention she mistakes for love. She will endure insult and assault, and it may never occur to her that she deserves anything else.

Deep down, she believes that the hero will never come. She has been compromised. She does not deserve a prince, for she is no princess.

It is for two women who fit this profile all too well that Jesus came. They had sinned and been sinned against. They had been hurt and made cynical by life. They were guilty and embarrassed. One deserved to die. The other may have wished to.

It is for men and women who fit this profile all too well that Jesus still comes—our conquering hero, strong and pure, risking life and limb to break the chains of oppression and set us free forever, to demonstrate once and for all that the pertinent issue is no longer the sins of our past but the God of our future. And one day (it may not be long), we shall ride with Him to His castle on a hill where we will all live happily ever after.

On one hand, it's important to remember that Jesus looks at you like the hero looks at the beautiful damsel in distress. That's how much He values you. He would rather die than live without you.

On the other hand, it's equally important to remember that Jesus looks at your neighbor the same way. The irritating receptionist, the traffic cop, your mother-in-law, the woman who stole your husband—Jesus died for them, too.

He doesn't just value good people; He values all people. And He calls us to do the same.

THURSDAY: Actions

God sure asks a lot of questions.

"Adam, where are you?" Does God really not know where Adam is? Or is God playing dumb?

"I'm over here hiding in the bushes because I'm naked." Adam had been naked since the day God made him, but now all of a sudden it's a big deal.

"Who told you that you're naked? Did you do something I need to know about?"

One time Jesus was walking with His disciples and they got into an argument about which of them was the greatest. Jesus turned and asked, "Hey, what are you guys talking about?" Like He didn't know.

"Why don't you go get your husband," He asked the Samaritan woman, knowing full well that she had been married five times, was 0-for-5 on the marital front and was shacked up with a guy now.

"Oh, I don't have a husband," she replied, and tried to leave it at that. She'd been talkative up to that point, but now—faced with the truth about herself—she found the value in brevity.

"Where are your accusers? Is there no one left to condemn you?" He asked the woman caught in adultery.

"They've all gone, sir," she said, trying to cover her shame.

Where are you? Who told you you're naked? Have you eaten from that tree? What are you guys talking about? Where's your husband? Does anyone condemn you?

Why does God insist on asking questions? He's obviously not looking for information. He already knows the answer before He asks. Here's why: He wants to know if we will come out of hiding and step into the light. Or will we retreat further into darkness?

See, Jesus can handle anything you've got. There's no mess so big He can't fix it. But He lives in the light, and if you want to deal with Him, well . . . that's where He is.

When you've sinned and your life is in shambles, you have two basic options: You can deny, cover up, stall for more time and (more than likely) end up digging yourself an even deeper hole. Or you can confess, come clean, be honest about how helpless you are in the situation and ask for Someone to show you the way out.

You can stay where you are. You can hold on for dear life and Jesus will go away eventually. But then there will be no healing, no restoration, no forgiveness.

The question God always asks is this: *Will you come out of hiding?*

FRIDAY: Prayer

Narrative

Lord Jesus, life in this broken world is fraught with so much sorrow and pain and with so many broken dreams and hopes. In our heart of hearts, we know what the world should be like and we long for that better world. Yet we do not have the power to make it happen, because we lack the inner resources to become the people You intended us to be. I thank and praise You that You have come into the world to rescue us from ourselves by drawing us to You. In spite of the ravages of human rebellion, You have come with compassion and grace to transform us into Your image and empower us to live a new kind of life with dignity, purpose and hope. In spite of our sinful and broken lives, You come to us with the gifts of acceptance, forgiveness and love. I magnify Your Name because of the awful price You paid with Your own blood to give us this new and eternal life.

Orthodoxy

Father, You have granted me the glorious gift of acceptance and welcome in Christ. Without Him, I was justly condemned and separated from Your holy presence. But through the powerful work of the Savior, You rescued me from the domain of darkness and transferred me to the Kingdom of your beloved Son. In spite of my guilt and sin, You reached out to me and lifted me out of the abyss. In my desperate need, You gave me the grace to acknowledge my condition and respond to Your loving call. You have declared me righteous in Christ and have reconciled me to You so that now I enjoy peace with You instead of estrangement and alienation. In light of Your great mercies, I want to present all I know of myself to all I know of You. Because of who You are and what You have done, I can trust You implicitly and place all my hope in You.

Orthopathy

Dear God, You are the Rescuer and Deliverer of my soul. Through Your Son, You stooped down in order to lift me up. I was dead in my trespasses and sins; my mind was blinded by the enemy to keep me from seeing the light of the gospel of the glory of Christ and I was held captive by the snare of the devil to do his will. But Jesus came to overthrow this bondage and to liberate me to be His beloved. You have graciously offered these gifts to all who call upon Your Name and receive the life that is in Christ Jesus. Just as You have accepted and forgiven me, may I also accept and forgive those who have sinned against me. Because You have liberated me from my captivity, may I also seek to be Your agent and ambassador to the people You have placed in my life. Instead of despising those who have done wrong, may I reach out to them in love and mercy.

Orthopraxy

Lord God, You know me from the inside out, and there are no thoughts I can have that are not fully evident to You. Nor can I escape Your manifest presence; You are always with me. The realization of these truths would be overwhelming to me if it were not for the righteousness of Christ that was credited to me when I received the gift of new life through trust in His Person and work. In Him, I no longer need to hide from You or try to cover up my faults. Thank You for the holy relief of being able to approach Your throne of grace with confidence and open access in times of need. You have loved me with an everlasting love, and in Christ, nothing can separate me from that love because it is uncaused and unmerited by me. I thank You for the assurance that Your penetrating gaze purifies me as it invites me to live in the reality of my new identity in Your Son.

37

One Week to Live

MATTHEW 21–25;
MARK 11–13;
LUKE 19–21;
JOHN 12

MONDAY: Story

It had been a busy week, and it wasn't over yet. Things had started off with a bang and a parade, with Jesus looking like some Bizarro World version of a conquering king—riding into town on the back of a donkey with hundreds (perhaps thousands) of peasants throwing down their coats before Him and waving palm branches. It looked like the Messiah was coming to claim Jerusalem.

But all was not well.

The Pharisees complained about the level of excitement (Pharisees frequently do). *Can't you get those kids to calm down and be quiet?* Jesus went toe-to-toe with the religious establishment and refused to back down. And He won . . . for the moment. The Pharisees lacked both the popular appeal and the official power to enforce their demands and could do nothing but stand there red in the face.

Jesus, however, did not rejoice in His temporary victory. Instead, He wept over the city of Jerusalem. He knew this would be the last time He would see the city like this. In a few short decades, Jerusalem would be ripped to shreds by the Romans. On top of that, He knew what this passionate week was going to cost Him. So He wept with undignified, gut-wrenching sobs.

Bright and early Monday morning, Jesus and His disciples made their way to the Temple. On the way there, He cursed a fig tree. Once He got there, He turned over the tables and benches where business was being transacted. People and animals scrambled this way and that. He had done this once before (see John 2:13–25), but apparently His initial cleansing of the Temple had little or no lasting impact. So as a sort of bookend to His public ministry, He did it again.

The Sadducees must have joined the Pharisees now in their anger and hatred of this man. But He had the people on His side. If they tried to stop Him, they might have a real fight on their hands. And the ever-present Romans weren't too far away, hands on swords, watching and waiting for their cue to quell a potential rebellion. And so they waited.

Tuesday was a day of conversation. Following two days of intense action, everyone wanted to have a word with Jesus. Some Greek people. Members of the Sanhedrin. Herodians. Sadducees. Pharisees. Regular folks. Everyone wanted to hear Jesus talk about who He was and what He intended to do. They questioned His identity, His authority, His politics, His eschatology, His ethics. The whole series of conversations built to a fever pitch, when Jesus launched into a tirade against the Jewish leaders (especially the Pharisees).

Afterward, He broke down in tears again. He had less than a week to live, and He knew it. Time was running out, and Jesus, meek and mild, seemed to have gone stark-raving mad!

If this is how the week begins, Lord only knows how it will end.

TUESDAY: Beliefs

If you only had one week to live, what would you do? What if you knew you could postpone your death by altering your schedule?

All Jesus had to do was lay low, and the whole thing would likely have blown over. It's not like the Jewish leaders were looking for someone to kill that week; they would have been happy to keep things quiet and avoid any kind of controversy.

And the Romans were reasonable: Stay in your place, pay your taxes, don't cause trouble, and no trouble will come after you.

But Jesus knew this was the thing He had come to do. Yes, the teaching was important. Yes, the miracles. Yes, the lifestyle. But none of it would make a difference without His sacrificial death.

The apostle Paul said that without the resurrection, we're the biggest fools of all time—celebrating a man who was executed! And he was right (see 1 Cor. 15:14–19). But there's no resurrection without the crucifixion. They're inseparable.

And so it was that Jesus, knowing full well that this week would end with Him dead and buried, having suffered the most humiliating and tortuous death imaginable, marched straight toward it, embracing His role in human history. Make no mistake about it: He chose this. No one did this to Him. He went willingly.

And here's the crazy kicker (it won't come as a surprise to any who have been following along): He didn't choose this path *in spite* of the fact that He was God. He chose this path precisely because He was (and is) God. This is exactly the kind of thing you'd expect Him to do.

Granted, no other god in any other religious system in human history would ever choose to die on behalf of the people who have spurned and rejected His loving advances for millennia. But this isn't any other god in any other religious system. This is our God, the God who humbled the Egyptians and parted the Red Sea, the God who drove the Canaanites from the Promised Land, the God who spared Isaac and redeemed Gomer, the God who loves relentlessly and refuses to give up on His dream of one day forming a community of people who are rightly related to Him and rightly relating to each other, a group of people whose very presence is a blessing to the whole, wide world.

He knew how the week would end. He knew how to avoid it. But He walked straight into the fiery furnace of hell for us. That's the kind of God He is.

WEDNESDAY: Values

Tuesday was a long day! It was one of those days when you blink and it's lunchtime, then you blink again and it's starting to get dark.

Jesus and His disciples found themselves in a series of meetings (some of us can relate to just how draining that can be!). But the day ended on a positive note.

As they were leaving the Temple, Jesus sat down in the court of the women and watched people as they approached the 13 trumpet-shaped, bronze receptacles. Each was labeled, telling what the donated money would go toward. Jesus saw wealthy people casually tossing in money, their coins sliding down the bronze, clanking metallically, attracting attention.

And that's when He saw her: Unnoticed by anyone else, an unassuming widow dropped two tiny coins in the coffer. Jesus got so excited that He called His disciples over to tell them her story. It must have seemed strange to them, given the scale of everything else that had been happening this week, that Jesus would get that worked up over a mere shaving of metal. But to Jesus, apparently, it was a very big deal.

Think about that for a minute: Jesus only had a few days left with His disciples. In about 48 hours His ordeal would begin, and it wouldn't end until He was dead and buried. We would understand if Jesus was a little preoccupied, wouldn't we? If Jesus was a little withdrawn or reserved or introspective, that would be understandable, right? Or if He was a little testy, pessimistic or cynical. After all, He had spent the better part of three years trying to get His message across to these dullards. But after all this time, still all they ever want to know is when He's going to set up the Kingdom, when He's going to overthrow the Roman government and who will get to sit next to Him when He finally holds court!

We'd understand if He just wanted to be alone for a while to collect His thoughts. Yes, He would get to that, but first He was determined to wring every last minute out of life while He could.

Jesus was always on the lookout for people who were getting it right. How did He even notice that one quiet widow amidst the sprawling chaos of His life? Well, if you study Jesus much at all, you'll notice a pattern. Do you know who the most important person for Jesus was at any given moment? *The person right in front of Him.*

One time when Jesus had just finished preaching, a guy with leprosy started calling His name. Jesus stopped everything to go over and spend time with him. One time when Jesus was on His way to heal a man's dying child, a woman touched the hem of Jesus' robe. Again, Jesus stopped everything to connect with that one sick woman.

It was His pattern. He was often busy—He had lots of things to do, places to go, people to see. But He was never too busy to notice people who were getting it right in small and quiet ways.

THURSDAY: Actions

The whole week was full to overflowing, pregnant with meaning and import. It would get even heavier as it moved toward the grand finale: the brooding tune of Thursday evening's meal, the somber sound of devastating loss that was that Friday afternoon, the silent and uncertain pause that was Saturday, the eternally resonating major chord of victory that was Sunday morning.

But before He got there, it appears that Jesus took a day off. Nothing is recorded about His whereabouts or activities on Wednesday. Perhaps He was making plans with a cryptic man who appeared to Peter and John carrying a water jug. Perhaps He was watching Judas wrestle with the demons that would prompt him to do his dastardly deed. Perhaps He spent the day praying and gathering His thoughts.

Regardless, it's instructive that Jesus chose to do nothing with one of His last days that the biblical writers deemed noteworthy. Because here we see another pattern in Jesus' life: He observed a rhythm of work and rest. He plunged Himself headlong into ministry, working from sun up to sundown, healing, teaching, feeding and touching. And then He withdrew from the crowds, carving out time for rest and solitude. Then once more into the breach He charged, only to retreat again when He felt it was time for a little R&R.

You can't really call the life He led "balanced." It's not like He had a Day-Timer or a Blackberry and scheduled every hour of His days: *Let's see, I spent an hour alone today, so that means I can spend an hour with people.* He just seems to have felt it, like a rhythm.

There are some personality types who are particularly prone to working all the time. If there's work to be done—one person who hasn't heard the good news about Jesus, or someone in the hospital who hasn't been visited—these people are on the go. They say things like, "I can rest when I'm with the Lord" or "I'd rather burn out than rust out." Either way, you're *out*, so we're not sure why either is an acceptable option.

For those of us who are more likely to work, work, work, it's important to see that Jesus, at this point, had only a few dozen hours left on this earth. And He chose to rest. He chose to do nothing of interest. He took a day off.

One of the reasons why taking a day off is so important is that it forces you to remember that everything isn't dependent upon you. Like Jesus, you have a Father in heaven who is constantly at work. The assurance of this is what makes rest possible.

Jesus could have been uptight and fussy, gathering His disciples for late-night cram sessions all week long. But He knew that the Helper would come and do

His work in His time. Jesus would do what He could and leave the rest up to His Father and the Holy Spirit.

Now if that's the way Jesus lived, do you suppose you could try to get some rest this weekend?

FRIDAY: Prayer

Narrative

Lord Jesus, the Law, the prophets and the other writings of the Hebrew Bible all pointed to You and anticipated, in unparalleled detail, the significant events of Your first and second comings. You are the Messiah. You came in humility as the suffering Servant in Your first advent, and I anticipate the day when You will come in power and glory as the reigning King in Your second advent. You are the Bread of life; You are the Light of the world; You are the Good Shepherd; You are the Resurrection and the Life; You are the Way, the Truth and the Life; and You are the True Vine. You did not come to be served but to serve, and to give Your life as a ransom for many. You came to seek and to save that which was lost. And You came to accomplish the work that the Father gave You to do. I glorify Your Name for who You are and for what You have done.

Orthodoxy

Dear Father, when I consider all the systems that men have developed since time immemorial to find ways of controlling the events of this life and of meriting a better destiny in the next life, I marvel at the uniqueness of Christianity. In other religions, people are the ones who offer sacrifices and good works to their god or gods. In Your Word, You reveal that You are the one who made the sacrifice of Your Son for us. In other religions, people are portrayed as good enough to earn their way to the ultimate. In the Bible, You reveal that all have sinned and fallen short of Your glory. Jesus Christ is the only true Savior the world has ever known; and as the sinless Passover Lamb, He alone can take away the sins of the world. I take refuge in Him and though I have not yet seen Him, I love Him.

Orthopathy

God of grace, Your enduring revelation in the written Word and the living Word displays a degree of concern and compassion that is too marvelous for me to fathom. I cannot see why You would take notice of us, let alone send Your Son into the world to redeem us with the blood of His cross. Your love surpasses comprehension, and Your Son reveals the lengths to which You would go to overcome the alienation of sin and welcome us as Your adopted children into Your heavenly household. Even while we were rebellious enemies, Christ died for the ungodly. Such love is too high; I cannot attain to it. It is too deep; I cannot plumb it. It is too wide; I cannot encompass it. Because You have loved us in this way, may we express that love in our love for others.

Orthopraxy

Jesus, I thank You that You never ask us to do what You have not already done for us. You taught us to love one another, and You first loved us. You taught us to forgive one another, and You first forgave us. You taught us to serve and sacrifice for others, and You first served and sacrificed Yourself for us. You taught us to obey the Father, and You obeyed Him perfectly. You taught us to pray, and You fully exemplified prayer in all that You did. You taught us to depend on the power of the Holy Spirit, and You accomplished all things in His power. You taught us to notice the obscure and the unlovely, and You first did that for us. You taught us to have patience and forbearance for others, and You demonstrated that throughout Your earthly ministry. You taught us to be kind and merciful to others, and that characterized all of Your life. May I grow in Your grace and become more like You.

38

Love and Feet

JOHN 13–16

MONDAY: Story

He had one last night with His friends, one last chance to talk to them about what mattered most, what they could not afford to forget. How could He take the wisdom of the ages, filtered through all the teaching, all the conversation, all the activity, and distill it down to one final lesson?

They had given up everything to follow Him for three years, and now the end was rapidly approaching. It was only a matter of hours now.

And to top it all off, they had been arguing all day about which of them was the greatest.

Maybe none of this stuff was sinking in at all. Maybe it would have to wait until after He was gone. Maybe then they would look back and remember.

While the disciples are fighting over who gets to sit where, Jesus silently picks up a towel and a bowl of water. Before anyone is aware of what's happening, the first sandals are off, and the hands that created the tree that would be turned into crossbeams, the hands that carved the mountain from which the iron was drawn to make the spikes, the hands that held everything together, were washing

287

the grime off road-weary feet. The hands were calloused, but they were tender with the kind of care only He could feel.

It got their attention.

Peter, in typical Peter fashion, went overboard: "You're not gonna do that to me!" he bellowed.

But Jesus was firm and resolute: "If you don't let Me do this, you're saying that you want nothing to do with Me."

Peter's pendulum swung to the other side: "Okay, if You're gonna put it like that, go ahead and gimme a sponge bath!"

Maybe they all had a good laugh. There was a lot of tension in the room, and laughter sometimes helps.

He worked His way around the whole room. Andrew. James. John. Bartholomew. Thomas. Philip. Matthew. The other James—the short one. The other Simon—the angry one. Thaddeus.

Judas.

Yes, Judas. Jesus washed the feet of the man who betrayed Him. That's what love does. That was the whole point.

TUESDAY: Beliefs

It's one thing to wash someone's feet if you like them, if they're nice to you, if you know you stand to gain something from it. Like if it was Donald Trump's or Oprah Winfrey's feet. (We don't wash feet anymore in our society, but we do other things in the hope that the other person will reciprocate.) It's practically unheard of to do something nice for someone you know is going to repay you in the cruelest manner imaginable. How did Jesus, knowing what Judas was determined to do, perform such an act of selfless love?

Just think about how odd the scene is here: Jesus—God in the flesh, Savior of the world, the One for whom all things were created—kneeling on the floor, performing a task that was considered beneath all but the lowliest of servants. This was a task so menial that nobody in this group would think of performing it; it might forever stigmatize the foot-washer, branding him in people's minds, creating an image of him with a towel around his waist like a slave.

It's quite a risk He's taking here. Their last mental picture of Him should be something more . . . powerful. Shouldn't it? (Can you imagine the President of the United States giving members of Congress a pedicure on his way out of office?)

How did Jesus do it?

The answer is embedded in the text: "Jesus knew that the Father had put all things under his power, and that he had come from God and was returning to God" (John 13:3).

First, Jesus knew that whatever power He had came from His heavenly Father. He didn't have to worry about losing status in the eyes of His friends. He didn't have to look the part of a leader. God was in control, and because of that, Jesus could risk showing them His love.

Second, Jesus knew where He had come from. He was confident that He had come from God, and that confidence enabled Him to know that what He was doing on earth was part of an unstoppable plan. God gives us the roles we play and takes them away at His discretion. We don't need to protect our power base. God will take care of that for us.

Finally, Jesus knew where He was going. He knew that His life wouldn't end in death; He was returning to His home with the Father, where God would place all things under His feet and would appoint Him head over everything (see Eph. 1:22). Jesus knew that as long as He continued to follow the leading of His Father in heaven, He would accomplish the purposes for which He was sent. No one could take away His destiny, and that made Him a very dangerous man!

He was so dangerous that He could love without reservation, without the need for reciprocation.

Knowing our origin and our destiny, knowing our true identity, wipes out the insecurity that so often keeps us from following Jesus into positions of service and enables us to live life with confidence and freedom.

WEDNESDAY: Values

Jesus washed the feet of a man He knew was going to betray Him. He didn't just wash the feet of those who were most likely to understand or respond well. He wasn't calculating the odds of a favorable response. He washed the feet of Judas because Judas was there, and his feet needed washing.

All too often nowadays, churches forget (or ignore) the people right in front of them. They're frequently content to serve themselves. They attract a certain group of people and cater to their demands out of fear that those people might leave. They allow themselves to be held hostage by insiders and never venture outside the walls of their building to serve the people around them who are in desperate need.

Service in churches has become a means to an end. When they serve, what they're really seeking is church growth—and if they can't get that, they'll settle for self-preservation. Service is a means to boost (or at least maintain) attendance figures. Service, in many churches, is a path to greatness. Maybe some day they'll be a megachurch (or at least they won't die as fast as that church down the road).

But in the kingdom of God, where Christ is the Head of the Church, service is not the path to greatness; it *is* greatness. Service is the only true greatness the kingdom of God has to offer.

Jesus says, "Now that I, your Lord and Teacher, have washed your feet, you also should wash one another's feet. I have set you an example that you should do as I have done for you" (John 13:14–15). Now, there are those who misguidedly wish to make a church ordinance of this, and they have mandatory foot-washing services. We shake our heads at them and say, "My, they sure have missed the point!"

It isn't a church ceremony Jesus was hoping to institute here; it's an attitude to learn and live. It's not something for us to sit back and ponder; it's something for us to figure out how to put into practice. Jesus' ministry of the towel is to be the Church's ministry of the towel.

This parable Jesus acted out Himself is about humility and an attitude of service. It's a warning that we must constantly rethink why we do the things we do. Are we serving others to gain their approval and honor and applause? Are we washing their feet in the hope that they will repay us with their faithful attendance and regular financial contributions? If so, we're missing the mark, sinning against the One who calls us to service.

We must be willing to identify with Jesus in the very act of humility and service. Otherwise, whatever it is we are involved with is not the kingdom of God. Jesus says, "What you've just seen Me do for you, go and do for others."

THURSDAY: Actions

Judas left soon after Jesus washed his feet, and Jesus had a heart-to-heart with the other 11 disciples. "Love is what it's all about," He said. "It's going to get unimaginably difficult for you after I'm gone. But love will win. Love will defeat treachery. Love will consume confusion. Love will defiantly withstand persecution. Love will win."

"And serve," He continued. "Service is not a path to greatness in God's kingdom. Service *is* greatness in God's kingdom."

He talked, and they walked. Through the Kidron Valley, by the vineyards there, passing the stream that ran red this time every year, red with the blood of the sacrificial lambs slaughtered for Passover.

He spoke about how dependent they would have to be on Him. This was puzzling for them in light of the fact that He had stressed His immanent departure. He assured them that He would still find a way to be with them. He would send a Helper, a Comforter, to live in them, reminding them of everything He had said and done, empowering them to do even greater things.

They looked at Him, not knowing what to say, not knowing what to do. They had never seen Him like this before.

He surely noticed their concern, because He told them, "Do not let your hearts be troubled. Trust in God; trust also in me" (John 14:1).

But how could they not be troubled? The One they'd given up everything for was going away. He had given them impossible commands to obey and examples they weren't sure they could follow.

"Love our enemies the way You have loved us? Wash peoples' feet—even the feet of those who would betray and abuse us?" Doing as He asked didn't seem very possible to them.

Perhaps it was because they were walking past vineyards that Jesus grasped hold of this illustration: "I am the vine; you are the branches. If you remain in me and I in you, you will bear much fruit; apart from me you can do nothing" (John 15:5). In other words, Jesus looked at this ragged group of men whom He loved so much and said, "I know you're scared and confused. I know there are problems and questions swirling about, and you wonder how you will survive to the end of today, let alone to the end of days. I know, but don't be afraid. You don't have to live in your own strength and power any longer. Cling to Me, and through the power of the Holy Spirit, you will grow."

Love. Serve. Trust. Abide.

He said it to them, and they believed Him. Then one of them wrote it down for us to hear. Now it's our choice whether we will believe Him, too.

FRIDAY: Prayer

Narrative

Lord, You know us better than we know ourselves, and yet You chose to serve us in the life and ministry of Your beloved Son. How can words express the magnitude of Your lovingkindness and mercy? You are in authority over all things, from the microcosm to the macrocosm. You order the stars, the galaxies and the clusters and superclusters of galaxies that are spread over distances so great that even to get a glimpse of the magnitude is terrifying. You sustain the sun, the planets and all that dwells on earth. You form life out of matter that has no life, and You shape our complex bodily systems, as well as our minds, personalities and moral capacities. You have made all things well, and even in this world that was subjected to futility, we see Your marvels and handiwork. I live in hope of the redemption of the body and of the whole of creation.

Orthodoxy

Lord Jesus, because You knew who You were, why You had come and where You were going, You were secure enough to serve even the lowliest of men. You knew that the Father had given all things into Your hands, and that You had come forth from God and were going back to God. You knew Your dignity and power, because the Father gave all things to You. You knew Your significance and identity, because You came forth from the Father. And You knew your security and destiny, because You were going back to the Father. In like manner, teach me to become secure enough to serve. For in You, I have received every spiritual blessing; in You, I am now a child of God; and in You, nothing can separate me from the love of God whom I will see face to face. I pray that this understanding will become increasingly real in my life.

Orthopathy

Lord God, just as Your beloved Son served us, I want to do the same for others. The more I grasp my new identity and dignity in Christ, the more free I become to serve others even when they do not reciprocate, and the less I am in the bondage of being defined by people's opinions and expectations. As I let You (and not people) define me, I am liberated to serve them, because I know who I am in Christ and have nothing to prove. May I grow in my spiritual apprehension of my identity in Christ, and may I invite the empowerment of Your Holy Spirit to make it possible to be truly other-centered. Teach me to develop a vision for what You are doing in the lives of others, and give me joy in helping them mature and reach their potential.

Orthopraxy

Jesus, You are the True Vine, and Your Father is the Vinedresser. As a branch derives its vitality from the vine, may I abide in You and draw upon Your life instead of trying to create life on my own. Only in this way will I be able to bear the kind of fruit that will endure and glorify the Father. I acknowledge that apart from You, I can do nothing that will remain forever and that will be pleasing to the Father. May I learn to walk in utter dependence on You as a conduit of Your life. Then I will have the joy of seeing excess life in the form of fruit that carries the seeds of its own reproduction and that nourishes others. May I know You in a personal and experiential way, and may that growing knowledge cause me to love You more. And as I love You more, may I joyfully obey Your commandments, so that I will bear much fruit and glorify the Father as Your true disciple.

39

The Last Night

MATTHEW 26:36–46;
MARK 14:32–42;
LUKE 22:39–46

MONDAY: Story

This night was unlike any other. The tension was palpable; everyone seemed on edge. There was bickering among them, and Jesus was in a strange mood. Their conversation had gone from death and betrayal to joy and peace. He kept telling them to love one another.

As they walked together through the cool spring night, Jesus spoke with a strange sense of urgency. When they got to the entrance of the garden overlooking the city, Jesus told everyone to wait for Him, silently tapping James, Peter and John. The four men went deeper into the olive grove until they came to a familiar place. There was a giant press nearby, and the fragrance of ripe olives hung in the air. How many olives had been crushed there, the heavy stones forcing oil from pulp?

Jesus looked at His closest friends in this world and said, "Wait here for Me. I'm going over there to pray."

They sank down, heavy from the accumulated stress of the week. Before they realized what was happening, they were asleep.

Jesus went farther into the garden and began to pray. But it was unlike any prayer before or since. It was a desperate, howling prayer. It was a begging, pleading, wrestling kind of prayer. He had always sought and done the Father's will. But now, in His darkest hour, He was—what? Uncertain? Hesitant? Maybe there was another way. Anything is possible.

He needed to be alone to sort this all out. But He also needed His friends close by. And they needed to be here; there were lessons to be learned, even in this. But the lessons could only be learned if they were awake. Jesus came back to them. "Wake up! Stay alert! There are important things happening tonight."

"Yes, Jesus," their mouths said, even as their eyes were beginning to close. In the brief glimpse they got of Him, He looked strange. Sweaty. Almost bloody—at least that's how one of them would later report it to a doctor friend.

Again He went, not more than a stone's throw from them, to pray. The sweat began pouring off His forehead like blood oozing from a freshly opened wound. The heavy stone that is the sin of the entire world, forcing blood, sweat and tears from this Man who would soon be beaten to a pulp.

"Still asleep?"

"Sorry, Jesus. It's been a long week."

And then He went back to talk to His Father again. This time, He was resolved. His face was as hard as flint. If it must be done, it must be done. If there is no other way, then so be it. He took a deep breath and, gathering His strength, stood up. He heard something in the distance and could just begin to see the light of torches approaching.

TUESDAY: Beliefs

Jesus knew what was coming and He knew when. He knew how little time He had left, and He knew how little of all this His disciples were actually absorbing. Even while they were walking from that Upper Room to the Garden of Gethsemane, they wanted to know if Jesus was getting ready to overthrow the Roman government. It had to have been discouraging for Him.

One of the side effects of discouragement is that it opens you up to temptation. When you're down in the dumps, anything that promises relief (even temporary relief) starts to look good.

The 52 Greatest Stories of the Bible

That's the place Jesus was in when He went to pray in the Garden. He was discouraged. He may have been frightened. He had worked so hard to get here, but He may have wondered if it would matter at all in the long run. Would any of this stick in the minds of these addle-brained disciples of His?

Maybe He *should* resort to force.

He could have done that—called a million angels down from heaven to slay the mob that was already on its way to Him. Had fire rain down from the sky. Toppled the Temple and established once and for all a Kingdom on earth.

Jesus had been tempted before, at the beginning of His ministry. He had gone out into the wilderness by Himself and fasted for 40 days. Satan himself showed up and tried to get Jesus to take a shortcut, to flex His muscles for all the world to see. Luke tells us that after Jesus won that showdown, the devil left Him alone for a while. But he was just waiting for a more opportune time (see Luke 4:13). Perhaps this lonely night was finally that opportunity. Here was Jesus, weakened and afraid.

It's not too much of a stretch to imagine the old devil sidling up alongside Jesus, whispering in His ear. "Go ahead, flex those muscles. Pulverize these people. Wipe this city off the map. They rejected You first. It's payback time!"

How tempting would that have been? Jesus could have gotten out of this ordeal right then and there. But what kind of message would that have sent? Jesus never used His power for personal gain, and He wasn't going to start now. He used His power to help others.

Sometimes there are no shortcuts through the fiery ordeal. Sometimes you just have to put your head down and keep moving forward.

And so Jesus, with a heavy sigh, repeated the words that He had probably said more than once before: "Nevertheless, Father, not My will but Yours be done."

WEDNESDAY: Values

The timeline's a little fuzzy, but as best we can figure it, Jesus spent about three-and-a-half years with His followers. For much of that time, He was a target for religious leaders who feared His influence among the people.

And then it all started to come to a head, with various religious groups coming together to figure out how to rid themselves of this man who was such a thorn in their sides.

Jesus wasn't alone during those years, however. He had some people who gathered around Him and formed a little community. They weren't a real promising group. Women. Fishermen. Tax collectors. The distressed, the indebted and the discontented. Not the best and brightest.

They followed Him everywhere, and they marveled at His teaching. They were especially fond of the food. And the miracles.

But then Jesus started talking about dying and how hard it would be to follow Him. He even told one guy to sell everything he had and give the money to the poor. And the religious leaders started stalking Him more closely.

That's when people started leaving.

"Are you guys going to leave, too?" He asked His friends.

"Where else are we gonna go?" Peter replied.

Not a ringing endorsement.

And Jesus knew that before it was all over, Peter would fold like a card table not once, not twice, but three times. His friends would turn tail and run away, leaving Him to face the cross alone. His kinsmen were about to hand Him over to the Romans to be executed; they would kill Him themselves if they were allowed. He was about to bear the weight of all the world's sin. He was distressed and distraught, and there was no one to whom He could turn.

So Jesus turned to His Father in heaven. He was the only One.

It's great to find strength in others, to gather together in little groups of people and find strength in friendship. It's fantastic that we can read a book or listen to a CD that encourages us. But when there's nowhere else to turn, the best place to turn is to God Himself. It's a skill we all need to cultivate. Time with God is essential in the life of a Christian, and prayer is a privilege we all need to value.

Jesus prayed to His Father in heaven while all His friends slept, and an amazing thing happened: "An angel from heaven appeared to him and strengthened him" (Luke 22:43).

THURSDAY: Actions

Jesus never did anything wrong. We're not talking morally, though that's true, too. Jesus never did anything illegal. He never broke a law. From everything we know, it appears that He paid His taxes and encouraged others to do the same. He never did anything wrong, but He was hunted like a fugitive, like a wanted criminal.

If He had brought the trouble on Himself, we might be able to say, "Well, that's what you get. You've made your bed; now lie in it."

But Jesus hadn't done anything wrong.

What do you do when you are harassed and harried and you don't deserve it? Believe it or not, one of the best things you can do is learn how to complain. That's right—you read that correctly: We are advocating that you learn how to complain.

Think you already know how to complain pretty well? Think that might just be your spiritual gift? The likely problem with the way you've been complaining is that you're complaining to the wrong source. We take our complaints to people. But what are they supposed to do? Pat you on the head and say, "Wow, it's hard to be you, isn't it?" They can't really do anything to help. Maybe they can offer some advice or a strong shoulder to lean on, or give you some money, for now. But that's about it. Most often, they can't really change the situation.

But God can.

He is the One with whom you need to register your complaints. Go directly to God. Discuss your discouragement openly and honestly with Him. That's what King David did in Psalms 142, 57, 34 and many others. In fact, scholars have divided the psalms into different categories (psalms of thanksgiving, enthronement psalms, psalms of wisdom, and so on). The largest single category of psalms is the Psalms of Lament—which is really just a fancy way of saying Psalms of Complaint.

What's interesting is that this type of literature is pretty unique to Judaism. No other ancient religion complained to its god(s). Other religions worshiped, praised and asked their god(s) to curse other people. They made requests and asked for blessings, health, prosperity. But only Jews could kvetch to their God.

And apparently, YHWH doesn't mind so much. He actually allows people to do this. He can handle it. And for those of you who didn't learn a few stories back and are still looking for examples—you've got one here. Jesus took His complaints straight to His father.

A lot of people just don't have the courage to do it. They stuff their discouragement down and pretend to be fine because complaining is not pious. They force a smile and pretend everything is blue skies and rainbows and sunbeams from heaven. They pray polite things that have nothing to do with what's really going on inside.

Not David. Not Jesus. We see in Jesus' prayer that night in the garden a remarkable level of honesty. You may not be comfortable calling it complaint, but you have to admit that He was certainly questioning God's plan and wondering if there wasn't another way.

Both David and Jesus knew that the only place you can meet the heavenly Father is in reality. And sometimes reality is a messy and confusing place. Jesus got in front of His heavenly Father and let Him know what was going on in His heart. So should you.

FRIDAY: Prayer

Narrative

Lord of hosts, I acknowledge that Your will is good and acceptable and perfect. Yet I often find myself wrestling with it, because I have my own ideas about how to order my life and what would be best for me, my family, my friends and my career. But I know that when I try to determine the content of my life, I set myself up for disappointment, because the only criterion I can use to see how well I am doing is comparison with others. And when I do that, it leads to a lack of contentment and the temptation to covet what other people have that I do not. I confess that it is only when I look to You to determine the content of my life that I know the contentment that comes from the realization that only You know what is really best for me, and that You are committed to bringing it about for my own long-term good.

Orthodoxy

God of all comfort, may I learn the wisdom of quickly turning to You and Your resources when I find myself in times of disappointment and discouragement. I know that when I face unhappy situations, I become particularly vulnerable to temptation. When I am despondent, I am tempted to medicate myself with resentments, short-term pleasures, self-indulgence, withdrawal and other sinful pain-avoidance strategies. And I know that these stratagems only exacerbate the problem. Knowing these things, I ask for the grace at such times in my life to look to You for my needs and to fully submit to Your good will for my life. May I rest in You and put my hope in Your promises and goodness. Only then will I know the peace that surpasses all comprehension and guards my heart and my mind in Christ Jesus.

Orthopathy

Lord, You have graciously given me meaningful relationships with other travelers during this earthly pilgrimage. You mediate Your grace and comfort through them when I become despondent, and this can be a great source of blessing. But I must first turn to You and find in You my greatest aid and encouragement in times of profound need. Your presence, grace and power lift me up when I stumble and keep me on the path of righteousness when I am tempted to set off in my own direction. May the Lord Jesus Christ and God my Father, who has loved me and given me eternal comfort and good hope by grace, comfort and strengthen my heart in every good work and word. I know that when I look to You, Lord, You uphold me with Your righteous right hand.

Orthopraxy

Loving Father, I find that I am tempted to grumble and complain when I encounter difficult circumstances. I may complain about bad luck or life being unfair or not getting any breaks, but ultimately, these are really indirect ways of challenging Your goodness in my life. I often wonder why You allow difficult things to occur to me and to others, and I really have no answers. But I know from the examples in the Bible that I would be far wiser to direct my complaints openly to You, and like Job and the psalmists David and Asaph, lodge my grievances and admit my confusion to You. In this broken and sinful world, there is so much undeserved suffering. But at least when I am open and honest with You, I know I am approaching the only One who can really do something in such times of need. Thank You for Your patience and kindness to those who bring their sorrows directly to You.

40

Crucifixion

MATTHEW 26:47–75; 27;
MARK 14:43–72; 15;
LUKE 22:47–71; 23;
JOHN 18–19

MONDAY: Story

He was praying when all hell broke loose. Suddenly, a mob appeared, armed guards—hundreds of them—marching with torches out to a garden to arrest an unarmed homeless man. It was ridiculous.

Judas led them straight to Jesus. He stood there awkwardly for a moment, looking unsure of himself, and then he kissed Him—puckered up his lips and planted one right on Jesus' face.

The soldiers moved forward to take Him into custody. Some of His disciples reacted, swinging wildly at someone's head. There was pushing and shoving and shouting. Then there was a lot of running away.

But Jesus stayed calm in the midst of the chaos. He seemed to be praying as it all came down.

There was a rushed trial and a rush to judgment. It had to have been obvious to everyone that the witnesses were being coached; they couldn't even keep their stories straight. No one seemed to be able to pinpoint precisely what Jesus was being charged with.

More pushing, more shoving, more shouting. They obviously wanted Him dead, but they knew they couldn't carry out that sentence. Only the Roman Governor had that power, so they took Him to Pilate, demanding that "justice" be served.

Everyone wanted something, except Him. He just stood there, allowing them to say whatever it was they were going to say. He answered when He was asked a direct question, but that was about it. No protest. No demands. It was as if He was resigned to what was about to happen.

Pilate knew trouble when he saw it, so after some preliminary questions, he shuttled this hot potato off to Herod. But all Herod wanted was a magic show. When it became clear that Jesus wasn't going to play along, Herod grew weary of Him and sent Him back to Pilate.

Now Pilate was in a pickle. The people were so insistent, so impatient for a condemnation to death. Flogging, which is as bad as you've heard, wasn't enough for them. Humiliation wasn't enough for them. They didn't want Him hurt; they wanted Him dead.

His friends left when it got bad. He had no one to advocate for Him. He was pronounced guilty and sentenced to die without a real trial. He was hit in the face, dragged through the streets of town, paraded through the marketplace half naked, beaten beyond recognition. And He just stood there. He said little. He resisted even less.

And then they took Him to a hill just outside of town, and there they crucified Him.

He prayed while hell reigned down on Him, tearing His flesh from His body, crushing His spirit.

The people gathered for a while. He said a few short sentences. He had a brief exchange with the two other criminals who died with Him that day. And then it was over.

But it wasn't over, really. It was just beginning.

TUESDAY: Beliefs

When Luke tells us the Christmas story, he begins with some background information to set the stage. He says, "In those days Caesar Augustus issued a decree that a census should be taken of the entire Roman world" (Luke 2:1).

Caesar Augustus was a fascinating character who did two remarkable things. First, he had himself declared "Savior of the World." That takes some chutzpah. Second, he declared world peace. It was known as *Pax Romana*. In 27 B. C., he closed the temple that was dedicated to the Roman god of war, and by doing so, made a statement: There will be no more war.

Ironically, the way he maintained the peace was to kill anyone who stepped out of line in the most violent ways imaginable.

We are going to have world peace around here if I have to kill every last one of you!

That's one way of doing things. And it continues in some places today. Peace is often kept through coercion, bullying and violence.

Everyone from politicians to Miss America seems to want world peace, and one way of going about it is to simply declare it and rule with an iron fist—in government, in churches, in homes. But the cross of Christ shows us another way—a better way.

Later in his retelling, Luke tells us about the shepherds keeping watch over their flocks by night. You remember that part, right? It's the part Linus reads in *A Charlie Brown Christmas*. The angel's words are particularly what we're interested in today: "Glory to God in the highest, and on earth peace to those on whom his favor rests" (Luke 2:14).

Jesus was born into a world where people who were in charge screamed, "We will have world peace if I have to kill every last one of you!" The One who is the true Savior of the world brought peace in a different way: by bestowing favor on us and by dying in our place.

Who deserves that favor from on high? Absolutely no one.

Who gets this favor from on high? Absolutely everyone who will receive it.

Caesar Augustus offered to kill in order to get peace.

Jesus of Nazareth offered to die in order to get it.

Guess whose peace still prevails?

WEDNESDAY: Values

We've spent several weeks thinking about Jesus. We've talked about things He did, stories He told, people He met. We've imagined Him walking the roads of His hometown, winding His way through other villages on His way to Jerusalem.

We've been to Jerusalem. We've tried to imagine Him sitting under an olive tree or climbing the steps of the Temple. We can almost see Him walking into

Bethany for one of His frequent visits to Mary, Martha and Lazarus's home, or hunkered over a fire on the shore at Tiberius.

But today, as we think about the story at hand, it's hard to look at Him. We know too much of the story. We know how the day will end—the same way it has ended for nearly 2,000 years now. It is inevitable. It is inescapable. It is the end of the week.

Today Jesus will die.

It's difficult for squeamish people to watch people who are in pain. Whether on television shows or in stage plays, seeing someone in pain often causes us too much internal angst. We want to turn away, plug our ears, close our eyes, imagine ourselves elsewhere.

Many of us went to see Mel Gibson's bloodbath, *The Passion of the Christ.* It was brutal and savage, and—while much of it was historically accurate—it wasn't very biblical in the way it portrayed the crucifixion. The writers of the Gospels don't go in for a lengthy meditation on the cruel suffering involved. They don't dwell on gory details or meticulous depictions. Even Luke, the Gospel writer who is normally given to medical descriptions, shies away from doing so at this point in his narrative. The apostle John was there; he actually witnessed the event, the horror of it, the agony of it. Yet he refuses to pander to our base desire for spectacle. There are no drawn out explanations of the flogging Jesus endured, no gruesome reminders of the sights and sounds of actual crucifixion. The bloodiness has been removed. There is no emotional manipulation in the biblical accounts of that day.

Perhaps they were too close to the actual events to write about them. People were still being killed in this manner when these four men, prompted by God Himself, set down their records of the events. There was no need to describe what was involved; everyone knew. Perhaps it was still too emotionally charged for them to write down the details; the wounds still fresh, talking about it in too much detail may have felt like picking at scabs that hadn't yet had time to heal.

Regardless of their reasons, the authors chose to edit the content of the storyline somewhat at this point. What actually happened was too awful, too terrible, too horrible to contemplate for very long. Yet it was too necessary, too wonderful, to skip over completely.

There are churches where Good Friday isn't commemorated. They don't like to talk about it. They want the rush of Easter, the joy of the Resurrection. But they are two sides of the same coin. You cannot have a resurrection until you have a death. There is no empty tomb unless there is first a figure on a cross.

THURSDAY: Actions

Think about the cross. Really think about it. See Jesus on it. Hear the sounds. Feel the terror.

Now realize this: You could be doing any number of things. You could be going for a drive or taking a walk. You could be sipping a glass of iced tea or playing a round of golf or having lunch with friends.

But instead you're sitting here contemplating an instrument of torture. The cross wasn't just designed to kill a man, but to keep him alive as long as possible so that he could experience as much pain as possible without passing out, until finally he died an excruciating death from suffocation as his lungs collapsed from the weight of his body suspended from iron spikes.

That's brutal.

You're sitting here, concentrating on a cross.

You could be doing something upbeat, something that has more to do with living. Everything in our world tells you that you can save yourself by getting on with the business of living. There's not a commercial or an ad in the world that entices you to buy something that will hasten your death. The whole point of advertising is that the products will enhance your life. Take that vacation. Get that new car. Find the best food. Stay looking young with all the wrinkle cream and hair dye available. That's what we want: a beautiful life—as long as possible, as rich as possible, as pleasant as possible.

So why are you here, thinking about an instrument of torture, a crossbeam of suffering? Are you crazy? Are Christians all nuts? Why not get out there and enrich your life? It can't be healthy to think about death. It's certainly not popular.

The truth is, there comes a time in everyone's life, a time when we become painfully aware that we cannot save ourselves by living. We are dying to live, but that desire—that hope that we can live a long, beautiful, comfortable, rich life—can never be fulfilled. It slips away. Life has a way of ebbing out of even the healthiest among us. And in the meantime, it can become so much less than what we tried to grab hold of.

All of a sudden, the life that we tried so hard to create, the life that we thought we had, is much less than what we hoped for. The truth is that what draws us to the cross of Jesus is something deep inside each of us that says, *Jesus' dying was the real currency that purchased your freedom from all this try-to-save-yourself-by-living frenzy.*

Trying to save yourself by living is like trying to buy groceries with Monopoly money. You've got the wrong currency. It may be good when you're playing the game, but it won't work when you want some real food. All the little properties and accumulated achievements that enable us to own this board and win this game have nothing to do with God's grand scheme.

If it were possible for humanity to save itself by living, we would have done it by now. We'd have collectively reached down and pulled ourselves up by our bootstraps. But it hasn't happened. And it won't. From Socrates to Dr. Phil, the world has taken a 5,000-year bath in human wisdom and come out just as dirty as ever.

So that's why you're here: You can't save yourself by living.

That's why God has come: to save the whole world by dying.

It doesn't sound like a very practical application, but do it anyway. Think about the cross. Really think about it. See Jesus on it. Hear the sounds. Feel the terror. And know that you have been spared.

FRIDAY: Prayer

Narrative

Father God, I thank You for the gift of open access to You through prayer. It enhances my fellowship and intimacy with You and it appropriates Your power for my life. Open communication with You brings mercy and grace in time of need, and it develops my understanding and knowledge of You. It empowers me to understand and accomplish Your purposes for my life, and it changes my attitudes and desires. In prayer, I acknowledge the greatness of Your character and my desire to become more conformed to Your likeness. Through communion with You, may I learn to affirm Your will in all things, even in trying circumstances. When my will conflicts with Yours, I know it is because I have a false idea of what my best interests look like. May I seek to align my will with Yours.

Orthodoxy

Lord, You are the source of true peace. In this fallen world, there is so much alienation through hostility, enmity, strife, anger, unforgiveness, impatience, selfishness, envy, slander and malice. And this lack of peace in relationships spreads like a virus to larger social arenas. It produces a world in which there is little real peace. Without You, I would have no hope of a solution, because this lack of peace with ourselves and others stems from a lack of peace with You. But You have opened the way to reconciliation by bringing peace through the death of Your Son. You did what we could never hope to do by opening up the way of access and acceptance before You. I thank and praise You for Your boundless love, mercy and forgiveness that have transformed me from a condemned criminal to Your beloved child.

Orthopathy

Lord Jesus, by Your love and grace You emptied Yourself by taking the form of a bond-servant and by becoming obedient to Your Father's will, even to the point of an ignominious and agonizing death on a cross. Such love transcends my grasp, but You willingly embraced the redemptive purpose for which You came to the earth. You could endure the shame of the cross because You could see beyond it to the joy that was set before You. Good Friday was the only way that could lead to Easter, because death had to precede resurrection. May I also learn to look beyond the pains of this life to what You are preparing for me. When I lose my life for Your sake, I find it. Nothing I give up for Your Name can compare with the glory that is to be revealed. May I learn the wisdom of humbling myself now, so that I will later be exalted.

Orthopraxy

Dear God, You have made it clear that none of us can save ourselves by living longer or better. If righteousness and union with You were possible through human attainment, then Christ's death was needless. But You have revealed that, apart from Him, no one is righteous; no one attains perfection, and no one can earn salvation. All of us fall short of Your goodness and glory, and while it is true that some clearly live better lives than others, even the best of us cannot attain to the perfection that makes it possible for us to have fellowship with You. I will thank You forever that in Your compassion for us in our desperate condition, You did not spare Your own Son, but delivered Him over for us all. Now that I have trusted in Him, He gives me His righteousness and holds me in His hand by interceding for me and protecting me.

41

Resurrection

Matthew 28;
Mark 16;
Luke 24;
John 20

MONDAY: Story

Early in the morning, the women went to the tomb. It was the first day of the week and they had a lot to do, so they got an early start visiting the body of Jesus, making sure everything was as it should be before embarking on their journey home.

Why did they go to the tomb? Because they assumed they would find Jesus there—dead. They had seen Him die. They had watched His body go into the cave. Dead people then, as now, tended to stay dead.

But something was not right. The stone was rolled away. And upon closer inspection, they found the grave clothes, but not the corpse. There was no body.

What in the world was going on?

Suddenly two men appeared, their clothes shining bright as lightning. "What are you doing here looking for a live person among dead bodies?"

We aren't looking for a live person; we're looking for a dead man.

"He has risen just like He said He would. Don't you remember?"

Hmmm . . . that does sound familiar. He did say something about that. More than once, if memory serves. But He also said that He was the Messiah, and Messiahs aren't supposed to die. Messiahs are supposed to kill the bad guys, not be killed by the bad guys. Wow, those clothes are bright!

"Hurry back and tell the others that Jesus Christ is no longer dead."

Bursting back into the room where the dejected followers of Jesus were, these women began to tell them what had just happened. But where do you even begin to explain the inexplicable? It didn't make sense. The stone was where? There were two men whose clothes were shiny who said what? It had been a long and traumatic week for everyone—especially the women. There had been the parade into the city, that incident in the Temple, the Passover, the death of Jesus, and now this. Maybe these women ought to lie down.

It was nonsense to everyone. Except Peter. Peter started thinking back to a conversation he'd had with Jesus a while back. Jesus had asked everyone, "Who do you really think I am?"

Peter had answered Jesus before he even realized his mouth was open: "You're the One—the Messiah."

And Jesus had applauded him for his answer. But then Jesus had started talking about death and resurrection. It hadn't made sense at the time. And when Peter tried to interrupt Jesus, there were harsh words exchanged.

Peter bolted from the room, John hot on his heels.

Arriving at the tomb, they saw the strips of linen—but not the body. What could this possibly mean? You don't suppose . . .

TUESDAY: Beliefs

If there's no resurrection, nothing else makes sense. The demands of holiness, the call to turn the other cheek, the yearning for something greater than this life has to offer—none of it makes any sense. The sinless life, astonishing teaching, unbelievable miracles, gruesome death—none of it makes any sense.

We're open to debate about Jesus. Was He a wise and moral teacher or one of many prophets sent from God? Was He a lunatic or criminally insane? Was He consumed with a messiah complex? Everyone can have an opinion, and everyone's opinion is equally valid.

Unless there's a resurrection.

In fact, if there's no resurrection, the earliest disciples had it right. Go home. Go fishing. Go back to doing whatever it was you were doing before. Let's call it a day. Close the book. Mourn for a little while the dream you had of things being different. Then eat, drink and be merry. Go ahead and slap your boss if he's bothering you. Run your credit card debt up as high as they'll let you. Steal something. Give in to every whim and indulge every desire.

Unless there's a resurrection.

Christopher Hitchens and Sam Harris and Richard Dawkins, today's most famous trio of atheists, are right: Religion ought to be outlawed. It's nothing but a source of misery and ignorance. We're either the most lame-brained gullible fools, or we're the victims of the most carefully guarded conspiracy theory ever concocted. They're right in saying religious people have something desperately wrong with us; we're sick and ought to be either cured or eradicated altogether.

Unless there's a resurrection.

All the promises, all the laws, all the waiting, all the discipline—it's all a bunch of nonsense; they're all just silly manmade rituals designed to keep people in their place. Keeping clean, maintaining your purity, abstinence, fasting, self-control— these are just some humanly devised method of preserving order in society.

Unless there's a resurrection.

If there's no resurrection, what in the world are we doing? We're the most nitwitted people on the planet. Life is what you make it. It's every man for himself. It's dog-eat-dog out there. You get what you deserve, and you better do unto others before they have a chance to do unto you. Be nice to those who will repay you. Forgive with strings attached. Take care of Numero Uno, and climb that corporate ladder by hook or by crook, stepping on whomever you have to in order to get that brass ring (whatever that is). Whoever dies with the most toys wins.

Unless there's a resurrection.

Let's be clear about this: We're not talking about a metaphorical, allegorical, symbolic resurrection here. We're talking a real-life, flesh-and-blood body that used to be dead but is now upright and walking and talking and conscious. *Resurrection.*

Without that, the life of Jesus doesn't make any sense. And neither does yours. It may be an interesting read for a while, but the ending will be terrible. You die. That's all. Your existence was nothing in the grand scheme of things. You will eventually be forgotten by history. Life is utterly meaningless.

Unless there's a resurrection.

WEDNESDAY: Values

Think back to the very first meal in the Bible. Eve found a piece of fruit that looked good to her. She took a bite and gave it to her husband, Adam.

That's how it all went wrong.

It was the wrong fruit from the wrong tree, and from then until now we've been regretting that very first meal.

One of the greatest things about Jesus was how He ate. The idea of sharing a meal with someone in Jesus' time involved more than just ingesting nourishment; it implied acceptance of the other person. Jesus got in trouble with people because He was willing to eat with just about anyone: the poor, the unimpressive, the despised—the bottom of the social barrel.

It was during mealtime that Jesus revealed His true character and nature.

He shared that last meal with His friends before He was betrayed and crucified, giving them new insight into His identity and mission. After His resurrection, He shared meals with them again. After encountering a pair of them on the road to a village called Emmaus, He stopped to eat with them. They didn't even realize it was Him until He took the bread, gave thanks for it and began to distribute it.

There's something about Jesus and mealtimes. That's when we come to know Him.

Since the very beginning, God's great desire has been to share in a relationship with these humans He created. They would walk together and talk without fear or hesitation. There was no shame; there was just fellowship—communion.

You can think of that companionship being symbolized by a table.

But then sin entered the world, rupturing the relationship. And where sin is present, death is always close at hand. Because Adam and Eve sinned and realized their nakedness, animals died that day, giving their lives to cover the humans' shame.

Sin and death, sin and death, century after century of sin and death. Death of relationship. Death of friendliness. Death of companionship.

You can think of that sin and death being symbolized by an altar.

Year after year, animals were sacrificed on the altar so people could live without the guilt and shame brought about by their sinfulness. All the animals, all the sacrifices, all the altars pointed forward to one central event: the crucifixion of Jesus. That was the ultimate altar upon which the ultimate sacrifice would ultimately be made.

But it can't end there. We must not stop with the altar. We must move beyond it to the table that has been restored because of this altar.

This is why we gather together around the table, to remember and celebrate the fellowship that has been restored, the communion that is now ours to share. We gather to commemorate the Lord's Supper, the Eucharist, not merely as a meditation on the sacrificial death of our Lord and Savior Jesus Christ, but also as a celebration of the restored community we enjoy as a result of His victorious and vindicating resurrection.

THURSDAY: Actions

For some reason, people did not immediately recognize Jesus after His resurrection. One reason is surely because He was the last person they expected to meet, walking around like a . . . well, like a living person again. As we said earlier, dead people didn't tend to do anything but stay dead back then. Just like now.

But there was another reason they didn't recognize Him: There was something about His physical appearance that was different. His body had changed somehow. His closest friends recognized His voice, but they were skeptical about His identity until He offered some proof.

The proof He offered came in the form of His scars (see Luke 24:39; John 20:20, 27).

Interesting, isn't it, that God brought Jesus back to life, supplying Him with a new kind of body but choosing to retain the scars from His former life (and death)?

Apparently, the resurrected life—which is one that all followers of Christ are expected to participate in—is not identified by its accomplishments, possessions or honorary degrees. Rather, the resurrected life is known by its scars. After all, we are not only called to participate in His resurrection; we are called to join Him in His death (see Matt. 16:24–25).

Jesus' life after His resurrection looked an awful lot like His life before His crucifixion. We see Jesus, after He has come back from the dead, serving others (see John 21), telling people about the kingdom of God (see Acts 1:3), and preparing and commissioning others to continue the work He had begun (see Acts 1:4–8).

And now He calls us to live as He did—to serve others in love, to tell people about the availability of His kingdom, to prepare others and commission them to continue the work He began and continues to do in and among and through us. We will encounter hardship, but we will endure it with gladness. We will bear in our bodies the scars of our own crucifixion so that the ongoing, everlasting life of Jesus may be seen in us as well (see 2 Cor. 4:10).

We will live in the shadow of the cross and in the light of the empty tomb. We will live as those who have been crucified with Christ, raised with Him and sent back to this earth on a temporary mission.

FRIDAY: Prayer

Narrative

Lord, Your enduring Word is a progressive revelation of Your character, Your ways, Your purposes and Your plans. The story of the Old Testament gradually unveils a messianic Figure who would be unlike anyone else. He would be both a Servant and a King. He would live and die and live again. He would open His mouth in parables and accomplish miracles that would demonstrate His authority over all things. He would be betrayed, sold for 30 pieces of silver, crucified and pierced through. He would be despised and forsaken of men, a Man of sorrows and acquainted with grief. He would be rejected and mocked by His own people. But He would overcome the bondage of death, and His death and resurrection would mean the death of death. Glory to You for His Incarnation, His life, His ministry, His miracles, His teaching, His redemptive death and His awesome resurrection.

Orthodoxy

Lord Jesus, Your death and resurrection are the foundation of my faith, the source of my meaning, hope and purpose, the wellspring of my salvation, the assurance of Your truth and the basis of my eternal life with You. Life without the resurrection would be a brief episode between nonexistence and oblivion. There would be no long-term, abiding, transcendent hope. Human life and history would be a tragedy of epic proportions. Without Your resurrection, Your life would have been a terrible waste of extraordinary human potential. We would still be in our sins and there would be no real hope as we hurtle toward bodily decay and death. But thanks be to God that You were declared the Son of God with power by the resurrection from the dead through the power of the Holy Spirit.

Orthopathy

Dear Lord, from the beginning of history, You have desired to have communion with Your people and have delighted in those who passionately wanted to walk with You. I thank You for the imagery of table fellowship that runs from Genesis to Revelation and portrays Your acceptance and communion with Your people. I thank You for the God-Man who ate and drank with His followers during the years of His ministry, just before His death and after His resurrection. And I thank You for the great celebration to come, when we will share in the marriage supper of the Lamb. And as we celebrate through the communion elements of bread and wine our salvation and fellowship with You and with the restored community of faith, may we rejoice in all You have done and in all You will do in the ages to come.

Orthopraxy

Father, I know that if the earthly tent that is my bodily house is torn down, I will have a building from You, a house not made with hands, eternal in the heavens. And while I am in this body, I groan for the new body You are preparing for me, which is no longer perishable but imperishable, no longer earthly but heavenly, no longer weak but glorious in resurrected power. For I know that my true citizenship is in heaven, and that my humble and decaying body will be transformed into conformity with the body of Christ's resurrected glory. And I know that in that day, I will see how the sorrows, suffering and scars of this life will be fully redeemed by that glory. Seeing this, I pray that I will be steadfast and immovable, always abounding in Your work, knowing that my toil is not in vain in the Lord.

42

The Sequel

Acts 1:1–11

For three years, they watched the greatest story of all time unfold before their very eyes. More than just passive observers, they were actually characters in the story. It was amazing, truly the adventure of a lifetime.

They watched this enigmatic man teach and live. He was confusing and challenging and always loving, even when He scolded them sometimes or sent them out to do hard things. He was the smartest and most amazing Man they had ever known. They didn't even know a life like His was possible until they saw it for themselves.

But then the unimaginable happened. He died. They saw Him betrayed and tried on trumped-up charges. They saw the flogging (or at least heard the awful details about it). Then they saw Him dead.

What do you suppose they thought?

We would understand if they thought that was the end. We would understand if they wondered what they were supposed to do next. We would understand if they decided to just go home, just go back to fishing. They must have been absolutely devastated.

But then the greatest ending to the greatest story ever told took place: the resurrection. What was Jesus going to do next? How do you follow a resurrection? What's the sequel to that?

There was only one thing they could think of that would top the resurrection, so they asked Him, "Are You going to finally kick the Romans out, seize the throne and make Israel once more the envy of all the other nations?"

Jesus had spent the last three years trying to impress on them the idea that the kingdom of God was not a political thing. But they *still* didn't understand. So He said, "It would be best if you hung around Jerusalem for a few days after I'm gone. The Holy Spirit will come and explain this stuff to you. Maybe He'll have better luck than I've had."

Jesus didn't say that last part—we kind of added it in.

They wanted to know what was coming next, so Jesus got really explicit with them. He said, "No one knows for sure when God is going to bring all this to a grand finale. So in the meantime, you just go around and be witnesses, just tell people what you saw and experienced."

In other words, Jesus said, "Tag! You're it! You're the sequel. Now go."

TUESDAY: Beliefs

It probably wasn't what they were expecting.

They may have assumed that they would get to continue sitting on the front row, watching the greatest Man who ever lived do what God sent Him here to do. But Jesus instead told them, "No more sitting on the front row watching. Get up there on stage. Get out there in the game and do what you've seen Me do. Tag! You're it!"

And then He left.

They must have wondered if He was joking. "Us? But we don't know what we're doing! We're messed up. We're unstable and dysfunctional. We're in need of remedial help."

But Jesus just left. And the disciples stood there for a while looking into the sky where He'd gone. "He'll be back in just a minute. He's messing with us. There's no way He's leaving us in charge."

Eventually two angels had to come and shoo them away. "You heard what He said. Go on. Get out there!"

Why in the world would Jesus have left things like this? Why them? Why would Luke write a whole book about their adventures? Why would God see fit to preserve that book for us today? Here's why: God—who is far wiser than any of us—has a plan, and His plan to rescue the world is the Church. That's His plan. Not a corporation or a university, not a nation or an economic strategy. It's the followers He left behind, and now it's us. The Church.

He still comes to His Church and says, "You'll be My witnesses, and your main assignment is to come to know Me and love Me and follow My Spirit and help others do the same." That's the plan. Any questions?

The earliest followers bet the farm on it. Many of them ended up dying for it. They endured persecution and humiliation and even martyrdom for it.

Why would they do such a thing?

Because they remembered when their lives weren't spent doing anything permanent. And one day this Jesus showed up and said, "I want to give you a bigger purpose—a bigger mission than just catching a few fish or collecting some taxes. How would you like to partner with God in the greatest mission ever conceived? It's not merely the restoration of Israel. It's the redemption of the entire world and the human race."

They said, "What do we have to do?"

He said, "Go be My witnesses in Jerusalem, Judea, Samaria, Rome, Paris, London, New York, Cleveland, Atlanta, Chicago, Grand Rapids, Dallas, Phoenix, Los Angeles."

And the crazy thing is that it actually started to work.

WEDNESDAY: Values

He told them He was coming back from the dead, but they weren't waiting for Him at His resurrection. They weren't hanging out near the tomb with banners that read WELCOME BACK, JESUS!

He came back and they didn't believe it was really Him until they saw the scars.

He came back with no fanfare in the quiet hours of a still Sunday morning. No one was around at the time—a few guards nodding off at their post, suddenly bowled over by whatever it was that rolled the stone away. None of the people who said they believed in Him so much that they would follow Him through the gates of hell were even there.

He said He was coming back, and they went fishing.

Then He reminded them about all the things He had taught them. He showed them the scars and convinced hundreds that He could conquer death. He revealed His true nature by serving and teaching and sending them out into the world.

And then He told them He was coming back.

Will we be waiting for Him at His appearance? We're not talking about selling everything and moving en masse to some mountaintop where we'll sit in a meadow stringing garlands of wildflowers and singing "Kumbaya" until He returns.

He has given us a task. He has told us plainly that our responsibility is to go out into the wide world (not retreat from it) and make disciples of people from every nation on earth. We're to baptize and teach and be salt and light. We're to help and feed and clothe. We're to do the kinds of things He did.

We're to be the Body of Christ.

But make no mistake about it: He's coming back.

And so we pray with the saints throughout the centuries: *Maranatha! Lord, come quickly!*

But there are people who aren't ready for Him to return. If He were to return today, they would be faced with the prospect of entering a Christless eternity. For their sakes, as badly as we want Him to return, we also want Him to wait awhile longer.

We're torn. We long for His appearing, but we relish the patience He is currently demonstrating. And until He does return, we should be about the business He has given us. And we should value the time we have. Jesus did not spend time treading water until it was time to die and return to the Father. Neither should we.

THURSDAY: Actions

Q: How many of the disciples' sermons are recorded in the Gospels?

A: None.

Jesus preached, but they didn't—at least not as far as we know. Acts 2 is the first record of the first sermon delivered by one of Jesus' followers. Of course, it's Peter, and he is amazingly bold!

Remember, he's in Jerusalem, and he's telling people about Jesus. He says, "God made Jesus—you remember Him, the guy you killed a few weeks back—God made Him both Lord and Messiah" (see Acts 2:36).

What kind of reaction do you suppose he and the other disciples were expecting with an opener like that?

The response was overwhelming. "They were cut to the heart and said to Peter and the other apostles, 'Brothers, what shall we do?' Peter replied, 'Repent and be baptized, every one of you, in the name of Jesus Christ'" (Acts 2:37–38).

Baptism wasn't a simple ceremony for them; it was a statement of a new identity. It meant being cut off from family and synagogue. It meant persecution and harassment—possibly even death. It was their way of saying, "I'm all in!"

Peter says, "Jesus is Lord and Savior."

They say, "What do we do now?"

Peter says, "Repent and be baptized. Bet the farm on Jesus."

And 3,000 people did.

Jesus said, "You'll be My witnesses in Jerusalem."

We read, "So the word of God spread and the number of disciples in Jerusalem increased rapidly" (Acts 6:7).

Jesus said, "You'll be my witnesses in Judea and Samaria."

We read, "Then the church throughout Judea, Galilee and Samaria enjoyed a time of peace and was strengthened. Living in the fear of the Lord and encouraged by the Holy Spirit, it increased in numbers" (Acts 9:31).

Jesus said, "You'll be my witnesses to the ends of the earth."

We read, "In this way the word of the Lord spread widely and grew in power" (Acts 19:20).

They were living out this incredible sequel and no one could stop them. The authorities tried, but we read, "When they saw the courage of Peter and John and realized that they were unschooled, ordinary men, they were astonished and they took note that these men had been with Jesus" (Acts 4:13).

Jesus said, "You will be my witnesses."

They had no strategic plan. No resources. No building. No staff. But they found out that if you can talk to people about Jesus—in open and honest language they can understand—things start happening. They found out that if you do the kinds of things Jesus did, you get similar results.

That's what the Church is called to be and do in every generation. Talk about Jesus. Obey and love and follow Jesus as closely as we can. Bet the farm on Jesus and His crazy plan to turn the world right side up.

Do what He did, and see what happens.

FRIDAY: Prayer

Narrative

Lord, I give thanks to You for the new life You have given me in Jesus. When I reflect on His life as portrayed in the Gospels, I see an entirely new quality of life, a new way of being, of thinking and of acting. And though He was fully God—still the second Person of the Divine Trinity—He was the most fully human being the world has ever seen. I ask that, as I learn more about Him through the renewal of my mind with the Word, I would also know Him more in an experiential way so that I will become more like Him. And now that I am in Christ, You have given me the holy commissioning to spread the gospel of the Kingdom in my time and through my arena of influence. May I be faithful to this heavenly calling so that I would go into the world where You have sovereignly placed me and be His witness in word and in deed.

Orthodoxy

Lord Jesus, You have called me to Yourself and made me a member of the Church, which is Your Body. Now I am a part of Your Bride, a living stone in a living temple, indwelt by the Holy Spirit and empowered to be Your vital agency in the world. As a member of Your Body, You have gifted me to do what I could never have done before—be an instrument through whom You mediate Your presence and love in this bent and broken world. Just as the lives of the disciples were radically and permanently transformed by Your resurrection and by Your Spirit, so I desire that transformation in my life. You have invited me to become a part of a greater purpose and a greater mission than I could have created for myself. As an agent of Your life and authority in this world, may I give my life away to others and be faithful until Your return.

Orthopathy

Dear Lord, when I reflect on the greatest Story ever told—the Story of the creation, the fall, Your redemptive plan to restore what was lost in the fall and the glorious consummation to come—I marvel at its scope, its genius and its majesty. Your sovereign power is so great that You can use even the vilest acts for a greater good, and You most decisively demonstrated this in the death and resurrection of Your Son. Jesus the Messiah, the Passover Lamb, the fulfillment of the prophets, the Sin-bearer and Redeemer of the world, will return in glory, majesty, might, dominion and authority, and every knee will bow to Him. Until that great day, You have given Your Body, the Church, a precious time of opportunity to manifest Your life, light and love in this world. As a member of that living Body, may I be Your faithful witness in my time.

Orthopraxy

God of glory, majesty and dominion, You have graciously accepted me as a living member of the Body of Christ, and You have implanted me in the communion of saints that will forever endure. Now that I have received a new identity in Jesus as a holy and beloved part of Your glorious and eternal plan, may I live out that new identity in my thinking, my speech and my actions. Empower me to be Your ambassador, Your witness of the transforming life that is found in Jesus, who is the Way, the Truth and the Life. May I love and obey Him and stake everything I have on Him without reservations or conditions. Empower me to live during this brief earthly sojourn in light of Your return and to treasure this as a unique time of opportunity that I will never have again. For it is only on this earth that I can share the gospel and serve people in need.

43

The Room Upstairs

Acts 2

MONDAY: Story

People don't usually like to wait. With that in mind, imagine the initial response to Jesus' last command: "Don't leave Jerusalem just yet. Wait a few days for the gift My Father is sending." Do you suppose they were happy about that? "Hooray! We get to wait! That was just what I was hoping He'd say!"

People have always had a difficult time waiting—especially when they don't have a lot of information. And Jesus didn't give His followers many details. Maybe He explained things a little better than the writers of the Bible let on, but it doesn't look like Jesus filled in the blanks for them very much.

Still, He said to wait, so they waited. They didn't know how long they'd have to wait. They didn't know what to do while they were waiting. They didn't know how or when (or even that) the gift would arrive. They just knew they were supposed to wait.

Fortunately, they didn't have to wait long—just 10 days. And, as it turned out, they didn't have to wonder, "Is this the gift that He was talking about?"

It was pretty obvious.

They were all in the same room, 120 of them, when they heard the wind start blowing really loudly. Then they saw fire (which is not always a good thing when you're in a crowded room). A pillar of fire entered the room, split into multiple parts and started moving toward certain people, specifically toward their heads.

You'd think this spectacle might have freaked them out a little. *Is it going to hurt? Fire tends to hurt. Fire and human hair aren't compatible.*

But it didn't hurt. It landed on everyone's head, and no one was hurt.

And then people started speaking different languages.

It was all pretty confusing. A sound like a violent wind. Tongues of fire. Speaking in other languages. What in the world did it all mean?

The details about the gift the Father was sending were still fuzzy and would be for quite some time, but there was no mistaking this: The time for waiting was over. The Gift had come, bringing life and purpose, power and energy. Those 120 followers emerged from that room an unstoppable force, committed to do what they had seen Jesus doing, to be His Body—His hands and arms and feet and mouth. They were going to continue what He started.

Waiting just outside that room were people from all over the world. The followers of Jesus met them and began doing what Jesus told them to do: "Just be My witnesses. Tell others what you've seen and heard."

That's precisely what they did.

Then something strange started to happen. Some of the people didn't believe them. Some thought they were drunk. Some thought they were crazy. But some listened, and some believed.

And the world has never been the same since.

Turns out, some gifts are worth waiting for.

TUESDAY: Beliefs

There's been a lot of confusion down through the years about the book of Acts. Is it just history or is there theology in there as well? Is it just an accurate description of what happened, or is this a prescription for the way things should still be?

We find it helpful, when we encounter something in the Bible that seems strange, to ask if there is anything else in the Bible that is strange in the same sort of way. For example, we read in Acts about this group of people who are together but not really doing anything. Then this wind blows through, fire lands on their heads and they begin speaking other languages. Think about it: People began speaking in languages they hadn't studied, speaking spontaneously in languages they'd never spoken before.

Sound familiar?

Right after the Flood, a group of folks got together and said, "'Come, let us build ourselves a city, with a tower that reaches to the heavens, so that we may make a name for ourselves and not be scattered over the face of the whole earth.' But the Lord came down to see the city and the tower that they were building. The Lord said . . . 'Come, let us go down and confuse their language so they will not understand each other'" (Gen. 11:4–5,7).

In Genesis, we find a group of people who had been told to go throughout the land, multiplying and advancing the borders of civilization. This was how they would glorify God.

But they didn't want to spread out. Instead, they wanted to stay together and figure out a way to get from earth to heaven on their own. They wanted to make a name for themselves. They wanted the fame and the glory that would come from having accomplished it. They didn't want to glorify God before the people. They wanted to glorify themselves.

So God confused their language and scattered them. God turned order into chaos.

In Acts, we find a group of people who are told to go throughout the land, multiplying and advancing the borders of God's kingdom. This was how they would glorify God.

So they went. They burst out of the upper room, celebrating the fact that God came from heaven to earth, offering them salvation apart from any works they could ever perform. They lifted up the name of Jesus. They had a zeal for spreading His glory.

To jumpstart their efforts, God made a common language so their message could spread more quickly. God turned confusion into order.

The curse was reversed. Where there was alienation, there is now reconciliation. Where chaos reigned, there is now harmony. What was upside down is now beginning, slowly but surely, to be turned right side up again.

WEDNESDAY: Values

Maybe the Holy Spirit needs a better publicist. Equal in standing with God the Father and God the Son, He doesn't get nearly as much press as the other two. They have most of the good worship songs directed toward them. Eloquent prayers are offered to the Father, through the name of the Son. People are baptized into Jesus. They seek a personal relationship with their heavenly Father.

The Holy Spirit is the quiet member of the Trinity, the shy one, the one people have a hard time describing and discussing. Christians throughout the centuries have acknowledged the existence of the Holy Spirit, but many have been content to focus our attention on the Father and the Son.

Some of us have gone to the other extreme, pushing the pendulum to the opposite end, seeking a powerful encounter with God the Spirit without pursuing intimacy with God the Father through a personal relationship with God the Son. We want the goosebumps, the warm fuzzy feeling, the signs and the wonders.

We either reject the work of the Holy Spirit or become obsessed with Him.

But to misunderstand the Person and work of the Holy Spirit is to misunderstand something fundamental to Christianity. The Father sent the Son into the world and empowered Him by anointing Him with the Spirit. When the Son had completed His earthly mission and returned to the Father, He sent the Spirit to continue His work through His followers.

The Holy Spirit is a Person, a Helper, a Comforter, a Counselor and an Advocate.

Still, there is so much confusion about Him. Does He do miracles? Is His only job description to teach us about God and convict us of our sin? Does He bring the goosebumps we feel in those intense times of worship and prayer?

Two things you can know for certain about the Holy Spirit: He will always point you to Jesus, and He will always work to form Christlike-ness in you.

Did the miracle point you to Jesus? Or did it point you to the miracle worker?

Did the lesson point you to Jesus? Or did it point you to the teacher?

Did the worship point you to Jesus? Or did it point you to the worship leader?

Did any of it make you think, feel and act more like Jesus than you did before?

These are the questions we should be asking, but because we misunderstand the purpose of the Spirit's activity, we tend to value the gifts He brings more than His presence.

Without the Holy Spirit's work, you won't grow. Today, thank God for the gift of the Holy Spirit, and invite Him to point you to Jesus and help you become more like Him.

THURSDAY: Actions

Jesus told the disciples they were to go out into the whole world. As they were going, they were to make disciples of others. But He warned them first: "Apart from me, you can do nothing" (John 15:5). Because He knew they would be lost without Him, Jesus made them a promise right before He left to return to the Father: "You will receive power when the Holy Spirit comes on you" (Acts 1:8).

In other words, the Christian life cannot be lived apart from the Spirit of Christ. Without a moment-by-moment reliance on the power and presence of the Holy Spirit, Christian living is simply impossible.

In the absence of such a personal relationship with the Holy Spirit, we reduce God to a set of biblical principles instead of a living Person who refuses to be boxed in, controlled or manipulated. Because we fear hearing from God personally, we say that God no longer communicates apart from the Bible, and we close off the surprising work of the Spirit in our lives.

The Spirit of God is never pushy, never rude and doesn't spend much time where He's not wanted or welcomed. So it happens that our desires create our beliefs, and our beliefs create our experiences. We don't expect to hear from the Spirit, and we convince ourselves that the Spirit will not speak to us. And we are not surprised when He doesn't. Our experiences reinforce our beliefs, which reinforce our feelings.

But what if we're wrong? What if the Spirit of God wants to communicate with us? What if the Spirit is waiting for a few people who will listen and respond to His prompting? What might He be waiting to reveal to the Body of Christ through one humble servant who is open to His leading?

You could be that person.

He would never ask you to do something Jesus wouldn't do. He won't make you do anything. He won't force Himself on you. He won't lead you into anything that contradicts the Bible.

But He may have something to say to you. Are you willing to listen and respond in obedience to what the Spirit has to say?

If so, ask Him to speak. Say, "Speak to me, Holy Spirit."

And listen.

FRIDAY: Prayer

Narrative

Lord God, teach me to desire You more than anything else, to will what You command, to hope in Your promises, to trust in You and to wait on You. It is difficult for me rest in You and wait for Your timing because I get impatient with the status quo. And when this happens, I focus more on the product I want rather than the process along the way to what You want. It seems that the process of preparation always takes longer than what I have in mind. But what use would it be to travel rapidly toward what I would later discover to be a dead end? You alone know what is best for me, and Your love for me always wills it for me. You give me the opportunities and the gifts I need for the next stage in the journey, and I ask for the patience to wait for Your timing, for You to open doors and for You to endue me with Your power as I need it.

Orthodoxy

Lord of heaven and earth, Your love is boundless, Your plans are perfect and Your goodness extends to all who wish to receive it. Though Your ways are past finding out, nevertheless they are always trustworthy. The tale of human history seems to be a series of attempts to make a name for ourselves in our strength, in our timing and in our effort, and like the Tower of Babel, it ends in confusion and chaos. But when You are welcomed into lives and into communities, You turn our chaos into Your creative order. May I be far more concerned about pleasing You and seeking to honor Your Name than about making a name for myself. Treasure in heaven is incomparably greater than earthly treasure. Nothing on earth can begin to compare with Your accolade of "Well done, good and faithful servant."

Orthopathy

Triune God, I confess that it is all too easy to overlook the Person and work of the Holy Spirit in my life and the life of the Church. He always points to Jesus, and His voice can be overlooked in the din of this world. And yet it would be impossible for anyone to live the Christian life without His presence and power. It is Your Spirit who reproduces the life of Christ within me, and I will only bear the fruit of the Spirit when I choose to walk in His strength. It is Your Spirit who was sent as the Comforter and Counselor, and He imparts to us the divine resources for righteousness and life-changing ministry. It is through the filling of Your Spirit that Your Word can be proclaimed with transforming power, and You have given Him to Your followers to continue the work of Your Son in this world. May I walk in His footsteps, dependent on Your Holy Spirit.

Orthopraxy

Lord, I bless and thank You that Your Spirit of wisdom and understanding, of counsel and strength, of knowledge and the fear of the Lord has been poured out within my heart through my new birth in Jesus Christ. Your Spirit convicts me when I disobey You, He comforts and encourages me when I am downtrodden, He illuminates me when I study Your Word and His indwelling presence protects and empowers me. I thank You for the manifold ministry of Your Spirit and for the spiritual gifts He has given to energize and edify Your living Church. May I value His presence even more than His gifts, but may I also learn to discern and develop the spiritual gifts He has imparted to me. I want to learn how to listen to His voice and expect His surprising work in my life and in the life of the community of faith.

44

The Ends of the Earth

Acts 4–8

MONDAY: Story

It didn't take long for those first followers of Jesus to figure this out: When you do what Jesus did, you're likely to get the same response.

Some people flocked to them. They were healing and sharing and telling people how to connect with their heavenly Father in a way that bypassed all the corrupt ritualistic forms and politically motivated religious leaders. There was momentum and freedom, and many people jumped on board.

Some were wary of them. All this fuss over a Messiah who was killed by the very enemy He was supposed to overthrow . . . it didn't make sense. Besides, movements like this had happened before. *Maybe*, they thought, *we shouldn't do anything hasty. Just let it go for a while and see if anyone's still talking about it next year.*

Some were downright hostile. This Jesus movement, these followers of the Nazarene—the whole thing suggested a total overhaul of the Jewish system in Jerusalem, a system that had been working pretty well for some people for quite some time. The Romans were content to leave them alone as long as they paid their taxes and kept quiet. Too much rocking the boat might incur their imperial wrath and rob the local leaders of their power. Best not to upset the apple cart.

There was just one problem: These Christians wouldn't shut up.

Everywhere they went, it was, "Jesus did this" and "Jesus did that" and "You had Him killed but He came back to life, and that proves that you're going about this thing the wrong way." They wanted to put an end to the sacrificial system, which was very good for the economy. They meant to tear down the organization, the whole hierarchy of it all . . . and replace it with what? With a simple group of people who come together to do what? To pray? To sing? To give? To share?

It sounded like anarchy to many peoples' ears. Women were permitted to talk in the presence of men. Regular day-laborers were assumed to have insight they could share with the scholars.

Worst of all, if what they were saying was true, it wouldn't be long before Gentiles were allowed to share in, well . . . everything. It was as if there was no special blessing for being Jewish. God's Chosen People no longer enjoyed the status of being His Chosen People. Imagine: God choosing people out there among all the Gentiles. Unthinkable!

No, the only course to take was to shut this thing down now before it gathered any more momentum, before it could convert any more naïve people.

At first, it was simple harassment. The Jewish rulers brought in some of the leaders and warned the Christians to stop. When that didn't work, the beatings began. But that only seemed to stiffen the resolve of these heretics.

But all was not lost. The first signs of a crack in the newly laid foundation came, believe it or not, from within. A disagreement broke out between some of the Greek-speaking Jews from outside of Jerusalem and those who spoke the more familiar Aramaic. It concerned the care of widows, and though it was quickly resolved, it did reveal the fact that there might soon be trouble in paradise.

It was around this time that Stephen—one of those Greek-speaking Jews—opened his big mouth in front of the Sanhedrin and the High Priest and got himself killed.

That was all it took. Now the Jesus followers left Jerusalem like rats leaving a burning ship. To all appearances, Christianity was unraveling before it ever really got going.

TUESDAY: Beliefs

Harassment, internal bickering and persecution threatened to kill the fledgling movement before it ever really got started. At least that's what it looked like from a human perspective. But do you remember what Jesus said right before He ascended into the clear, blue sky? He told them, "You will receive power when the Holy Spirit comes on you; and you will be my witnesses in Jerusalem, and in all Judea and Samaria, and to the ends of the earth" (Acts 1:8).

Notice that Jesus didn't command them to do anything; He told them how it was going to be. There were no conditions attached, no rules to follow. He said, "This is what is going to happen."

So persecution breaks out and the disciples begin to leave Jerusalem. Where do they go? First they go to Judea and Samaria. Eventually they scatter to the ends of the earth.

And what do they do? They tell people what they saw and heard and experienced. As they go, they tell about what Jesus said and did, and as others wanted to experience the same kind of life these messengers describe, they baptize people into His Name.

Sounds almost as if they are carrying out the Great Commission, fulfilling Jesus' prediction about their future.

If we've seen anything over the past 44 weeks, it's this: When God tells you something is going to happen, you can take it to the bank. In good times and in bad, regardless of whether the authorities endorse your message or persecute you because of it, God's promises are rock-solid security.

He doesn't promise us a stress-free lifestyle with no hardships or suffering. He doesn't assure us that everyone will like us and embrace our message. Instead, He promises that He will never leave us; we'll never have to face the suffering alone. And He promises to eventually bring us home.

He has a perfect track record thus far; there's no reason to think He'll start breaking His promises anytime soon.

WEDNESDAY: Values

Jerusalem was a pretty comfortable place . . . for a while. The followers of Jesus met together every day, sharing meals and money among everyone. They were generous and made sure everyone had basic needs supplied. They were a unified force, enjoying daily numeric growth. There were miraculous signs and wonders happening everywhere they turned.

Life was good!

But perhaps they had forgotten what Jesus left them behind to do. They weren't supposed to hang around Jerusalem and let people come to them if they wanted to know about how to have a relationship with God the Father through His Son, Jesus.

They were supposed to *go*.

They had been commissioned to venture out into the wide world, taking this life-changing message of Jesus with them as they went. They weren't supposed to pursue comfort and respectability; they were supposed to pursue God's mission of expanding the borders of His kingdom in this world.

But it was so nice there in Jerusalem. It was safe and familiar. They knew their way around. They knew people there, family and friends. Jerusalem was a nice place to live, a safe place to raise a family. It was nice and safe and familiar and comfortable.

But it wasn't God's plan.

So God allowed the heat to be turned up in Jerusalem. Like a mother eagle who teaches her offspring to fly and then breaks up the nest so that they can't come back, God allowed Jerusalem to become an uncomfortable place for followers of Jesus. In this way, His plan of having them take the message to the ends of the earth would be fulfilled.

God values people more than He values their comfort. God values mission more than He values safety.

That can be a very uncomfortable message for folks who live in nice houses in the suburbs, for people who drive nice cars and throw more food away each week than a lot of people consume, for people who pursue wealth and happiness, and who hunger and thirst for a nice, safe place to raise their kids.

There's nothing wrong with having money. There's nothing wrong with living in a nice house in a safe neighborhood or driving a nice car. But what do we value more? Do we value our safety and comfort more than we value God's plan? Are we content to stay huddled up when God calls us to get out there and run a play? Do we expect others to come to us instead of actively going out among them?

What would it look like for you to value people more than you value your own comfort? What would have to change for people to know that your priority is accomplishing God's purposes in your generation?

THURSDAY: Actions

Sometimes God's people are arrested and beaten for their faith. Sometimes ruling powers of this world make them choose between renouncing their faith and death. Sometimes good people get thrown into bad places for doing the right thing.

There's a spiritual war going on, and we shouldn't expect life to be comfortable. The fact is that most of the people reading this (and the two guys writing it) live in a level of luxury that is unprecedented in human history. But the notion that once you come to Christ you'll never have to face difficulties, sickness, loss of job, poverty, depression, divorce, the death of a child or persecution for your faith is patently absurd.

Jesus Himself said, "In this world you will have trouble" (John 16:33). In fact, in the Sermon on the Mount, He said, "Don't worry about tomorrow; tomorrow will worry about itself. Each day has enough trouble of its own" (Matt. 6:34).

Trouble today *and* trouble tomorrow? Thanks a lot, Jesus!

That's not the end of the story. But we cannot skip over it and jump to the happy ending just yet.

Evil is a real presence in our world; it is not an illusion. The forces of evil are powerful and clever, and they are intent on prying people away from God. There is a war going on, and it is not pretty.

Here's the reason this is so important: Most of us have never really known poverty. Few of us will ever have to worry about being thrown in prison and tortured for our beliefs. We live in relative comfort and ease, in an age of unprecedented wealth and affluence. Certainly, this is a blessing in many ways. Many of us live in nice homes and eat good food, have drinkable water and access to good medical care.

But our comfort can be a kind of curse, as well. It's made us soft. It's made us forget that there are people, even people in our world today, who don't have it so good. More people have been murdered for their faith in Jesus in the last 100 years than ever in history. There is a war going on still. Persecution is not just something the Church experienced in the book of Acts. Neither is it something that will happen one day during the Tribulation. It goes on today in places like Sudan, Indonesia, China and Afghanistan. It will continue until Jesus returns.

So, here's the challenge for you: Stop taking your comfortable lifestyle for granted. Receive it as a gift from God, but don't expect it to last forever. Don't feel guilty for having nice things and for making good money, but realize that you're called to use that wealth to further God's purposes in this world (see 1 Peter 4:10). Remember those who are still persecuted for their faith. Pray for those who go to bed hungry tonight or who are imprisoned.

If you're interested in doing more than sending happy thoughts, you might want to visit a couple of websites and get some information on how you can roll up your sleeves and get involved:

Voice of the Martyrs: www.persecution.com
Compassion International: www.compassion.com
The 410 Bridge: www.410bridge.com

FRIDAY: Prayer

Narrative

Lord Jesus, You have called Your followers to be Your witnesses even to the remotest part of the earth. You have also instilled within us the divine power of the Holy Spirit to accomplish in and through us what we could never dream of doing alone. Nothing is more satisfying than to see radical and permanent life change in others, and You have called us to enjoy that immense privilege. As we seek to be faithful to the process, we can leave the results in Your hands. We know that some will respond with enthusiasm, others with indifference and still others with hostility. We know that we cannot manipulate the outcome, and that we should not be surprised when we encounter opposition when we share the Good News about Jesus, especially in an age that has elevated tolerance above truth. Your Word is truth; may we not depart from it.

Orthodoxy

Father, I am so often tempted to put my hope in all the wrong things. I am tempted to hope in people to gain security, to hope in possessions to gain significance and to hope in position and performance to gain satisfaction. But all of these will let me down, because I can only discover these things in You, not in the world. And now, Lord, for what do I wait? My hope is in You. When I am distressed and disappointed, may I hope in You; when I am betrayed and misunderstood, may I hope in You; when I lose my possessions, may I hope in You. I will exult in hope, knowing that Your promises can never be thwarted by circumstances and setbacks. You will never desert me, nor will You ever forsake me. I will hope alone in Your perfect and unchanging character, knowing that You will carry me safely to Your eternal kingdom.

Orthopathy

God of grace and comfort, when I consider the state of the Church in the world today, I realize that its greatest vitality is no longer in Europe and North America, but in Asia, Africa and South America. The secularization, materialism and pragmatism of the West has diminished our spiritual power, and we have compartmentalized our faith to the degree that there seem to be few real differences between professing Christians and the rest of the population. I confess that we have become more concerned about our comfort than about our character and convictions, and we have become soft. I pray that we would cultivate hearts of gratitude for Your many provisions, and that we would be more generous in investing the resources You have given us for the spread of the gospel so that we participate more dynamically in the Great Commission.

Orthopraxy

Lord Jesus, Your followers in this world have experienced more persecution in our time than ever in the history of the Church. Yet you have used this persecution to bring about greater commitment and zeal and to dramatically bring in a harvest of worldwide proportions. You foretold, "This gospel of the kingdom shall be preached in the whole world as a testimony to all the nations, and then the end will come" (Matt. 24:14). We are privileged to see the great harvest at the end of the age before Your return. I thank You that Your Word is alive and active around the world. This is a time of unprecedented spiritual warfare, and we desperately need to submit to You and put on the full armor of God. For the weapons of our warfare are not of the flesh, but divinely powerful for the destruction of fortresses.

45

A Man Named Saul

ACTS 9:1–31

MONDAY: Story

Christianity was at a tipping point. Some viewed it as a heretical sect within Judaism. Others viewed it as a fulfillment of Judaism. Some wanted it to become a replacement of Judaism. There was confusion, some bickering and now the mounting threat of persecution.

Christians began moving away from Jerusalem. They settled in places like Caesarea, Samaria and Damascus (some even said there was a sizeable gathering all the way up in Antioch—nearly 500 miles away), thinking they might find a safer, more sympathetic community among people who didn't live in the shadow of Herod's Temple . . . but such safety was short-lived.

One of the most determined anti-Christians, a tent-making rabbi named Saul, went to the high priest and requested a warrant to scour the surrounding regions, looking for people who dared breathe the blasphemous name of Jesus. The Jewish leaders, having heard about how Christians were stirring up all sorts of turmoil in the synagogues (even suggesting that people no longer had to travel to Jerusalem to offer sacrifices in the Temple) granted Saul's request. The warrant was issued.

Saul (who in the Greek language he mostly spoke was also called "Paul") planned to travel to these cities, confront these heretics in the synagogues, quiet the trouble they created and bring them back to Jerusalem, where they would stand trial before the Jewish leaders. Just like their Leader had. If things worked out well, Saul reasoned, they might face the same humiliating ending Jesus had met.

But there was just one thing this Saul guy hadn't thought about: *What if they were right and he was wrong*?

He gathered his supplies for what would probably be a 10-day trip. Food, water, clothing—and not just for himself but for his entire entourage. It was a dangerous time and it was safer to travel in a group. Plus, one never knew what these followers of Jesus might do. Rumors had circulated that they even ate flesh and drank blood!

Having heard the one named Stephen arguing with the high priest, Saul was familiar with the gist of the argument he was likely to encounter upon his arrival. On the journey, lost in thought, perhaps he allowed his mind to work out the details of his rebuttal. If they quoted Isaiah, he would quote Jeremiah. If they quoted the psalmist, he would quote the law. If they . . .

Suddenly, a blinding light flashed in the sky, throwing Saul to the ground. There was nowhere to hide from it. It was positively suffocating in its brilliance. Everyone was terrified. Saul felt like he was on fire.

"Saul!" a Voice thundered.

The man in question was too terrified to respond.

"Saul!" the Voice repeated. "Why are you mistreating Me?"

Saul must have thought this was the end for him. But who in the world was talking? Who would say such a thing, and who would know his name—let alone his mission?

You don't suppose . . . ?

"It's me, Jesus . . . the One you're abusing!"

Saul's greatest fears were suddenly realized. His mind was racing. He heart was pounding.

"Get up! Go into the city. Someone there will tell you what to do."

And then it was gone. The light, the Voice, everything returned to normal . . . except for the panic. The fear remained. The terror became a part of Saul, burrowing deep into the core of his being.

He couldn't see. He could barely think or speak. He refused to eat or drink for three days.

And then a man named Ananias showed up, claiming that Jesus had sent him to restore Saul's sight.

Sure enough . . . as soon as Ananias finished speaking, Saul's eyes were opened.

He wasn't sure about much of anything anymore. But he knew this much: He was blind, and now he could see.

TUESDAY: Beliefs

Jesus had Saul right where He wanted him. A bright light shone from the sky, knocking the proud man off his high horse. Saul was blind and helpless. Jesus appeared and called Saul by name. Saul was absolutely terrified!

Hopefully, we know by now that it's not in Jesus' nature to be vindictive or vengeful. His primary motive is not to scare people. He could have done that all the time when He was here on earth, but He didn't. Instead, as Saul later wrote, "God's kindness leads us to repentance" (see Rom. 2:4).

Jesus had Saul right where He wanted him. He was broken and blind and helpless. Jesus could have done whatever He wanted to Saul right then and there. He could have killed him or permanently maimed him.

But that's not how Jesus operates.

Instead, He threw Saul a lifeline. He offered Saul another chance, a new beginning. He offered Saul (a man who deserved to die for persecuting innocent people) salvation. He offered Saul the possibility of an intimate relationship with God the Father through Himself. He even offered Saul the gift of the Holy Spirit's indwelling presence.

It was the opportunity of a lifetime.

Interestingly enough, Jesus didn't explain to Saul how to enter into this new relationship. Instead, He told him to go into town and wait for someone to come and help. Jesus could have explained the whole deal to Saul right there. He could have told him what to pray and how to pray it. He could have given him the Holy Spirit on the spot. He could have told him to go and be baptized.

But He didn't. That's not how it works. No one in the New Testament ever comes to faith in Jesus apart from another human being's help.

Why would we think it's any different today?

There's nothing wrong with Christian radio or Christian television programming *per se*. There's nothing wrong with tracts and literature designed to help people make that connection with God. But nothing will ever replace the original strategy Jesus set in place for growing His kingdom of followers: One person telling another person who tells another person who tells . . .

WEDNESDAY: Values

"I like Jesus, but I don't like the Church."

We've heard many people say this. We've even heard pastors say this! And maybe they've got good reasons. Certainly, the Church hasn't always looked a lot like Jesus. We bicker and brawl. We split theological hairs and exclude people who don't agree with us. We divide over dumb things like what kind of music to use or what women can and can't do or what color to paint the foyer. There are a multitude of reasons why a person might say they don't like Church.

You'll never hear Jesus say it, though.

In fact, one of the statements Jesus made to Saul on the road to Damascus demonstrates how Jesus feels toward His Church: "Saul, Saul, why do you persecute Me?"

Saul, of course, had no idea what this Voice was talking about. He asked, "Who are You, Lord?"

Jesus replies, "I am Jesus, whom you are persecuting."

That was probably confusing for Saul. He wasn't persecuting a person; he was persecuting a group of people who followed a Person.

But Jesus said, "If you're messing with them, you're messing with Me."

These early followers of Jesus weren't perfect. They had squabbles over who was important. They were very prejudiced against people from other nationalities. They had knock-down, drag-out arguments over silly things like what you could and could not eat and whether or not you had to observe certain religious holidays.

But Jesus said, "Those are My people, and as imperfect as they are, if you mess with them, you're messing with Me!"

He still says the same thing about His people today. Is the Church perfect? Far from it! Will it ever be? Not until Jesus comes back. But Jesus loves Her, with all Her warts and spots and wrinkles and blemishes. She is His plan to save the world.

Saul, who became known more widely as Paul, apparently got the message. In his later writings, he referred to the Church as "the Body of Christ" (see Rom. 12; 1 Cor. 12; Eph. 4–5; Col. 3).

Would you say to Jesus, "I like You, but I don't like Your Body"?

Remember, you mess with the Church, you mess with Jesus. And if you accept Jesus . . .

THURSDAY: Actions

Saul was a terror before he met Jesus. Luke wrote, "Saul was still breathing out murderous threats against the Lord's disciples" (Acts 9:1). He was like a wild and ferocious beast in his passion to destroy these people who were spreading the news about Jesus.

In other words, Saul would have been voted "Least Likely to Convert to Christianity."

And yet he did. He didn't just convert to following Christ; he became the greatest missionary the world has ever known. He took the message to the very epicenter of the ancient world: the city of Rome. He suffered tremendously for the sake of his mission, but he did so willingly for the sake of advancing the borders of God's kingdom to the ends of the earth.

And that brings up an interesting thing for us to consider: Who is too far away from God? Who is so unlikely to convert to Christianity that it's not even worth your time to pray about them? Howard Stern? Osama Bin Laden? Richard Dawkins? Madonna? Your spouse? Your ex? Your brother-in-law? Your dad? Your next-door neighbor? Who is so far out there, so far gone, that you're not even going to waste your breath talking to God about them?

Jesus loves porn stars and the drunk in the gutter. He loves Muslims and atheists. He loves mass murderers. He loves people who get divorced, and He loves people who gossip about people who get divorced. He loves everyone. And no one—not a single person who still has breath in his or her body—is too far away for the grace of God to reach.

So don't say no for someone else.

We're so willing to say, "Oh, not that guy. He'll never be interested in having a personal relationship with God. I'm not gonna waste my breath on him."

Don't say no for him. Pray about him. Ask God to open a door of opportunity, and be ready to walk through when it opens.

Spend time today thinking about those who you would vote "Least Likely to Convert to Christianity." Pray for them. Some of them may be celebrities. Others may be people you work with or know casually. Pray for them. Ask God to soften their hearts to His message. Ask God to begin the process of drawing them to Himself. Then ask God to include you in that process.

FRIDAY: Prayer

Narrative

Dear Lord, it is good for me to review my spiritual journey from time to time so that I memorialize the significant people and events You have used in the process of gradually forming me into the person You intend me to become. Although You made me, I have acted as though I am self-made. I was meant for You, yet I have lived as though everything was meant for me. You called me for Your purposes, yet I have sought my own purposes. But when You were pleased to reveal Your Son to me, You opened up an entirely new way and a new set of options that were formerly closed to me. Now I can live for You and pursue Your purposes, because You have turned my spiritual blindness to sight. In Christ, You have given me a new derivation, a new dignity and a new destiny.

Orthodoxy

God of mercy and grace, without You I was on a path that led only to disappointment, emptiness and death. In Your severe mercy, You brought me to a realization of my condition and my real need, and You caused me to see my spiritual bankruptcy. Through the way of brokenness, You graciously drew me to an understanding of my inadequacy and futility. It was only then that I could see clearly enough to reach out for Your grace and transforming power. I thank You for the circumstances and the people You used to bring this about, and I realize that You have now given me the great privilege of acting as Your agent of reconciliation so that I can participate in Your process of bringing others to faith in Christ. I give thanks for Your many gifts, and I ask You to guide and empower me to share them with others.

Orthopathy

Lord, when I consider the history of the Church through the centuries, it amazes me that You have chosen to use such an imperfect and inefficient vehicle to spread the gospel of the Kingdom throughout the world. Yet in spite of all the selfishness, pride, envy, strife, malice, deceit, errors and misunderstandings that have characterized Christendom, Your purposes in the world cannot be thwarted. It would be so much easier for You to spread the gospel directly without our involvement, but You have chosen to love and nurture the living Body of Christ, which is Your Bride, the Church. In spite of our imperfections and foolishness, You have chosen to love us and live through us. I look forward to the day when You will sanctify and cleanse us so that we can be holy and blameless when we are with You.

Orthopraxy

Father, there are so many forces of opposition against the gospel of Christ in this world, and the multiple attacks on Christianity have become more fierce in our time than ever. When I think of some of the people who are bitterly opposed to the gospel, it seems that nothing could break through such hatred for the truth. But then I remember remarkable instances of the dramatic conversion of people who were at enmity with you. Like Saul on the road to Damascus, who was transformed by the power of the resurrected Christ, no one is beyond Your reach. You can change the unlikeliest of people into trophies of Your love and grace. May I therefore not hate those who are opposed to the gospel, but pray for their conversion. I ask for the grace to see people in light of eternity, and never to underestimate the power of prayer and witness.

46

For Gentiles

ACTS 10–11

Let's review: It all started with an idea God had to create a group of people who would live in harmony with Him and with each other. Their very presence would be a blessing to the world.

But it went bad very early on, when sin entered the world through the terrible choice of the first man and his wife.

Still, God has proven to be unrelenting in His pursuit of this idea. He promised then and there that He would send a Deliverer who would set things straight again. A few hundred years later, He spoke to Abraham and said, "I'm going to bless you, and through you I'll bless everyone on the whole planet."

The first half of this book tells the story of what God did in, among and through Abraham's descendants, the Jewish people. He gave them a place. He gave them a Law to live by. He gave them His presence. He made them the envy of all the surrounding nations.

And they blew it. In the grand tradition of Adam and Eve, these people just had to have it their own way. So God gave them over to others, disciplining them for their rebellion but never forgetting the promise He had made to them.

When the time was just right, Jesus appeared. He was Jewish, by the way—extremely Jewish. And the books that talk about Him are also very Jewish. He was circumcised like a good Jewish boy. He studied the Torah like a good Jewish boy. His ministry began in a synagogue, where He read a passage out of the Jewish Bible. He even said that He had come to gather up all the lost sheep of Israel (see Matt. 10:6).

His closest followers, the ones He handpicked, were all Jewish, and after His death and resurrection and ascension, on the Day of Pentecost, there was a great crowd of Jewish people gathered in Jerusalem. These are the ones who heard that first sermon by Peter, and more than 3,000 of them responded by placing their faith in Jesus. When they went home, they didn't stop being Jewish. They kept meeting in synagogues and all that.

We're about 90 percent of the way through the Bible's Story, and so far there's not much in there that's not really, really Jewish. There's been quite a bit about YHWH blessing the descendants of Abraham, but there hasn't been that much about Him blessing the rest of us through them.

There have been a few previews: the story of Ruth from Moab; the story of Jonah going to Nineveh; Jesus talking to the Samaritan woman. Other than that, though, there hasn't been much indication that God has been aiming outside of Israel.

But with this story, the larger Story takes a dramatic turn. Saul has just been knocked off his high horse and converted for one primary purpose: to carry the good news about God to non-Jewish people (see Acts 9:15).

Saul's conversion is just the first of many dominoes that will fall in rapid succession. First Saul becomes a Christian, then comes the first high-profile Gentile convert: a military officer named Cornelius. The next thing you know, the whole thing is out there running wild. The Christians in Antioch (which is where the word "Christian" was first used) start intentionally targeting Gentiles with their message, building a truly cross-cultural missional outpost, raising money and sending out missionaries who always go first to Jewish people and then talk to anyone who will listen.

God had this idea way back when; He made this promise.

And He meant what He said.

TUESDAY: Beliefs

The story of Cornelius's coming to faith (see Acts 10) is one of the happiest stories in the Bible. Here was a man who was neither Christian nor Jewish; he was a God-fearing Roman. He tried to do good. He prayed a lot. But he wasn't affiliated with any of the established religions.

Cornelius sounds a lot like some of the people who live in your neighborhood.

One afternoon, he received a vision of an angel who told him that God had noticed his prayers and good deeds. Oddly, the angel didn't give him the message he needed. Instead, the angel told him how to make contact with a man named Peter, who could give him the message.

That sounds a lot like Saul in our previous story. Again we see how no one in the New Testament comes to faith apart from another human's help.

Shortly after Cornelius received one vision, Peter received another. Peter's was an odd one involving a crazy command by God to do something that Jewish Peter thought was a sin. This is what learning theorists call "cognitive and moral dissonance." God confused and frustrated Peter so that He could teach Peter something.

In this case, God was forcing Peter to reconsider his categories. *What is sin? What is out of bounds? Who is too far away?*

God didn't let Peter mull these questions over for very long, though. While he was thinking about it all, the guys from Cornelius's house showed up: "We're here to bring you to see our boss."

Cornelius was Roman—as in Italian. He sent some guys to see Peter. Peter went with them. 'Nuff said, *capiche*?

When Peter went to Cornelius's house, Cornelius literally fell at Peter's feet. He figured Peter had been sent by an angel, that he was a messenger from God or something—maybe Peter expected and deserved special treatment.

But Peter's response was great. He said, "Stand up, I'm just a regular guy like you."

That's just good mental health right there. So many Christians feel unqualified to do the work of evangelism because we feel so normal, so regular, so unspiritual. We're just regular folks. We're not "evangelists." We don't have big hair or expensive suits.

Peter said, "I'm just a man like you."

James, the brother of Jesus, would later write, "Elijah was a man just like us. He prayed earnestly that it would not rain, and it did not rain on the land for three and a half years. Again he prayed, and the heavens gave rain, and the earth produced its crops" (James 5:17–18).

Elijah was just a man like you. Peter was just a man like you. People like you are the only kind of people God uses.

WEDNESDAY: Values

Peter was summoned by a man named Cornelius. God Himself told him to go. God told Cornelius to send for him. And Peter had arrived.

Cornelius was not Jewish. Up to this point, all of the followers of Jesus had been Jewish (except for the folks in Samaria, who were half-breeds). This posed a dilemma for Peter. Would he go inside Cornelius's house? That would be a big deal. Jewish people weren't supposed to go inside a Gentile's house. They weren't supposed to eat together or have extended conversations.

What's a good Jewish boy to do?

What would you do?

We still have our dividing lines. We may not always divide along the lines of ethnicity—although skin color is still a big deal in a lot of places. We may divide along the lines of religious affiliation or political ideologies. We may draw our lines with socioeconomic markers or even theological positions.

You may think, *I can't talk to them; they're Mac users! They're Calvinists! They're Democrats!*

Peter could have launched into a diatribe about the things that divided them. He could have preached a good, old-fashioned "Turn or burn!" sermon. But he didn't. Instead, look what he did: "Talking with him, Peter went inside" (Acts 10:27).

Perhaps the most important phrase in this story is simply this: "Talking with him."

Peter didn't talk *to* Cornelius. Peter didn't talk *at* him. Peter talked *with* him.

And look what he said: "You are well aware that it is against our law for a Jew to associate with a Gentile or visit him. But God has shown me that I should not call any man impure or unclean" (v. 28). Cornelius and his friends were from the wrong religious and ethnic background, but Peter knew now not to call anyone impure or unclean.

Truth is, everyone is impure and unclean—Jew and Gentile alike—Christian and non-Christian. But no one gets called impure or unclean. Not Gentiles. Not lepers. Not women. Not AIDS patients. Not Republicans. Not Democrats. Not feminists. Not New Agers. Not Muslims.

No one gets called impure or unclean.

There was a time when simple conversations, steeped in humility ("I'm a man just like you") and couched in the context of acceptance could persuade. It was through conversations like Peter had with Cornelius that the world was changed.

Later in his life, Peter would write, "Always be prepared to give an answer to everyone who asks you to give the reason for the hope that you have. But do this with gentleness and respect" (1 Pet. 3:15).

Do we even know how to have conversations like that anymore—with gentleness and respect? Can we stop talking past others, talking at others, talking down to others long enough to talk *with* them?

The power of a simple conversation, the give-and-take and exchange of ideas without name-calling is a marvelous thing. It's how the Early Church spread. It's how the Church would spread today if we'd give it a chance.

THURSDAY: Actions

Peter, a Jew, went to visit Cornelius, a Gentile. In doing so, he broke protocol; he broke the law among Jews that said such a visit was anathema. But he did it because God had called him to do it. It was certainly uncomfortable and disorienting, and Peter must have surely felt out of place. But he did it anyway, and in the process, he confessed that he was learning new things about God, too.

He must also have been putting this experience together with Jesus' final words to him: "Go! Get out there in the wide world and take My message to everyone!"

Peter and the rest of the early followers of Jesus probably thought Jesus meant them to take the message to all the Jewish people who lived in the wide world. But this experience shed new light on His command. Maybe when Jesus had said "everyone," He actually meant "everyone." Not just Jewish people everywhere, but all people everywhere.

We commonly refer to non-Christians as "lost people." The term comes from Jesus' stories about the lost sheep, the lost coin and the lost son recorded in Luke 15. Sadly, the term, which in those stories meant loved, precious and sought after, has become synonymous with "impure" or "unclean." Sometimes we call people *lost* with such derision in our voices, passing judgment on them as if we're so much better for having been found. God doesn't look at them and say, "Good riddance!" They are treasured and missed.

It's enough to make you wonder who's really lost. After all, if you sent a letter to someone and it never arrived, you would say the letter was lost—not the intended recipient.

God has sent us into the world as His letter to people He misses greatly (see 2 Cor. 3:3). We're His ambassadors, sent out to make known His loving and gracious intentions to everyone (see 2 Cor. 5:20). And when He says "everyone," He means "everyone." And yet so few of us actually arrive at our destination.

In light of that, who is really lost?

Jesus promised His followers that He would always be with them, and that's a promise we can claim, as well. But there was a command attached to the promise. Do you remember what it was? It's called the Great Commission (see Matt. 28:19–20).

Jesus will be with us as we spread the message. There are lessons we can only learn as we, like Peter, follow Jesus out of comfortable positions and places, allowing the Holy Spirit to stretch us. He will be with us as we engage in spiritual friendships with people like Cornelius, learning as we teach, refusing to place ourselves on a higher plane and showing respect for those to whom we have been sent. Jesus will be with us as we go to *everyone*.

Do we really believe what He says or not?

FRIDAY: Prayer

Narrative

Lord God, You called Your servant Abram to take the risk of leaving everything he knew in his country, including his relatives, to go to a land he did not know. You called him to a far higher purpose than he could have pursued on his own, because You invited him to be a part of Your great Story rather than his own comfortable existence. And You promised to make this man who had no children into a great nation, and to bless him and make his name great so that he would become a blessing not only to his own people, but ultimately to all the families of the earth. Your fulfillment of this covenant promise came about in completely unexpected and unpredictable ways—in ways that demonstrate Your divine creativity and sovereign authority over history. For Abram became Abraham, and his seed led to the Lord Jesus Christ, who blessed both Jews and Gentiles.

Orthodoxy

Father, I praise Your Name that You have given me eternal life in Jesus Christ, a new quality of life that is meant to flow out of my inner being and bear lasting fruit in the lives of others. I delight in the liberating truth that I do not need to be an impressive person who has accomplished significant things by the standards of this world. Instead, You use ordinary people to accomplish extraordinary things, because the power of Your kingdom is of an utterly different nature than the powers known to the world. I do not need to be wise, mighty or noble to be used in profound ways by You. I thank You for the many examples in the Bible that make this clear. May I look to You, follow You, know You, discern Your desires for my life and submit my will to Your desires, knowing that You want to bear abiding fruit in and through me.

Orthopathy

Lord, we have always lived in cultures that erect barriers between people. Social, economic, racial, gender, political and worldview barriers divide us and make us feel either arrogant or inferior. I thank You for the life and ministry of the Lord Jesus, who broke through these artificial boundaries in His love, acceptance, forgiveness and service to the last, the least and the lonely. And I give thanks for the way Your followers, according to the book of Acts, were willing to carry the Good News from the Jews to the Samaritans, and on to the Gentiles. Teach me to treasure all the people I encounter and to love them enough to seek their greatest good. I want to be gracious and kind when I share my faith, not talking *at* people, but *with* them. May I build redemptive bridges of friendship based on common ground with people who do not yet know Jesus.

Orthopraxy

Dear Lord, through my new birth and identity in Your Son, I now have an entirely different orientation in life. I have become a steward, and I no longer manage my possessions, but Yours. I have become an ambassador, and I am no longer on my own business, but on the business of Your kingdom. Because I am a new creature and now Your ambassador in Christ, You have given me the ministry of reconciliation in this world. Through Your resources, You have made me adequate as a servant of the new covenant to become a living letter about Christ that can be known and read by others. Jesus, as You promised in Your Great Commission, You will be with me always as I serve as an agent of Your life-giving Word. Give me a growing willingness to move out of my comfort zone, and stretch me by Your Holy Spirit to see and do new things in Your power.

47

Conflict Resolution

ACTS 15:1–35

MONDAY: Story

The earliest Christians were fundamentally Jewish people. There were Jewish people who lived in Jerusalem, and there were Jewish people who lived in other parts of the world who happened to be in Jerusalem when Peter and the others burst out of their upper room and declared the greatest news of all time.

But they were all Jewish people.

And then came this guy named Cornelius, and this issue that had been lurking beneath the surface bubbled up: If a Gentile heard about Jesus, would that Gentile have to become Jewish first in order to become a Christian?

This issue brought up a whole bushel of issues. What about circumcision? What about sacrifices? What about the Temple and the dietary laws and the Sabbath and all the stuff that comes with being Jewish?

The underlying question was this: *Is faith in Christ enough, or should there be something else—something more?*

Jewish people had always made provision for outsiders who wanted to join them, but the provision involved some external ritual—namely, circumcision.

Now, however, saying that a person had to be circumcised in order to be saved sounded like Jesus didn't really accomplish everything, like maybe He needed some help from us, a little boost.

That didn't sound right.

As you might imagine, there were debates and discussions and diatribes. (Religion has always been a touchy subject, and the first century was no exception.) But because the earliest leaders of the Church relied so heavily on the Holy Spirit's guidance, cooler heads prevailed. Gathering all the concerned parties in Jerusalem, a meeting was held to sort things out. They discussed the issues openly and honestly. Their conclusion was clear and decisive.

Jesus Christ, their Messiah, had accomplished everything necessary for salvation through His sinless life, sacrificial death and victorious resurrection. Nothing else must ever be added to that. In doing so, He opened the way for people of every nationality and ethnic background to come to God. The only way to God is Jesus. Period.

With that in mind, it also seemed wise for them to make two suggestions: First, if you want to follow Jesus, you have to commit to holy living. Second, it's a good idea to be sensitive to one another and not do things just to aggravate each other. These aren't conditions of your Christianity; they are expressions of your Christianity. The motivation for living this way isn't obligation; it is love.

Seems like Jesus had said something about love, hadn't He? Oh, yeah—that bit about love being the way people would know we are really His followers.

TUESDAY: Beliefs

In essentials, unity; in non-essentials, liberty; in all things, charity.

So much wisdom is packed into the three short phrases of this centuries-old dictum! It certainly expresses the thought of the Early Church leaders who gathered that historic day in Jerusalem.

The matters they discussed and debated there would decide the future of this new movement. Would it remain just an offshoot of Judaism, or would it be given the wings necessary for it to fly to the ends of the earth? And what exactly was it they would export to the world? Would it be a modified version of Judaism, or would it be a new thing altogether?

The wisdom reflected by the early leaders of the Church allowed the momentum established by Barnabas and Saul's first missionary journey to continue, opening the door for evangelistic activity to continue throughout the world. You are able to read this (and we are able to write it) because of the result of that meeting in Acts 15.

There are essentials to this Christian faith, and in these essentials we must have unity.

God is holy. Humanity is broken and unable to save itself. Jesus, being both fully God and fully human, is the only way for broken humanity to be repaired and restored in its relationship to Holy God. Such repair and restoration is freely available to all those who place their trust in Jesus Christ as Lord and Savior. These people are Christians, and they must progressively grow in holiness and love.

This much is non-negotiable. In these essentials we must have unity.

Must someone believe in the verbal-plenary inspiration of the Scriptures? Must they affirm our position on End Times or charismatic gifts or the role of women in the Church? Must a person quit smoking or drinking or viewing pornography in order to be saved?

No. In fact, it could be argued that a person cannot do many of these things *until* they are saved!

There are essentials for salvation, and there are other things that are by-products of that salvation. There are essentials, and there are matters of opinion. There are essentials, and there are things that are open for debate.

Only God can give us the wisdom to practice unity in essentials, liberty in non-essentials and charity in all things. And He will give us that wisdom if we ask Him for it.

WEDNESDAY: Values

In the beginning, God placed Adam and Eve in a beautiful garden where everything was good—except for one thing. It wasn't good for Adam to be alone.

So God created Eve, and community was born.

But they chose to reject God's way of life and ended up estranged not only from their Creator but from one another, as well. Adam blamed Eve for the whole mess, and suddenly there was shame and fear in their relationship. From then until now, human relationships have been fraught with anxiety and suspicion, defensiveness and division.

Sin separates us from God and alienates us from one another. Conflict and hostility threaten to permeate every level of society, from marriages to nations. History can be read as a testament to sin's ability to tear asunder what God intended to join together.

But sin will never be allowed to have the last word. God has a plan that has been unfolding since Genesis 3 to reconcile us back to Himself and to one another. He made a promise to Abraham, and we've seen how all of Abraham's descendants were brought together in great unity. Granted, they kept tearing at the fabric, trying to unravel what God was sewing. But God was more stubborn than they were.

Still, it wasn't clear to them that His intention was for more than just Abraham's children to be blessed with the chance to enjoy healthy relationships. There was a "mystery" about this, and it would only be made clear through God's Son, Jesus (see Eph. 3:4–6).

Jesus came from the lineage of Abraham. He went to the Jewish people first, but He also brought Good News to the Gentiles—Good News of great joy for *all* people! That's what the angels announced at His birth.

After Jesus returned to His Father in heaven, the Holy Spirit was poured out on those first followers on the Day of Pentecost, and the Church was established. That day, there were people gathered from all over the world. God began His new community by drawing people from many nations to faith in Jesus. That new community was the Church, it is the Church, and it has always, from Day One, transcended barriers of race, language and culture.

Those who wanted the Gentiles to adhere to their customs in order to be unified were grieving the heart of God, who wants nothing more than for His children to enjoy His presence and live at peace with one another. They were denigrating the completed work of Jesus on the cross by suggesting that unity would only be gained through human activity.

Throughout human history, people have tried to accomplish unity. But they've never been successful. It's far too costly. It cost Jesus His life. He paid a high price to purchase not just our personal redemption, but the ability now for us to know, accept, serve and celebrate one another.

We cannot initiate such unity through our efforts. Our best attempts always fall short. Only the Spirit of God can create unity. Our job, then, becomes to maintain it (see Eph. 4:1–6).

We could start by making unity a core value.

THURSDAY: Actions

We've come to the conclusion that you simply cannot avoid controversy in the Church. It seems like it's been that way since the very beginning, and if you try to steer clear of it, you almost always end up making it worse! So it behooves us to consider how to deal with conflict, rather than attempting to bury our heads in the sand and pretend that if we sit really still, maybe Jesus will come back and resolve things for us.

The Council at Jerusalem, recorded in Acts 15, is a really good example for us to follow. This was a sharp dispute with a lot of passion and debate. Some of these people were really angry! But they never allowed it to get ugly. We never read about any gossip or slander. No one was vindictive or sarcastic. No one attacked anyone's motives. They showed tremendous honor, acceptance, respect and civility.

In spite of conflict, they modeled a Christlike spirit and attitude toward one another.

However, they understood that this was something more than just human conflict resolution. Their goal wasn't to appease all the people there. It wasn't a democracy. They were trying to discern the will of God.

Certainly, God speaks through the collective wisdom of His people, so we must listen to one another. But we shouldn't allow a majority vote to settle issues for us. There are some who are better at discerning the leading of God than others. It appears in Acts 15 that everyone was allowed to speak, but not everyone was allowed to decide.

Another factor that surfaces in the speeches recorded for us in Acts 15 is this: They knew the peace was being disturbed and eventually it became clear who was causing the disturbance.

First Peter says, "Brothers, you know that some time ago God made a choice among you that the Gentiles might hear from my lips the message of the gospel and believe. God, who knows the heart, showed that he accepted them by giving the Holy Spirit to them, just as he did to us. He made no distinction between us and them, for he purified their hearts by faith" (Acts 15:7–9).

Then Barnabas and Paul tell "about the miraculous signs and wonders God had done among the Gentiles through them" (v. 12).

Finally James speaks: "Brothers, listen to me. Simon has described to us how God at first showed his concern by taking from the Gentiles a people for himself" (v. 14).

Who is disturbing the peace? Who is the Agitator?

God.

And as they looked at what God was doing, instead of what Peter or Paul or the Gentiles or the Judaizers were doing, they saw clearly their course of action. God was calling them to join Him in what He was doing. He wanted to know if they valued Him and His work more than they valued their traditions.

They met. They talked. They listened. They argued respectfully. They deferred to those who were wise. Most importantly, they asked themselves what God was up to in their midst and how they could join Him in that work. And then they decided. They declared their willingness to adapt their methods in order to meet their mission, to sacrifice their traditions if need be for the sake of partnering with God in expanding His kingdom to the ends of the earth.

That's how you handle conflict in the Church.

FRIDAY: Prayer

Narrative

Lord God, Your Word clearly demonstrates the need for a quality of righteousness that cannot be earned by us but must be credited to us. All of us fall so short of Your glorious character that the differences between the best and the worst people who ever lived are trivial in comparison to the standard of perfection that You require. The Mosaic Law was a tutor to lead us to our need for faith, because no one can be justified in Your sight by the works of the Law. The Law reveals the problem of sin; but only in Christ, who is the fulfillment of the Law, can righteousness before You be found. I praise and glorify Your Name for Your righteousness, which comes through faith in Jesus Christ for all those who believe. Through His gift of redemption, You have justified all people who transfer their trust from themselves to Him.

Orthodoxy

Father, so many divisions and disputes have been generated by issues, practices and traditions that are not part of the fundamentals of the faith. Your Church is a glorious unity in diversity, but when we major on the minors, the spirit of factionalism replaces that of unity and peace. I ask for the boldness and courage to stand up and contend for the essentials of the faith, even if it means a lack of peace. I do not want to compromise the truth of the gospel for the sake of peace. But I also ask for the graciousness to demonstrate kindness and tolerance for believers who disagree with me about the non-essentials. I acknowledge that there are some things that are not clear enough in Your revelation for us to understand fully, but these are not the clearly revealed core issues of the faith. In all things, may I be loving and gracious to others.

Orthopathy

Lord, I pray for a spirit of humility and gentleness and of patience and tolerance in my own faith community, so that Your love will prevail as we seek to preserve the unity of the Spirit in the bond of peace. It is only as we walk by the Spirit that we can attain this quality of unity that cannot be achieved by human efforts. May we put away selfishness and empty conceit and seek to be united in love and in spirit. Give us such an affection and compassion in Christ that we are intent on one purpose, which is Your honor and pleasure. May we walk by the Spirit and bear the fruit of peace, patience, kindness and goodness. For it is only by Your Spirit that we can overcome the estrangement that is caused by the selfishness and willfulness of sin. May we be perfected in unity so that the world may know that Christ is in our midst.

Orthopraxy

Father, You have taught us that relational harmony is so important that it must be achieved before effective worship can take place. As far as it depends on me, may I seek to be at peace with others and to pursue prompt reconciliation by lovingly speaking the truth. May I develop a greater capacity to forgive so that I will not allow wrongs to be barriers to my relationships. And may I not seek to defeat or humiliate my opponents, but to win their friendship and understanding. Let me look for and build on areas of common ground, and seek to clarify meaning and build understanding, so that I will pursue the things that make for peace and the building up of others. May I be a peacemaker and an others-centered servant who is more concerned about the needs of people than about winning arguments.

48

Freedom

THE BOOK OF ROMANS;
THE BOOK OF GALATIANS;
THE BOOK OF EPHESIANS;
THE BOOK OF PHILIPPIANS;
THE BOOK OF COLOSSIANS

MONDAY: Story

Christianity was no longer a branch of Judaism. It was its own thing. It had roots in the Jewish faith, but it had begun the process of breaking with its past to form something new. Or perhaps Judaism broke with what had been God's plan all along. Perhaps it was not Christianity that was the new thing, but Judaism without the leadership of YHWH.

Regardless, what God was doing now in places like Antioch and Galatia and Ephesus and Rome would be a decidedly good thing for the vast majority of the world. However, it would prove to be a serious obstacle for law-abiding, Christ-following Jews. The Law of Moses, the Temple sacrifices and holy days—these had been objects of reverence for them, and they had paid dearly for their devotion throughout the centuries. Were they to just cast them aside now that Jesus Christ has come and rendered them obsolete?

What was becoming clearer and clearer, at least among the leaders of early Christianity, is that true religion was never supposed to be about the rules and the rituals; it was always meant to be about *relationships*. God wanted a people who were rightly related to Him and rightly relating to others. The rules and the rituals were supposed to facilitate that. Somehow, the tail had begun to wag the dog.

A simple letter from the Council in Jerusalem wasn't enough to appease the consciences of some who felt compelled not only to maintain their own personal observance of Jewish law, but to bind it on others as well. These people came to be known as "Judaizers." They plagued the apostle Paul everywhere he went by opposing his teaching that acceptance by God is available to people from all ethnic backgrounds by grace through faith in the completed work of Jesus. And they denied his status as an apostle.

Sadly, many young believers fell prey to their message that God's approval must be earned and maintained by rigid observance of the Jewish Law. They had to become Jewish in order to gain God's favor.

Needless to say, this infuriated Paul. Once, in something approaching a fit of rage, Paul wrote, "I can't believe how easily you've been turned away from the true message about Jesus to this lie they're telling about God!" (see Gal. 1:6–7). He continued, "You were running a good race," and then asked rhetorically, "Who cut in on you and kept you from obeying the truth?" (see Gal. 5:7).

For some reason, some folks in the first century apparently found grace unsettling. They felt as if they needed to do something more in order to be accepted by God.

Aren't you glad we finally got past that kind of thinking? Oh, wait . . .

TUESDAY: Beliefs

The entire letter to the church in Galatia is written with passion and anger, correcting the corruption of the Good News that was being spread by the Judaizers. Paul states his case as clearly as he can: "If righteousness could be gained through the law, Christ died for nothing" (Gal. 2:21). In other words, Christ's work is sufficient. We dare not think that keeping the Law can add a thing to what He has done. What matters now is not whether or not you live your life according to the Jewish Law, but whether or not you live your life in Christ under the direction and guidance of the Holy Spirit.

Later, Paul incorporated these same thoughts into his letter to the Christians in Rome. They were struggling with similar issues in both places, so he went to great lengths to demonstrate the futility of seeking to be declared righteous by keeping the Jewish Law (see Rom. 3:9–20).

The Judaizers weren't content to stay in Galatia and Rome; they spread their corruption into every area that the message of Jesus had reached. To the church in Ephesus, Paul states, "For it is by grace you have been saved, through faith—and this is not from yourselves, it is the gift of God—not by works, so that no one can boast" (Eph. 2:8–9). He says that Jesus has destroyed the things that separated Jews from Gentiles "by abolishing in his flesh the law with its commandments and regulations" (2:15). In Philippi, Paul warned the church, "Watch out for those dogs, those men who do evil, those mutilators of the flesh" (Phil. 3:2). In Colossae, Paul instructed the church, "Therefore, do not let anyone judge you by what you eat or drink or with regard to a religious festival, a New Moon celebration or a Sabbath day" (Col. 2:16).

Your standing with God is not determined by your ethnicity or your observance of Jewish Law; it is determined by your identification with the finished work of Jesus Christ and the life you now live under the influence of the Spirit.

Sadly, legalism is still practiced in many churches today. Maybe it's not about kosher foods or circumcision, but we've managed to create our own boundary markers. For some, it's social drinking or smoking. In some circles, it's going to movies, listening to certain kinds of music or dancing.

Most of us have moved beyond those debates, but there are other, subtler forms of legalism still at work among us. For example, if you've made it this far in our book, you are to be commended. But we're guessing at least some of you got behind somewhere along the line. You got busy and skipped a few days. Maybe you made it up by reading several days' worth of material in one sitting, or maybe you just fast-forwarded to the next story.

Here's the thing: Sometimes people feel guilty about missing their daily devotional or "quiet time." They feel distant from God—even unloved by Him for that day. They can't wait to get back to their scheduled reading so that they can once again find themselves in God's good graces.

Guess what? That's legalism. You *are* loved by God. Reading your Bible and saying your prayers doesn't make you any more loveable to God than you already are.

The discipline is important, but the discipline doesn't make you acceptable to God. Jesus Christ makes you acceptable to God. Live life in Him, and you never need to feel the burden of Quiet Time guilt again!

WEDNESDAY: Values

As Americans, we love our freedom. We value and cherish our freedom. Soldiers are willing to die to protect our freedom. We go to great lengths to make sure that the freedom we currently enjoy will be passed down to the next generation.

We love freedom, but do we really understand it?

The concepts of slavery and freedom are deeply woven into the Story of the Bible. Beginning with the 400 years in Egypt, God demonstrated His desire to see His people free. But there was a particular reason *why* He wanted them free: He wants them to be set free so that they can worship Him (see Exod. 5:1; 7:16; 8:1; 8:20; 9:1; 9:13; 10:3). In other words, the Hebrews were set free from one thing (Egyptian slavery), but they were also set free for something else (to worship YHWH).

Like those Hebrew slaves, we find ourselves enslaved, as well. Without Jesus, we are enslaved to sin and self to such an extent that we cannot free ourselves (see John 8:34). Because of our bondage, we are unable to live the life God created us for.

In the Bible, freedom is always *from* something; but it is also *for* something. God wants to set us free from our bondage to anyone or anything that keeps us from living life in His kingdom. God wants to set us free for a lifestyle characterized by what He calls "the fruit of the Spirit," that is, love, joy, peace, patience, kindness, goodness, faithfulness, gentleness and self-control (see Gal. 5:22–23).

Freedom *from* . . .

Freedom *for* . . .

The apostle Paul was adamant about this. All who place their faith in Christ have been set free from sin and are now free to live life in the Spirit (see Rom. 8:1–11; Gal. 5). God has set you free from your sin, free from your past, free from religious convention, free from regret and guilt and shame and fear and anxiety. But you're not just free from all that; you're free *for* some things now. God has set you free for a life of worship, a life of service, a life of joy and peace and love and generosity.

The important thing to remember is that if you never engage in the thing you've been set free for, you'll end up enslaved again to the thing you've been set free *from*. If you never move forward into worshiping God by living a life of freedom in the Spirit, you'll end up enslaved to sin and self all over again.

Value your freedom. Cherish that freedom. Fight for your freedom. Protect it and guard it. But know that it's not complete until you move into the life you've been set free for.

THURSDAY: Actions

I'm free to do what I want any old time.

Who knew The Rolling Stones' song from 1965 would come to resonate so deeply with a people? Who would have imagined they would sing it for more than 40 years and that it would eventually become the tune for an advertising campaign for a credit card company?

But is that really freedom? Or is that just egocentric individualism run amuck?

We live in a free society, but are we free to do whatever we want whenever we want? The answer is, in one sense, yes. We are free to hurl obscenities at the driver who cuts us off. We are free to steal from our offices. We are free to cheat on our spouses and on our taxes. Sort of.

But there are consequences.

You may get caught. Your spouse may divorce you. Your boss may fire you. The IRS may audit you, and the driver in front of you may get out of his car and punch you in the nose.

Worse, no one may ever find out. You may never get caught, but there will still be consequences. You'll become an even more impatient, untrustworthy, self-indulgent person who lives isolated and alienated from others.

In other words, if you allow your freedom to become license for over-indulgence, you'll end up enslaved to your appetites. The choice isn't between limitation and freedom. Rather, the choice is whom you will allow to set your limits.

The apostle Paul says that you can set the limits for yourself. You can use your freedom in that way, to indulge yourself. However, that approach is disastrous when you try to live it out—especially when you try to live it out in the context of community with others (see Gal. 5:13–15).

His solution is not to give up your freedom; his solution is to concentrate less on what you've been set free from and more on what you've been set free *for*. If Jesus has set you free, you're free to follow the leading of the Holy Spirit now rather than your own selfish interests. And if you follow the leading of the Spirit, you have no need for the Law to tell you what's right and wrong. The Holy Spirit can be trusted to guide you wisely and well (see Gal. 5:18).

Selfish living sounds good for a while, but it always leads to boring repetition. It cheapens life and love. It's characterized by frenzied activity with diminishing returns, momentary but fleeting fits of happiness. It inevitably leads to loneliness and jealousy and an increasing inability to love or receive love from others. It always promises more than it can deliver.

You're now free to live like that, if you like.

But you're also free now to live a different way, a better way. You're free to live life in the Spirit. You can live a life of affection and enthusiasm. You can have a peace that defies your circumstances. You can endure hardships with joy. You can stand up for your convictions fearlessly and show compassion to others. You can keep your commitments and enjoy relationships without manipulation.

You're now free to live like that, if you like.

That kind of life won't come about through any kind of legalistic observance of rules, though. Legalism only gets in the way. The way to gain that kind of life—the kind of life you've always wanted but have never been able to achieve on your own—is by surrendering on a daily basis to the guidance of God's Spirit.

FRIDAY: Prayer

Narrative

Lord, what You inaugurated through Your beloved Son is utterly unique in human history. Christianity is not a set of regulations and rituals that are intended to earn favor and merit with God, with the gods or with some other version of the Ultimate. That is the nature of humanly devised religions, and it only leads to bondage and uncertainty. But the Lord Jesus Christ opened up an entirely new way, through which we can have direct access to You, not by our merits, but by His grace. The heart of Christianity is not a set of rules and observances, but a living relationship with You. But Your Word clearly reveals the human inclination to add to grace, because we think we need to accomplish something to earn acceptance with You. Deliver us from the folly of putting ourselves on a treadmill by denying the all-sufficient work of Your Son.

Orthodoxy

Lord God, when Your kindness and love for the people You created appeared in the Person of Your Son, You saved us, not on the basis of deeds we have done in righteousness, but according to Your mercy, by the washing of regeneration and renewal by the Holy Spirit. Now that we have been justified by Your grace, we have been made heirs according to the hope of eternal life. We have been justified by faith and not by the works of the Law, and only the righteousness of Your Son in us can make us acceptable before You. Teach us, Lord, with increasing clarity that not only is grace through faith in Christ the basis for our salvation, but that grace through faith in Christ is also the basis for our sanctification in the spiritual life. It is as we abide in Christ that His fruit of good works will become evident in and through us.

Orthopathy

Lord Jesus, You set me free from the yoke of slavery and delivered me from the bondage of the world, the bondage of sin and the bondage of self so that I could be liberated into newness of life. The more clearly I see myself in Christ, the more free I am from the guilt and pain of the past and from the anxieties of the future. Now that I have been adopted into Your family, You have given me a new identity and a new inheritance. By Your grace, may I learn to live out of the resources You have given so that I will move forward into the new freedom You have given and be less inclined to revert to the bondage of the past. May I become increasingly attracted to what You want for me and less attracted to the lures of the things that formerly ensnared me.

Orthopraxy

Father, Your Word teaches that the freedom You have given us in Christ is not the libertarian freedom to do whatever we want to do. That form of freedom leads to selfishness and the painful consequences of self-indulgence. When we try to do things in our way and in our timing, this ultimately diminishes our freedom, because we are attempting to live life on our own terms. Too many of us who profess to be followers of Christ are trying to play by two sets of rules at once. But You have made it clear that we must choose to serve only one master. Service to the world and to self is not freedom, but bondage. But service to Christ Jesus is the source of perfect freedom. As I follow You and live life in Your Spirit, new options open up before me. Now as I walk by the Spirit, I can choose to be pleasing to You and to reflect the righteousness of Your Son.

49

Love and War

The Books of 1 and 2 Peter

MONDAY: Story

As you've seen by now, Christianity wasn't just another branch of Judaism—like the Pharisees or the Sadducees or the Essenes or the Zealots—after all. It was its own thing.

And so the persecution began.

It began mostly as Jew-on-Jew crime in Jerusalem. James, the brother of Jesus, the leader of the Church there in the Holy City, was stoned to death on authority of the high priest, his meticulous observance of the Law no longer able to make up for the fact that he aligned himself with the Gentile-loving Christians.

Christians like Paul throughout the Jewish world looked to Rome for protection, and it was granted as long as the Romans believed Christianity to be under the umbrella of Judaism. But as more and more Gentiles came to faith in Christ, they came under more careful scrutiny. In a few short years, the Roman emperor Nero saw Christians as a convenient scapegoat for a dastardly crime committed by none other than the emperor himself: the burning of Rome!

Now you might think that the most powerful nation in the history of Planet Earth would be able to win this little skirmish. But these Christians proved a plucky lot, willing to endure terrible hardships and finding joy amidst their pain, peace in spite of their circumstances and the gumption to bless those who cursed them.

As you can imagine, this infuriated the Romans.

Christians were rounded up and killed. Nero had them wrapped in animal skins and thrown to packs of wild dogs. He thought it would be ironic to have them crucified like the One they claimed to follow. He lit them on fire and suspended them on poles to serve as torches for his outdoor parties.

But these Christians wouldn't stop. Somehow they thought that no matter how bad things got in this life, there was something better waiting for them on the other side. They believed that the sufferings would appear to be brief in light of the eternal life that was theirs because of their faith in Jesus. They saw the persecution they endured as a refining process.

After all, Jesus Himself had suffered at the hands of Jewish and Roman leaders; why should His followers expect to escape the same treatment? He suffered, and He was vindicated by His Father in heaven. If they could summon the strength to suffer as He had, they would surely be vindicated in a similar fashion.

This stumped the Romans.

All they could think to do was more of the same—only harder. So they cracked the whip again and again and again. Nine times in 250 years, they swept the land, seeking to rid themselves of Christianity once and for all.

But an amazing thing happened: Love won.

Love bested the worst Rome could dish out. Love outlasted power. Love demolished strength. Out of everything that had ever been or will ever be, these three will always remain: faith, hope and love. But the greatest of these is love.

TUESDAY: Beliefs

You can turn on your radio any day and hear Christian stations claiming to be "safe for the whole family." We know what they mean, but who in the world ever said Christianity was supposed to be *safe*? Jesus said the exact opposite. He said we shouldn't be surprised if our faith got us into trouble. The world wasn't always kind to Him; it won't always be kind to His followers.

Safety isn't bad, and Christian parents are often called to protect their children and provide safe environments for their families. But safety can easily become idolatrous if and when it replaces a willingness to follow God's leading in every area of our lives.

Those who follow God with this radical commitment level will sometimes find themselves persecuted. That is a simple fact of life. Persecution isn't just something the Church experienced back in the early days; it goes on all the time. There are Christians being imprisoned and killed for their faith, even now. Even in places like the suburbs of America, society can be somewhat hostile to people who take God seriously. The light of the gospel has broken in, but this world is still a dangerous, unfriendly place that often refuses to treat us kindly.

So how are we to live? Should we just withdraw from society, hole up, hide away and forward a lot of paranoid, Chicken Little, the-sky-is-falling emails to one another?

It's a good thing God doesn't think the way we think. He saw a world that was hostile toward Him, and His response was to send His Son into that perilous world to die on its behalf. In fact, the whole Bible Story shows us, time and time again, how God calls people out of safety and comfort into places of danger and risk.

How did they survive? Faith was their survival kit.

Faith asks us to face the future with the courageous tenacity to persevere in doing what God has called us to do, looking forward to the fulfillment of God's promises, regardless of whether or not those promises will be fulfilled in our own lifetimes.

It's relatively easy to keep the faith, when life's good. When the sun is shining and you're in good favor with your boss and your neighbors—well, God is good then. But when your faith gets you in trouble, it's easy to start wondering about the validity of these outlandish promises God has made. Life on this planet doesn't always feel like abundant life for even the most passionate Christian.

Still, the promise has been made. Jesus is returning, and when He does, every knee is going to bow and every tongue is going to confess that He is Lord and in charge (see Phil. 2:10–11). He has put His reputation on the line.

One day it will all come full circle, and the hardships we endure now will prove worthwhile (see Rom. 8:18–25; 2 Cor. 4:16–18). That day has yet to arrive, and until it does, we must remain forward-facing, leaning into whatever today holds in store for us, filled with faith in a God who has secured and is preparing for us a future beyond our wildest expectations!

WEDNESDAY: Values

When trouble comes, it's easy to focus on what you do not have. You do not have relief. You do not have comfort. You may not have the physical freedom you once enjoyed. Such a focus easily turns to complaining and grumbling.

But that's a terrible way to live. Even if it's accurate, it's not helpful. It doesn't accomplish anything. It doesn't make you feel better. In fact, complaining and grumbling are self-sustaining activities; vocalizing your dissatisfaction reinforces your dissatisfaction and makes you want to vocalize it even more.

By the time the apostle Peter got around to writing his first letter, there were Christians scattered all over the known world who were enduring terrible persecution, a kind you and I probably can't even imagine. Jesus had told them He would be right back, but it had been decades, and there was no sign of His return. Worse, they were being hunted down and murdered for their faith.

Where was Jesus in the midst of all this? They didn't have Him, at least not in the flesh. They didn't have relief. They didn't have comfort. They didn't have the physical freedom they once enjoyed.

They began to focus on what they didn't have, and it wasn't long before it turned into complaining and grumbling. Some were even beginning to doubt this whole Christianity thing.

Peter countered this by reminding them of what they had received. Rather than focusing on what they lacked, he advised, they should focus on what was theirs because of their faith in Christ. For example:

> Praise be to the God and Father of our Lord Jesus Christ! In his great mercy he has given us new birth into a living hope through the resurrection of Jesus Christ from the dead, and into an inheritance that can never perish, spoil or fade—kept in heaven for you, who through faith are shielded by God's power until the coming of the salvation that is ready to be revealed in the last time. In this you greatly rejoice, though now for a little while you may have had to suffer grief in all kinds of trials. These have come so that your faith—of greater worth than gold, which perishes even though refined by fire—may be proved genuine and may result in praise, glory and honor when Jesus Christ is revealed. Though you have not seen him, you love him; and even though you do not see him now, you believe in him

and are filled with an inexpressible and glorious joy, for you are receiving the goal of your faith, the salvation of your souls (1 Pet. 1:3–9).

Peter calls his readers to hope—not to dream or wish, but to *hope*—in Christ. His desire is that we rest in the promises of God and rejoice in the assurance that the future will be better. Amid present and difficult dangers, we are justified in viewing the future with optimism because we are securely attached to the God who deals in futures.

Nero and Rome may do their worst. The Chinese government may imprison, and the ACLU may seek to remove any vestiges of our nation's Christian influences. They do not get the last word—God does. And because of our relationship with Him, we will emerge from the fires of trial victorious.

Cling to that hope! Cherish that hope! Live in and out of that hope!

THURSDAY: Actions

Few biblical truths are as self-evident as Jesus' statement, "In this world you will have trouble" (John 16:33). At some point, you will face discouragement. It may be something as simple as a rift in a relationship or as serious as harassment for expressing your faith. Regardless, you will be opposed by the devil, by the forces of this present darkness that work to sabotage God's agenda.

There is no denying that there is a war going on. It is bigger than the war on drugs and more divisive than the war on terror. It is a culture war, and we are engaged in it.

What will win such a war? It won't be violent rhetoric or legislating a Christian agenda. It won't be telling the other side how and why they're wrong and we're right. In fact, those who have engaged society with an arrogant attitude like this have done more harm than good. The only way to win a culture war is by embodying the sacrificial love of Jesus.

We tend to view our enemies with suspicion, to hide from them or attempt to impose our will on them. We do not want our enemies to know our weaknesses. In fact, truth be told, we hate our enemies. We pray that God will hold them accountable for the atrocities they've committed.

But God's wartime strategy is remarkably different. Think of it like this: The people in the world (including us) were enemies of God (see Rom. 5:10). We were at war with God (a futile notion if ever there was one!). And what was God's plan for ending that war? He sought us out, wooing us with His love, giving us freedom to embrace or reject His message. He became weak in our presence, humbling Himself to the point of death. Out of His great love for us, He asked that we not be held accountable for the things we had done.

In short, God was willing to go to unbelievable lengths to win us back. Not to win the war, but to *win the warriors*, even as they continued acting out their hostility and aggression toward Him.

What would it look like for us to engage in the current culture war with the same depth of love for those on the other side as God demonstrated toward us?

How do you win the culture war? Love the other side.

Don't embrace their beliefs, values or behaviors. But love them. Seek their best. Serve them. Forgive them. Show them hospitality and courtesy. Use whatever you've been given to meet the needs of others (see 1 Pet. 4:7–11). In other words, treat them the way Jesus has treated you. Then, whether you change their minds or not, you will know that God is shaping you, transforming you from within into the kind of person you were created to be.

FRIDAY: Prayer

Narrative

Lord, You have warned us not to be surprised when we share the sufferings of Christ and encounter fiery ordeals during our sojourn in the present darkness of this world. The forces of this world system are opposed to the gospel of Your kingdom, and when we do not fit in this system because of our commitment to Christ, we know that we can become targets of opposition, ridicule, and other forms of persecution. May we immerse ourselves especially during these times in biblical faith, hope and love. May we hold fast to the truths of the gospel, to the Person and work of Christ, and to the power of the Spirit. May we hope in Your promises that we will not receive in this life by welcoming them from a distance and confessing that we are strangers and exiles on the earth. And may we display the love of Christ to those who oppose us.

Orthodoxy

Lord Jesus, You taught Your followers that they would have tribulation in the world. But You also counseled them to take courage, because You have overcome the world. Just as the world persecuted You, it will persecute us, Your Body, and this is more evident around the world today than ever before. But as Your servant

Paul taught, we who are in Christ can exult in our tribulations, knowing that tribulation brings about perseverance, proven character and hope that does not disappoint. When we go out as agents of Your Great Commission, we know that in spite of opposition, nothing can thwart Your work. May we learn to mature in faith by trusting You regardless of the consequences we see in this life. We know we are headed for a glorious and eternal future with You that cannot be compared to the temporary results in this world.

Orthopathy

Father God, I am so tempted to focus my attention on what I do not have instead of being thankful for the many blessings You have already bestowed on me. Too often, I approach life from a perspective of deficiency rather than sufficiency. And when I fail to be steadily grateful for Your many tender mercies, I succumb to the sin of grumbling and complaining. Too often, I make my joy contingent on the outcomes I want, rather than the promises You have made. I confess the sin of grumbling and murmuring against Your provision and plans when these do not meet my expectations. I realize that unless I see all of life as a gift from You, I will develop an entitlement mentality that expects things You have not promised. Teach me to focus on Your promises for a future with You that will transcend anything I could hope for in this world.

Orthopraxy

Lord God, it takes little faith to realize that trouble in this fallen world is unavoidable. And now that I have come to faith in Jesus Christ, I know that opposition and tribulation may well increase, especially when I seek to be Your ambassador of reconciliation in the lives of people I meet. When I encounter personal adversity or hostility and when I consider the broader adversity and hostility to the gospel in this world, may I choose to respond in love and not in fear or hatred. May I remember that people are not the enemy; they are victims of the enemy. Give me the grace to embody love for others in spite of what they say or do, and to express the sacrificial love of Jesus by treating others in the way Jesus treated me. My confidence is in You, and I will steadfastly hold fast to You rather than wringing my hands over the evils in this generation.

50

Matter

The Book of 1 John

MONDAY: Story

As the early Christians became further and further removed from their Jewish roots, they opened themselves up to the false beliefs of their newly converted Gentile neighbors. The primary challenge came from a religious group whose wrong ideas about creation led them to reinterpret the teachings of Jesus and the apostles through the lens of a Greek philosophy known as "Gnosticism."

While there was a fair amount of diversity among these Gnostic groups, the belief that unified them was the idea that the material world was inherently corrupt. They reasoned that the one true God would never allow Himself to be contaminated by our base, physical reality. In fact, He would never have created such filth in the first place.

When these people read the Old Testament, they concluded that YHWH must be an inferior God. After all, He created everything and thought it was pretty good. YHWH described Himself as having physical characteristics such as hands and eyes (see Exod. 7:5; Ps. 34:15). The *real* God, they reasoned, would be appalled to be thought of in such a way.

Continuing along this line of reasoning, most of them figured that Jesus couldn't have been both divine and human; those two categories were mutually exclusive in their minds. A sort of sub-category of Gnosticism developed, known as Docetism (from the Greek word *doxa*, which means "to seem"). Docetists claimed that Jesus only seemed human. Others claimed that Jesus was a human who only became divine when the Holy Spirit came upon Him at His baptism, and then went back to being human when the Holy Spirit left Him at His crucifixion.

They were trying to protect God from being polluted by this material world. To them, anything physical was evil and inconsequential; only "spiritual" things mattered. A person was really a spiritual being trapped inside a physical shell of a body, trying desperately to get out and be reunited with the "real God," who only lived somewhere "out there." The way to escape and get to God was to deny yourself anything physical (don't get married, never have sex, don't enjoy your food, and so on). If you refused to indulge your whiny physical body, it would leave your spirit alone.

Another group of these Gnostics went to the opposite extreme, figuring that if they could appease their bodies, maybe the impulses would be sated and leave their minds alone. They reasoned that they could get away with committing sexual immorality as long as their minds were pure. *You're not really your body anyway*, they believed. *The body is just a prison the spirit lives in, so it doesn't really matter what a person does with his or her body. Feed it or starve it—it's going to burn up anyway.*

Sound familiar?

TUESDAY: Beliefs

The Christian faith rests on literal, historical events, the most important of which are the Incarnation and the Resurrection. Both events involve one central feature: the physical body of Jesus Christ. Both were acts of God, rooted in history and witnessed by many of Jesus' contemporaries.

But these two anchor points for the Christian faith have been hotly disputed throughout the centuries since their occurrence. In the earliest days of the Church, they were disputed by some Gentiles who came to a kind of belief in Jesus but refused to believe that He was fully human. They were known as Docetists, and they believed an early form of what would later become full-blown Gnosticism.

They believed anything material was automatically and completely evil. Conversely, they believed that only spiritual things were good. Your body? Evil. Your soul? Good. This physical world? Bad. The spiritual world with angels and all that? Good.

The apostle Paul firmly rejected this heresy. For example, he told a young protégé, "They [the Gnostics] forbid people to marry and order them to abstain from certain foods, which God created to be received with thanksgiving by those who believe and who know the truth. For everything God created is good, and nothing is to be rejected if it is received with thanksgiving, because it is consecrated by the word of God and prayer" (1 Tim. 4:3–5; see also Col. 2:8–23).

But none of the writers of the New Testament spoke against this heresy more clearly or loudly than the apostle John. He countered the argument that Jesus wasn't fully divine until the Spirit entered Him by saying, "The Word became flesh and made his dwelling among us" (John 1:14). He countered the argument that Jesus only *appeared* to be human by saying that anyone who denied that Jesus Christ came in an actual body was so opposed to God as to become Antichrist (see 1 John 4:1–3).

We believe, along with Christians throughout history, that God created a physical world. Jesus lived in a physical body. Neither this physical world nor our physical bodies hinder us from being in a relationship with God. He created them, validated them and seeks to redeem them. Our problem is sin, not physical matter. It is sin we are called to avoid, not stuff.

You can't avoid stuff; you *are* stuff. You must not fall for either extreme of neglecting or indulging your physical body in order to elevate your spiritual self. It doesn't make you a more spiritually mature person to ignore the basics of hygiene and health. Jesus came to share in our physical birth so that we, through our identification with Him in His physical death, can be assured of our sharing in His physical resurrection.

These physical events have led us to spiritual life.

The way the early Christian writers responded to the heresy of Gnosticism lets us know that when it comes to your spiritual life . . . well, there's really no such thing as a "spiritual" life—there's just *life*, and it's all spiritual.

WEDNESDAY: Values

Adam woke up in the Garden that very first day, staring into the eyes of the God who had just breathed into his body the breath of life. Later, God created another human to share this thing called fellowship with Adam. Together, Adam and his new mate, Eve, enjoyed not only each other's company but God's company, as well.

There was fellowship all the way around! And it was very good.

Then sin entered the picture, and fellowship was broken. The man and woman were alienated from one another and from God. They found themselves out in the cold, no longer able to see the face of God. He didn't show up like He used to and walk with them in the cool of the day.

Obviously, God wasn't content to let the story end there with a severed relationship. God began a plan way back then to restore the fellowship. He gave His people the sacrificial system to pay for their sins, and He gave them the Law to show them how to live.

Of course, when God was revealing these to Moses, the people were rebelling and worshiping a golden calf. Fellowship remained broken.

At that point, God actually told the people to go ahead and take up residence in the Promised Land without Him (see Exod. 33). But even then, God's people understood that fellowship with God was of far greater value than anything else, so they declined His offer.

One of the reasons it was important for the Early Church to emphatically refute Gnosticism is that if God can have no fellowship with physical matter, then it is impossible for God to have fellowship with us.

Jesus defined eternal life for us once, but His definition doesn't sound like many of ours. He said, "This is eternal life: that they know you, the only true God, and Jesus Christ, whom you have sent" (John 17:3). Eternal life is not about being in heaven. It's not about being delivered from the mess that so often accompanies life on earth. It's not about finally being rid of that pesky earthsuit you're made to wear.

Eternal life is fellowship with God. That's what the whole Bible Story is about.

The purpose of the gospel is to bring men and women out of darkness and into the light of God's glory, to reunite us with our Creator and enable us to enjoy fellowship with Him and with one another again. If you miss this, you've missed the whole point of the Story.

Sadly, few people actually value their relationship with God and with others as the main event. They tend to act as if the main point is the mansion that will be theirs in heaven or the things they can gain as a result of their fellowship with God and others.

But fellowship isn't a means to anything else. Fellowship is *the thing*, the main point of all that Christians believe.

THURSDAY: Actions

Because physical matter is actually a part of God's creation, we should receive it as a gift from Him. We are free to savor it as it is, without needing to "Christianize" it by stamping a Bible verse on it, hoping to make it suitable for Christian consumption. If God created it, we can safely assume it's okay to enjoy in its proper context.

No one should enjoy the outdoors more than Christians do. Whether you prefer the mountains or the beach or the desert, get out there and take a walk or plant a garden or have a picnic with the kids. And while you're out, give thanks to God.

Or go to the movies, a museum or a concert. No one should enjoy art more than Christians do. Don't think the art has to be overtly Christian, either. It need not be proclamational for it to be enjoyable. It doesn't need to have an altar call at the end for it to be worthwhile; because when filmmakers or artists or musicians create, they are reflecting the creative impulse of the Creator, in whose image they are made.

There are certain things Christians should give up because they're wrong and they lead us in the wrong direction. But we can enjoy the work of God's hands. In fact, some Christians of old said it this way: Our first responsibility as humans is to find pleasure in God's world—to know God and enjoy Him forever.

Maybe you connect with God when you're up to your wrists in topsoil or up to your ankles in sand and saltwater. Maybe you find the most peace dropping a fishing line in the tall reeds at the far edge of the pond or hiking the trails up to the timberline. Maybe it's listening to Vladimir Horowitz playing Mozart or staring at *The Starry Night* by Vincent Van Gogh.

However you connect with God most deeply, take a moment to thank Him for His amazing creation. Be grateful that He put you here to enjoy real things.

And remember this: If God were unable to come into contact with physical matter, He couldn't have come in the flesh. He couldn't have participated in a bodily resurrection, and He couldn't have any fellowship with you. Aren't you glad that He did, and aren't you glad that He does?

FRIDAY: Prayer

Narrative

God of promise, You have been working throughout history to overcome the alienation and estrangement that took place at the Fall. Your glorious redemptive plan that led to the incarnation of Your Son provides the only basis for our for-giveness, atonement and eternal life.

But since the days of His earthly ministry, there has been a concerted effort by the enemy of our faith to distort the biblical teaching about His identity. Teach-ers have denied Jesus' full deity on the one hand or denied His full humanity on the other, and this still happens now. We are such creatures of extremes—the extremes of Jesus as God but not man, and of Jesus as man but not God; the extremes of asceticism and of indulgence; the extremes of seeing matter as evil and of worshiping the earth. But only the biblical revelation of the full God-Man is enough to save us from our sins.

Orthodoxy

God of all creation, even though creation has been subjected to the futility of the curse, it is still Yours, and You will redeem nature when You reveal the children of God in the redemption of our bodies. The material world is still good, because it comes from Your hand, and You have made us to be incarnate beings. And when the Word became flesh, He dwelled in our midst and identified Himself with the human condition, except for our sin. This incomprehensible identification with us in His incarnation, death and physical resurrection is the glorious foundation for our hope. By becoming one of us, He could take our sins upon Himself on the cross. And through His bodily resurrection from the dead, He made it possible for us to be resurrected as well. Thanks be to God for this wondrous gift.

Orthopathy

Father God, I thank You that Your gift of eternity begins in this life with the reception of the righteousness of Your Son through faith. In Christ, my alienation and estrangement with You due to my sin are overcome and replaced by the gifts of justification and of peace with You. Through my redemption and adoption into Your spiritual family, I have received the great blessings of Your presence and of fellowship with You. As the triune God, You Yourself are a relational community of three Persons. This profound mystery is the basis for all relationships, because it takes more than one person for there to be love and communion. In Christ, You have welcomed me into this fellowship, and the greatest glory of heaven will be to be with You in Your unmediated presence, beholding Your boundless beauty and majesty and enjoying You with others.

Orthopraxy

Lord of heaven and earth, of all things visible and invisible, Your Word affirms the beauty, glory, marvels and goodness of Your created order. The heavens declare Your majesty and power, and it is through Your creation that You have revealed Your invisible attributes, Your eternal power and divine nature to all people. The earth is full of Your possessions, and in wisdom You have made them all. The heavens and earth abound with resplendent wonders on every level, including the fearfully and wonderfully made human body. May I learn to enjoy and praise You through the splendors of Your creation, and may I celebrate Your goodness in the many gifts of this life, such as food and fellowship, as well as great art, music and literature that have been crafted by Your image-bearers. All of life is spiritual, whether material or immaterial, and I will worship You in all things.

51

Revelation

REVELATION 1–3

MONDAY: Story

Nearly 40 years after Jesus was killed, Jerusalem was destroyed . . . again. There was a dispute among some of the aristocracy over some taxes. Some overzealous revolutionaries got wind of it and seized control of the city. Roman forces were dispatched to crush them. In the spring of 70 A. D., just as a sea of faithful Jewish people descended upon Jerusalem for the Passover (which was, ironically, a celebration of their liberation from slavery), the siege began.

For months, the city languished in starvation, disease, random acts of violence and internal strife. By August, the entire city—including the Temple—was demolished. Hundreds of thousands of Jewish people were dead.

Thirty-seven years, Passover to Passover, from the execution of Jesus, the city of Jerusalem was wiped off the map.

The immediate reaction of Christians everywhere was horror. But while they were genuinely horrified, they couldn't help but think that perhaps those in Jerusalem had brought this on themselves by rejecting the Messiah. Jesus had predicted this would happen.

But Jesus had predicted a lot of things.

He said His kingdom would overcome the kingdoms of this world. He said all power and authority had been given to Him. He gave His followers the distinct impression that He would be back soon. It had been more than a generation now. His followers had lived and died, suffering persecution and humiliation, and He still had not returned.

The 12 disciples Jesus had hand-picked were all gone now except for John—and he was stuck on an island in exile. There was a rumor circulating that he might never die, but there was another rumor that his health was poor. Who knew what the truth was anymore?

Persecution was no longer occasional or in a few places; it was everywhere all the time. The new emperor was demanding that people worship him as lord. Failure to do so could result not only in the loss of home or job, but one's very life!

Heretics (whether Gnostics or Judaizers) kept churches in turmoil. Immoral practices leaked into Christian worship from pagan temples. In a few places, cultural acceptance of Christianity and financial respectability caused some to water down the teachings of the apostles.

John, the one human alive who had the authority to quell these rumblings, was living in a cave on 60 square miles of rock, far from the people he loved—the people who desperately needed his wisdom.

Thankfully, the Lord had John sit down and record what he was about to see.

TUESDAY: Beliefs

Think about how hard it must have been as a member of one of the fledgling churches at the end of the first century, trying to weather the corrupting influences within and the growing harassment from without. You might be tempted to wonder if it was all worth it. And you might wonder where God was in the midst of all this chaos.

Then imagine you receive a letter one day addressed from the island of Patmos. It's from John!

You crack open the seal and begin reading, finding out that John has recorded a vision given to him by God, a vision of the risen Lord Jesus. His first words to you are these: "Grace and peace to you from him who is, and who was, and who is to come" (Rev. 1:4).

Peace is precisely what you don't have!

But John's words were precise: First grace, then peace.

John, the beloved apostle, was cast aside to rot on an island prison, cut off from the people he loved and distressed by what he had heard about their situations. The churches of Asia Minor were feeling the hatred of Rome and the challenges of living faithfully in a faithless generation. What did they need to hear most?

It wasn't a detailed account of future events, intended to be decoded centuries later. It wasn't a threat of divine retribution to be meted out on the heads of those who opposed the message of Jesus. It wasn't a lovely allegory to anesthetize the Church's pain and suffering.

It was a portrait of the risen Lord Jesus, our Hope and our Future.

As we've seen throughout the Bible Story, the central plotline has always involved God's plan to create a community of people who are rightly related to Himself and rightly relating to one another. The main character, as it turns out, is Jesus Christ. His identity is hinted at throughout the Old Testament, and then stated explicitly and emphatically in the New Testament.

In the final portion of the Bible Story, this glimpse into the future is revealed: In the world to come, God's people will finally live the way God intended. Sin and evil will be eradicated. The corruption that infected God's creation will give way to a new heaven and a new earth (more on that next week). We'll have new bodies, incorruptible bodies and incorruptible minds.

So much will change and be totally new.

But this much will be the same: the central character will still be Jesus Christ.

It is the *grace* of God, most clearly made manifest in the Person and work of Jesus Christ, that is the only possible foundation for a *peace* that promises to last throughout all eternity. We enjoy the grace that is ours now, even as we eagerly await the peace that will be ours in time.

First grace. Then peace. Always Jesus.

WEDNESDAY: Values

The apostle John was old and tired when he wrote Revelation. He had given his entire life to serving and following God. He had literally walked with the Lord, listening as his Rabbi and Friend told astonishing stories. He watched as Jesus performed unbelievable miracles, wept as Jesus died and rejoiced as Jesus reappeared. He joined the others in their initial confusion over Jesus' final departure. He was in the Upper Room when the Holy Spirit came like the sound of a rushing wind and tongues of flame landed on everyone's head.

He had spoken in a foreign language on the Day of Pentecost.

He had been in Jerusalem when news about Stephen's death was reported, and when Paul and Barnabas and Peter reported about what God was doing among the Gentiles.

He had taken care of Jesus' mother, Mary. And he had gone to Ephesus and served the Christians there.

Now he was old and he was tired.

It's easy to imagine him sitting on that hot rock in the middle of the Aegean Sea. Did he ever wonder if it was all real? Had it really happened the way he remembered it, or had the sun baked his brain into thinking these things? It had all been so long ago . . .

What John needed more than anything else was Jesus.

The churches in Asia Minor were discouraged when they received their letter from John. They had given time and energy and money to serve and follow God. They had listened to John recount these stories. They had witnessed their fair share of miracles. They had wept and rejoiced, celebrated and mourned. Lately, though, there had been more grief than anything. They were confused and wondered whether or not Jesus would ever actually come back.

Maybe John was wrong about all this. Maybe he hadn't seen it. Maybe he was so old that his thoughts were jumbled up. It had all been so long ago . . .

What those seven churches needed more than anything else was Jesus.

Odds are, some people reading these words right now are old, tired, discouraged or confused. You've given so much and done so much. You have listened and experienced and witnessed firsthand so many things. But you have more ashes than beauty these days. And maybe you're wondering if it all just might be too good to be true. *Is this whole thing a fairy tale? Will Jesus ever come back, and will it ever balance out?*

Once upon a time, you had been so sure. But that was so long ago . . .

What you need more than anything else is Jesus.

THURSDAY: Actions

Seven different churches with different people, different leaders, different challenges, different strengths, different weaknesses. These are the folks to whom

John writes, hoping to infuse them with hope by giving them a glimpse into what will shortly begin to take place.

So many different issues to deal with, so many different knots to untie. And yet the challenge to each church is the same: *Overcome.*

- Those who will overcome will eat from the tree of life (Rev. 2:7).
- Those who overcome will not be hurt at all by the second death (2:11).
- Those who overcome will eat hidden manna and be given a white stone with a new name written on it (2:17).
- Those who overcome will have authority over the nations and will be given the morning star (2:26, 28).
- Those who overcome will be dressed in white (3:5).
- Those who overcome will be made into pillars in the temple of God (3:12).
- Those who overcome will sit with Jesus on His throne (3:21).

Overcomers are promised unique rewards because they are unique men and women. They've managed to muster their gumption, employ their imaginations, steel their resolve and withstand temptation, persecution and spiritual warfare. They've taken everything the evil one could dish out, and they've done more than survive.

They have overcome it all by the grace of God.

In spite of their real and painful circumstances, they have lived life convinced of a greater reality than that which can be seen.

Just as these promises were meant to cheer the hearts of those tired Christians nearly 2,000 years ago, they are meant to cheer our hearts today. We are called to be overcomers, to do more than survive until Jesus returns. We are called to accomplish the victory that is ours by virtue of our relationship with our victorious King.

We must heed John's warning, though: Not everyone will overcome. Some will compromise their faith. Others will live in fear. Lest we falter in our own faith, let us listen again to the words of Jesus. He says to us, "I know."

- He knows our deeds, our hard work (Rev. 2:2).
- He knows the stands we have taken for His cause (2:2).
- He knows our hardships and poverty (2:9).
- He knows where we live (2:13).

- He knows our actions, our love, our faith, our devotion and our endurance (2:19).
- He searches our hearts and minds. He knows our suffering and our weakness, having experienced them Himself. In fact, Jesus is the ultimate Overcomer.

Those of you who would become overcomers, here is your charge: Allow Christ to live in, among and through you. This is comfort and challenge. The promise-keeping Promised One promises to give us ultimate victory and vindication as we allow Him to overcome through us, to make us like Himself.

FRIDAY: Prayer

Narrative

Lord, when I read the epistles of the New Testament, I am struck by the content of these letters that dealt with serious problems in the Early Church. The errors of legalism, early Gnosticism, immorality and divisiveness were rampant, and each of these posed a serious threat to the purity and propagation of the gospel. And the social, cultural and moral conditions in the Roman Empire also opposed the spread of Christianity. Your Church was challenged by internal and external turmoil, and from a human perspective, should never have survived. And yet it has, and Your gospel has now spread to every nation on earth. And I know that in spite of the internal and external challenges Your people face today, the gates of Hades will not overpower Your Church. I thank You for Your sovereign grace in the past, present and future.

Orthodoxy

Lord Jesus, You are the First and the Last, and the Living One; You were dead, but You are alive forevermore, and You have the keys of death and of Hades. You are the Lion from the tribe of Judah, the Root of David and the Overcomer. You are the Lamb who was slain and whose blood purchased for God people from every tribe and tongue and people and nation. You are worthy to receive power and riches and wisdom and might and honor and glory and blessing. The kingdom of the world has become Your kingdom, and You will reign forever and ever. You are called Faithful and True, and in righteousness You will judge and wage war. You are King of kings and Lord of lords. You are the Alpha and the Omega, the

Beginning and the End. And You are coming quickly, and Your reward is with You. Amen. Come, Lord Jesus.

Orthopathy

O Lord, there are times when I allow fear and doubt to grip me and cause me to wonder about the reality of my faith. But then I remember Your faithfulness to Your people from the beginning; Your redemptive plan that consummated in the cross of Your Son; His unique life and miracles and teachings and resurrection; and Your great works of provision, protection, comfort and guidance in my life. When I call these things to mind, I can affirm that nothing in heaven or on earth can separate me from Your love in Christ Jesus. Knowing that I am in Your grip, I can be steadfast and immovable, always abounding in Your work, knowing that my toil is not in vain. You will continue to make me more like Your Son, and no loss or grief in this present world can even be compared with what You are planning for those who love You.

Orthopraxy

Dear God, I want to cultivate an eternal perspective as I journey through this temporal arena. May I learn to pursue the eternal reality of the unseen future over the current reality of the visible present. Knowing that reward in the Kingdom of heaven is based on faithfulness to the opportunities You give me in this life, I want to treasure each opportunity and see all of life as a stewardship. While I cannot grasp the full nature of the rewards You promise to the overcomers who abide in, love and obey Christ, I believe the greatest dimension of reward will be relational intimacy. The nature and depth of my relationships with people in heaven will be a great joy. But the greatest reward will be my capacity to know and experience You. May You be the object of my deepest love so that I will pursue You above all else.

52

The Last Story

REVELATION 21–22

MONDAY: Story

The Story began with God creating a place. Out of nothingness, He spoke and earth was formed. From that earth, He fashioned a Garden more beautiful than anything we've been able to create since. Into that Garden, He placed a man and, shortly thereafter, a woman. Their lives were full of meaning and purpose, void of frustration and fear.

But it didn't last long.

You know the story by now. Sin entered the world and wreaked havoc and destruction. Violence and anxiety, turmoil and tumult—these things have characterized human existence since the events recorded in the third chapter of the Bible Story, punctuated here and there with glimpses of a better way. Like previews of a coming attraction, these scenes are short and designed to whet our appetites for the day of its glorious appearing.

Then it happens. God sovereignly moves and begins recreating a new heaven and a new earth. Nothing gets in His way, and nothing can bring a stop to what He has initiated. Evil is consigned to destruction forever so that it can have no influence in this New Creation. Human history as we know it is brought to a conclusion, and those whom God has redeemed from every culture and generation eagerly await what He has in store.

And what He has in store does not disappoint. It's new and amazingly different, but also strangely familiar (it's earth, after all). It is not people with halos and white robes floating on clouds and strumming harps. It is not an endless church service. There is nothing static about what God does. It's dynamic. It's breathtaking. It's better than anything we could ask for or imagine.

It's a city nearly the size of the United States of America, except it's a perfect cube. On the old earth, there were specifically designated holy places; the new earth is a holy place. On the old earth, there were pockets into which the glory of God periodically broke through; the new earth is *filled* with His glory. It is a magnificent city filled with the radiance of God's greatness.

This city is inhabited by people with bodies that are not subject to aging, sickness or death. These bodies have minds that are untainted by the effects of sin and impure motives or thoughts. And the people are innumerable. They are amazingly diverse and yet unified by one constant—the shared access they have to the throne of God.

Like Adam and Eve in the very first story, God's redeemed will once again live in unbroken intimacy with Him, with each other and with the world around them. It will be an idyllic existence.

How great will that be?

TUESDAY: Beliefs

The book of Revelation is quite a story! Lots of people argue over how much of it should be taken literally or how much to take figuratively. Will the new city of Jerusalem literally be 1,400 square miles? Will there actually be streets of gold? Will we actually wear white robes? There are lots more questions than there are answers in what John wrote down, but there are still things we can know and trust from reading the end of the Bible.

For example, we know that God wins. God began human history, stands outside human history and will bring human history to a conclusion when it suits His purposes. Evil may look like it has the upper hand, but God promises (and He's powerful enough to deliver!) that evil will one day be destroyed once and for all.

We also know that there will still be work for us in eternity. Before you start to worry about what kind of job you'll have, think about this: There won't be any frustration. Can you imagine work with no stress, no anxiety, no fear, no frustration? No paperwork or busy signals, no traffic jams or spam in your email folder, no more office politics, no blue Mondays, no pink slips—just the fulfillment and joy that come from knowing you're doing what you were always created to do. There will be learning without Test Anxiety. There will be growth without growing pains. Life will be ordered, and work will be fulfilling. That's a pencil sketch of some of what awaits you; imagine what the full-color, three-dimensional version will be like!

Few things cause as much heartache on this old earth as interpersonal conflicts. It's so easy to be misunderstood or to feel slighted in some way by another person, and over time, those things add up and can cause a lot of unnecessary stress. More good news: There's none of that in eternity. There's no shame, no deceit, nothing impure. There's no room for unhealthy ego or manipulative motives. Your relationships with other people will have no secrecy, no hidden agendas, no triangulation, no neediness about them at all—not even your relationships with your in-laws!

But wait . . . it still gets better!

We get to see God's face.

No one has ever been allowed to see God's face. Not Abraham. Not Moses. Not even the apostle John, who wrote the book of Revelation, could handle the overwhelming light of God. But in eternity, all of God's people are able to live fully in His presence and see Him face to face.

In our world, God makes His presence available to us, but He allows us to choose whether or not we want a relationship with Him. In eternity, God will gather together a group of people—His redeemed community—whose hearts and minds have been illuminated by His truth and melted by His grace. God will no longer be a visitor; He will be a resident. He will no longer live in a few of us; He will live with all of us.

Perhaps the most amazing thing is that the invitation into that kind of eternity is open to each and every one of us. The most baffling thing is that some folks decline.

What about you?

WEDNESDAY: Values

God's intent has always been to live in relationship with us. Why this should be so is beyond our ability to comprehend, but it is plainly taught through every story in the Bible.

God values relationships. When Jesus was asked to sum up the entire message of the Bible, He said it was all about having a right relationship with God and rightly relating to other people (see Matt. 22:34–40). It's important to remember that the two are so entwined that they cannot be separated. In eternity, we will not only be living as individuals in relationship with our heavenly Father; we'll be living among others as part of the community of the redeemed.

We would be wise to ponder the idea that many of the people we will live with *there* are people we have the opportunity to live with *here*. It seems odd that we might suddenly begin to value them when we meet them in eternity if we have not valued them here. Perhaps beginning to do so is part of the ultimate sanctification. Perhaps we should begin practicing now what will be reality then.

It is also clear from the end of the Bible Story that God values comfort. Not the kind of comfort we think of as laziness and leisure; God is shown comforting His people, especially those who have endured pain and sadness. As His agents on this old earth, as those who actively seek to bring a portion of eternity into the here and now, we should be about the same business of comforting those who grieve. Those who have been hard-pressed and downtrodden in this world finally find rest in God's presence.

God values people from every nation. So should we.

God values every language. So should we.

God values diversity. As hard as this is for some of us to hear, so should we.

God's new city is remarkably designed with its cubic architecture and its tree-lined streets. There is room for all of God's children in their new home. And the design is both new and traditional at the same time. It is new in the sense that nothing like it has ever been conceived before; it is traditional in all the ways it gives honor to things like the 12 tribes of Israel and the 12 apostles. Its very name implies the new and old coming together: New Jerusalem.

As in the very first story, we also see that God loves creativity. His new city has a remarkable design that goes beyond merely functional. It's beautiful and complex. Whether its gates are actually made of pearls or the city itself made of gold, God clearly intends for us to know that it will be a place of beauty and wonder, complexity and whimsy.

Creativity. Order and design. Diversity. Rest. People. Community. These are the priorities of God's heart as it is revealed in the first two chapters of the Bible. Amazingly, the very same priorities are revealed in the last two chapters of the Bible.

Are they ours as well?

THURSDAY: Actions

We're all dying. It's inevitable. As hard as we've tried, humans have simply never been able to find that elusive cure for death. With all of our medical technology, we've managed to stave it off for a few days at most, but it is an indisputable fact: The mortality rate among humans is 100 percent.

For those of us who have placed our faith in Christ, we have the assurance that what comes next is taken care of for us. We need not fear death, because heaven awaits us on the other side.

But most of us have some time standing between where we are now and where we'll be then. God does not simply get us saved and then take us home. There's some living to be done between now and then, and we need to think carefully about how our final destination affects our present situation. After all, we haven't just been saved *to* something; we've been saved *for* something.

For starters, we should add our voices to those of Christians throughout the ages in praying, "*Maranatha!* Lord, come quickly!" That's appropriate. But to that prayer we should add the saying that Jesus taught His earliest followers to pray: *Your kingdom come and Your will be done on earth as it is in heaven* (see Matt. 6:10).

In other words, it's okay to pray "God, get us out of here!" but we must also pray that, in the meantime, God will bring some of "up there" into our "down here." Moreover, we must be willing to roll up our sleeves in order to work for that reality. Let's set about bringing something of heaven into our present world.

Cultivate the world. Order it and set it right. Engage the culture rather than withdrawing from it. Faith demands that we engage others and work for their betterment. Hope will sustain us as we engage in this endeavor. Love determines the rules of our engagement.

Remember, our salvation brought about reconciliation with God in every area of our lives. Art, literature, science, education, sleep, entertainment, work—nothing is off limits from the lordship of Jesus Christ. We have reason to believe that we will engage in most if not all of these activities in heaven. Let's learn how to engage in them in heavenly ways right now.

It's physically impossible to face in two directions at the same time, but we must learn to do this spiritually. We live in the "in-between" times, in the already/ not yet of God's kingdom. It has come, it is coming and one day it *will* arrive in all its fullness.

Until it does, let us be salt and light, penetrating society and influencing it for good. Let us make a difference in our world, partnering with God in its redemption, pushing back the darkness and advancing the borders of His kingdom in our generation.

And let's try to take as many to heaven with us as we can.

FRIDAY: Prayer

Narrative

O Lord my God, You are exalted above all things we can conceive and imagine. Time and space are a part of Your created order—You brought them into being, and You dwell in all times and places. You are the eternal Now, the great I AM, the Beginning and the End, the Alpha and the Omega, the First and the Last. You are present everywhere and You rule all things from the microcosm to the macrocosm. You spoke, and energy and matter came into being. Your boundless power and wisdom are evident in Your works, and all things derive their being from You. The beauty, radiance and wisdom that abound in Your creation all point beyond themselves to You, their Creator and Sustainer. I ask for the eyes to see Your goodness, beauty and truth as I behold plants, trees, animals, insects, sunrises and sunsets, landscapes and the starry sky.

Orthodoxy

What we could not have learned from the glories and marvels of Your world, You have revealed through Your Word. We know from the heavens and the earth that you are all-powerful, utterly wise and everywhere present; Your eternal power and divine nature have clearly been revealed. But it was only through Your special revelation in Scripture that we could know that the One who has dominion over all things is also the Lover of our souls. Your Word is a love letter to the people You created to enjoy forever in loving communion with You. May I be diligent to be a student of Your Word so that it will renew my mind and give me an eternal perspective as I meditate on Your timeless truths.

Orthopathy

Your creation is a magnificent unity in diversity, profound in wisdom, awesome in understanding, marvelous in purpose and rich in elegance. You revel in variety, subtlety, intricacy, information and beauty. All things work together in both the physical and spiritual realms. I thank You for creating and calling me to become conformed to the image of Your Son, and I pray for the grace of holy desire to pursue by Your power what You have called me to become in Christ. I thank You for friendships and alliances with likeminded people, and I am grateful for the manifold gifts and ministries in the Body of Christ. Give me a growing heart for Your people so that I will be embedded in others-centered community as a lover and servant of the people You love.

Orthopraxy

You have called me to participate in Your purposes through the work I have been given to do during my earthly sojourn. May I do my work with care and excellence in the desire to be pleasing to You. I realize that all things become spiritual when they are done in Your Name. May I honor You in my choices and activities and view the works of my hands as a mode of worship. I want whatever I do in thought, word and deed to be honoring to You and edifying to others. I ask for a clearer sense of purpose and calling, and for the power to accomplish that for which You have placed me on this earth.

Notes

Chapter 1 The First Story

1. Rich Mullins, "Here in America," Universal Music-MGB Songs, Los Angeles, CA, 90064.

Chapter 4 Birth of a Nation

1. YHWH (usually translated as "I AM") is God's personal name, spoken by God Himself to Moses through the burning bush (see Exod. 3:14). It's derived from the Hebrew verb *hayah*, which means "to be" and is by far the most common name for God used in the Old Testament. In an English translation of the Bible, each time you see LORD in small capitals, you are encountering YHWH.

Chapter 29 A Real Live Human God

1. Josephus, *Jewish Antiquities*, 17:271–272.
2. "This Is My Father's World," by Maltbie D. Babcock (1901).

Chapter 34 Unconventional

1. George Herbert, "The Elixir," from *The Oxford Book of English Mystical Verse* (Oxford: The Clarendon Press, 1917).

Dr. Kenneth Boa is engaged in a ministry of relational evangelism and discipleship, teaching, writing and speaking. He holds a BS from the Case Institute of Technology, a ThM from Dallas Theological Seminary, a PhD from New York University, and a DPhil from the University of Oxford in England.

Dr. Boa is the president of Reflections Ministries, an organization that seeks to encourage, teach and equip people to know Christ, follow Him, become progressively conformed to His image and reproduce His life in others. He is also president of Trinity House Publishers, a publishing company that is dedicated to the creation of tools that will help people manifest eternal values in a temporal arena by drawing them to intimacy with God and a better understanding of the culture in which they live.

Dr. Boa is the author of numerous books, of which his more recent releases include *A Guided Tour of the Bible, Sense and Nonsense About Angels and Demons, Sense and Nonsense About Heaven and Hell, Handbook to Leadership: Leadership in the Image of God, Passionate Living: Praises and Promises* and *Passionate Living: Wisdom and Truth.* He is a contributing editor to *The Open Bible* and *The Leadership Bible* and is the consulting editor of the *Zondervan NASB Study Bible.* Dr. Boa has received the Evangelical Christian Publishers Association's Gold Medallion Book Award for *An Unchanging Faith in a Changing World* (1998), *The Zondervan NASB Study Bible* (2000) and *Faith Has Its Reasons: An Integrative Approach to Defending Christianity* (2001). He also writes *Reflections,* a free monthly teaching letter (see www.reflectionsministries.org).

Dr. Boa lives in Atlanta, Georgia, with his wife, Karen.

John Alan Turner has studied theology, psychology and philosophy at such universities as Pepperdine University, Pacific Christian College, Bear Valley Bible Institute and the London School of Theology, earning a ThM with emphasis in New Testament Studies. He has appeared on American Family Radio and *The Coral Ridge Hour* television broadcast. His articles have appeared in several magazines, including *Integrity Journal, New Wineskins, ParentLife* and *Stimulus:*

The New Zealand Journal of Christian Thought and Action. He is also the coauthor of *The Gospel According to the Da Vinci Code* and *Hearts and Minds: Raising Your Child with a Christian View of the World*.

In addition to maintaining his busy writing schedule, John also serves as the president of Faith 2.0, an organization committed to helping people live better lives by re-examining what they really believe. He has also recently fulfilled the role of teaching pastor at The Bridge, a non-denominational church in suburban Atlanta. He will be filling a similar role for River Park Community Church, a brand-new church plant in Oxnard, California, set to launch in September 2008.

John made one of the best decisions of his life when he married Jill on October 2, 1993. Jill works as an editor and writer for the children's curriculum 252Basics and was the lead writer for the character-based curricula *Core Essentials* and *Shake this Planet* (used in public school systems in more than 20 different states). Together, the Turners are raising their three daughters, Anabel, Eliza, and Amelia, and a dog named Coco. John enjoys jazz, baseball, and reading—though not necessarily in that order.

For more information on the authors, visit
Ken Boa's website: www.KenBoa.org
John Alan Turner's website: www.faith20.org
or check out John's blog: http://blog.faith20.org